THE
ADMINISTRATIVE
PRESIDENCY
REVISITED

SUNY Series in Environmental Public Policy
Lester W. Milbrath

SUNY Series on the Presidency: Contemporary Issues
John Kenneth White

THE ADMINISTRATIVE PRESIDENCY REVISITED

Public Lands, the BLM, and the Reagan Revolution

Robert F. Durant

State University
of New York
Press

Published by
State University of New York Press, Albany

© 1992 State University of New York

For information, address State University of New York
Press, State University Plaza, Albany, NY, 12246

Library of Congress Cataloging-in-Publication Data

Durant, Robert F., 1949–
    The administrative presidency revisited : public lands, the BLM,
and the Reagan revolution / Robert F. Durant.
        p.   cm.
    Includes bibliographical references and index.
    ISBN 0-7914-9859-7 (alk. paper) : $54.50. — ISBN 0-7914-0960-0
(pbk. : alk. paper) : $17.95
    1. American Presidency. 2. United States—Natural Resources. 3. New
Mexico—Natural Resources. 4. United States. Bureau of Land Management.
5. Reagan, Ronald. I. Title.
HD243.N5D87   1992
333.1'0973—dc20   91-14098
                                                                          CIP

10 9 8 7 6 5 4 3 2 1

To Tom, Esther, and Joseph Baca:
There is a friend that sticketh closer than a brother.
—Proverbs *18:24*

CONTENTS

List of Tables and Figures ix
Preface xi
Acknowledgments xv

PART I. THE ANATOMY OF AN ADMINISTRATIVE
PRESIDENCY 1

Chapter 1
A Passion to Prevail 3

Chapter 2
Prometheus Unbound or Sisyphus Redux? 29

Chapter 3
Public Lands, the BLM, and the Reagan Revolution 51

PART II. A VIEW FROM THE GRASSROOTS 79

Chapter 4
Politics, Position, and Power Production 81

Chapter 5
Backdoor Privatization, "Cow Welfare," and
the BLM 103

Chapter 6
     Toward Becoming a "Good Urban Neighbor"? Or,
     "You're Not a Man Till You Do a Land Exchange"   129

Chapter 7
     Thou Shalt Not Covet Thy Neighbor's Water   163

Chapter 8
     Wilderness, King Coal, and the San Juan Basin   193

PART III.   BEYOND FEAR OR FAVOR: LESSONS FOR
THEORY AND PRACTICE   229

Chapter 9
     Missing Links, Links Gone Missing, and Natural
     Resource Management   231

Chapter 10
     "Fire Alarms," "Garbage Cans," and the
     Administrative Presidency   275

Notes   323
References   355
Index   385
About the Author   401

LIST OF TABLES AND FIGURES

TABLES

1-1	Major Legislation Affecting the Management of U.S. Public Lands, 1872–1978	14
3-1	BLM Personnel by State, FY 1980–FY 1986	62
3-2	Total BLM State Personnel by Administrative Level, FY 1980–FY 1986	63
3-3	BLM State Office Personnel as a Percentage of Total Statewide BLM Personnel by Division and State, 1981	64
3-4	BLM State Office Personnel by Function, FY 1980–FY 1986	66
3-5	BLM Personnel by Administrative Level, New Mexico, FY 1980–FY 1986	69
3-6	BLM State Office Selected Personnel Skill Mix, New Mexico, FY 1980 and FY 1986	70
3-7	BLM District Office Selected Personnel Skill Mix, New Mexico, FY 1981–FY 1986	71
3-8	BLM Resource Area Selected Personnel Skill Mix, New Mexico, FY 1980–FY 1986	72
3-9	Selected Indices of Natural Resource Development on BLM Lands, New Mexico, FY 1976–FY 1988	74
8-1	Comparison of Andrus (1979) and Watt (1982/83) Coal-Leasing Regulations	198
9-1	Decision Settings and Appropriate Governance Networks	252

10-1   Decision Parameters of Different Types of
Presidential Agenda Items   280

10-2   Bureaupolitical Dynamics of the Administrative
Presidency by Type of Agenda Item   290

FIGURES

9-1   Traditional and Alternative Production
Structures   269

10-1   A Typology of Agenda Items   278

10-2   Bureaupolitical Response as a Function of the
Noncompliance Delay Effect (NDE)   295

10-3   Political Appointee–Careerist Relations: A
Strategic Perspective   311

PREFACE

With bureaucratic performance widely recognized as problematic yet critical to presidential objectives, and with executive-legislative stalemate almost routine in a redistributive era of policy choice and hyperpluralism, recent presidents have turned to the "administrative presidency" to energize, direct, and control domestic policy. While the study of this phenomenon has increasingly attracted substantial scholarly attention, significant gaps remain in our understanding of its implementation processes, potential, and pitfalls.

This book attempts to develop a theoretical foundation for understanding and applying the administrative presidency across both domestic and foreign policy domains by taking a decidedly different approach and analytical focus than those of its predecessors. Specifically, it uses President Ronald Reagan's efforts to reorient natural resource policy in the West as a "policy window" for examining the politics, processes, and prospects of the administrative presidency. The book's analytical focus is the way the Bureau of Land Management's (BLM) efforts to reorient public land policy affected a single yet pivotal Western state: New Mexico. Using a comparative case study design, this "bottom-up" perspective affords an uncommon view of the administrative presidency across six policy arenas: rangeland management, energy leasing, water resource management, wilderness preservation, urban economic development, and public land acquisition.

Why be concerned with the experiences early in his administration of a president long since departed for sunnier climes in Southern California? Why another study of perhaps the most academically scrutinized presidency in recent memory? One reason is that Ronald Reagan was the quintessential practitioner of the administrative presidency, wielding its tools with a comprehensiveness, vigor, and relentlessness unparalleled in his predecessors. Another reason is more forward-looking. With the presidency likely to remain the epicenter of public accountability for an impatient and unforgiving citizenry, the administrative presidency promises to retain its allure to embattled Republican or Democratic chief executives—be they liberal, moderate, or conservative. This book's findings, conclusions, and prescriptions will completely please neither Reagan's supporters nor his critics. Neither will it totally comfort proponents of the administrative presidency, nor assuage those wary or contemptuous of it. Indeed, the analysis reveals both good and bad news for those on all sides of the debate over the strategy's assumptions, as well as its instrumental and normative implications for the contemporary administrative state.

Others may be disappointed that this book fails to examine the impact of the administrative presidency on the morale and character of the federal career service in the BLM. Certainly, this is an important dimension of the strategy's impact during the Reagan Administration and beyond on what Hugh Heclo terms "the larger organizational life of government."[1] To the extent that the administrative presidency leads to lower morale, early exits from the public service, and more difficult recruitment of new employees, the quality of our lives as citizens in the administrative state suffers as well. Yet such linkages are difficult to establish, vulnerable as they are to spurious and confounding effects. And even when links are empirically demonstrated, one's judgment about their implications is typically colored by one's view of the appropriate trade-off between political responsiveness and professional expertise. Thus, I leave this task to others, focusing instead in chapter 10 on how a public service model of political appointee–careerist relations might be developed in the federal government.

The specific cases selected for illustration and analysis in this study of the administrative presidency obviously do not represent a random sample of those experienced in New Mexico, let alone the West as a whole. Such a research design is impractical. What is more, it is unnecessary given the study's purposes: to generate propositions, analytical frameworks, and strategies through in-depth exploration of significant implementation experiences. Eschewed as well is any attempt to evaluate how wise or imprudent were the Reagan Administration's policy goals. Our concern only is how well- or ill-served these goals were by the administrative strategies wielded by Reagan's appointees.

Four criteria informed the selection of cases. First, those included were chosen to maximize the range of resource policies open to comparison, thus minimizing the pitfalls of single case analysis. Second, each case had to afford an opportunity to observe the administrative presidency in a resource issue area that was (a) persistently heralded as significant by Reagan appointees, and (b) widely recognized by knowledgeable observers as a focus of the Administration's reorientation effort in the West. Third, each of the BLM's experiences had to be identified by multiple and diverse interviewees, as well as by an exhaustive search of New Mexico newspapers, as among the most significant and critical initiatives of their kind in the state during both the Carter and Reagan administrations. This ensured a focus on policy reorientation efforts that were litmus tests for the sincerity, acumen, and consistency to principle of Reagan's appointees as they applied the administrative presidency to reorient the policies of the Carter Administration. Lastly, from those cases passing the first three criteria, "finalists" for analysis were selected to maximize the range of implementation outcomes and bureaupolitical dynamics experienced in New Mexico.

The data informing the inquiry are the product of two investigative techniques. To chronicle the course of events, I conducted extensive documentary searches of internal agency memoranda and administrative studies; interagency communications and correspondence by interested parties; congressional hearings; General Accounting Office (GAO) reports; Office of Technology Assessment (OTA) studies; minutes of BLM advisory board meetings; and periodical and legal journal accounts of the cases involved, as well as of the general field of natural resource policy. What is more, to help identify and chronicle the most significant cases in New Mexico that overlapped both the Carter and Reagan administrations, I conducted a microfilm search of two major New Mexico newspapers dating from 1976 through 1987. The *Albuquerque Journal* has the largest circulation in the state and is located in northern New Mexico. The *Las Cruces Sun-News* is located in southern New Mexico, serves the second largest county in the state, and reports widely on regional issues and state matters of interest. Once particular cases were selected, I supplemented this analysis with a search of the *El Paso Times,* a major newspaper in west Texas.

In addition, I conducted semistructured interviews with 73 individuals involved in or familiar with the specific cases or with the generic issues they raise. Those interviewed include: (1) present and former representatives of federal, state, and local government agencies; (2) elected officials at each level of government; and (3) affected and interested private sector actors. To encourage candor, I offered anonymity to all interviewees. Those waiving this offer are listed in the Reference section of this book. These interviews were useful particularly for selecting the specific cases, identifying relevant case material, reconstructing events, and indicating the nuances of relationships among the actors.

ACKNOWLEDGMENTS

The aid, counsel, and cooperation of many individuals has made this book possible. Project expenses were covered by generous financial support from three sources: the Lawrence L. Durisch Memorial Fund, University of Tennessee–Knoxville; the Arts and Sciences Research Center, New Mexico State University; and the College of Arts & Sciences, University of Georgia.

Many colleagues contributed valued emotional support or critical advice during various phases of this project. Especially helpful were William A. Taggart, New Mexico State University; Joyotpaul Chaudhuri, Arizona State University; Frank J. Thompson, State University of New York at Albany; Jerome S. Legge, Jr., Thomas P. Lauth, Robert T. Golembiewski, Hal G. Rainey, J. Edward Kellough, and William Chittick, all of the University of Georgia; Paul F. Diehl, University of Illinois at Urbana–Champaign; John Kingdon, University of Michigan; Richard Rose, University of Strathclyde; and Thomas D. Ungs and David Welborn, both of the University of Tennessee. Also, critiques by Francis E. Rourke, Johns Hopkins University, and Grace Franklin, Ohio State University, gave early direction and focus to the study. Obviously, all errors of commission, omission, and interpretation in this book are my responsibility.

Aside from these professional debts, I owe a more personal note of gratitude to Tom and Esther Baca, and their son, Joseph. Tom served as an administrative assistant to former U.S. Senator Harrison (Jack) Schmitt (R–NM), as Director of Real Property and Development in Las Cruces, New Mexico, and as Superintendent of the New Mexico Regulation and Licensing Department. A public servant with an uncommon scholarly bent, Tom was always there for me—providing introductions to key actors in and observers of the cases; providing useful insight into events and relationships related to the Las Cruces Industrial Park–Elena Gallegos case; and suggesting other avenues for investigation. Moreover, the

Bacas' home became my "home away from home" for three years after I had joined the University of Georgia with many research ends left untied in New Mexico. I cannot thank them enough for the kindness, hospitality, and support they provided me over the years. Most important, they were good friends under trying personal circumstances for me. No doubt, the findings and conclusions tendered in this book will not totally please the Bacas. Nonetheless, I dedicate this study to them and their friendship.

Finally, I wish to thank several individuals for their technical assistance on this project. I am indebted to the following: Carol Boyse, Lynn Deming, Don Haynes, Mary Horka, Ferne Bridgford, Wes Brownfield, David Hamilton, Alan Haufmeister, Michelle Deany Holmes, John Lopez, Robert Sanchez, Ann Schvaneveldt, Leslie Lowe, Robert Aldinger, Tim Wu, Joe Lamb, Patricia Lundstrom, Herb Walker, Tammy Ward, Beth McClelland, John O'Looney, Geneva Bradberry, and Marian Thomas. Special thanks go as well to Clay Morgan, my editor at SUNY Press, and Susan Geraghty for their guidance in bringing this project to completion.

In the end, of course, it is the support of family members over the years that has been most important. Special thanks to Jennifer, Mark, and Gladys Durant, as well as to my sister, Shirley Redmond, for sacrificing so much and asking so little in return.

Selected portions of this book have been adapted from journal articles that I have authored or coauthored over the years. I therefore wish to thank the American Society for Public Administration (ASPA) for its permission to draw heavily from "Thou Shalt Not Covet Thy Neighbor's Water: The Rio Grande Basin Regulatory Experience," *Public Administration Review* *(PAR)*, vol. 45 (November/December 1985), pp. 821–831. Special thanks as well go to ASPA for allowing me to use aspects of my articles, "Toward Assessing the Administrative Presidency: Public Lands, the BLM, and the Reagan Administration," *Public Administration Review* *(PAR)*, vol. 47 (March/April 1987), pp. 180–189, and "Beyond Fear or Favor: Appointee-Careerist Relations in the Post-Reagan Era," *PAR*, vol. 50 (May/June 1990), pp. 319–331. Likewise, I am indebted to Paul F. Diehl, my coauthor, and Cambridge University Press for allowing me to borrow extensively from "Agendas, Alternatives, and Public Policy: Lessons from the U.S. Foreign Policy Arena," *Journal of Public Policy*, vol. 9, no. 2 (April/June 1989), pp. 179–205. Finally, chapters 9 and 10 incorporate aspects of my articles "Fire Alarms, Garbage Cans, and the Administrative Presidency," *Administration & Society,* vol. 23 (May 1991), pp. 94–122 (copyright © 1991 by Sage Publications, Inc.) and "From Complacence to Compliance: Toward a Theory of Intragovernmental Regulation," *Administration & Society,* vol. 17, no. 4 (February 1986), pp. 433–59 (copyright © 1986 by Sage Publications, Inc.). Reprinted by permission of Sage Publications, Inc.

PART I

The Anatomy of an Administrative Presidency

CHAPTER 1

A Passion to Prevail

Assessing the leadership quandary confronting modern presidents, Bert Rockman avers that "a [political] system designed to rein in the opportunities for temporary majorities to achieve their goals, in practice, tends to prevent presidents from achieving theirs."[1] Indeed, recent scholarly research is replete with pessimism concerning the ability of any chief executive to successfully propose, enact, and implement a coherent domestic policy agenda without constitutional reform, uncommon bargaining skills, or uncanny good luck.[2] Scholarly references, however, to the "hemorrhaging of presidential power," the "illusion of presidential government," and the "no-win presidency" in no way diminish popular expectations that incumbents will "provide leadership in defining the policy options available to us, [make] the appropriate choices among these options, and [transform] those choices into effective government action."[3] Indeed, as Theodore Lowi suggests, the "personal president" has become the epicenter of public accountability in the Second American Republic.[4]

With bureaucratic responsiveness to their objectives problematic, with executive–legislative stalemate almost routine, and with the federal judiciary a formidable competitor in agenda setting, chief executives now resort regularly to the "administrative presidency" to energize their domestic policy agendas. As portrayed by Richard Nathan, this presumably "low-visibility, low-political-cost" administrative strategy for executive leadership is based largely on three interrelated premises.[5] First, congressional and bureaucratic opposition to presidential initiatives is the rule rather than the exception, and must be countered aggressively by incumbents lest their agendas be beached on the shoals of indifference, inertia, or outright sabotage. Second, presidents can nimbly sidestep congressional and bureaucratic intransigence by pursuing their policy goals administratively rather than by statute as they effect agency rule making, budgetary, personnel, and reorganization decisions. Finally, strong, decisive, and unrelenting presidential control of the career bureaucracy and its administrative processes is a necessary condition for presidential success since agency operations constitute policy.[6]

Upon assuming the presidency, Ronald Reagan relentlessly applied an administrative strategy to the pursuit of his policy goals in a fashion and to an extent unprecedented in terms of its strategic significance, scope, and philosophical zeal. Broadly speaking, his administration attempted to alter the size, scope, and ends of the federal government by simultaneously (1) changing budget and personnel patterns in ways supportive of the President's agenda; (2) amending, rescinding, or relaxing the enforcement of administrative regulations to suit Reagan's deregulatory instincts; (3) appointing "movement" conservatives, intimate associates, and kindred philosophical spirits to key posts throughout the bureaucracy to direct and control its operations; (4) pursuing major intradepartmental reorganizations designed to symbolize and institutionalize the purposes of the president; (5) monitoring agency performance through elaborate managerial control systems; and (6) devolving policy, enforcement, and financial responsibility for various federal programs to the states. Referred to as "supply-side management" by some, and as the "dismantling of America" by others, Reagan's strategy was the epitome of Nathan's administrative presidency.[7]

Not surprisingly, the administrative strategy pursued by Ronald Reagan and his more recent predecessors has proven quite controversial. At issue is the quintessential dilemma of the contemporary administrative state: How can a polity best reconcile its needs for bureaucratic responsiveness and accountability; presidential leadership of the bureaucracy; and nonpartisan, professional, and effective administration? To some, the administrative presidency affords an overdue restoration of presidential leadership, purposiveness, and prerogative.[8] To others, the strategy represents an untoward assault on congressional intent; the U.S. Constitution; and politically neutral, expertise-based policymaking and enforcement.[9] And to still others, the approach signifies only missed opportunities to effect more permanent policy reform through a vigorous legislative strategy.[10]

Despite the salience of the administrative presidency as a tool for executive leadership, and the magnitude of the issues it raises for a democratic society, significant gaps remain in our understanding of its processes, potential, and pitfalls. First, while a rich and often insightful literature on the topic is evolving, analysts have focused on certain aspects of the approach and slighted others. For example, the policy formulation and legitimation processes of the administrative presidency in Washington have attracted a great deal of popular and scholarly attention during the Reagan years.[11] In contrast, analysts rarely have focused on the triumphs, travails, and consequences of its implementation processes in the field.[12] As a consequence, we are relatively well-versed in how political appointees, the Congress, and the federal courts have influenced presidential initiatives. However, we know little about the political machinations, managerial nuances, and implications of the administrative presidency once its initiatives have evaded or weathered early legislative or judicial challenges.

Second, we have not systematically developed and applied what Bruce Buchanan calls "competent process standards" to the administrative presidency.[13] That is, most scholars studying the topic have left unexplored the extent to which presidents have wielded the managerial levers of power with strategic savvy and ultimate policy accomplishment. Early studies of the Reagan years, for example, were necessarily speculative and assumed implicitly that if administrative objectives were accomplished—e.g., budget cuts were enacted—successful policy reorientation could not be far behind. To some degree, researchers have subsequently tested these expectations, but largely without linking specific administrative strategies and implementation processes to policy outcomes.[14] Some, for example, focus exclusively on the intraorganizational consequences of the administrative presidency (i.e., the managerial effect of personnel reductions-in-force),[15] while others address its policy effects either speculatively or tangentially.[16] Still others rely exclusively on time-series analyses or aggregate data comparisons (e.g., the number of enforcement actions taken by regulators) to measure outcome differences across administrations or between federal and state implementation patterns.[17] As students of evaluation might properly insist, however, inferring presidential "savvy" and program effectiveness solely from performance measures or pretest-posttest research designs is fraught with hazards.

Finally, while an impressive multidisciplinary effort to study the administrative presidency has occurred, we still lack an empirically grounded theoretical foundation for understanding, implementing, and critically evaluating this strategy. Students of the presidency, of court-agency relationships, and of public administration generally have increased significantly our understanding of the logic, tactics, and issues involved in an administrative strategy. They have done so, however, mostly by focusing on and describing the processes of the "institutional presidency"—i.e., the staffing, strategy, and policy initiatives of the White House Office, the Executive Office of the President, and (occasionally) political appointees within the federal bureaucracy.[18] In contrast, scholars have yet to concentrate on developing theoretical frameworks that capture the implementation dynamics of the administrative presidency both in Washington *and* in the field. This omission is significant. It is in the field that the administrative presidency's ultimate success or failure is typically decided, and where its consequences for democratic values are profoundly felt.

This book seeks to contribute to our evolving understanding of the administrative presidency by using natural resource policy as a "window" for doing three things: (1) exploring the strategy's implementation dynamics; (2) assessing its implications for the larger organizational life of government; and (3) advancing theory development in this increasingly important area of governance. Specifically, this book chronicles and assesses aspects of the Reagan Administration's efforts to implement administratively a drastic reorientation of natural resource policy in the West. During his tenure in office, President Reagan relied primarily on an administrative strategy to shift public land policy from the Carter Administration's emphasis on environmental protection and conservation to an agenda of resource production, economic development, and states' rights. To provide a novel, manageable, yet informative analytical focus for understanding this effort, this book systematically examines how and with what consequences Reagan's policy, management control, and retrenchment initiatives interacted during their implementation in a single yet pivotal western state. Specifically, the study places in a regional context and examines in detail five disparate and illustrative cases culled from the implementation experiences of the Bureau of Land Management (BLM) in New Mexico. In the process, the purposes, logic, and dynamics of resource policy reorientation are reviewed across several major issue areas: public rangeland management, energy leasing, water resources management, wilderness preservation, urban economic development, and public land acquisition.

The purposes of this study are fourfold. First, it seeks to chronicle what can happen, and why, when a president tries to reorient policy significantly by using an administrative strategy. Second, it assesses the degree to which the particulars of Reagan's administrative strategy were linked effectively to his resource management goals in the West. In the process, this examination suggests an alternative to the conventional bureaucratic approach to resource management, to "top-down" implementation strategies, and to the policy prescriptions of the New Resource Economics.[19] Third, this study uses the Reagan Administration's implementation experiences in New Mexico—along with the findings of prior research—to begin developing a comprehensive theoretical foundation for grasping the promise, performance, and pitfalls of the administrative presidency as a device for executive leadership within the federal bureaucracy. Finally, this book explores the consequences of the administrative presidency for the core values of public administration in a democratic society.

A focus on the implementation experiences of the BLM seems especially promising given its checkered past, its turbulent task environment during the Carter Administration, and the salience of its operations to President Reagan's deregulatory agenda for the West. Indeed, as Jeanne Clarke and Daniel McCool contend, Reagan's deregulatory initiatives affected the Bureau more drastically than they did any other natural resource agency in the federal government.[20] Created in 1946 when two failing and suspect agencies—the General Land Office and the Grazing Service—were combined by executive reorganization within the Interior Department, the BLM assumed responsibility for managing more land than any other agency in the federal government.

Likewise, a focus on specific experiences of the Reagan Administration in New Mexico seems especially appropriate and useful. On the eve of the Reagan presidency, one-third of New Mexico's land was under BLM stewardship; its statute books contained one of the West's first federal land divestiture laws; and its Texas, Arizona, and Colorado neighbors unabashedly coveted the state's scarce water supplies. As a result, New Mexicans were profoundly interested in, affected by, and instrumental in developing aspects of the Administration's reorientation agenda.

As the "decade of the environment" dawned in 1970, the BLM confronted a task environment poised for rapid, convulsive, and profound change. By mid-decade, federal legislation had wrought a resource management agency assaulted by diverse interests engaged in an epic struggle for the organization's mind and soul. And by decade's end, the "sagebrush rebellion"—a grassroots political movement averse to BLM policy, management, and enforcement styles—dominated the resource agenda of many Western states. Among other things, members of the movement demanded that Congress expeditiously transfer all unappropriated BLM lands to state ownership. Their rationale: Federal stewardship created serious natural resource conflicts; distorted state priorities; and imposed arbitrary and unreasonable limits to community, agricultural, mineral, and energy resource development.[21] A professed "sagebrush rebel" during the 1980 presidential campaign, Ronald Reagan relished and promised to implement a fundamental change in the BLM's regulatory mission, management priorities, and enforcement style.

The remainder of this chapter sets the stage for analysis. First, it presents an abbreviated review of the leadership quandary facing contemporary presidents in the administrative state. Next, it identifies the origins of President Reagan's agenda for natural resource policy by examining the evolution of public land management in the West. The chapter concludes by presenting the central research questions and methods framing the study.

PRESIDENTIAL LEADERSHIP: AN ANALYTICAL PERSPECTIVE

While the concept of executive leadership has long intrigued scholars in a variety of disciplines, its essence remains largely elusive and enigmatic. Even sympathetic observers conclude that, "After years of trying, we have been unable to generate an understanding of leadership that is both intellectually compelling and emotionally satisfying."[22] Witness, for example, four perspectives presently claiming to capture best the essence of presidential leadership in the United States. For convenience, one might refer to these as the "heroic," the "deterministic," the "substitutionist," and the "attributionist" models of executive leadership.[23]

Clearly, recent scholarship reflects the "heroic" tradition by viewing the president as either "savior" (FDR, Kennedy, and Johnson prior to 1966) or "satan" (Nixon as well as Johnson after 1966).[24] Thus, while researchers in this tradition differ over how well- or ill-served the Republic is as a result, they all portray the presidency as a strong, purposive, and premiere force in our political system.[25] In contrast, other scholars offer a more deterministic perspective that emphasizes vexing economic, sociocultural, and political forces that constrain presidents from exercising much, if any, influence.[26] More specifically, secular trends such as presidential-congressional relations and partisan realignment interact with moderate-term business cycles, issue-attention cycles, and foreign policy cycles to condition significant policy changes. As a consequence, "No leader [is] more than a catalyst for events . . . which would have occurred with or without [the] heroic personality."[27]

The substitutionist and attributionist schools of leadership are also well-represented in the literature on the American presidency. In substitutionist terms, the "perpetually dickering" president is either "Samson" (weak, which is bad for the Republic) or "Seraph" (weak, which is good for the Republic).[28] Specifically, scholars in this genre see presidents as persuaders whose success or failure depends on their ability to be transactional leaders—e.g., coalition builders—who adroitly influence and broker the interests of disparate actors within our Madisonian system of fractionated problems and fragmented authority. Complicating this task, however, are factors that variously substitute for and thwart executive leadership. These include (1) bureaucratic rules, routines, and cultures; (2) professional norms and values; and (3) policy communities and issue networks. Thus, while researchers in this tradition disagree over how good or bad presidential weakness is in promoting the public interest, each disabuses us of the notion that presidents reign supreme in a tidy system of hierarchical relationships.

As for the attributionist perspective on presidential leadership, Lowi provides a provocative analysis of the "personal president."[29] He focuses on how, why, and with what consequences the public readily attributes inordinate power to its presidents—despite compelling evidence to the contrary. Lowi argues that citizens today are overwhelmed by the complexity of government and by ill-understood socioeconomic and political forces. As a result, a perplexed public magnifies presidential prowess out of a need to feel that someone is "in charge" and can cope with these impersonal forces. For their part, presidents consciously stoke these expectations in order, initially, to gain electoral support and, subsequently, to create the "high drama" necessary to garner legislative support for their policy agendas. What is more, because they fully expect to be held accountable for their hyperbole by an impatient and unforgiving electorate, presidents unfailingly move to centralize White House control over policy issues and managerial processes.

Regardless of which model best captures the leadership quandary facing contemporary presidents, the most common assessment of their plight by public administration specialists has been Hamiltonian in its assumptions and Brownlowian in its prescriptions. To wit, scholars view "energy in the executive" as a prerequisite for a vital and purposive political system; but to effectively become such a catalyst, the "president needs help."[30] What kind of help? For most studying this issue, the answer has been clear, consistent, yet ill-suited to our Madisonian system of divided authority, responsibility, and loyalty. That is, "presidentialists" have pursued a hierarchical, control-oriented vision of "efficient, executive-centered government" that resembles in retrospect a racehound chasing a mechanical rabbit: Each reform has only obtained broader grants of authority for presidents to pursue expanded responsibilities that in turn require additional authority for them to perform successfully. Still, presidents *do* successfully enact and implement their policy objectives, with most now convinced that administrative as well as legislative strategies are essential to their success.

Perhaps at no time has the administrative presidency been more rabidly applied in pursuit of an incumbent's agenda than in the Reagan Administration. And perhaps nowhere did this Administration more enthusiastically, contentiously, and with less apology apply the strategy than in the area of natural resource policy. Here, several of the President's most passionately committed and resourceful devotees labored to increase natural resource production, enhance states' rights, and quell the strident complaints of traditional public land users by amending bureaucratic budgets, routines, and worldviews rather than congressional statutes. In Part II of this book, we shall examine what the New Mexico experiences reveal in the field about the specifics and consequences of this strategic choice. Before doing so, however, it is useful to place President Reagan's deregulatory agenda for natural resource management in historical perspective.

THE EVOLUTION OF A DEREGULATORY AGENDA

David Rosenbloom argues that public executives must strive heroically in their work to reconcile three analytically distinct traditions in public administration: the managerial, the political, and the legal.[31] The managerial tradition stresses a hierarchical organization structure that promotes economy and efficiency, tight control of the bureaucracy, and a neutrally competent, expertise-based administration. In contrast, the political tradition values bureaucratic responsiveness, accountability, and representativeness informed by the "values, conflicts, and competing forces" of our pluralist society. Lastly, the legal tradition focuses our attention upon the equity or fairness issues involved in the exercise of agency discretion. Thus, the courts are counted upon to review and remedy bureaucratic processes and decisions to prevent agency misfeasance, malfeasance, or nonfeasance of duty. It is thus not surprising that these three administrative traditions, with their disparate outlooks and values, provide a most enlightening framework for appreciating the deregulatory furor confronting the BLM on the eve of the Reagan presidency.

The Political Tradition: From Dominant to Multiple Clientelism

The political plight of the BLM in the late 1970s was partly a product of secular changes in the demographic and cultural context of natural resource management in the West. Three of these developments were most telling. First, public land issues gradually turned from local management affairs into national policy issues. As recreational lifestyles changed, ecological awareness expanded, and Washington eyed energy resources on public lands as substitutes for precarious OPEC oil supplies, natural resource management in the region became a national concern and priority.[32] Not surprisingly, Congress especially intensified its scrutiny of BLM's policies and operations, since lands the agency managed were among those most coveted for their natural resource bounty.[33]

A second factor affecting public land politics was the demographic shift to the West during the past quarter century. With energy costs spiraling, with tax increases and expenses for land, labor, and capital depressing personal income and corporate profits, and with retirees seeking less frigid climates, frostbelt emigrees flocked to urban areas in the Sunbelt. For the BLM and Western members of Congress, this immigration fashioned a more diverse constituency, one with a decidedly different public lands agenda from that held by traditional ranching, mining, and timber users in the region.[34] Consequently, the Bureau's prodevelopment constituency—dominated historically by the livestock and hardrock mining industries—ran pell-mell into a more metropolitan clientele with an agenda stressing environmental, aesthetic, and amenity values over resource consumption.

Finally, financial distress plagued the Western livestock industry during the 1970s. As a result, many ranchers either left the business or moved to more hospitable climates in the South where the humidity begets grasslands that support more cattle per acre.

Not only did this situation reduce the ratio of rural to urban residents in many Western states, but it also caused many ranchers to see competing uses of the public lands as distinct threats to their survival. In this zero-sum framework, more forage needed for wildlife management meant less grassland available for nurturing and expanding one's own herd. Similarly, the more access granted to hunters, energy companies, and recreationists, the more acute the damage to sparse rangelands and the more disruption to grazing patterns and productivity. What the ranching industry feared most, however, was a plan conservationists championed: to impose sizeable and immediate cutbacks in the amount of grazing permitted on public rangelands. With a ranch's market value linked to the number of livestock permitted to graze on adjoining federal lands, with the value of existing permits a component of a ranch's original purchase price, and with ranch values the basis for bank loans to permittees, the issue of grazing reductions aroused the passionate political ire of ranchers, real estate brokers, and bankers in the West.

Not unexpectedly, the confluence of these trends spawned a surge of legislative action in Washington. Congress repeatedly enacted legislation affecting the substance, scope, and techniques of public land management in the region (see Table 1–1). While ensuing chapters discuss the specifics of these statutes as they relate to the BLM's experiences in New Mexico, it is important to note here their most profound political effect: the legal enfranchisement of nontraditional uses and users of the public lands. In this regard, the Federal Land Policy and Management Act of 1976 (FLPMA) stands as the single most important contribution to the BLM's emergent "multiple clientelism" in the 1970s and beyond. Indeed, as Paul Culhane and Paul Friesma suggest, the Act provided "an unmistakable cue that the public lands should be managed for purposes beyond livestock grazing."[35]

Among other things, FLPMA (the BLM Organic Act) required the Bureau to recognize the legitimacy of both market and nonmarket land values, and consequently to consider and reconcile the often conflicting demands of traditional and nontraditional public land users. Moreover, the Act compelled the BLM to plan and perform in ways that were as consistent as possible with state and

TABLE 1–1
Major Legislation Affecting the Management of U.S. Public Lands,
1872–1978

Statute	Description
General Mining Law (1872)	Provides for access to and location of claims for specific "hardrock" materials on the public lands, including U.S. Forest lands. Allows for exploration, development, and patenting of claims under prescribed conditions.
Antiquities Act (1906)	Prohibits removal or destruction of antiquities from public lands.
Mineral Leasing Act (1920)	Provides for leasing of oil, gas, sulphur, coal, potash, sodium, phosphate, and oil shale on public lands, including U.S. Forest lands and land where the surface may be patented (i.e., leased) but the federal government retained the minerals. Allows both competitive and noncompetitive leasing procedures.
Recreation and Public Purposes Act (1926)	Provides for the disposal of public lands through sale or lease to certain non-profit entities for the location of recreational or public purpose facilities. Examples are state parks, county sanitary landfills, boy scout camps, and buildings where public hearings are held.

(*continued*)

TABLE 1–1 (*Continued*)

Statute	Description
Color-of-Titles Acts (1928 and 1932)	Provides for granting title to public land occupied and improved by citizens inadvertently for a period of 20 years or longer. Establishes procedures for qualification and for payment of some fees for land transferred to private ownership.
Taylor Grazing Act (1934)	Provides for a tenured system of permits or leases to individuals to graze livestock on the public lands within specified conditions and carrying capacities. Also allows for range improvements, such as fences, wells, etc.
Acquired Lands Mineral Leasing Act (1947)	Provides for mineral leasing on lands acquired by the federal government, such as military reservations, Bankhead-Jones Act lands, etc.
Classification and Multiple-Use Act (1964)	Provides for a system of classification for all of the public lands into categories for management and/or disposal. This act has expired; however, the classifications made remain in effect.

(*continued*)

TABLE 1–1 (*Continued*)

Statute	Description
Wilderness Act (1964)	Establishes a wilderness preservation system and sets requirements for future management of these areas to protect wilderness values. Applies to most federal and managing agencies, although the BLM was not included until 1976.
National Historic Preservation Act (1966)	Establishes a system for identifying, protecting, and managing certain historic sites, buildings, etc.
National Environmental Policy Act (1969)	Requires the preparation of an environmental assessment or statement to analyze the effects to the environment of any major federal action. Current statements on livestock grazing are being done under the requirements of this act.
Land and Water Conservation Fund Act (1970)	Allows for collection of fees for certain designated federal recreation sites, the money collected to be used to purchase additional recreational areas or for major improvements to existing sites on cost sharing basis with non-federal agencies.
Rare and Endangered Species Act (1973)	Establishes a listing of and procedures for protecting specific rare and/or endangered species of plants, fishes, animals, and birds.

(*continued*)

TABLE 1–1 (*Continued*)

Statute	Description
Archaeology and Historic Preservation Act (1974)	Requires specific steps be taken to recognize and protect archaeological, cultural, and historic sites on public lands.
Federal Coal Leasing Amendments Act (1976)	Establishes procedures for leasing federal coal, which incorporate competitive leasing, land use planning, "diligent development," revenue sharing, surface reclamation, and other environmental safeguards.
Federal Land Policy and Management Act (1976)	Provides for retention of most public land by the federal government and requires that the concepts of multiple use and sustained yield be applied to the management of these lands.
Surface Mining Control and Reclamation Act (1977)	Regulates surface mining. Established the Office of Surface Mining within the Department of the Interior. Provides for surface owner consent prior to mining where privately owned surface overlies federal coal.
Public Rangelands Improvement Act (1978)	Provides for appropriations for range improvements to the public lands.

local land-use plans, and to maximize public participation in agency decision making. To be sure, since at least the early 1960s, the agency had weighed informally the preferences of these users, as changes occurred in the Bureau's task environment. FLPMA, however, provided a statutory mandate to consider specific values related to outdoor recreation; watershed protection; fish and wildlife management; and the preservation of natural, scenic, cultural, and historical treasures. In the process, the Act legally affirmed the principle that multiple, diverse, and typically competitive BLM constituencies have a justiciable right to influence natural resource policy. What FLPMA did not supply, however, was a framework for assessing the priority of uses or users in particular situations. Consequently, a prolonged and bitter conflict arose over which land management ethic—"multiple use–sustained yield" or "fullest and best use"—would prevail, in what form, and in whose interest.

The Managerial Tradition: Toward a Science of Natural Resource Management?

Woodrow Wilson—president, scholar, and activist in the early progressive reform movement—once wrote that government "must administer our resources as a good trustee would administer a great estate for the support of the living and the benefit of those yet unborn."[36] For Wilson, Gifford Pinchot, and other Progressive conservationists of this era, wise and disciplined use of our natural resources was essential to human survival. As such, resource management could not be left either to the vagaries of the market or the power asymmetries of the pluralist bargaining process. Instead, experts applying scientific principles and sophisticated quantitative models should husband our natural resources to satisfy both the immediate and long-range needs of a variety of resource users through apolitical, expertise-based scientific management.

For the BLM, however, implementing these multiple-use and sustained-yield principles of resource management in an apolitical fashion has proven most difficult and controversial, given the land management legacy bequeathed to it by our nation's six analytically distinct yet overlapping eras of natural resource policy: acquisition, disposal, reservation, custodial, intensive management, and consultation-confrontation.[37] Remnants of each era doggedly confronted, complicated, and rendered adversarial the managerial responsibilities of the BLM as Ronald Reagan assumed the presidency.

Toward Privatization. The first two eras—acquisition (1792–1867) and disposal (1812–1933)—fostered a crazy-quilt pattern of land ownership and competing interests that contemporary BLMers must somehow reconcile to manage effectively the public lands. Propelled during the acquisition era by the rhetoric of "manifest destiny," the federal government amassed nearly 1.8 million acres of land through direct purchase, peace treaties, and international agreements.[38] As the nation's debts mounted, however, Congress instructed the General Land Office to sell federal lands as needed for revenue. But with ownership titles from territorial days frequently unclear, and with productive capacity only marginal on most arid lands, sales were few in number, widely dispersed, and plagued by land fraud and speculation.

Following this episode, Congress moved vigorously to encourage permanent settlement and economic development of the region. Under various iterations of a federal homestead program, settlers gained title to land at nominal fees once they had successfully farmed allotments of varying sizes for specified periods of time.[39] While modest numbers of widely scattered land tracts located near water supplies were disposed of quite readily, the program's impact was stifled substantially when it offered homestead land in arid Western climates where the allotments were too small to support livestock grazing.[40] Related efforts to lure miners and foresters to the West were equally disappointing, since Eastern lands near population centers were more profitable for development.

Thus, contrary to the expectations of their designers, land disposal programs managed only to further balkanize land ownership in the region. What is more, the situation grew worse when Congress began issuing land grants to states and railroads for economic development. State grants often abutted private, municipal, or federal properties managed for differing and frequently conflicting purposes. Similarly, railroad grants spawned "checkerboard" patterns of ownership as corporations received as investment incentive miles of alternating land tracts adjacent to their routes. In sum, by the end of the disposal era, vast amounts of the West remained in federal hands. Moreover, these properties were nestled among nonfederal lands, in noncontiguous blocks, and in random sizes and patterns that too often made efficient, effective, and apolitical land management the exception rather than the rule.

Toward Minimalist Management. The next two eras of natural resource administration—reservation (1890–1940) and custodial management (1910–1950)—were likewise fraught with problems for future administration by the BLM. In withdrawing from development a variety of pristine resource areas during these years, the federal government explicitly legitimized and institutionalized a scientific approach to resource management. At the same time, it sparked an interagency rivalry over natural resource administration that has worked to the chronic disadvantage of the BLM throughout its history. As Congress began to designate timber lands as national forest reserves, Progressive conservationists persuaded legislators that these resources required professional management informed by the multiple use–sustained yield principle of scientific forestry. To this end, Congress transferred responsibility for the reserves from the Interior to the Agriculture Department, in the process giving birth to the U.S. Forest Service. In doing so, however, it also effectively split responsibility for public land management between the Forest Service and the Interior Department, with the former touted widely as a "model" to be emulated by its drastically less professionalized, less technocratic sister agency.

For today's BLM, the programmatic and political consequences of these developments are profound. As Clarke and McCool observe, natural resource agencies imbued with the image, if not the reality, of a multipurpose mission and scientific ethos tend to fare better in Congress at budget time than their less-well-perceived rivals.[41] In fact, they ordinarily acquire a "favored agency status" relative to the others, one that widens appropriation gaps and power differentials among the agencies as the years pass. Thus, by 1980, the BLM managed four times the acreage of the Forest Service, but with one-third the budget and one-seventh the personnel.

A second legacy of the reservation and custodial eras is an elaborate water regulatory framework that directly affects public land management in the West. Ever since the disposal era, Congress had generally accepted the premise that regulatory authority over in-state water resources passed from the federal government to the states as each entered the Union. Thus, for federal resource agencies operating today in the region, this means submitting to a water regulatory system premised on the doctrine of "prior appropriation and beneficial use." Although the specifics of the state systems vary, most assign water rights to the first applicant who seeks to appropriate the water for a beneficial economic use. Customarily, users forfeit their rights if they do not actually use the water as stipulated within a specified time. Thus, in principle, state regulators scientifically determine the quantity and quality of available surface- and ground-water supplies. They then impartially allocate these waters on a "first-come, first-served" basis that, in turn, is premised on a "use it or lose it" principle. In practice, however, supply-and-demand uncertainty frequently abounds, and political conflict often ensues over the quantity, quality, and proper allocation of this scarce resource.

As a final legacy, the reservation and custodial eras bequeathed to the Interior Department a "minimalist" management ethic animated by user demands rather than by aggressive demand management. Most assuredly, this ethic fostered an enduring belief among traditional users that Interior's proper role is to promote, not regulate their activities. Take, for instance, the federal government's traditional approach to public range management. Prior to the 1930s, ranchers enjoyed free access to public lands adjoining their properties and proceeded to graze cattle at rates and in numbers that far exceeded the carrying capacity of these lands. In fact, most graziers grew dependent on unrestricted access to the public domain for their very livelihood. However, in the wake of the Dust Bowl disaster, and to block the access of sheepherders to the public lands, the cattle industry ultimately agreed to limited regulation under the Taylor Grazing Act of 1934.

The Taylor Grazing Act charged the Grazing Service—overwhelmingly staffed by former ranchers—with establishing district advisory boards. Dominated by local cattlemen, these boards

made decisions regarding grazing access, levels, and fees that differed fundamentally from those made by the Forest Service with its
data-based, multiple use–sustained yield grazing policies. More
specifically, they effectively ratified historical grazing levels, assigned public land-use exclusively to ranchers with adjoining water
supplies, and routinely ignored federal range studies that recommended sizeable grazing reductions. In fact, these boards even
requested that Congress slash Grazing Service (and, later, BLM)
budgets in order to undermine aggressive regulation, deflect legislative scrutiny, and enhance their own control over range policy.
Toward the "New" BLM. The final two eras of natural resource
administration—intensive management (1950–1960) and consultation-confrontation (post-1960)—are integrally related and highly
significant, since they provide a legislative foundation for multiple-
use management by the BLM. Recall that intense, diverse, and
complex pressures for increased land use began during the 1950s
and spiraled over the next two decades. Initially, the Bureau coped
with this situation without explicit multiple-use authority and with
a mosaic of disposal-oriented statutes, nonprofessional personnel,
and pro-development constituencies. This gradually began to
change, however, after Congress enacted the Land Classification
and Multiple-Use Act of 1964. This statute instructed the BLM to
inventory and classify public lands for either disposal or federal
retention. In addition, it temporarily charged the agency with
managing retained properties according to multiple-use principles
and brought on board the first significant numbers of university-
trained range management specialists. Thus, as Sally Fairfax concludes, the Bureau by the mid-sixties was indeed striving to develop the ambition and the ability to regulate public rangelands
aggressively.[42] Nonetheless, the Multiple-Use Act expired in
1970, leaving the agency without a compelling statutory mandate
for multiple-use management until Congress enacted FLPMA in
1976.

As noted above, FLPMA permanently reformulated the agency's mission, radically altered its decision premises, and over the
ensuing decade regularly incited the passions of the Bureau's emerging multiple clientele. Not only did it shift BLM's priorities toward land retention rather than disposal, but it also authorized the

agency to designate local planning regions, to base its management decisions upon land-use plans, and to institute multiple-use advisory councils to offset the power of the district grazing boards. To develop these planning documents, multidisciplinary teams of BLM professionals had to collect and analyze inventories on existing resource conditions and trends. Then, applying environmental and economic criteria, they had to make multiple-use land decisions informed by broad-based public participation.

While synoptic planning approaches always have great intuitive appeal, the simplicity of their formats belies the cost, complexity, and controversy surrounding their implementation. Indeed, for a financially strapped and chronically understaffed BLM, long-range planning has sparked more than its share of controversy and internecine conflict among agency professionals.[43] Reminiscent of the spirit and tactics of the Progressive reform era, the Bureau under the Carter Administration pursued a technocratic approach with abandon, commitment, and a modicum of success. It did so, however, encumbered by the agency's minimalist legacy of suspect data inventories, competing resource theories, and controversial modeling techniques. As a result, the agency aroused the sustained ire of litigious public interest groups across the West.

The Legal Tradition: Public Land Management and the Revolt Against Bureaucracy

Since the early 1970s, interrelated developments in court–agency relationships have dramatically affected public managers' behavior: the judicialization of administration, the emergence of procedural and substantive rationality as standards for judicial review of agency actions, and the rise of the public law litigation model of bureaucratic reform.[44]

Judicial access and activism have meant mixed blessings for the BLM. To be sure, many in the agency welcomed and profited politically from these developments when lawsuits directly buttressed the Bureau's budget requests and fledgling multiple-use mandate. For example, in *Natural Resources Defense Council v. Morton*, a federal judge ruled that a single environmental impact statement (EIS) for the BLM's total grazing program did not satisfy the procedural requirements of the National Environmental Policy

Act (NEPA).[45] Since the Bureau had failed in its EIS to consider the effects of grazing on discrete local environments, the court ordered the agency to perform 212 separate environmental statements. Fully aware of the funding and workforce implications of its decision, the court stipulated that "lack of resources can not be an excuse to ignore or pay mere lip service to the NEPA requirements," and "the issue of any shortfall in performance will become a matter for discussion" in Congress.[46]

In this fashion, the federal judiciary helped to coax a conservation agenda from recalcitrant elements within the BLM, to legitimate agency requests for badly needed funding, and to accelerate and diversify the Bureau's professionalization. The herculean task of preparing EISs on the scale and within the time frame stipulated focused BLM energies and resources on land-use planning and intensive recruiting of wildlife biologists, soil scientists, archeologists, paleontologists, and planners. Unlike traditional BLM personnel, these recruits held professional values that stressed nonconsumptive over consumptive uses of the public lands. What is more, during the Carter years they regularly sparred with their more development-minded colleagues for policy ascendency within the Bureau.

In other instances, however, lawsuits taxed the patience and jeopardized the policy initiatives of the "new" BLM. For example, the conservative Mountain States Legal Foundation repeatedly used methodological arguments to challenge the Carter Administration's efforts to reduce grazing, oil, and gas leasing on public lands, while environmentalists successfully challenged its effort to stimulate coal leasing in the wake of the Arab oil shock in the late 1970s.[47] Clearly, one could not intentionally craft a regulatory predicament more ironic for the BLM. Precisely as the agency began to amass the will, additional resources, and statutory foundation to practice scientific management, citizens and federal judges grew more suspicious of, less willing to defer to, and more likely to substitute their own judgment for bureaucratic expertise. And most significantly for Ronald Reagan, their perspective ultimately translated into staunch electoral support for his pro-development, deregulatory, and states' rights agenda for natural resource management.

CENTRAL RESEARCH QUESTIONS

How successful was President Reagan's use of the administrative presidency in reorienting natural resource policy in the West? As John Leshy suggests, relying only on aggregate statistics to compare the Reagan Administration's resource development record with its predecessors' is extremely unwise.[48] First, the Reaganites were uniquely positioned to capitalize on policy changes made during previous administrations, changes that could not be fully implemented or felt until the 1980s. Second, aggregate data mask the impact of factors—such as court injunctions, weather conditions, and world energy markets—that are beyond any administration's control. Finally, these measures are insensitive to the nuances of implementation style and attitude that so enraged the "sagebrush rebels." These caveats notwithstanding, however, it is clear that the "ravaging of the West" so bemoaned by environmentalists and political cartoonists never occurred under the Reagan Administration. Indeed, even when more modest standards are applied to Reagan's stewardship, most independent analyses echo Leshy's first-term assessment that the Administration's performance "did not [match] the relative clarity and ambitiousness of its program goals."[49]

Certainly, assessments of this nature beg several questions for those interested in the administrative presidency. First, is any of the responsibility for this outcome attributable to the Administration's managerial strategy itself, or is it merely the product of macropolitical missteps by Secretary Watt and his successors, judicial reversals of Reagan's deregulatory agenda, or contextual factors beyond anyone's control? Second, what bureaupolitical dynamics tend to characterize various attempts at reorienting policy administratively? Third, from a more theoretical perspective, do these dynamics tend to vary across policy initiatives? Fourth, do particular variables help account for these differences in bureaupolitical dynamics? Fifth, under what conditions and using what implementation strategies will the administrative presidency prove most successful in the natural resource policy arena? In other policy arenas? And finally, what are the side effects of the administrative presidency for Heclo's "larger organizational life of government?"[50] In particular, what are the implications of this strategy for executive leadership and democratic values in our Madisonian system of checks and balances, issue networks, and judicialized administration?

To explore these issues within the larger context of natural resource policy in the West, this book uses a comparative case study design that applies a "direct" and formative evaluation approach adapted from the literature on strategic planning.[51] Thus, we can assess the internal consistency of the strategic goals and tactical maneuvers pursued by Reagan appointees, with performance measures providing only the leitmotif against which these officials carried out the administrative presidency. At issue: How consistent were the Reagan Administration's operational choices (i.e., agency reorganizations, rule making, budget cuts, and personnel actions) with its strategic choices (i.e., its natural resource goals and objectives).

The remaining chapters in Part I frame the analysis. Chapter 2 places Ronald Reagan's approach to the administrative presidency in historical perspective across a range of policy domains, types, arenas, administrations, and levels of success. Chapter 3 then explores how the Reagan Administration's reorientation effort, as conceived in Washington, affected the organization, operations, and staffing of the BLM in New Mexico.

The specifics of the case analyses follow in Part II. Chapter 4 examines the Reagan Administration's experiences as it sought to simultaneously decentralize policy authority within the BLM and to deregulate oil and gas production in New Mexico through structural reorganization. Chapter 5 analyzes the Administration's concurrent efforts in New Mexico to provide regulatory relief for Western ranchers, to increase range production, and to trim agency expenses by privatizing maintenance costs for range improvements. Chapter 6 reviews how two prominent Administration initiatives interacted in New Mexico: "unlocking" urban areas for economic development and discouraging the purchase of additional wilderness, forest, and national park lands. This is followed in Chapter 7 by an accounting of how budget retrenchment, cost-sharing of water projects, and evolving case law combined to complicate the Administration's pledge to preserve states' rights in water regulation. Chapter 8 ends this section by chronicling the Administration's plight as it sought to significantly increase coal exploration and leasing in wilderness study areas in northwest New Mexico.

The book concludes with Part III assessing the practical and theoretical implications of its findings. In the process, Chapters 9 and 10 offer analytical, strategic, and theoretical perspectives on both natural resource management and the administrative presidency.

CHAPTER 2

Prometheus Unbound or Sisyphus Redux?

By the end of the first term of the Reagan Administration, scholars, practitioners, and pundits alike concluded that they were witnessing a watershed event in the evolution of the administrative presidency. Some even suggested that Reagan's "striking success" in fashioning a "workable administrative framework placed him in a pivotal historical position" that could "establish him as the most administratively influential president of the modern period."[1] To enhance our appreciation for the intellectual foundations, controversies, and singular qualities of Reagan's "supply-side management" approach to the administrative presidency, this chapter examines the strategy's evolution across various administrations, policy arenas, and presidential priorities.

SUPPLY-SIDE MANAGEMENT, THE ADMINISTRATIVE PRESIDENCY, AND THE REAGAN REVOLUTION

As James Carroll, A. Lee Fritschler, and Bruce L. R. Smith summarize its broad elements, supply-side management is the logical corollary of supply-side economics:

> As the supply of managers is reduced there will be less tendency for the government to manage programs directly and hence fewer activities undertaken by federal departments and agencies. Fewer services to administer in turn means less pressure to appoint managers and build large management teams within government. . . . Government can get along with fewer managers because it will leave to career administrators the 'details' of administration while appointive officials chart broad policy directions. [Consequently], within the department or agency, a small number of senior managers set policy goals for "flatter" organizational structures [as] . . . the classes of

"manager" (political) and "operator" (career) are more sharply separated, and fewer intermediate level positions exist. . . . Thus, the supply-side manager's tool kit is complete: diminished expectations of government; an atmosphere of budgetary constraint and of centralized control of decision making; and a focus on a small number of central objectives deemed to be of overriding national importance.[2]

In sum, the "minimalist state" moorings of the Reagan Revolution were tightly coupled to a "minimalist" management philosophy, one tethered tautly to the implementation tools of the administrative presidency.

Organization Tools: The "Realpolitik" of Administrative Reform

For decades, structural reorganization of the executive branch has fascinated activist chief executives bent—most often—on realizing short-term tactical, symbolic, and political advantage, and—less often—on strategically enhancing their policy preferences. The literature and folklore of presidential reorganization spans policy and program types and chronicles a variety of purposes, strategies, and tactics. One popular variant of the approach involves presidents trying to enhance policy control, survival, or coordination by locating nascent, floundering, or uncooperative units within the purview of White House officials. For example, both President Kennedy's Food for Peace Program (FPP) and President Johnson's War on Poverty were given the imprimatur of presidential priority when the FPP director was named special assistant to the President, and the Office of Economic Opportunity was placed in the Executive Office of the President (EOP). Similarly, President Carter's energy "czar," James Schlesinger, operated as a White House advisor with the authority to coordinate the activities of all energy agencies prior to the creation of the Department of Energy. And by creating the National Security and Domestic Policy Councils, Presidents Truman and Nixon, respectively, sought to overcome bureaucratic parochialism and enhance White House control over policy formulation.

Presidents also have tried to "punish" wayward bureaus by allowing White House or EOP staff members to monitor, challenge, or curtail their internal management, budget, and personnel practices. In effect, they have created what Richard Pious aptly terms cabinet "oversecretaries": White House officials delegated administrative responsibilities that supercede those of cabinet secretaries and bureau chiefs.[3] Quite interestingly, however, it appears in retrospect that a paradox often exists between White House involvement in agency affairs and presidential policy control. Not only do staff politics, processes, and parochialisms often foil these efforts, but staffers' concerns with agency detail routinely displace the larger policy concerns of the Chief Executive. Thus, it is not surprising that President Carter's transition team soundly critiqued this situation in the mid-1970s as "a jumble of different kinds of entities which serve different purposes and exist for different reasons."[4]

A second variant of the reorganization approach involves creating new or combining existing bureaucracies to fashion administrative environments more conducive to presidential goals. Recent examples of this tactic are President Eisenhower's creation of the National Aeronautics and Space Administration, President Nixon's creation of the Environmental Protection Agency (EPA) and the Occupational Safety and Health Administration (OSHA), and President Carter's creation of the Departments of Energy and of Education. Referred to by scholars as "old style" reorganization—i.e., restructuring that cuts across departments and requires enacting legislation by the Congress—the structural approach to policy reorientation is hardly for the impatient, the politically unastute, or the weak of spirit. Indeed, it typically elicits formidable opposition from beneficiaries of the status quo—whether in Congress, the bureaus themselves, or agency clientele groups.

Finally, presidents have tried to use reorganizations to diminish congressional oversight of executive branch activities and to foil unwelcome legislative overtures. For example, when President Nixon established the Office of Management and Budget (OMB) with a director who served as a presidential counselor, he was formally attempting to preclude Senate oversight and thereby to enhance agency responsiveness to presidential priorities. Similarly, Presidents Ford, Carter, and Reagan deftly pursued internal OMB reorganizations that established new layers of political appointees (known as "program associate directors") bent on promoting presidential prerogatives. At other times, however, presidents have avoided, resisted, or warily approached reorganization, especially when the status quo advanced presidential control over policies dear to an incumbent's heart. One thinks immediately, for instance, of President Roosevelt's efforts to ensure bureaucratic redundancy, overlap, and duplication in order to facilitate bureaucratic conflict—conflict that only he ultimately and strategically could resolve. Likewise, President Nixon and Henry Kissinger institutionalized rivalries among the Joint Chiefs, the Secretary of Defense, and the military services to advance their own personal control over national security policy.

How effective is the "old style" reorganization approach to presidential leadership? For years, scholars and practitioners have debated inconclusively the impact of these efforts.[5] For example, many in the so-called "realpolitik" school of organizational reform discount them as quixotic exercises; they are resoundingly gutted, defeated, or frustrated in their implementation by members of Congress jealously preserving their access to existing bureaucratic fiefdoms. Others of this persuasion impugn the ability of time-consuming reorganizations to realize projected savings or to bring about fundamental policy or attitudinal change. To be successful, they argue, personnel, procedural, and administrative reform on a similar scale must accompany astute structural reform. Still others in this genre chide as "irrelevant" the managerial orthodoxy supporting most reorganization proposals. To wit, Harold Seidman and Robert Gilmour write of "the tactical and strategic uses of organization structure, processes, and procedures as an instrument [sic] of politics, position, and power."[6] Moreover, these scholars contend that while presidential success in promoting policy redirection through structural change requires a coherent organization strategy premised on these realities, presidents typically proceed instead in a piecemeal, reactive, and opportunistic fashion.

The pessimism of the "realpolitik" school is buttressed as well by the writings of several leading management scholars.[7] They conclude that we have reached the limits of our competence within the conventional bureaucratic model that normally informs presidential reorganization proposals. As Robert Golembiewski explains, opting for departmentation by function or program rather than by work process effectively means opting for managerial *control* instead of organizational *accomplishment.* He argues that by intentionally fragmenting work flows among subunits of the organization, the conventional model prevents any single agent from handling a complete transaction or policy goal. As a result, subunit (or program) cooperation is necessary to accomplish statutory goals and responsibilities. Unfortunately, cooperation tends to be the exception rather than the rule as implementors somehow must transcend enduring professional or program jealousies, loyalties, and interests. As a consequence, presidents seeking policy or program redirection by placing similar functions or programs "cheek to jowl," as the "administrative orthodoxy" prescribes, are usually disappointed.

Still, enough theoretical, empirical, and anecdotal evidence supports the worthwhileness of structural reform to whet the appetites of determined presidents, political appointees, and interest groups. Some theorists suggest we need to revamp our thinking about reorganization proposals by placing them on a longer time horizon, by appreciating the educative function they perform, and by being more sensitive to the interpretive coherence they afford to political life in a complex democratic polity. James March and Johan Olsen, for example, insist that "any specific major reorganization project is likely to fail, but persistent repetition of similar ideas and similar arguments over a relatively long period of time appears to make a difference" in gaining congressional approval.[8] In addition, these scholars identify a variety of "secondary returns" for presidents who pursue their proposals with commitment, patience, and perseverance. For instance, agencies that are targets for reorganization frequently change or modify their behavior in the desired direction to head off structural reform. What is more, presidents tend persistently to reap political benefits whether their proposals succeed or fail in the short run: "Announcing a major reorganization symbolize[s] the possibility of effective leadership, and the [public's] belief in that possibility may be of greater significance than the execution of it."[9]

During the Reagan presidency, political appointees never viewed "old style" reorganization as an effective instrument for reorienting public policy. Instead, they focused on *intra*departmental and *intra*agency reorganizations that unilaterally and immediately altered hierarchical relationships, responsibilities, and communication channels. More precisely, they doggedly revamped formal authority and informal communication networks to circumvent obdurate and strategically located career executives who opposed the President's agenda within individual agencies. For instance, appointees at the Justice Department's Land and Water Resources Division effectively diminished the status, organizational independence, and enforcement zeal of hazardous waste personnel by merging this unit with the Division's environmental enforcement section. Likewise, Department of Energy officials either eliminated altogether units dealing with conservation and renewable energy resources, or merged them with units that were unsympathetic to these pursuits. Meanwhile, Reagan appointees at the Employment and Training Administration, the Federal Communications Commission (FCC), and the Mine Health and Safety Administration desperately tried to circumvent pockets of bureaucratic resistance by shifting functional responsibilities to different units and levels within their organizations.

Authority Tools: "Reaganizing" the Federal Bureaucracy

One of the most popular, time-worn, and controversial control devices wielded by presidents is their power to appoint nearly five thousand noncareer officials to key executive posts within the federal government. Indicative of the critical importance attached to this function, recent presidents have created increasingly more systematic and sophisticated appointment mechanisms within the White House.[10] On the assumption that management, policy, and program control is elusive without political control, presidential activists try earnestly to fill agency leadership positions with kindred spirits loyal to their political, policy, or philosophical outlooks. These appointees in turn are expected to institutionalize faithfully the president's agenda in daily personnel, rule making, enforcement, and resource allocation decisions.

Examples abound of both adept and disappointing applications of the presidential appointment power. In the defense policy arena, for example, Morton Halperin cites President Eisenhower's frustration at being unable to appoint an Army Chief of Staff willing to support enthusiastically his massive nuclear retaliation doctrine—a strategy envisioning sizable army troop reductions.[11] Similarly, President Nixon's appointment of Walter Hickel as Interior Secretary initially brought kudos from resource developers. Yet Hickel rapidly aroused their ire by tilting natural resource policy in a decidedly conservationist direction during his abbreviated tenure. In contrast, President Carter ably recruited civil rights, occupational health, environmental, and consumer protection activists to staff the Equal Employment Opportunity Commission (EEOC), the Occupational Safety and Health Administration (OSHA), the Environmental Protection Agency (EPA), and the National Highway Transportation Safety Administration (NHTSA). And unlike his experience with Hickel, President Nixon reaped policy dividends by transferring Elliot Richardson from Secretary of Health, Education, and Welfare (HEW) to Secretary of Defense to disrupt Richardson's uncommonly cordial relationship with HEW careerists.

Despite its popularity, "politicizing" the bureaucracy is a highly controversial approach to presidential leadership, especially when wielded in ways reminiscent of President Nixon's counter-bureaucratic strategy. There are those, for instance, who excoriate the strategy as an ill-conceived assault on neutral competence; an assault that ironically strips chief executives of the expertise, professionalism, political savvy, and institutional memory that they ultimately need to be effective.[12] Heclo, for example, despairs over "a real and growing danger that as demands on government performance are growing, and as the need for continuity, executive branch coordination, and independent analysis is increasing, the standards of neutral competence are being eroded."[13]

Similarly, James Pfiffner questions the ability of presidents to attract and retain sufficiently mature, talented, and seasoned individuals for the less prestigious and less lucrative subcabinet positions previously assigned to careerists. Supporting Pfiffner, Patricia Ingraham also warns that extremely high turnover rates among appointees actually *diminish* presidential control; these novices are more dependent on career personnel for expertise.[14] What is more, adds Heclo, presidents and their emissaries are served best when they view neutral competence as "loyalty that argues back." In his view, appointees should rely on agency professionals to sort out the substantive and political pluses, problems, and pitfalls of policy initiatives before irreparable damage is done to presidential popularity, agendas, and places in history.[15]

In contrast, however, another group of observers finds much to commend political control of the federal bureaucracy, with some even advocating increased estrangement between political appointees and career executives as politicizing progresses. Jack Knott and Gary Miller, for example, worry that the Progressive reform era's emphasis on depoliticizing the bureaucracy went too far in insulating careerists from political accountability and the will of the electorate.[16] Likewise, Richard Nathan and Terry Moe remind us that critics ignore the institutional and political imperatives that make politicizing the bureaucracy attractive to presidents, that render calls for depoliticizing unrealistic, and that make repoliticizing a prerequisite to bureaucratic innovativeness.[17]

Lastly, other scholars take the extreme position that appointees must diligently avoid being inundated by the bureaucratic perspective; presidential priorities can be disarmed or disrupted by risk-averse careerists.[18] For instance, Michael Sanera readily concedes that political appointees can employ a variety of management strategies—some even involving the participation of careerists when stewarding the president's agenda through the bureaucracy. Yet his approach zealously guards the policy prerogatives of political appointees, cautiously allows access only to loyal careerists, and immutably distrusts public managers. Indeed, Sanera extolls the virtues of what he terms "jigsaw puzzle management":

> Whether he is implementing a planned agenda or formulating a new one, the political executive will be involved in politically controversial subjects. This means that control over the process must be retained by the political executive and his immediate political staff. . . . Career staff will supply information, but they should never become involved in the formulation of agenda-related objectives. Similarly, once controversial policy goals are formulated . . . [career] staff see and work on the individual pieces, but never have enough of the pieces to be able to learn the entire picture.[19]

Upon assuming the presidency, Ronald Reagan pursued an energetic, enterprising, and philosophically based politicizing strategy that far eclipsed all his recent predecessors' efforts, with the probable exception of FDR. Indeed, many concluded that Reagan's cabinet and subcabinet appointments were the most partisan and ideological of any president of the past twenty years. Thus, for example, the President adeptly appointed five members of the hawkish Committee on the Present Danger to arms control agencies within the State Department, and likewise named supply-side economists such as Paul Craig Roberts and Norman Ture to strategic posts at the Treasury Department. In addition, Reagan's appointments of John Lehman, Fred Ikle, and Richard Perle to the Defense Department helped ensure a buildup in naval forces, a determined defense mobilization, and confrontational East-West trade relations, respectively.

Similarly, in the social regulatory realm, the President pursued a two-pronged politicization approach to policy reorientation. On the one hand, he routinely appointed individuals who were conspicuously weak in substantive policy expertise, but rich in free-market philosophy and animus toward regulatory missions—e.g., Edwin Edwards at the Department of Energy, Albert Angrisani at the Employment and Training Administration, Timothy Muris at the Federal Trade Commission, and Ford B. Ford at the Mine Health and Safety Administration. At the same time, Reagan unapologetically appointed representatives of regulated industries to leadership positions at key agencies—e.g., John Crowell at the Forest Service, Thorne Auchter at OSHA, Mark Fowler at the FCC, and Robert Burford at the Bureau of Land Management.

While no doubt significant, these high-profile political appointments were but the tip of the iceberg in the President's comprehensive plans for "Reaganizing" the federal bureaucracy. Taking advantage of the unprecedented opportunities for managerial control afforded by the Civil Service Reform Act (CSRA) of 1978, Reagan's strategy was fivefold: first, establish an almost tentacular White House control mechanism for subcabinet appointments to staff and line positions; second, impose reductions-in-force (RIFs) and hiring freezes to increase significantly the ratio of noncareer to career executives and managers in domestic agencies; third, reduce the number of policy-making careerists by systematically down-grading middle management positions to lower classifications; fourth, dramatically alter the skill mix of professionals in various agencies to modify institutional cultures; and finally, empower philosophically attuned political appointees to wield unabashedly their managerial prerogatives in pursuit of the President's agenda.

With regard to the White House appointment process, President Reagan—unlike many of his predecessors—did not delegate authority to his department heads to make subcabinet appointments. Too often, he felt, presidents so inclined watched later in despair as loyalty to cabinet secretaries and *their* policy agendas displaced presidential preferences. Moreover, the architects of the Reagan Revolution were confident that "true believers" could be most effective if placed strategically in low-profile managerial posts (e.g., assistant secretary for administration, deputy assistant secretary, and GS-13 to GS-15 Schedule C positions) where daily operational decisions effectively constitute policy making. From these slots, Reagan loyalists could advance the President's agenda—presumably without intense, sustained, or hostile scrutiny from opposing interest groups or advocacy coalitions. Concurrently, Reagan's controversial Director of the Office of Personnel Management (OPM), Donald Devine, immediately recentralized to OPM a number of staffing delegations for middle management positions that the Carter Administration had entrusted to agency administrators.

As for RIFs, downgrading of positions, and altered skill mixes, the Administration handily executed sizable, targeted, and strategic cuts in many domestic agencies. For example, during Fiscal Years 1981 and 1982 alone, nearly twelve thousand federal employees lost their jobs through RIFs, with the total loss soaring to ninety-two thousand by the end of 1983. In addition, "voluntary" resignations spiraled as many careerists grew disgruntled with frequent job transfers, "punitive" geographical reassignments, position reclassification to lower General Schedule (GS) positions, and stifled opportunities for career advancement in increasingly politicized bureaus. Especially hard hit were the Departments of Agriculture, Interior, Health and Human Services, and Commerce.[20] What is more, the outlook for federal careerists during Reagan's second term appeared especially bleak. As the President's first term ended, the Administration announced plans to cut 40,000 additional middle-management positions (GS-11 to GS-15) by reclassifying them to lower grade levels.

Finally, the Reagan Administration completed its "counterstaffing model" of appointee-careerist relations by filling noncareer Senior Executive Service (SES) positions with relatively inexperienced individuals prone to short tenures in their respective positions. This was done to keep political executives from "marrying the natives" and to create for top appointees a cadre of bureaucratic "fire fighters" loyal to President Reagan. While this strategy's intensity varied from year to year, definite patterns emerge. Carolyn Ban and Patricia Ingraham's research on noncareer SES members in the federal government between 1979 and 1986 found an average tenure-in-office of 1.7 years, with fully 40 percent of government executives occupying their positions less than one year.[21] Even more striking were tenure data for specific agencies. For instance, nearly sixty percent of these appointees at the Veterans Administration and the OPM either moved from one position to another or left government altogether after less than one year in office. Consequently, on average, fully one-third of Reagan's political executives changed or left their jobs in each year studied.

The epitome of the President's supply-side management philosophy, these draconian personnel actions paralleled the Administration's efforts to alter agency staffing patterns and promotional opportunities to foster implementation of the President's goals. To these ends, Reagan appointees intensified the efforts of the Ford and Carter administrations to introduce a meaningful degree of "economic rationality" into the regulatory process by increasing the presence, influence, and authority of microeconomists in many social regulatory agencies. Simultaneously, many appointees—such as Mark Fowler at the FCC—reduced the role of attorneys in regulatory agencies by drastically simplifying licensing procedures and creating paraprofessional positions to process more simplified licensing applications. These efforts, in turn, were complemented by OMB's "massaging" of agency personnel ceilings and pay-grade distribution requirements.

How extensive was the "Reaganizing" of the federal bureaucracy? Two trends over the duration of the Reagan presidency are quite revealing: the increasing number and strategic placement of political appointees, and the declining number of career civil servants during the same period.[22] In 1980, 14.5 percent of all federal civilian executives were political appointees in Executive Schedule, noncareer SES, or limited-term SES positions, while the comparable figure for 1986 was 15.4 percent. Correspondingly, the number of career executives declined by 4.6 percent, while Schedule C appointments rose in grades 13 to 15 from 1,456 to 1,643—nearly a 13 percent increase.

Still, one has to place these data in historical context to appreciate fully the dimensions of Reagan's initiative. In analyzing the distinct increase in political appointees over the past decade, Ingraham concludes that the largest spurt came quite naturally under the Carter Administration as it began implementing the SES provisions of Carter's cherished CSRA. Nonetheless, the Reagan Administration quickly surpassed its predecessor's abbreviated track record; the percentage of filled noncareer positions in the federal government was 8.3 percent in 1980, rose to 10 percent by 1983, and settled at 9.5 percent two years later. Moreover, the Reagan Administration's record far exceeded its immediate predecessor's percentages in two additional categories: first, noncareerists in high-level Schedule C appointments and, second, political appointees in central management agencies (viz., OMB and OPM).

Ingraham's data also disclose a second important dimension of the Reagan strategy: differential "packing" of political appointees across departments and agencies. Here, the ratio of political to career employees is prominently higher in agencies expected to bridle or balk at program reorientation. So, while noncareerists occupied at least 20 percent of executive-level leadership positions in each of these organizations (exclusive of Schedule C positions), specific concentrations of political appointees varied from 22 percent at the Justice Department to 45 percent at the Department of Education. Moreover, while the proportion of political appointees held constant (or even decreased) in some agencies across the Carter and Reagan presidencies, the latter was the first administration able to apply during its entire tenure the significantly more protean management control provisions afforded political appointees by the CSRA. Specifically, it was notably easier for Reagan's appointees to transfer loyal and disloyal careerists within their own agencies; to hire career and noncareer employees committed to Reagan's philosophy; to shift executive-level positions into the President's priority areas and away from those he deemphasized; and to reward agency personnel for performances consistent with presidential priorities. All in all, these developments portray an unerringly consistent and broad-based strategy of politicization, a strategy designed to "increase presidential control of the central management functions, . . . to facilitate networking (and control) between top political appointees and the operating levels of federal agencies," and to unshackle Reagan loyalists bent uniformly on implementing the President's minimalist state agenda.[23]

Treasury Tools: From Reactive to Proactive Budgeting

For years, prominent students of the presidency have recognized that skillful use of a president's budgetary powers can profoundly influence bureaucratic priorities, predilections, and performance. Consequently, recent incumbents have tried to bolster their control of the executive budget process by centralizing review, first, within executive departments and, more recently, within the OMB itself. Recall, for example, Robert McNamara's efforts to diminish administratively the military's procurement influence by establishing a Planning, Programming, and Budgeting system at the Department of Defense (DoD) during the Kennedy years; or Harold Brown's attempt to control the development of strategic and tactical nuclear weapons by imposing preliminary budget ceilings at DoD. Equally illustrative in the domestic policy realm are Howard Phillips' designs on "zeroing-out" expenditures for the Office of Economic Opportunity during the Nixon presidency, and the OMB's scuttling of comprehensive health and urban policy initiatives because of their inordinate costs during the Carter Administration. In addition, seasoned observers will recall how disgruntled presidents persistently turn with varying degrees of vengeance and success to their impoundment, rescission, and deferral authorities under the Economic Stabilization Act and the Budget and Impoundment Control Act of 1974.

To many presidentialists, however, these attempts at presidential primacy have been too episodic in nature, narrow in scope, and reactive in style. Indeed, critics of this persuasion suggest that executive budgets have been less the personal agendas of presidents and more the mere aggregation of departmental requests premised largely on the biased pluralism of subsystem politics.

Others contend that presidents ordinarily have difficulty altering established funding patterns due to congressional norms, procedures, and statutory legerdemain. Indeed, budgetary norms such as "fair share," "historical base," and "reciprocity" combine powerfully with subcommittee government, entitlement programs, and multiyear authorizations to render the federal budget stubbornly resilient to dramatic changes in priority. What is more, because presidents traditionally live within their predecessors' budgets during the first year in office, and because the next budget cycle takes about 18 months to complete, a president's impact on spending is largely deferred until late in the first term. Yet even then, presidential preferences are frequently beached on the shoals of congressional politics, diffidence, or indifference—fates now imminently more likely given the Budget and Impoundment Control Act of 1974.

Crafted in an era of fiscal stress and presidential excess, the Budget and Impoundment Control Act sought to rein the Chief Executive's authority to impound funds, to bolster Congress' ability to impose "top-down" spending restraint on its members, and to heighten Congress' influence over expenditures by matching the EOP's prowess in multiyear economic forecasting. For beleaguered presidents, this means coping with several daunting and stamina-taxing consequences. First, presidential budgets are typically "dead on arrival" when submitted to Congress, thus enmeshing the White House—and especially the OMB—in interminable budgetary bickering. Second, Congress often passes continuing budget resolutions rather than appropriations bills, thus further proscribing presidential impoundment powers. Third, congressmembers sometimes enact omnibus spending rather than individual appropriations bills, thus rendering presidential vetos less immediately threatening to profligate legislators. Fourth, Chief Executives are confronted by a "fiscalization" of the legislative agenda, one that focuses their attention on macroeconomic aggregates rather than program management and impact. And finally, because presidents must premise their budgets on multiyear economic projections, their efforts are necessarily "prey to the vagaries of assumptions about a fluctuating economy, errors in econometric forecasting, different interpretations about the direction and speed of economic trends, and even manipulation."[24]

These debilitating trends notwithstanding, many scholars still contend that presidents are hardly helpless or hapless during budgetary proceedings. In fact, compelling empirical and anecdotal evidence suggests that the budget has been—and arguably ought to be—the central strategic component of the administrative presidency. For instance, scholars have challenged the methodology underlying characterizations of the budgetary process as incremental. They argue that different conceptualizations of the historical base, and of "controllable" and "uncontrollable" budget segments, are operative at different times, and thus mask the nonincremental nature of shifting presidential budget priorities.[25]

Methodology aside, however, others claim that "bottom-up" conceptions unwittingly ignore recent procedural changes that can work to a president's political advantage. Thus, as fiscal stress burgeons, as budget deficits spiral, and as trade imbalances oscillate, "top-down" budgeting procedures for broad-scale fiscal planning are instituted both within the executive branch and the Congress. These innovations, in turn, irrevocably alter traditional definitions of what constitutes "controllable" and "uncontrollable" budget items. Specifically, the budget reconciliation process can provide great leverage to embattled incumbents trying to control and set priorities in expenditures previously deemed uncontrollable.

Similarly, top-down budgeting trends within the executive branch have perceptibly buoyed the spirits of presidentialists. In response to the "displacement of the presidential budget," Reagan's most recent predecessors had already diminished the OMB's traditional role as a neutrally competent advisor with allegiance to the *presidency* rather than to particular presidents. Indeed, by the time Ronald Reagan assumed office, the politicizing of the OMB was well underway and its advocacy role for presidential priorities well-established.[26] Still, the Reagan Administration's top-down executive budgeting was by all accounts unsurpassed in proportion, centralization, and systematic coordination with other aspects of the administrative presidency.

The uniqueness of Reagan's effort is best appreciated by examining the top-down procedural innovations meticulously crafted early on by Administration officials. Their most radical departures were twofold. First, they submitted their own rather than President Carter's lame-duck budget to Congress. Second, they imposed ceilings on overall spending, average pay grades, and personnel for individual agencies prior to receiving departmental requests. While challengeable by agency officials, few appeals were made. And these were often argued by careerists with scant political resources, clout, or credibility.

Meanwhile, the White House staff "hit the ground running," effectively muting cabinet opposition to the OMB's cuts by (1) moving swiftly before secretary-designees could "marry the natives," and (2) hearing budget appeals in a small-group setting dominated by the President's aggressive, tireless, and austerity-minded OMB director, David Stockman. Moreover, the President effectively set the leitmotif against which appeals would take place by freezing expenditures in programs earmarked for budget cuts in the months and years ahead. Concomitantly, none soon will forget the Administration's legislative prowess in shaping the FY82 budget to its liking by adroitly manipulating the congressional budget reconciliation process. In the end, the Omnibus Reconciliation Act of 1981 heralded the beginning of a historic reversal of priorities that had driven federal spending for decades; billions were slashed from discretionary social programs and a massive defense buildup was initiated. Further, Reagan's appointees worked energetically to reverse the Carter Administration's funding priorities *within* both the foreign and domestic policy domains. For example, within the defense budget the Administration slashed Carter's funding recommendations for general purpose forces (e.g., training and personnel) by 4.7 percent, while it resoundingly increased the procurement budget for strategic nuclear forces by fully one-third. Meanwhile, the President adeptly pursued his domestic "supply-side" and "New Right" social agendas by reducing intergovernmental federal aid to mid-1970 levels and by slashing federal funding for family planning and day-care services.

Obviously, the breadth and depth of budget cuts realized in FY82 did not—and could not—continue apace during the remainder of Reagan's presidency. Yet the OMB did effectively institutionalize top-down budgeting norms, processes, and "strategic" budget deficits in its quest to parry spending appetites in "non-priority" policy areas. For example, the OMB engineered crippling budget and staffing cuts in civil rights agencies; the EEOC and the Office of Federal Contract Compliance sustained budget reductions of 10 and 24 percent as well as staffing reductions of 12 and 34 percent, respectively. Similarly, between FY81 and FY84, EPA sustained a draconian 44 percent cut in its enforcement budget for air, water, and hazardous-waste pollution, while its total enforcement budget was cut by 28 percent. At the same time, EPA curtailed its funding assistance to the states just at the time President Reagan proposed devolving federal enforcement responsibilities to state agencies. And precisely as the Administration called for more research on acid rain and other environmental pollutants, EPA was pummeled by a 50 percent cut in its research budget. In fact, both EPA and the Office of Surface Mining actually absorbed budget cuts at rates matching those of the Civil Aeronautics Board—an agency destined by statute for dismantling during Reagan's first term.

Communication Tools: "Unloosening" the Regulatory Ratchet

Ralph Hummel has written that presidents bent on controlling bureaucracy must "dictate the words and grammar used for human communication."[27] With presidents notoriously leery of negative political fallout from the exercise of bureaucratic discretion, and with a generation of scholarship chronicling how bureaucratic operations constitute policy making, it follows logically that communication processes would become a major star in the constellation of presidential control devices. Indeed, the administrative presidency often flounders or flourishes depending on how skillfully its practitioners communicate their purposes not only in bureaucratic processes, procedures, and substantive rule making, but also in three distinct communication arenas: among bureaucracies, within bureaucracies, and between bureaucracies and their clients.

The Bureaucracy Problem. Today, policy analysts, practitioners, and pundits commonly indict "government overload" as an untoward consequence of the administrative state. In particular, distressingly overcrowded "policy spaces" abound that compromise any administration's ability to effectively address, coordinate, or reconcile often disparate public purposes. Today, for example, issues in international trade policy span, and often elude reconciliation by, the Department of Commerce, the Treasury Department, the Office of Trade Representative, the Department of Agriculture, and the State Department. Thus, as Richard Rose has noted, it is not that government has no objectives; it has too many of them.[28]

Similarly, centrifugal tendencies within organizations can also frustrate, embarrass, and wreak political havoc on presidential incumbents. As Benny Hjern and David Porter suggest, hierarchical conceptualizations of bureaucracies are disastrously anachronistic; contemporary public agencies are flush with tensions between the organizational imperatives of agency generalists and the disparate substantive and procedural imperatives of the program specialists operating within them.[29] In short, the incommensurate "words and grammar" of each often complicate or preclude concerted or coordinated organizational effort between them. In addition, organizational and program imperatives impose processes, incentives, rules, and roles on street-level bureaucrats that promote rigidity, goal displacement, hierarchical distortion, and regulatory unreasonableness. Deeply enmeshed in the dominant subculture, these bureaucratic pathologies routinely complicate, distort, or even thwart the communication and acceptance of presidential prerogatives by affected constituencies.

Administrative Reforms. To counteract these entropic communication forces, presidents traditionally have sought to coordinate the administrative state through cabinet government, budgetary and managerial reforms, executive orders, and episodic intervention by the White House Office. Yet all appear inadequate to the task. For example, cabinet government ordinarily flounders as secretaries either "grandstand," "marry the natives," or stoke interdepartmental rivalries. In addition, agencies and programs titularly within a department secretary's purview often have direct statutory authority that supercedes that of the secretary. Thus, with their authority incommensurate with their policy responsibilities, appointees often cannot deliver on promises to coordinate—even when coordination is in their interest.

Similarly, budgetary and managerial reforms regularly deteriorate into "paper exercises," "paralysis by analysis," or agency gamesmanship. Witness, for example, the fates of PPBS, Zero-Base Budgeting, and Management-By-Objectives as pursued by Presidents Johnson, Carter, and Nixon, respectively. Here, the "words and grammar" of "decision packages," "multiyear program analysis," and "program objectives" propelled top-down and inter-bureaucratic communication systems, but with negligible policy results. In the same way, federal agencies usually deflect or reinterpret executive orders and White House intervention in order to protect or "buffer" their organizational essence or "core" from purportedly "tangential" White House concerns.

With procedural reforms, executive fiats, and cabinet government so problematic in effect, recent presidents have tried to place their imprimatur on bureaucratic policies by administratively altering policy assumptions and content. In foreign and defense policy, for example, shifts in the assumptions underlying strategic doctrines enunciated by the Eisenhower and Kennedy administrations have spawned nuclear weapons implications that sorely challenge arms negotiators today. Specifically, shifting from a massive to a graduated nuclear retaliation doctrine meant a U.S. counterforce strategy requiring significantly more warheads, more accurately targeted missiles, and a reactive U.S. posture linked inextricably to Soviet actions.[30] In domestic policy likewise, presidents have altered policy assumptions with significant consequences. Take, for example, the assumptions underlying the "poverty problem." As these shifted from Hoover's "poverty as a character problem," to Johnson's "poverty as a political problem," to Nixon's "poverty as an expectations problem," national policy shifted from free market solutions, to "maximum feasible participation," to "benign neglect."

The Record. How appropriately and effectively has this shift to administrative rule making enhanced presidential power? To some, such as Seidman and Gilmour, this approach seems especially apropos and effective given the ascendancy of the "regulatory state": The federal government today "determines *what* services should be provided and regulates how they *should* be provided, but leaves actual [service] delivery to private contractors or state and local governments."[31] In their view, the implications of this development for presidents are clear: administratively amending, rescinding, or promulgating rules and regulations in ways consistent with one's policy agenda offers a particularly potent tool for executive leadership. Too, others believe that promulgating bureaucratic rules, regulations, and processes consonant with presidential prerogatives actually "*enhances* (emphasis added) public accountability and responsiveness, given the tendency of industrialized states to become increasingly controlled from bureaucratic, technocratic, [and interest group] power centers."[32]

In contrast, those uncomfortable with "legislating" bureaucratically express both democratic and instrumental objections to arbitrarily changing the "words and grammar" of agency rule making, adjudication, and enforcement. Ironically, a former Nixon advisor, Bryce Harlowe, best summarizes the normative argument: "It is one thing to support and strengthen the president's capability to perform his pivotal role within the constitutional system; [it] is quite another to restructure the government so the president . . . is running the whole government from the White House."[33]

More pedestrian concerns are expressed by Eads and Fix, who excoriate administrative strategies as shortsighted since they are decidedly less authoritative, binding, and irreversible than legislation.[34] The Reagan Administration, they contend, egregiously erred by using an administrative rather than a legislative strategy for deregulation; the former needlessly aroused public alarm, alienated Congress, and squandered an unprecedented opportunity to redress regulatory unreasonableness through legislation. While others disagree with this assessment, most do concede that judicial review of agency rule making is a most formidable and vexing obstacle for any administrative strategy to overcome.[35] That is, with the "hard-look" doctrine now determinative, summarily reversing existing rules and regulations without synoptic and compelling evidence becomes problematic.

These caveats notwithstanding, the Reagan Administration applied an administrative strategy with a fervor and comprehensiveness unparalleled by its predecessors. At the level of the institutional presidency, three singular efforts stand out: (1) creating interdepartmental cabinet councils; (2) using the OMB as a clearinghouse for rule-making initiatives promoted by the agencies; and (3) having the Office of Policy Development "control, channel, and monitor" Reagan's policy initiatives during their implementation.[36] Initially, the Administration established cabinet councils in five specific policy areas, including natural resources. Designed to promote camaraderie among cabinet appointees, to overcome departmental parochialism, and to keep tangential issues from crowding out presidential priorities, each cabinet council was staffed by a secretariat and subdivided into working study groups. These effectively set the policy agenda for each of the councils.

Similarly, the Office of Policy Development tracked all major policy developments, kept resources tightly focused on Reagan's priorities, and suggested ways to avoid or overcome bureaucratic snafus or resistance. Finally, Reaganites at OMB went way beyond the Nixon, Ford, and Carter administrations in applying the benefit-cost criteria of Reagan's Executive Order 12291 to stymie agency rule making. Rather than merely consider cost, agency personnel now had to demonstrate that regulatory benefits exceeded costs substantially.

The Administration also attempted to alter policy and enforcement directions within individual bureaucracies by strategically amending the decision premises of the career service. Thus, for example, Secretary Weinberger promoted a redrafting of export control regulations to reduce the supply of Western credits and technology to the Soviet Union. Similarly, he endorsed a "horizontal escalation" strategy that reset regional priorities for general planning in the event of global warfare with the Soviets. Yet Reagan's appointees reserved the most studied, relentless, and painstaking use of the strategy for their assault on domestic policy. With one hand, for example, they reduced intergovernmental funding for social services, child nutrition, compensatory education, Medicaid, and Aid to Families with Dependent Children; with the other, they stiffened eligibility requirements, relaxed targeting regulations, and imposed market interest rates on states borrowing federal funds. In short, if supply-side management set the parameters of the Reagan Revolution, agency rule making enunciated, implemented, and institutionalized its specifics within the federal bureaucracy.

CONCLUSION

This chapter has chronicled the assumptions, logic, and controversy attending the administrative presidency as it has evolved across administrations, policy arenas, and presidential purposes. In the process, we have seen how the Reagan Administration logically extended its predecessors' tactics, but in ways and in combinations that dwarfed their scope, persistence, and ideological commitment. Thus, while individual presidents might have wielded discrete components of the administrative presidency more vigorously, none wielded them collectively with more zeal and bravado. And while his administration's supply-side management successes were less dramatic than he or "movement" conservatives would have liked, they nonetheless surpassed what most predicted possible at the beginning of Reagan's tenure.

Yet supply-side successes do not translate automatically into policy reorientation. They must be linked to substantive policy goals and be carried out with political finesse. How well did this occur in the public lands policy arena? Chapter 3 begins our analysis by assessing the strategy's impact on the organization and staffing of the BLM in New Mexico and the West.

CHAPTER 3

Public Lands, the BLM, and the Reagan Revolution

Donald Regan—former Treasury Secretary and Chief-of-Staff in the Reagan White House—once wryly drew an analogy between combat survival tactics and his approach to administrative politics in Washington. He noted that "Troops on outpost keep concealed as much as possible. . . . One quickly learns that the best target [to attack] is the person who 'stands on the skyline'."[1] No more eager or zealous footsoldiers patrolled the political skyline for President Reagan than James Watt, his associates, and their successors at the Interior Department.[2] Ultimately, these natural resource appointees persisted and, in some respects, prevailed, especially on their supply-side management agenda. And in doing so, their assault—albeit pursued more gingerly and more removed from the "skyline" in the post-Watt era—adroitly exploited the ideological diversity that characterizes the contemporary environmental movement.[3]

With environmental ranks flush with disparate and unresolved conservationist, preservationist, and anti-capitalist philosophies, Interior Secretaries James Watt, William Clark, and Donald Hodel portrayed themselves as the true legatees of Pinchot's Progressive conservationist tradition. In fact, Reagan's appointees excoriated their critics for abandoning sustained-yield principles in favor of an elitist, steady-state, preservationist mentality. In Hodel's words, environmentalists "clamor for a return to a more primitive life, to choking off our individual and collective aspirations for ourselves and our children."[4]

This chapter examines precisely how Reagan's appointees sought to institutionalize their philosophy within the Interior Department during the 1980s. It does so by focusing on three aspects

51

of the administrative presidency: organizing, financing, and staffing. Informing the analysis are two important implementation perspectives: the view from the center (policy makers in Washington) and the view from the periphery (policy implementors in the West).

THE VIEW FROM WASHINGTON

The Interior Department

In January 1981, Ronald Reagan's "happy band of deregulators" brought the Sagebrush Rebellion to Washington. Most were imbued with a nonrebuttable presumption that markets are (1) the most efficient, effective, and responsive means for allocating scarce resources to society; (2) that unbridled government spending was most responsible for inflation; and (3) that government rather than market failures increasingly spawned societal ills. Enraptured by this philosophy, Reagan appointees at the Department of the Interior proselytized and rushed to effect the President's four "d"s: debureaucratization, deregulation, decentralization, and devolution of federal responsibilities to the states. As one former Deputy Assistant Secretary at Interior remarked, the "Reagan Revolution was about shrinking the size of the federal government, not merely slowing its rate of growth nor fine-tuning specific federal programs."[5]

In another sense, however, the Administration's philosophical diversity—not its purity—complicated Reagan's natural resource agenda. That is, just as the environmental movement lacked cohesiveness, the Reagan Revolution exhibited its own philosophical contradictions. Some within it, such as James Watt, were "pragmatic" free marketeers with visceral and virulent antipathy to those in the environmental movement ("the greatest threat to the ecology of the West," said the Secretary). Formerly chief legal officer of the Mountain States Legal Foundation, Watt's personal economic philosophy was summarized best in the foundation's motto: "Private rights, private freedoms, and private enterprise."

Still, Watt's enthusiasm for markets and deregulation was tempered by a "balanced budget" philosophy of economic growth—much to the chagrin of Sagebrush Rebellion purists and philosophical devotees of unfettered market mechanisms. More precisely,

Watt subordinated almost everything else to the Administration's supply-side economic and management agendas.[6] Convinced that public land divestiture would substantially deplete federal land revenues, this avowed sagebrush rebel announced that a transfer of large tracts of federal lands to state ownership was not needed and not the Administration's "first priority." Neither were statutory changes in the Federal Land Policy and Management Act (FLPMA), the Public Rangelands Improvement Act (PRIA), or any other natural resource legislation. What *were* needed were changes in the Bureau of Land Management's attitude of distance, arrogance, and disregard for local interests. More precisely, the Administration proposed to hone a "good neighbor" policy predicated on "consultation, coordination, and cooperation" with states, localities, and users, a policy capable of replacing the "dictatorial, uncompromising attitudes of [public land] bureaucrats" during the Carter years.

Clearly, Watt and others of his persuasion were sensitive to the link between natural resource management and economic growth. Yet their philosophy was the mirror image of that espoused by the early Progressive conservationists, who believed that prudent stewardship of natural resources was a precondition for a strong, vibrant economy. Specifically, many at Interior saw a vibrant economy as a precondition to wise stewardship. As one assistant secretary of Interior proclaimed, "[We] are unashamed devotees of the free enterprise system . . . [and] our first priority must be to cut the [federal] budget and get the economy working again."[7] Thus, amid outcries from environmentalists and their congressional allies, Reagan's "minimalist-state" appointees supported draconian budget cuts for (1) land acquisition, (2) regulatory enforcement, (3) environmental planning, (4) resource management, and (5) federal water projects. Indeed, when it requested an overall 15.3 percent cut in Interior Department funding in FY82, the Administration set a retrenchment tone that endured throughout the Reagan presidency. This proposal included a 15 percent reduction for resource studies in Alaska, a 27 percent cut in enforcement funding for the Office of Surface Mining, a 20 percent decrement in funding for wildlife impact studies for the Fish and Wildlife Service, and a 7 percent retrenchment in BLM personnel assigned to oil, gas, coal, grazing, and public land inventories.[8] In addition, the Administration consistently argued that shifting these tasks to private industry and the states would produce more efficient and accurate inventories, as well as more effective enforcement of environmental laws. Their ultimate goal: Shrink the Interior Department's share of federal agency outlays from a Carter Administration average of 0.8 percent to 0.4 percent by FY91.

Political realities, however, often preclude presidents from applying the same philosophical litmus test to all appointees. Inclinations for consistency rapidly give way to the realities of promises made to campaign contributors, supporters with disparate ideologies, and solons sitting on key congressional committees. Consequently, not all natural resource appointees at Interior were economic conservatives. Some, for example, championed the views of the President's "privatization" constituency, while others represented the political pragmatism of many moderate Western Republicans. Those advocating privatization vigorously espoused the policy prescriptions of property rights, public choice, and Austrian economic theorists, a philosophical amalgam known widely as the New Resource Economics (NRE).[9]

In practice, devotees of the NRE propose taking as many resource management decisions as possible away from the bureaucracy; their faith lies instead with the collective wisdom of the marketplace. Public land managers, they assume, are rationally self-interested entrepreneurs who rely for succor on rapacious legislative and interest group actors who themselves have insatiable appetites for public largesse. As a result, these bureaucrats make resource decisions which exacerbate rather than mitigate ecological damage. How so? Federal public land managers operating without the discipline of the market neither benefit nor suffer sufficiently from the consequences of their resource decisions as long as they remain responsive to legislative sovereigns and their constituencies. In fact, without price information, even the most public-spirited managers must make natural resource decisions without clear notions of marginal trade-offs.[10]

Thus, while traditional "budget-balancing" conservatives within Interior bridled against public land sales, privatizers such as Steve Hanke lobbied aggressively for large-scale federal sales at fair market value. Likewise, NRE proponents argued for creating markets in water rights, where water would "flow" to its highest economic use regardless of state boundaries. In contrast, states' rights advocates within the Administration were troubled by such proposals; their interests lay in promoting and protecting state supremacy in water resource management.

Finally, a third cadre of Interior appointees were distinctly more motivated by the political ramifications of their actions, especially since many owed their positions to and staked their political futures upon the political sensitivities of this most ideological of recent administrations. "Politicos" at heart, they shared their party's predisposition for market rather than government solutions. Nonetheless, they were eminently more willing to subordinate market ideology to the political necessities of compromise, conciliation, and constituency building or maintenance. Thus, political realities dissuaded these appointees from supporting large-scale auctioning of the public lands at free-market prices unless preferential treatment was extended to ranching or community interests.

Garrey Carruthers of New Mexico, Reagan's first Assistant Secretary for Land and Water Resources, is perhaps the best illustration of this type of appointee. Carruthers had served in the Ford Administration, was Republican state party chairman in New Mexico, and initially supported John Connelly over Reagan in the 1980 presidential primaries. In addition, once his stint at Interior was over, he would successfully seek the governorship of New Mexico. Most tellingly, however, his coordination of President Ford's 1976 primary campaign in southern New Mexico, his association with moderates as party chair, and his refusal to endorse Reagan after Connelly dropped out of the 1980 race caused the President's transition team in New Mexico to oppose his nomination as Assistant Secretary. Indeed, staunch Reaganites still were irked by the internecine donnybrook that had torn the state party asunder during the 1976 campaign.

At that time, Reagan personally had nixed a proportional representation plan for the New Mexico delegation to the Republican national convention in New Orleans. In doing so, however, he effectively excluded from the delegation then-little-known, first-term Senator Pete Domenici and veteran congressman (and later

Interior Secretary for the Bush Administration) Manuel Lujan, Jr. Ironically, Republican control of the Senate in the wake of Reagan's victory propelled Domenici to the chairmanship of the powerful Senate Budget Committee. Likewise, Lujan became ranking Republican on the House Insular and Interior Affairs Committee. With the Senate Budget Committee so critical to Reagan's supply-side economic agenda, and with Lujan's committee vital to the President's plans for natural resource development, ideological opposition in New Mexico to Carruther's nomination was easily subordinated to Reagan's practical considerations about governing. With Domenici and Lujan advancing Carruther's candidacy, Watt tapped the politically ambitious New Mexican for the assistant secretary position overseeing—among other things—the operations of the BLM.

This is not to suggest that disparate philosophies paralyzed the Administration. Often the goals of the three perspectives—pragmatic free marketeers, privatizers, and political pragmatists—reinforced each other. Each, for example, saw a need to reduce "cow-welfare" (i.e., grazing permit and land improvement subsidies) for weekend graziers. Yet on the means, timing, and pace of federal withdrawal they often differed in ways leading to delay and ad hoc compromises that muted policy impact and satisfied no one. Budget balancers and NRE advocates, for example, sought as rapidly as possible to wean ranchers from subsidies, while moderates favored more slowly phased—and hence more politically palatable—grazing cutbacks.

While disparate philosophies persisted throughout the Reagan years, his appointees at Interior were united in their animus toward "regulatory unreasonableness," their passion for supply-side management, and their faith in administrative rather than legislative strategies for reorienting natural resource policy. Consequently, they perennially meted out stiff funding cuts for parkland acquisition, wildlife habitat protection, environmental studies, regulatory enforcement, and recreation grants. Interior officials also pursued their agenda by altering organization structures and downgrading personnel positions. Thus, to symbolize boldly and swiftly the lower priority Reagan assigned to environmental planning, his appointees fused the Planning and Environmental Division with Interior's Resource Division. In addition, Reagan's appointees abolished the Heritage Conservation and Recreation Service, the Water Resources Council, and the Office of Water Resources and Technology (OWRT). Eventually, the Administration shifted the Heritage Service's gutted wild and scenic river functions to a minor office at the National Park Service. Likewise, appointees replaced the Water Resources Council with the Office of Water Policy (an agency reporting directly to the Interior Secretary) and failed to replace OWRT altogether. The rationale for such actions? Most believed that individual states and private industries—as the primary beneficiaries of the research and development these agencies provided—should be primarily responsible for funding these activities. Too, they argued, shifting funding responsibilities to states and private industries would produce R&D in a much more efficient, effective, and responsive manner.

In pursuing Reagan's agenda, Watt and his successors also wielded personnel actions with a vengeance. Acting, for example, on the advice of the Heritage Foundation that control of the Interior Department is equivalent to control of the Solicitor's Office, the Secretary fired 14 "environmentally oriented attorneys" in that unit. Ostensibly designing his actions to correct "improper hiring which occurred in the last days of the Carter Administration," Watt admitted that the employees fired were not necessarily the same persons hired over budget. In addition, the Office of Personnel Management (OPM) reported that during Reagan's first term over thirty-nine thousand voluntary and involuntary separations occurred at Interior alone. Most notably, his appointees strategically used reductions in force (RIFs), reductions in grade, forced furloughs, and reorganizations to stimulate resignations from the Department. Moreover, they implemented RIFs in ways guaranteed to have a chilling effect on opponents of the Administration's agenda; dismissal notices were issued to many more individuals than were actually scheduled for termination. Indeed, OPM later estimated that for each person "riffed," three additional employees underwent related job actions. In the process, riffed and bumped personnel not only received substantial reductions in status and responsibility, but also accepted positions for which they were over- or underqualified. In all, employment at the Interior Department related to natural resource planning fell 6.6 percent during the Reagan years. Thus, although the number of full-time permanent employees actually increased at Interior during Reagan's tenure, growth occurred predominantly in positions related to energy and mineral production.

To supplement these personnel actions, then—Under Secretary Donald Hodel instituted a sophisticated management-by-objectives (MBO) system at Interior for goal setting and implementation. Initially, Interior's six assistant secretaries crafted seven overarching policy goals that clearly emphasized anthropocentric over biocentric resource purposes: (1) open federal lands to public access for appropriate use or users; (2) increase energy and mineral resource production; (3) "manage, reserve, and restore" the National Park System for public use; (4) promote resource development on Indian reservations; (5) increase the supply and quality of water in cooperation with user groups; (6) create "balanced" ecosystems through proper wild-plant-and-animal management; and (7) develop and implement sound managerial practices.[11]

Next, the assistant secretaries developed objectives for their divisions, broke these into unit tasks and subtasks, and extended the MBO process to the field office level in some divisions. Kenneth Smith, former Assistant Secretary for Indian Affairs, cogently reflected the Administration's control-oriented perspective on MBO systems by noting that implementors must "bear down to make it happen." In essence, "You have to spend time . . . asking about target dates, are we on target, and continuously use it, because if you stop, everybody else will just go back to the easy way."[12] To these ends, Interior supplemented its MBO procedures with a highly sophisticated management information system that tracked by computer the implementation status of critical management objectives. Political appointees could identify what tasks needed to be done, who in the bureaucracy was responsible for them, and how each was progressing.

In sum, Reagan's appointees at Interior pursued a decidedly "top-down" or "forward-mapping" approach to implementation during the President's first term. As described by Richard Elmore, the top-down perspective is recognized by its "implicit and unquestioned assumption that policy makers control the organizational, political, and technological processes that affect implementation"[13]—a most dubious assumption under the best of circumstances. Viewing bureaucratic discretion as threatening at best and an assault on democracy at worst, forward-mapping relies on sinewy hierarchical controls to "assure" faithful policy implementation.

BLM Headquarters

Turning specifically to the BLM, one sees readily how Reagan's supply-side management philosophy dominated the Washington scene. Reagan's appointee as BLM Director, Robert Burford, was a Colorado rancher who had jousted repeatedly with the BLM, most often over his own grazing violations. He also had been a key legislative sponsor (with Ann Gorsuch) of Colorado's failed Sage-brush Rebellion bill, and quite logically emerged as conservative Joseph Coor's first choice for Secretary of the Interior. Burford contended throughout the Reagan years that "ranchers, foresters, and industry have a far greater dedication to land protection than environmentalists credit them with." In fact, when a 1981 Council on Environmental Quality study cited overgrazing as a major rea-son for desertification of western lands, Burford refused to concede the severity of the problem. Instead, he averred that "the capacity for . . . increasing production in rangeland is tremendous" and that he intended to promote and expedite forage and timber pro-duction, as well as intensive management of ranges, forests, and other renewable resources.[14]

Likewise, in energy development, Burford's major priorities were to "streamline" mineral leasing on public lands and to make it more efficient. Himself a leasor of mineral rights to energy com-panies, Burford immediately raised the bureaucratic status and public visibility of the Bureau's Energy and Minerals Division in a series of intra-agency reorganizations. Moreover, he appointed to head the Division a Colorado attorney who had previously cham-pioned synfuel development in the state. And as Chapter 4 will discuss in detail, Burford later acquiesced in a massive reorganiza-tion of mineral leasing responsibilities initiated by Secretary Watt. So devastating was this reorganization to BLM's budget and tradi-tional skill mix (nearly a fifty percent reduction in funding, given the loss of offshore leasing royalties) that some wondered if Burford were conspiring to dismantle his long-time bureaucratic nemesis.[15]

Burford further fueled these worries during Reagan's second term by pressing ahead with a controversial BLM–Forest Service Land Interchange Proposal. Promoted as a vehicle for enhancing public service, improving management efficiency, and reducing agency expenditures, the proposal called for transferring jurisdiction over nearly twenty-five million acres of land between the agencies to eliminate waste, overlap, and duplication in land management.[16] For the BLM, however, the proposal envisioned a 5.4-million-acre net loss of surface management responsibility to its archrival, the Forest Service, as well as a 204-million-acre reduction in its subsurface management authority. In the process, the Bureau would also lose 450 permanent positions to the Forest Service.

Following OMB's lead, Burford further sought to institutionalize Reagan's pro-development agenda by altering the Bureau's funding priorities, professional skill mix, and administratively top-heavy structures in the states. As for funding and personnel priorities, he routinely sanctioned cuts related to wilderness reviews, resource inventories, and planning, while he increased allocations for onshore mineral development. His proposed FY82 budget, for instance, called for a $1.5 million increase for accelerated oil and gas leasing, with a coincident decrease for environmental inventories. Similarly, he consented to a $1.6 million budget decrease for activities related to Environmental Impact Statement preparation—despite court-imposed deadlines for their completion. Overall, the Administration budgeted a $1.5 million reduction in BLM planning activities, a 29 percent cut in its recreation and wilderness management program, and a 400-employee cut in the Bureau's Wilderness Inventory Program. Most significantly, however, the FY82 budget was only a harbinger of things to come. Funding requests for renewable resources, planning, and data management in the FY83 through FY87 budgets held steady at pre-FY78 levels. Indeed, BLM's FY87 budget request for planning and data management was but 78 percent of President Carter's FY81 budget request, while requested funding for renewable resource management stalled at 82 percent of that year's proposal.

The imprimatur of the Administration's supply-side management effort is indelibly etched on BLM's personnel actions in the eleven Western states. Nine states lost BLM personnel between FY80 and FY86, with losses ranging from 40.1 percent in Utah to 1.9 percent in Colorado (see Table 3–1). In fact, over one-third of the states absorbed cuts in excess of 20 percent of their 1980 allotments, with an average loss of 17.1 percent. The only two states with expanded workforces by the end of the Reagan years were New Mexico and Wyoming (14.1 percent each), two "OPEC" states[17] targeted for intensive energy leasing. The trend data (reported in Table 3–2) also illustrate the focus of Reagan's administrative presidency on personnel decentralization, an effort bent on reducing the influence of presumably environmentally oriented BLM state directors and staff over day-to-day management decisions at the grassroots. What is more, the data indicate that New Mexico was among the most centralized BLM states in the West as Reagan assumed the presidency (see Table 3–3).

The BLM organizational structure in each state has three geographical tiers: a state office (SO), district offices (DOs), and resource areas (RAs). In theory, resource areas are "on-the-ground" managers, while district offices provide support services to the RAs, offer them technical guidance, and assure quality control by periodically monitoring their work. State office officials set general policy guidelines within parameters enunciated by the BLM in Washington, evaluate state programs, and provide limited support functions to districts and resource areas when needed. In practice, however, role ambiguities plagued the BLM in most states during the Carter years, as the agency struggled to assimilate its expanded responsibilities under FLPMA and PRIA. Ultimately, resistance to their initiatives prodded Carter's appointees to stress state office oversight of district and resource area activities. Indeed, so aggressively did they do so that by 1981 an internal BLM study called for role clarification efforts at all administrative levels to counter overlap, duplication, and task confusion in the states (see Chapter 4).

Brandishing studies of this nature as justification, Reagan's appointees announced their plans to decentralize decision-making authority to the RA and DO levels—where traditional BLM clien-

TABLE 3–1
BLM Personnel by State, FY 1980–FY 1986

State	FY80	FY82	FY84	FY86	Net Change FY80 to FY86	Net Percentage Change
Alaska	966	979	936	883	−83	−8.6%
Arizona	410	412	389	379	−31	−7.6
California	799	622	607	621	−178	−22.3
Colorado	669	660	696	656	−13	−1.9
Idaho	554	488	458	433	−121	−21.8
Montana	609	540	567	543	−66	−10.8
Nevada	677	587	515	494	−183	−27.0
New Mexico	611	606	730	704	+93	+14.1
Oregon	1,638	1,595	1,464	1,414	−224	−13.7
Utah	893	558	579	535	−358	−40.1
Wyoming	603	531	645	688	+85	+14.1

Source: Data obtained from Bureau of Land Management, State Office, Santa Fe, New Mexico, 1987.

Note: Total number of on-board PFT and WAE positions.

TABLE 3–2

Total BLM State Personnel by Administrative Level, FY 1980–FY 1986

Administrative Level	FY80		FY82		FY84		FY86		Net Percentage Point Change
	N	%	N	%	N	%	N	%	
State Offices	3,146	36.6%	2,786	35.9%	2,671	34.2%	2,597	34.4%	-2.2%
District Offices	3,206	37.3	2,423	31.2	2,568	32.9	2,466	32.7	-4.6
Resource Areas	2,252	26.2	2,449	31.6	2,430	31.1	2,337	31.0	+4.8
AK Fire Service	-0-	-0-	103	1.3	147	1.9	148	2.0	+0.7
Total	8,604	100.0%	7,761	100.0%	7,816	100.0%	7,548	100.0%	—

Source: Bureau of Land Management, State Office, Santa Fe, New Mexico, 1987.

Note: Based on number of on-board PFT and WAE positions.

TABLE 3–3
BLM State Office Personnel as a Percentage of Total Statewide BLM Personnel by Division and State, 1981

Division	AZ	CA	CO	ID	MT	NM	NV	UT	WY	Median
State Director	2%	2%	3%	2%	2%	3%	1%	2%	2%	2%
Planning and Environmental Coordination	3	2	3	3	4	5	3	3	3	3
Resources	5	5	7	3	6	5	4	5	5	5
Resources & Special Projects (combined)	8	7	10	6	11	10	7	9	8	8
Technical Services	8	8	13	8	10	13	10	8	12	10
Management Services	12	8	10	8	12	12	9	9	14	10
Total State Office	30%	25%	35%	24%	35%	37%	27%	28%	36%	30%

Source: Compiled from BLM, *Final State Office Organization Study* (Washington, DC: Deputy Director for Services, Division of Management Research, Bureau of Land Management, October 2, 1981), Exhibit 10, p. V-7.

Reading from left to right, the states are: Arizona, California, Colorado, Idaho, Montana, New Mexico, Nevada, Utah, and Wyoming.

teles could most effectively influence agency actions. As part of this effort, they proposed decreasing the number of personnel in state and district offices and increasing their numbers in BLM resource areas. To what extent did this occur in the West, and how reflective of Reagan's prodevelopment agenda was this effort? The data indicate (see Table 3–2) that state office staffing as a percentage of total BLM employment in the West declined by 2.2 percentage points between FY80 and FY86, while district office staffing declined by 4.6 percentage points. In contrast, resource area staffing increased by 4.8 percentage points in the region.

Moreover (as Table 3–4 reveals), state office staffing patterns were highly consonant with presidential priorities to deemphasize environmental values. For example, percentages of SO personnel involved in renewable resource management planning and administration fell by 7.3 percent and 5.1 percentage points, respectively. In contrast, and indicative of the economies of scale realizable by centralizing functions in energy production, the percentage of SO personnel involved with land operations remained constant and substantial (nearly 42 percent). Similarly, staffing for minerals management soared from zero to 14.8 percent after the Reagan Administration moved the Minerals Management Service into the BLM (see Chapter 4 for details).

THE VIEW FROM NEW MEXICO

On the eve of the Reagan presidency, the BLM administered in New Mexico nearly 13 million surface acres and some 25 million acres of subsurface mineral estate. These properties generated over $218 million in federal revenue from mineral leases and permits, grazing fees, and timber and land sales, with New Mexico receiving nearly $106 million as its share of these receipts. Likewise, New Mexico led the nation in fees received from energy leasing on public lands. Concomitantly, significant environmental, aesthetic, and amenity values were abundantly at risk within its borders. These are vividly reflected in the number and acreage of study areas eligible for wilderness designation under Section 603 of FLPMA: BLM considered withdrawing 37 tracts of public land, totaling 786,391 acres, from grazing, timber harvesting, or miner-

TABLE 3–4

BLM State Office Personnel by Function, FY 1980–FY 1986

Function	FY80 N	FY80 %	FY82 N	FY82 %	FY84 N	FY84 %	FY86 N	FY86 %	Net Percentage Point Change
State Director[a]	237	7.5%	190	6.8%	171	6.4%	140	5.4%	−2.1%
Resources[b]	622	19.8	410	14.7	347	13.0	324	12.5	−7.3
Minerals	0	0.0	0	0.0	375	14.0	384	14.8	+14.8
Operations[c]	1,314	41.8	1,399	50.2	1,094	41.0	1,082	41.7	+0.1
Administration	776	24.7	510	18.3	528	19.8	508	19.6	−5.1
Other	197	6.3	277	9.9	156	5.8	159	6.1	−0.2
State Office Subtotal[d]	3,146	100.1	2,786	99.9	2,671	100.0	2,597	100.1	
Total State	8,604	36.6%	7,761	35.9%	7,816	34.2%	7,548	34.4%	−2.2%

Source: Bureau of Land Management, State Office, Santa Fe, New Mexico, 1987.

Note: Based on number of on-board PFT and WAE positions.

[a] Staff assigned to State Director.
[b] Renewable resources related to range, wildlife, soil conservation, hydrology, etc.
[c] Including cadastral surveys, engineering, construction of water projects, roads, fire control.
[d] State Office subtotal. Subfigures do not always total 100% due to rounding.

al development. Finally, rife with checkerboard patterns of Western landownership, parts of the state were prime candidates for economic development should land sales, acquisitions, and exchanges be consummated.

What is more, BLM actions in New Mexico during the Carter years stoked much of the "fire and fury" associated with the Sagebrush Rebellion. Thus, it is hardly surprising that the BLM's structure, operations, and management philosophy in the state drew the sustained, persistent, and critical scrutiny of the Reagan Administration. For example, when the first three grazing EISs issued in New Mexico cut grazing rights so deeply that experts predicted an annual decline in ranch income of nearly $1.7 million, a deep and abiding disdain for the BLM blossomed among ranchers in the state.

Similarly, many New Mexicans felt their energy production doldrums were unnecessarily compounded by the Carter Administration's backlog of unprocessed coal lease applications, by charges of corruption in Interior's oil and gas lotteries, and by allegations that federal mineral mismanagement had cost producing states at least $400 million a year in lost royalty payments. And perhaps most galling to prodevelopment enthusiasts, one of the nation's richest coal reserves lay untapped in New Mexico's San Juan Basin—a region rich in wilderness study areas, paleontological treasure, and unresolved Navajo Indian land claims. Finally, many New Mexicans were outraged at the Carter Administration's water policy for the West. As Reagan assumed the presidency, New Mexico labored to cope with the region's painstaking transition from a water-supply to a demand-management era. Consequently, many New Mexicans excoriated Carter's "hit list" of water projects in the West, his efforts to hike users' shares of federal water project costs, his designs on curtailing new dam construction, and his claim to unreserved federal water rights on BLM lands.

How did the Reagan Administration's top-down, supply-side management philosophy affect BLM's management operations in New Mexico? Certainly, a variety of administrative measures are instructive, including the downgrading to a staff agency of the Division of Planning and Environmental Coordination. Arguably, however, President Reagan's natural resource agenda is revealed most vividly in BLM's personnel actions in the state. Recall that New Mexico and Wyoming were the only two Western states to gain employees (+14.1 percent) during the Reagan years. Indeed, while New Mexico ranked seventh in total number of BLM employees in FY80, by FY86 it ranked third. In addition, New Mexico was considerably ahead of other Western states in assigning personnel to field offices. While the percentage of BLM employees assigned to the state offices fell by 2.2 percentage points across all Western states (see Table 3–2), those assigned to the SO in New Mexico fell by 6.3 percentage points (see Table 3–5). Declines of a similar magnitude also occurred in district office assignments (−6.0 percentage points), while the percentage of BLM personnel assigned to resource areas in New Mexico spiraled by nearly 12 percentage points. In contrast, assignments to these levels for the region as a whole were −4.6 and +4.8 percentage points, respectively (Table 3–2).

These data also reveal that by FY86, New Mexico had slightly lower than average percentages of SO employees working in both minerals management (12.3 percent compared to 14.8 for the West as a whole—see Tables 3–5 and 3–4, respectively) and renewable resource functions (11.1 percent compared to 12.5 percent for the region as a whole). Moreover, the state outpaced its Western neighbors in changes related to state office staffing responsibilities: The percentage point decline in personnel associated with renewable resource planning was approximately twice the rate for the West as a whole (−15.1 to −7.3 percentage points), as was the percentage decline in administrative staffing (−9.8 to −5.1 percentage points).

Even more telling, however, are data profiling how Reagan appointees altered the skill mix of resource professionals in New Mexico. Turning, first, to state office personnel, planning, oversight, and environmental protection capacities dwindled between FY81 and FY86 (see Table 3–6). Axed entirely by FY86, for example, were environmental coordinator positions. Meanwhile, slots for natural resource specialists, wildlife biologists, and community- and outdoor-recreation planners declined by one-half to two-thirds of their FY80 levels. In contrast, the number of BLM personnel associated with energy production—geologists, mining engineers, and petroleum engineers—increased significantly. Likewise, the Administration's quest for regulatory relief wrought sub-

TABLE 3–5

BLM Personnel by Administrative Level, New Mexico, FY 1980–FY 1986

Level	FY80 N	FY80 %	FY82 N	FY82 %	FY84 N	FY84 %	FY86 N	FY86 %	Net Percentage Point Change
State Office	240	39.3%	235	39.0%	245	33.6%	234	33.0%	−6.3%
State Director[a]	20	8.3	14	5.9	10	2.5	11	4.7	−3.6
Resources[b]	63	26.2	42	17.8	24	9.7	26	11.1	−15.1
Minerals	—	—	—	—	24	9.7	29	12.3	+12.3
Operations[c]	80	33.3	130	55.3	127	51.8	116	49.4	+16.1
Administration	77	32.0	49	20.8	60	24.4	52	22.2	−9.8
District Offices	207	34.0	174	29.0	201	27.5	200	28.0	−6.0
Resource Areas	164	26.2	197	33.0	284	39.0	270	38.0	+11.8%

Source: Bureau of Land Management, State Office, Santa Fe, New Mexico, 1987.

Note: Based on number of on-board PFT and WAE positions.

[a] Staff assigned to State Director.
[b] Renewable resources related to range, wildlife, soil conservation, hydrology, etc.
[c] Including cadastral surveys, engineering, construction of water projects, roads, fire control.

TABLE 3–6
BLM State Office Selected Personnel Skill Mix, New Mexico,
FY 1980 and FY 1986

Position	FY80	FY86
Civil Engineer	2	2
Community Planner	3	1
Realty Specialist	3	2
Outdoor Recreation Planner	4	2
Resources Manager	0	1
Botany Specialist	0	0
Wildlife Management Biologist	3	1
Environmental Scientist/Coordinator	6	0
Environmental Protection Specialist	2	3
Anthropologist	0	0
Archaeologist	2	1
Natural Resources Specialist	9	3
Range Conservationist	5	2
Soil Conservation Specialist	0	0
Soil Scientist	1	1
Petroleum Engineer/Technician	0	0
Mining Engineer	0	2
Petroleum Engineer	0	3
Natural Gas Regulation Specialist	0	0
Hydrologist	2	1
Geologist	2	8

Source: Branch of Personnel Management, BLM State Office, Santa Fe, New Mexico, 1987.

stantial cuts in positions associated with range and soil conservation efforts.

A strikingly similar picture emerges when one looks at the skill mix of BLM professionals in New Mexico's district offices. The number of community- and outdoor-recreation planners, soil scientists, wildlife biologists, botanists, resource managers, and environmental protection specialists were reduced drastically between FY81 and FY86 (see Table 3–7). Indeed, while range conservation positions held steady between FY81 and FY84, their

TABLE 3–7
BLM District Office Selected Personnel Skill Mix, New Mexico,
FY 1981–FY 1986

Position	FY81[a]	FY82[b]	FY83	FY84	FY86
Civil Engineer	6	6	2	0	10
Community Planner	9	4	3	3	3
Realty Specialist	29	29	28	28	3
Outdoor Recreation Planner	18	12	10	10	3
Resources Manager	3	1	0	0	0
Botany Specialist	2	1	0	0	0
Wildlife Management Biologist	26	18	14	14	3
Environmental Scientist	0	1	5	7	0
Environmental Protection Specialist	9	7	16	11	2
Anthropologist	0	1	1	1	0
Archaeologist	11	13	13	14	n/a
Natural Resources Specialist	20	30	23	19	5
Range Conservationist	66	63	49	59	5
Soil Conservation Specialist	0	0	3	2	0
Soil Scientist	11	6	3	3	2
Petroleum Engineer/Technician	0	0	24	36	7
Mining Engineer	1	1	7	7	3
Petroleum Engineer	0	0	14	14	5
Natural Gas Regulation Specialist	0	0	0	2	2
Hydrologist	3	4	1	3	2
Geologist	19	6	25	27	18

Source: Branch of Personnel Management, BLM State Office, Santa Fe, New Mexico, 1987.

[a] Personnel figures for FY81 represent the last New Mexico Annual Work Plan (AWP) submitted under Carter.
[b] FY82 figures represent those included in the first Reagan budget.

numbers dropped precipitously from 66 to 5 positions by the end of FY86. Likewise, the staffing of natural resource specialists dropped from a high of 30 positions in FY82 to a low of 5 positions by the period's end. Meanwhile, realty specialist positions held fairly constant until FY84, but were nearly extinct by FY86. In contrast, and directly resulting from the BLM-MMS reorganiza-

TABLE 3–8
BLM Resource Area Selected Personnel Skill Mix, New Mexico,
FY 1980–FY 1986

Position	FY80[a]	FY81[b]	FY86
Civil Engineer	3	0	6
Community Planner	1	1	0
Realty Specialist	24	23	20
Outdoor Recreation Planner	16	12	9
Resources Manager	0	0	0
Botany Specialist	0	0	0
Wildlife Management Biologist	10	12	7
Environmental Scientist	0	0	2
Environmental Protection Specialist	0	0	9[c]
Anthropologist	0	0	0
Archaeologist	7	12	10
Natural Resources Specialist	2	3	7[c]
Range Conservationist	42	43	46
Soil Conservation Specialist	1	0	0
Soil Scientist	0	0	2
Petroleum Engineer/Technician	1	0	11
Mining Engineer	0	0	1
Petroleum Engineer	0	1	18
Natural Gas Regulation Specialist	0	0	0
Hydrologist	1	1	1
Geologist	7	8	6

Source: Branch of Personnel Management, BLM State Office, Santa Fe, New Mexico, 1987.

[a] Personnel figures for FY81 represent the New Mexico Annual Work Plan (AWP) submitted under Carter.
[b] FY82 figures represent those included in the first Reagan budget.
[c] New position classification developed for transferred U.S. Geological Survey Conservation Division personnel.

tion, slots for petroleum engineers spiraled from zero to 14 by FY84 in the districts, dropping off to five in FY86.

Of course, with the Administration shifting personnel to resource areas, it is possible that environmental, planning, and resource inventory personnel were transferred, not cut, from district offices. However, district office cuts and shifts in skill mixes were ratified in the resource areas (see Table 3–8). For example, wildlife biology positions in New Mexico's RAs declined by fully thirty percent after falling nearly to zero at the district office level. Likewise, after sustaining a nine-position cut in the districts, the number of soil scientists increased by only two positions in the resource areas. In addition, while realty specialists and range conservationists suffered dramatic reductions at the DO level, their numbers remained roughly the same in the RAs. In contrast, energy-related staff—including 29 additional petroleum engineers and petroleum technicians—rose substantially at the RA level by FY86. And while the number of environmental protection specialists jumped from zero to nine (thus offsetting losses at the district level), those added were primarily transferred, reclassified Geological Survey personnel who held a more dominant-use, production-oriented ethos than their counterparts in the BLM (see Chapter 4). In any event, such staffing was clearly incommensurate with the level of energy leasing and production envisioned by the President, his emissaries, and his pro-development constituencies.

To summarize, the impact of the Administration's reorientation effort on the managerial operations of the BLM in New Mexico was profound, relentless, and consonant with the anti-environmentalist rhetoric of the Reagan Revolution. Unlike most Western states, New Mexico experienced a significant increase in personnel, most assuredly because of its status as a resource-rich OPEC state. Too, the character of that growth was clearly consistent with the pro-development, deregulatory, decentralization, and anti-planning agenda of the Reagan Revolution. Lastly, the data support those who contend that the Reagan Revolution continued apace at Interior long after Secretary Watt's hasty, embarrassing, and premature exit. Indeed, the pace of retrenchment actually quickened in range conservation, planning, and environmental areas in the post-Watt era.

CONCLUSION

This chapter has chronicled the logic, supporting ideas, and particulars of Reagan's "supply-side management" agenda for creating

TABLE 3–9

Selected Indices of Natural Resource Development on BLM Lands, New Mexico, FY 1976–FY 1988

Index	Fiscal Year					
	1976	1977	1978	1979	1980	1981
Authorized Livestock Use (animal unit-months)[a]	1,470,259	1,480,503	1,425,707	1,412,041	1,299,256	1,647,971
Competitive Oil and Gas Leases Issued (# and acreage)	74 (19,818)	129 (36,146)	64 (19,634)	70 (13,740)	60 (15,534)	144 (38,747)
Noncompetitive Oil and Gas Leases Issued (# and acreage)	1,446 (1,956,669)	1,071 (1,162,087)	799 (803,177)	784 (777,230)	948 (1,482,978)	1,317 (2,742,956)
Coal Production (short tons)	1,209,845	2,259,422	3,827,901	4,660,225	6,546,224	8,872,863
Oil Production (barrels)	27,326,359	27,760,479	26,213,083	24,611,522	22,879,275	21,928,018
Natural Gas Production[b]	599,029,418	632,159,549	622,154,601	614,786,347	598,438,409	631,324,878

[a] Data represents immediately preceding grazing fee year (e.g., FY 1976 = grazing year 1975).
[b] Million cubic feet.

(continued)

TABLE 3–9 (Continued)

Index	Fiscal Year					
	1982	1983	1984	1985	1986	1988
Authorized Livestock Use (animal unit-months)[a]	1,647,971	1,335,713	1,590,109	1,694,496	1,689,096	1,711,930
Competitive Oil and Gas Leases Issued (# and acreage)	64 (11,004)	224 (44,604)	372 (61,418)	320 (67,604)	236 (41,816)	311 (163,906)
Noncompetitive Oil and Gas Leases Issued (# and acreage)	1,288 (4,452,695)	150 (362,539)	84 (214,968)	NP	NP	133 (289,176)
Coal Production (short tons)	4,847,398	2,290,379	3,048,000	NP	NP	NP
Oil Production (barrels)	19,294,318	NA	15,787,287	NP	NP	NP
Natural Gas Production[b]	664,840,935	NA	474,204,098	NP	NP	NP

Source: Bureau of Land Management, *Public Land Statistics* (Washington, DC: U.S. Government Printing Office), FY 1976 through 1986, 1988 editions.

[a]Data represents immediately preceding grazing fee year (e.g., FY 1976 = grazing year 1975).
[b]Million cubic feet.
NP = Publication of these categories discontinued by Reagan Administration after FY 1984. Represents impact of a series of congressional moratoria (see Chapter 8).

the minimalist state in natural resource policy. How well- or ill-served by these supply-side tactics were the President's natural resource goals? The data in Table 3–9 afford a crude barometer of selected BLM production trends in the state during the Carter and Reagan presidencies. While somewhat mixed, these data are consistent with the conclusions of Leshy and others that the Administration's accomplishments were distinctly more modest than the rhetoric of its friends or its foes might suggest. Moreover, as subsequent chapters in Part II chronicle, the Administration's experiences in New Mexico suggest that these results were not only the product of political missteps by Watt and his successors, of market conditions beyond anyone's control, of judicial reversals of the Administration's deregulatory agenda, and of the type of policy reorientation sought administratively. Ironically, they were partially attributable as well to his appointees' success in realizing their supply-side management agenda. Specifically, an implementation paradox developed to plague the administrative presidency in the natural resource policy arena: the more Reagan's appointees successfully used this strategy to pursue regulatory relief, the more difficult it became for them to meet their resource production, states' rights, and economic development goals in New Mexico.

Simultaneously, these cases also alert us to several additional paradoxes dogging conventional approaches to the administrative presidency. Referred to in Part II and developed explicitly in Part III, these address the more generic ironies of reorienting policy administratively. First, the more Chief Executives and their appointees pursue policy reorientation administratively, the more likely they are to set off fire alarms prompting resistance from the Congress, disgruntled clienteles, unsympathetic agency careerists, and an aroused, litigious public. Yet, if they don't pursue aggressive and skillful administrative strategies, their agendas are distinctly vulnerable to members of Congress "micromanaging" agency operations in pursuit of their own agendas. Second, the greater the success of appointees operating and strengthening hierarchical control systems, the greater the power of program bureaucrats, and the less influential are political appointees. And third, the more successful appointees are in applying the administrative orthodoxy (i.e., hierarchical bureaucratic controls) to agency operations, the less successful they are in assuring account-ability to majoritarian, rather than parochial, societal interests.

The cases presented in Part II provide the reader with a sense of the historical background, issues, logic, and outcomes associated with the Reagan Administration's public land management experiences in New Mexico and the West. To highlight both the similarities and unique aspects of the cases, as well as to facilitate a more theoretically grounded discussion later in Part III, each chapter concludes with a brief synopsis of (1) the type, magnitude, and pace of the policy reorientation envisioned by the Administration; (2) how closely and successfully linked its tactics were to the President's long-term strategic policy objectives; and (3) the very disparate nature, scope, and outcome of the bureaupolitical conflict spawned by the initiative.

PART II

A View from the Grassroots

CHAPTER 4

Politics, Position, and Power Production

During the 1970s, responsibility for on-shore minerals management was divided between two agencies frequently at odds within the Interior Department. One—the Bureau of Land Management—reported to the Assistant Secretary for Land and Water Resources and performed such pre-lease tasks as site selection, determination of when leasing should occur, and review of lease bids for acceptability. The other—the Conservation Division of the U.S. Geological Survey (USGS)—reported to the Assistant Secretary for Energy and Minerals and prepared economic and scientific appraisals of acceptable bids. The Division also performed such post-lease tasks as on-site leasing regulation, mining plan reviews, and royalty collection.

The rub, of course, was this. Over the years, split responsibility for leasing within Interior led to internecine distrust, jurisdictional disputes, and crippling procedural delays. These, in turn, fostered lease application backlogs, made oil thefts and fraud less detectable, and seriously diminished timely and accurate royalty payments to federal, state, and tribal governments for the depletion of their energy resources.

This chapter chronicles how the Reagan Administration's efforts to reform this system collided with each other, as well as with the President's supply-side management agenda, to severely undermine policy reorientation in New Mexico. In the process, the chapter reveals three primary flaws in the way Reagan appointees linked strategic goals to operational or tactical choices. First, the Administration's supply-side management philosophy seriously delayed and compromised its ability to decentralize authority to pro-development field operatives. Second, by assigning on-shore

81

leasing responsibility to the BLM, Reagan strategists placed the development and enforcement of critical oil and gas regulations in the hands of an agency long bent on enhancing the influence of the ranching industry over energy development. And third, by conducting both of these initiatives simultaneously, each made the other's goals more problematic.

THE PAST AS PROLOGUE: DISENCHANTMENT IN THE LAND OF ENCHANTMENT

Without question, the 1980s witnessed a sea-change in popular opinion: Government rather than market failures began to fire popular imaginations. Perhaps nowhere was this trend more clearly articulated by President Reagan than in the energy policy arena. Wrote critic Richard Corrigan, "Unlike Presidents Nixon, Ford, and Carter, Ronald Reagan doesn't see energy as an urgent problem needing federal action. . . . Instead, he puts his faith in the free market."[1] Still, as William Hogan argues so compellingly, "After seven years with two energy crises, eight energy czars, and at least as many energy plans, the nation was ready in 1980 for President Reagan's promise of more energy production from less government involvement in energy markets. . . . Government was said to be the cause of energy crises, not the cure."[2]

While others have painstakingly chronicled the reasons for discontent in the West with President Carter's energy policies, our purposes require an appreciation of New Mexico's specific concerns. By 1980, nearly five percent of U.S. on-shore oil and gas production originated from federal lands in the West, with most pumped from established wells in Wyoming and New Mexico. In addition, nearly sixty percent of the nation's low-sulfur coal lay beneath federal properties in the region, with 82 percent of New Mexico's bounty (both high- and low-sulfur) located on federal lands. Moreover, by 1990, New Mexicans expected to rank fourth among all Western states in total contribution to national supplies.

Nonetheless, during the 1960s and 1970s, the state had directly experienced the effects of Uncle Sam's restrictive oil, gas, and coal leasing policies in the West. Indeed, responding to its ranching constituency's historical animosity to the negative effects of drilling operations (e.g., trespass, sedimentary runoff, acidic leaching), the Bureau had waged a three-front assault on oil and gas leasing. First, the agency stringently limited seismic exploration on public lands. Second, the BLM's leadership curtailed the construction of public access routes to remote areas targeted by energy companies for geophysical studies. And third, even when it issued leases, the Bureau typically imposed detailed stipulations on site operations (e.g., restoring mined land to original contours, site-selection restrictions for access roads, and "no surface occupancy" restrictions on leased lands). Thus, Pete Hannigan's perspective as Executive President of the New Mexico Oil and Gas Association is consistent with a 1981 General Accounting Office study critiquing "overly restrictive" BLM leasing covenants. Complained Hannigan, "There's an awful lot of bureaucratic red tape involved, the kind of things that make it difficult to work on [public] lands."[3]

Likewise, many New Mexican politicians bridled at President Carter's proposals in the Emergency Natural Gas Act of 1977 for deregulating the price of interstate natural gas, converting industrial and utility plants from oil to natural gas, and conserving energy. Indeed, the state's congressional delegation—Republicans and Democrats alike—scorned the Act for (1) not providing incentives for oil and gas exploration; (2) exacerbating existing gas shortages in New Mexico and "federalizing" intrastate gas regulation; and (3) costing four thousand New Mexicans their jobs.[4] Put most caustically by New Mexico's junior U.S. Senator, Harrison "Jack" Schmitt (R-NM), Carter's plan was "way off course and seemingly devoid of common sense."[5]

From New Mexico's perspective, however, the worst lay ahead. Over the next two years, New Mexico's energy production dipped, charges of corruption plagued Interior's oil leasing operations in the state, and coal leasing delays burgeoned. Specifically, New Mexico's already stagnating oil production declined by five percent, its natural gas production fell an additional four percent, and BLM's national backlog of coal lease applications burgeoned to thirteen thousand. Thus, with energy leasing revenues the largest single source of state funds, New Mexico's senior U.S. Senator, Pete Domenici (R), bristled, "We have a national policy right now that is almost as bad as no policy at all. . . . [It's] holding up the development of coal resources and is only contributing to our inability to become energy independent."[6] Similarly, when Carter's Interior Secretary, Cecil Andrus, suspended oil and gas lotteries in 1980 after charges of corruption in the awarding of leases, Domenici fumed. Labeling Andrus' action "ridiculous" and "incomprehensible," the Senator excoriated the Interior Department for not faithfully implementing existing regulations designed to root out corruption.[7]

With foreign oil dependence touted by the CIA as an "invitation to national suicide," with leading scientists at a Senate hearing chaired by Senator Schmitt calling for increases in public land exploration, and with Western states lambasting Carter for "stunting" coal research and "usurping" state authority, Administration officials relented belatedly. On the eve of the 1980 presidential election, Andrus released for energy development 16.6 million acres in nine Western states, including New Mexico (3 million acres). His overture, however, was too little and too late to prevent its critics from helping sweep the Carter Administration from office.

TOWARD REGULATORY REFORM? THE ADMINISTRATIVE ORTHODOXY REVISITED

Once in office, Reagan appointees at Interior confronted three primary choices critical for assuaging Sagebrush Rebels in New Mexico and the West generally. First, how could the BLM reorganize its structure and processes to streamline, rationalize, and decentralize its operations to the field? Second, how could the Interior Department do the same to eliminate waste, fraud, and abuse in its energy leasing program? Finally, how could the Administration best deliver enforcement relief to energy companies in the post-lease regulatory period?

The Role Clarification Issue

Reeling in 1979 from its new multiple-use responsibilities under FLPMA and PRIA, the BLM began an internal study of its own structure, processes, and organizational elan. At issue was the suitability of the Bureau's existing organizational arrangements and managerial approaches for its spiraling, complex, and conflict-ridden responsibilities. Carter's BLM Director, Frank Gregg, issued a twofold charge to the BLM study team: (1) investigate relationships among resources, operations, planning, environmental coordination, and administration; and (2) recommend changes where necessary. To these ends, the Bureau Management Team (BMT) first randomly surveyed BLM's 5,458 district and resource area personnel across the West. Next, they conducted semistructured interviews with a 1,300-member subset of this population. Finally, after Reagan's inauguration, BLM evaluators conducted a similar examination of state offices in the region.

What the BMT found brought little comfort to an organization grappling to keep pace with "rapidly increasing demands for its services and a strong national trend toward less government, tight budgets, and restrictive personnel ceilings."[8] For example, district office (DO) and resource area (RA) interviewees were disgruntled with such operational issues as (1) budget size, development, and restrictions; (2) merit principle violations; and (3) inadequate training. Thus, twenty percent of the respondents indicated that they received no BLM training in the area they were assigned to work in, and another twenty percent rated inadequate the training they did receive.

Likewise, respondents rated BLM's financial management and subactivity system too complex, rigid, and inadequately linked to Annual Work Plans (AWPs) developed within DOs and RAs. And well they might; multi-year funding requests for New Mexico alone—broken out by office, subactivities (more than forty in number), and program elements—produced a twenty-five hundred page document! The result, it seems, was "much too much information for a [line] manager to assimilate. . . . They [thus] redelegate this responsibility to program leaders . . . [who] gladly accept this responsibility and use the budget as a means for program advocacy. . . . Consequently, there is a steady erosion of line management authority to program managers/program leaders."[9]

Equally disconcerting was the BMT's assessment of role understanding, satisfaction, and coordination among Bureau employees. Put simply, role confusion was rampant. In turn, role confusion frustrated employees—especially those within the Resource Management and the Planning and Environmental Coordination Divisions. In each, BMT members chronicled: (1) the demoralizing consequences of multiple, duplicative, or conflicting task assignments; (2) scarce input by specialists into, or their lack of control over, program operations; (3) inadequate definition of what properly constituted "adequate program oversight and guidance"; (4) adversarial relationships among program specialists and RA managers; and (5) a need to continually revamp Annual Work Plans crafted more appropriately at the resource area level.

Witness, for example, the dilemma confronting the Resource Management Division:

> Personnel in the Division were expected to perform as supervisors over their programs; [to serve] as evaluators over those same programs; to provide advice, guidance, and assistance; to write resource documents, review [them], and assume the lead responsibility for resource projects; to provide staff support on resource projects; to collect inventory data; to provide information; and to compile and monitor the AWP. These types of work assignments conflict with each other, and add to the overlap, duplication, and general role confusion between the District and Resource Area staffs.[10]

Likewise, the BMT reported that in many district offices, the Planning and Environmental Coordinating Division:

> had expanded its role beyond what was originally intended. In the cases where the Division has expanded its role, it has been assigned lead responsibility for preparing [environmental impact statements] or other types of planning activities. This goes well beyond the coordination and guidance role authorized and is an expansion into current roles for the Divisions of Resource Management and the Resource Areas. In addition, there has been duplication of professions already available in Resource Areas and the Division of Resource Management, which further contributes to role confusion within the District. [Moreover], planning . . . has wandered up and down throughout the field organization. Mostly, it has tended to creep up through the organization rather than down.[11]

The dysfunctions of "creeping centralization" were also well-documented in a subsequent BLM state office study conducted after Reagan's inauguration:

In the past, the State Office role, out of necessity, was heavily oriented toward operations and review of District Office work. [Today, however,] the same professional skills are now found in the Resource Area, the District Office, and the State Office. . . . As a consequence, work planned or accomplished at the Resource Area level is often reviewed by the District Office and then by the State Office. . . . the State Office is neglecting long-term policy-setting, technical training, and *periodic* program evaluation responsibilities because it is too operational in its product and decision reviews.[12]

Thus, BLM managers spent too much energy resolving internecine squabbles among program specialists who failed to identify with a multiple-use management ethos. Moreover, managers grew too chary of delegating authority and engaged too readily in full-scale reviews of decisions best made on the ground.

Study Team Recommendations. How best to address these shortcomings? Not surprisingly, the BMT fell back on the administrative orthodoxy: Classify positions more precisely; clarify lines of authority; redelegate authority commensurate with responsibility; and departmentalize (or divisionalize) on the basis of function or program, rather than work process. In effect, team members recommended precisely what rational choice students of public bureaucracies contend is a self-defeating reform producing "individual rationality and collective irrationality."[13] Specifically, the BMT counseled *more* bureaucracy as the solution to bureaucratic dysfunctions typically associated with functional bases of departmentation. That is, while organization by functional area (e.g., operations and administration) or programs was the source of many of the BLM's most stubborn problems, the team suggested more of the same, only done better.

Let us be clear, however. The team's recommendations were well-grounded in the conventional wisdom of our time. What is more, several were progressive, if not cutting edge, proposals. For example, they emphasized using project teams as collateral structures for circumventing the pathologies of conventional bureaucratic structures. Progressive, as well, was the recommendation to develop a "cultural overlay" of participative management at the Bureau. But participative management is only a process or technique; substantive values must inform it (e.g., multiple-use management based on resource plans rather than program elements) to be effective. Indeed, as Robert Golembiewski, Henry Mintzberg, and Tom Peters contend, organization by function, process, or program carries the seeds of its own destruction by exacerbating parochialism and conflict among functional or program units animated by disparate reward structures. Moreover, this approach typically results in policy centralization rather than decentralization, as responsibility for resolving sub-unit conflict pushes a greater number of decisions to higher organizational levels.

Caveats like these are especially germane when proposing structural and procedural remedies for the BLM, since its statutory responsibilities support and depend upon each other. Ultimately, the Bureau's success depends upon integrating functions it assigns to various sub-units, entities which may or may not be able, predisposed, or willing to cooperate. For example, to increase natural resource production, management plans for specific activities (e.g., ranching or mining) must be completed. These, in turn, must be premised on timely and comprehensive resource management plans that, themselves, are premised on substantively and legally adequate resource inventories. All this, of course, depends on sufficiently staffed, trained, and funded personnel systems across sub-units with appropriate skills in resource production and environmental protection. To discount, dismiss, or ignore these interdependencies is to place one's production goals decidedly at risk. In sum, further fortifying a functional organizational structure and a budgetary process focused on program elements, as the BMT's recommendations did, promised only to further balkanize, not integrate, the Bureau.

The Recommendations Revisited. As seized on and implemented by his appointees as consistent with Reagan's pro-development agenda, the BMT's recommendations held profound implications for the Bureau. First, BLM personnel had to reorient state and district offices toward formulating rather than implementing policy, toward facilitating operations rather than controlling them, and toward periodic rather than sustained monitoring of sub-unit activities. All three of these goals, of course, diametrically opposed existing organizational cultures. Second, fully implementing the BMT's recommendations meant nearly thirteen hundred transfers of staff throughout the Bureau to its resource areas, with the proportionate grade and budgetary impacts spawned by staffing shifts of this magnitude. More precisely, average pay grades in the RAs had to increase significantly, since more journeymen-level and full supervisory positions were necessary to foster manageable spans of control. Finally, decentralizing such skills, operating authority, and environmental protection responsibility to the RAs was controversial for environmentalists both within and outside the BLM. They feared that local ranchers might capture the agency even more completely.

How successful was this effort bureauwide? The most systematic assessment of its consequences occurred in 1986 in a follow-up Role Clarification Study.[14] Conducted concurrently with BLM initiatives to slim down state organizations in response to Reagan's sizeable FY87 budget cuts, BMT evaluators noted that more operational work was occurring at lower organizational levels, staffing typically was adjusting to fit workloads at those levels, delegations of authority were now clear and "basically accepted," and updated BLM manuals more clearly conveyed an accurate perception of role definitions.

Still, formidable problems remained. Indeed, the BMT characterized implementation as less than envisioned, uneven in application, and undermined by serious shortcomings. Alas, the report affords a discomforting sense of *déja vu:*

> There is good understanding and acceptance of delegations of authorities to the three tiers [SOs, DOs, and RAs]. However, duplicate reviews and confusion about office roles do exist. . . . District Offices should be service-oriented to Resource Areas and should stop duplication of operational roles and regular reviews of lower level work. . . . Resource management decisions are being made by both line and staff officials . . . [a situation] particularly true with minerals decisions. [In short,] roles, responsibilities and functions identified for organizational levels in the 1981 studies have not been consistently implemented.[15]

Reminiscent of earlier concerns, the 1986 study also warned that "If BLM organizations are to be workload-based, and funding for these workload-based organizations is to be left to something other than chance, then [line] management [rather than program specialists] must be directly involved in the choice of program priorities, workloads, and the allocation of budgets to those chosen priorities."[16] Wrote one specialist,

> The [financial] system must serve [generalist] line managers. This goal is distinctly different from assuring that . . . [Bureau program specialists] promote various programs as ends in themselves (e.g., promoting wilderness outside of a balanced resource management context, promoting oil and gas outside the framework of multiple-use management, etc.).[17]

No one, however, expected this situation to change easily, rapidly, or comprehensively in the near future. Indeed, BLM budget analyst Geoff Middaugh put the bureaupolitical realities of the situation best:

> At present, many of our subunits are based on a program structure. In addition, these [subunits] and programs develop clienteles and constituencies that perpetuate their status quo. This, in turn, gives [program managers] more "power" and "authority" at the expense of [generalist] line managers. The result is that [the] Washington Office program staffs have vertical control over their programs and exert vertical program control over states. . . . There is tremendous organizational inertia to perpetuate this system, since WO program staffs can operate in their organization vacuums and only have to nurture their congressional contacts to perpetuate their jobs. . . .[18]

Were these the "sour grapes" rantings or the counter-offensive of state- versus Washington-based BLM careerists disgruntled with the supply-side, pro-development agenda of the Reagan Administration? Partially, perhaps. Yet neither should one underestimate another factor informing this situation in the BLM: the Reagan Administration's more targeted efforts to reform oil and gas leasing on public lands by merging the Bureau and the Minerals Management Service (MMS).

Politics, Position, and Energy Production

As noted, the BLM in New Mexico was among the most centralized in the West during the Carter presidency. Recall, as well, that the state soundly outpaced its cohorts during the Reagan presidency in reducing state and district office personnel and increasing the percentage of resource area employees. Still, the raw percentages reported camouflage the obstacles posed to meaning-ful decentralization in the state by the Reagan Administration's own actions. In fact, one 1986 internal BLM document argued persuasively that the Bureau of Land Management-Minerals Man-agement Service reorganization "complicated and curtailed to a large degree" these efforts to decentralize bureauwide.[19]

To fully appreciate the background, logic, and irony of the BLM-MMS reorganization, one has to appreciate its origins in the "fire alarm" oversight activities of the U.S. Congress.[20] According to McCubbins and Schwartz, "police patrol" oversight occurs when members of Congress persistently, systematically, and ex-haustively scrutinize agency activities within their committees' pur-view. In contrast, fire alarm oversight is triggered episodically by constituents disgruntled by bureaucratic failings, real or imagined. Specifically, legislators exercising fire alarm oversight seek to claim credit for meeting constituency demands without engaging in com-prehensive, time-consuming, and mostly thankless police patrol oversight. To do so, they await constituency outcries of bureaucrat-ic malfeasance, misfeasance, or nonfeasance before initiating more formalized, focused reviews of agency activities.

Precisely these conditions prevailed in mid-1981 with regard to the federal coal leasing program cobbled together by the Interior Department. With allegations rampant regarding theft and mas-sive underpayments of oil and gas royalties for use of federal, state, and Indian lands, Congress established the Linowes Commission (hereafter cited as Linowes I) as an investigating body. Premised on its own investigation, GAO studies, and nine congressional hear-ings, Linowes I indicted the government's royalty management sys-tem as "thoroughly in need of overhaul."[21] To remedy this situa-tion, the Commission recommended removing the royalty management function from the U.S. Geological Survey (USGS). Operationally, this meant stripping the Conservation Division from the USGS, in the process creating a new agency capable of eventually housing all of Interior's minerals management activities.

Why split the Conservation Division from the USGS? Commis-sion members felt that a new organization—imbued with a clear mission, independent budget authority, and skilled personnel—could more vigorously oversee leasing activities once unshackled from the institutional culture of the USGS. Wrote the Commission: "the [scientific] management skills of USGS leadership are not those required for strong royalty management."[22] Most tellingly, USGS's institutional culture was deemed inherently incompatible with regulatory responsibilities:

> The USGS is an esteemed scientific organization . . . [whose] primary mission is to explore and map the geologic resources of the United States. . . . Indicative of [this mission], Directors of the Survey have always been outstanding scientists in the field of geology. . . . [Likewise, the Conservation Division's] staff consists primarily of engineers and others of related professions [given that] . . . its primary mission . . . is to ensure the efficient recovery of mineral resources from [the public lands]. . . . [Thus], until recently, the royalty management program was completely 'integrated'—or perhaps *submerged* (emphasis added)—in the rest of the Conservation Division.[23]

Interestingly, the Commission flirted with, but quickly dismissed as "mistaken," the idea of totally transferring oil and gas royalty management functions to the BLM. On one hand, the BLM was "already seriously overburdened" with critical land management tasks. Thus, additional responsibilities could "hamper the accomplishment of [the Bureau's] other missions." On the other hand, the "stepchild" nature of coal leasing responsibilities within the BLM boded ill. Put succinctly, the USGS and the BLM exhibited strikingly dissimilar managerial cultures, approaches, and operating procedures. Indeed, so diametrically opposite were they that Reagan's policy reorientation would flounder without herculean efforts to change the Bureau.

Why was this true? First, while the BLM's tradition of decentralized management is suitable for grazing, wildlife, watershed, and other surface management responsibilities, it is distinctly unsuitable for federal coal management. More precisely, because coal management involves national and regional market and policy concerns, it requires at least the regional organizational basis used by the old Conservation Division. The BLM, in contrast, is organized on a state basis. Second, coal management requires levels of expertise acquired only after years of sustained, persistent, professional commitment to the enterprise. Yet the BLM traditionally transfers and rotates its personnel among management regions and tasks in ways ill-suited to developing such a commitment. Third, coal management requires an organizational culture steeped in subsurface rather than surface land management values, one like the USGS's. The Bureau, in contrast, has singled out good surface land managers for its highest organizational recognition and rewards. Finally, coal management requires a modicum of national and regional planning since, for example, federal coal produced in Wyoming frequently competes with that produced in New Mexico. Yet BLM planning staffs tended mostly to focus on land use plans having a local or site-specific focus.

These caveats notwithstanding, Reagan appointees rushed pell-mell into precisely such a reorganization. Saying he was "streamlining" minerals management operations, Secretary Watt first created a new agency within Interior, the Minerals Management Service (MMS). Simultaneously, he placed the new unit within the organizational purview of the Assistant Secretary for Energy and Minerals. In the process, Watt—following a Linowes Commission recommendation—transferred royalty management responsibilities to the MMS and relocated the Conservation Division within it.

Subsequently, Watt again appeared to advance considerably the Commission's recommendations by transferring off-shore oil and gas leasing from the BLM to the MMS. Still unaddressed, however, was the stubborn issue of split responsibility for on-shore minerals management. Clearly, the only thing left to complete the total consolidation recommended by Linowes I was a transfer of on-shore responsibilities to the MMS. Instead, however, Watt moved the old Conservation Division from the MMS to the Bureau of Land Management! Then, after Watt's resignation, Secretary William Clark transferred the MMS to the new Assistant Secretary for Land and Minerals Management. In the process, Clark eliminated the Office of Assistant Secretary for Energy and Minerals, assigning its remaining functions to a newly established Office of the Assistant Secretary for Water and Science. Thus, for the first time in Interior's history, the BLM had total control over on-shore leasing functions, while a single assistant secretariat had all three organizational entities dealing with minerals management within its jurisdiction (the BLM, the MMS, and the Office of Surface Mining).

As Steven Maynard-Moody and his associates insightfully argue, the "style" of a reorganization either profoundly affirms or disconfirms existing organizational values, assumptions, and subcultural dominance.²⁴ Applying this perspective to the BLM-MMS reorganization, it is difficult to fathom how the Administration's "bold" initiatives could possibly have advanced their stated purpose: accelerating oil, gas, and mineral production. By ignoring Linowes' warnings about transferring minerals leasing responsibilities to the BLM, Watt had placed responsibility for subsurface energy production in a surface management agency unsympathetic if not congenitally hostile to these ends when in conflict with rangeland interests. Specifically, the USGS historically blamed on-shore leasing backlogs on the Bureau's responsiveness to ranching and environmental constituencies hostile to energy development! One might also interpret Secretary Clark's actions as symbolically, operationally, and ironically "demoting" on-shore energy production when he dissolved the Office of Energy and Minerals and combined its functions under an assistant secretariatship for Land and Minerals Management.

So why were the Linowes Commission warnings not heeded? And what prompted Clark to craft as he did his historic reorganization of minerals management responsibilities? At one level, these results appeared to signal and implement a philosophical commitment to energy production goals. After all, eliminating split responsibility for minerals leasing and placing these responsibilities under one assistant secretary were impressive accomplishments long sought by the energy industry as ways to diminish overlap, inefficiency, and production delay. Moreover, while the BLM Director was a Colorado rancher, he too had benefitted from energy leasing on his own property. Yet, inspecting more closely the context of Watt's actions reveals a less obvious, yet politically potent, benefit for the President in assigning on-shore leasing responsibilities to the BLM.

Reagan's appointees had already stripped off-shore leasing duties and on-shore royalty collection responsibilities from the Bureau, in the process nearly halving the Bureau's budget. Thus, while these budget cuts involved lost receipts rather than personnel cuts, BLM's friends and foes alike spoke openly of the agency's potential demise under the Reagan juggernaut. To further strip the agency of responsibilities might have triggered the type of fire alarm oversight that already placed Secretary Watt on the defensive in 1983.

Still, even this does not completely account for why Watt transferred on-shore leasing from the MMS to the Bureau. Neither does it explain his successor's reorganization efforts. For additional insight, one must turn to a third factor: the personal political ties and agendas of two of Reagan's subcabinet appointees at Interior, New Mexicans Frank DuBois and Garrey Carruthers. DuBois, considered briefly for the directorship of BLM, joined Carruthers as his assistant when the Bureau job went to Burford. Most relevant to the reorganization issues raised here, however, DuBois envisioned returning to New Mexico eventually to become that state's powerful secretary of agriculture. Likewise, as chronicled in Chapter 2, Carruthers harbored strong gubernatorial aspirations. Thus, each man coveted and courted the support of ranching and agricultural interests in that state by advancing Sagebrush causes while at Interior.

So animated, and with powerful ranching interests wishing greater control over the adverse impacts of energy leasing on rangelands, both men staunchly advocated maintaining and, then, consolidating on-shore leasing within the ranchers' advocacy agency, the BLM. What is more, Carruthers—taking advantage of Secretary Clark's inexperience in natural resource management—quickly consolidated the ranching industry's influence over mining interests. Specifically, Carruthers convinced Clark to sign off on a reorganization proposal accomplishing what the ranching industry had sought unsuccessfully for decades: direct BLM control over all aspects of on-shore energy leasing. Gained as well was an assistant secretariatship capable of reconciling rancher interests with the energy and land management goals promoted by the BLM, MMS, and Office of Surface Mining.

Regardless of how well these structural reforms advanced the personal or programmatic agendas of politicos or the ranching community, they did not comport well with Reagan's professed long-term energy production goals. Indeed, many transferees from the Conservation Division felt that the Bureau did not aggressively pursue its expanded mineral production responsibilities after reorganization.[25] Those interviewed for this study complained that they or their colleagues were consistently under-utilized, and that they had swapped professional and budgetary subservience in the USGS for the same in the Bureau. What is more, their morale suffered further as their reduced discretion, responsibilities, and decision-making authority translated into lower pay. And all this occurred after many interpreted their initial reassignment to the MMS as final, a first step toward gaining professional and budgetary dominance in the "overwhelmingly production-oriented" agency called for by the Linowes Commission.

That this reorganization affirmed ranching rather than energy values also received empirical and anecdotal support from representatives of the oil, gas, and mineral industries across the West. Initially heartened by and supportive of Watt's efforts, they gradually grew disgruntled with the Bureau's regulatory and enforcement zeal. Most acute was their displeasure with the agency's implementation of the Federal Oil and Gas Royalty Management Act of 1982 (FOGrMA).[26] Charged by FOGrMA with enhancing site security and preventing royalty payment fraud on public lands, the Bureau was attacked by the energy industry and members of Congress for inordinately tightening and over-zealously enforcing production, site security, and environmental regulations. Simultaneously, internal agency critics alleged that ranching and environmental elements within the Bureau had seized upon the FOGrMA rule making opportunity to discourage energy development.[27] "Fire alarms" all, complaints such as these eventually spawned full-scale congressional oversight hearings on BLM's leasing operations. Make no mistake, however. The surface management affirming qualities of the BLM-MMS reorganization—while significant—were not its only implications for public land management, for Reagan's energy agenda at BLM, nor for the Reagan Revolution as a whole. To appreciate how and why, one has to address the interactive consequences of the BLM-MMS reorganization, Burford's Role Clarification initiative, and Reagan's supply-side management agenda in New Mexico.

New Mexico's Public Land Management Conundrum

For an agency historically resource-starved, the most significant managerial dilemma of the BLM-MMS reorganization for New Mexico was a welcome one: how to integrate a sizeable influx of skilled minerals management professionals and to program a bountiful 25 percent increase in funding for the Mineral and Land Resources Division in FY 1984 and FY 1985. By 1986, however, the dilemmas posed by this surfeit of resources were clear. Indeed, participants in and informed observers of New Mexico's travails by then concluded that the Bureau's "good fortune" had "complicated and curtailed to a large degree" the successful implementation of the 1981 Role Clarification Study across all BLM activities.[28]

Two reasons for this conclusion are paramount. First, Reagan's success in reducing staff numbers across the West conspired as well to "adversely affect" Burford's plans to decentralize authority to BLM district and resource area managers. Second, energy experts noted that "continued role confusion" and losses of expertise through employee transfer and resignation acutely compromised the Administration's energy production goals. Indeed, so crippled did his energy agenda become that oil and gas production on federal on-shore properties during Reagan's first six years in office was no better than Carter's record.[29]

Actually, signs that the Administration's reorientation efforts were going awry in New Mexico occurred even prior to the BLM-MMS reorganization. As John Lopez, Personnel Director for BLM in the state, recalled, transferring authority and agency personnel to RAs required two things: retraining personnel and enhancing managerial capacity in the field. More precisely, transferees needed training in hands-on skills relating to processing applications for drilling, performing environmental assessments, and conducting categorical exclusion reviews.

Furthermore, the Administration's rule-of-three criterion for span-of-control issues created a *taller* rather than a flatter hierarchical structure as transferees arrived. Thus, contrary to the supply-side management philosophy, the agency needed *more* rather than fewer middle managers. Moreover, these had to be sufficiently imbued with requisite skills and Reagan's pro-development philosophy. Thus, the ultimate irony: Precisely when funding for reskilling, developing managerial capacity, and relocating personnel to DOs and RAs was paramount if Reagan's appointees were to realize his goals, Reaganites at OMB, OPM, and the Bureau were reducing funding severely for these activities. In Lopez' words, "It soon became clear that decentralizing authority to the extent and [at the] pace envisioned by the Administration was impractical without more training funds and personnel, yet the Administration was cutting back in both these areas."[30]

Another sign that reorientation was amiss surfaced in a second Linowes Commission study of Interior's fair market value assessment procedures (hereafter referred to as Linowes II).[31] Impaneled by Congress in mid-1983, Linowes II investigated widespread charges that the Reagan Administration—either by design or incompetence—sold coal leases in the Powder River Basin of Wyoming and Montana for $60 to $100 million less than their true value (see Chapter 8 for further details). Critics, including the General Accounting Office and the House Appropriations Committee, charged that this "fire sale" occurred in a "soft" coal market and after confidential appraisals of the leases got into coal industry hands. Incensed, Congress swiftly invoked a two-year suspension of regional coal sales until Interior clarified fundamental issues related to coal leasing.

Based on six months of study and 23 hearings, Linowes II spoke directly to the untoward consequences of the BLM-MMS reorganization as it affected coal leasing states such as New Mexico. Specifically, the Commission concluded that the organizational structure and managerial procedures occasioned by the reorganization were hindering Reagan's pro-development energy agenda. True, the Administration's success in totally eliminating by FY86 the inordinate backlog of coal lease applications was a formidable one and consonant with Reagan's pro-development pledge. Moreover, despite a 23 percent reduction in on-shore oil and gas exploration during FY86 alone, as well as a 40 percent decline in drilling permits processed as oil prices collapsed, BLM's doubling of oil and gas leases between 1981 and 1984 was also a significant accomplishment. Still, Linowes II documented compellingly how the Bureau implemented the BLM-MMS reorganization in ways affirming existing BLM values, assumptions, and dominant subculture.

Calling upon the Interior Department to monitor the situation, the Commission's report concluded:

It is an urgent priority for the BLM to find and promote personnel
with the professional training and experience to manage critical mineral resources for the Nation. [The BLM-MMS transfer] provides the
Bureau with many additional skilled professionals. It now falls to the
Bureau to take full advantage of their knowledge and abilities, a
difficult task because the two organizations have different traditions
and past ways of operating. . . .[32]

The report also indicted as inadequate the Bureau's salaries for
minerals professionals, its continued use of site-specific and disastrously ad hoc planning processes, the Bureau's penchant for too
frequently transferring minerals management personnel among
different policy areas and tasks, and the agency's tendency to un-
derutilize transferees (e.g., petroleum engineers reclassified as environmental specialists, inspectors of ranch fencing, or monitors of
electrical transmission lines).

Lastly, Linowes II reported that considerable role confusion
still plagued the Bureau's energy program, a conclusion supported
by ten management studies conducted by the Bureau between
1983 and 1985. The culprit? An incessant series of reorganizations
at Interior during the 1970s and 1980s, with the Reagan Administration alone responsible for four of these, including the BLM-
MMS experience. Undermining the Administration's energy production agenda, these efforts ironically produced a significant loss
of technical expertise as employees resigned or transferred.[33] As
the BLM itself concedes, appraisal teams for oil, gas, and coal
exploration should have at least seven professionals, including an
economist, a mineral appraiser, a mining engineer, a geologist, and
a mathematical statistician. Yet, if these standards are applied, the
Bureau's three regional offices were operating at less than sixty
percent capacity as late as one year into Reagan's second term.

Reorganizations, however, do not account alone for the role
confusion and employee disaffection dogging the Bureau during
these years. Also to blame was the herculean task of reconciling the
disparate world views, structures, and procedures of the BLM and
the Conservation Division during the BLM-MMS reorganization.
Recall that the Bureau used a line-staff organizational structure
premised on state boundaries, while the Conservation Division
was housed in a functional organization with regional boundaries.
Thus, in implementing the BLM-MMS reorganization, the Bureau

tried to force transferees and assignments into its on-going line-staff organizational structure. The result, according to the 1986 Role Clarification Study, was a "mixed delegation [of authority] to District Managers, Area Managers, Assistant District Managers for Minerals, and Deputy State Director[s] for Minerals, *causing contin[ual] confusion among staffs*" [emphasis added].[34]

CONCLUSION

This chapter has chronicled the Reagan Administration's efforts to fundamentally reorient energy policy in the West while simultaneously decentralizing managerial authority and implementing a supply-side management agenda within the BLM. In the process, neither the Administration's goals of remedying "regulatory unreasonableness," decentralizing on-the-ground managerial authority, or increasing energy production on New Mexico's public lands occurred to the extent anticipated by the President's pro-development constituency. Why was this true? Prior research on the Reagan presidency has posited correctly that political missteps by Watt and his successors, as well as larger economic and market forces, decidedly limited the impact of the Administration's effort. The "bottom-up" perspective on the administrative presidency offered in this chapter, however, indicates other more mundane yet significant strategic and managerial reasons for these shortcomings.

Our analysis suggests that even without those debilitating factors identified in previous research, internal tensions among the Administration's goals and implementation tactics rendered successful reorientation problematic. More precisely, two of the Administration's goals—decentralization and energy development—were implemented in ways that actually compromised the other. What is more, each goal suffered significantly from (1) the supply-side management penchant of the Reaganites, (2) the machinations of politicos bent on personal electoral gain in their home states, and (3) BLM's implementation of the Watt-Clark reorganization initiatives in ways affirming its traditional surface management values and constituencies.

In terms of supply-side side effects, the Administration's budget cuts stalled meaningful policy and administrative decentralization in New Mexico. Budget cuts, personnel reductions, and persistent reorganizations crimped retraining of transferees to the DOs, further muddled role clarification efforts, and stymied the creation of a skilled and sufficiently staffed middle-management cadre. All these initiatives, of course, were prerequisites for decentralizing authority within the BLM on the scale heralded by Reagan appointees.

Bureaupolitically, and despite the scale of the endeavor, the nature and scope of the political conflict associated with BLM management reform was almost imperceptible. Couched heavily in the prescriptions of BLM's own administrative staff, pushed initially by the Carter Administration, and consonant with evolving administrative theory, the logic, scope, and intent of the reform effort offered little grist for challenge by opponents. Its legitimacy had been established gradually, persistently, and thoroughly within policy networks over the years. At the same time, the initiatives jibed well with the agenda of the Bureau's most sustained, persistent, and vigilant clientele: the cattle industry. And with the BMT's recommendations grounded in the administrative orthodoxy, they never aroused the ire of program specialists. Why not? The BMT preserved unscathed the latter's functional fiefdoms. What remained, then, were the bureaucratic politics and consequences of personal and industry agendas related to the BLM-MMS reorganization: locating on-shore leasing within BLM; the agency's regulatory zeal; and industry-spawned, non-majoritarian "fire alarms" successfully seeking congressional redress.

But how typical were these managerial and political phenomena in other efforts by the Administration to reorient natural resource policy? As the remaining four cases in this section will demonstrate, the Administration's approach was quite consistent, yet the bureaupolitics of policy reorientation varied significantly. How so, why, and with what lessons for the administrative presidency? For insight, we turn next to the similar fate in New Mexico of the President's goals for public rangeland management in the West.

CHAPTER 5

Backdoor Privatization, "Cow Welfare," and the BLM

One can trace much of the initiative, emotionalism, and dynamism of the Sagebrush Rebellion directly to the rangeland management practices of the Carter Administration as it implemented the Federal Land Policy and Management Act (FLPMA) in the West. Moreover, much of the Rebellion's symbolism sprang directly from the Bureau's earlier actions in New Mexico. Chided a former state chairman of the New Mexico Farm and Livestock Bureau, "Give us half the amount for range improvement spent [by the Bureau on administrative tasks] and . . . the [shoddy] conditions of the public lands would be a dead issue in five years."[1]

Animated by such antipathy, and encouraged by Reagan's appointments of Watt and Burford, most Western cattlemen anxiously awaited a pro-development bonanza from the Reagan Revolution. This chapter reviews and critically evaluates the logic, processes, and consequences in New Mexico of the way Reagan's appointees used the administrative presidency to pursue these goals. It discusses the ways the Administration's supply-side management, privatization, and rangeland improvement initiatives combined to complicate and diminish the impact of its rangeland production goals across New Mexico and the West.

THE PAST AS PROLOGUE: OR, "IF YOU WANT GOVERNMENT OFF YOUR BACK, GET YOUR HAND OUT OF ITS POCKETS"

The animus of western cattlemen toward the federal government— and most especially toward the BLM—during the Carter Administration was neither novel nor easily assuaged. Indeed, the themes and tactics of the Sagebrush Rebels in the late 1970s were tested, timeworn, and well-honed. Thematically, the Rebels offered a threefold argument: ill-advised Western rangeland policies were developed by hostile "Easterners" in Washington, maladministered by neophyte BLM "professionals," and misguidedly applied to placate those viewing the West as a "recreational playground" rather than a source of economic succor.

To fully appreciate the rancor provoked among cattlemen by Carter's policies, witness the biting commentary in 1981 of Sherman Harmer, then secretary-manager of the Utah Cattleman's Association. Tracing "anti-cattlemen" attitudes at the Bureau back to the tenure of Interior Secretary Stewart Udall in the early 1960s, Harmer railed:

> There has been no communication between the BLM and the livestock interests. The Taylor Grazing Act said that you *assist* the livestock industry, not *kill* it. . . . The BLM hires kids straight out of college who suddenly become experts and tell seasoned ranchers how to manage the rangelands . . . [they and their families] grazed for a half-century or more. It's just gotten out of hand."[2]

To which New Mexico Cattle Growers Association leaders, Bud Eppers and Bob Jones, as well as fellow ranchers Larry Franklin and State Representatives Hoyt Pattison (D-Lea County) and Dan Berry (D-Lea County), added as late as 1982:

> I [Franklin] approach it [BLM] as a scam. . . . They are not in the ranching business and they want to tell us how to ranch. . . . In meetings I've been to, there was not a whole lot of data to back up their claims. When you confront them, when you fight and get down to numbers, figures, and digits [supporting their decisions], they have to back out because they don't have the data. . . . The BLM is run by autocratic bureaucrats who have no understanding or care about people who operate the land.[3]

Tactically, the approach of the Rebels ranged from primordially visceral to cunningly cerebral as the Bureau moved during the 1960s and 1970s from a minimalist to an intensive management philosophy. According to Bob Jones, BLM employees literally "took their lives in their hands" when venturing into southeastern New Mexico (the heart of the Rebellion in the state) to "inform rather than consult" with ranchers about their decisions. "Some of the less articulate members of the 'Crowfoot Vigilantes'," recalled

Jones, "came to me and offered to shoot them on sight."[4] In contrast, the more articulate demonstrated the political and legal prowess of the most veteran and adroit Washingtonian infighters.

While others have chronicled comprehensively the particulars of the Sagebrush Rebellion in the West, it suffices presently to sample the Rebels' concerns, passions, and political aplomb in New Mexico during the Carter years. To this end, a case involving rangeland management in the Rio Puerco resource area is archetypical. One of Carter appointee Guy Martin's goals as Assistant Secretary for Land and Water Resources at the Interior Department was to shift away from the Ford Administration's emphasis on forestalling grazing reductions through federally subsidized capital improvements (e.g., fencing, water pipelines, and brush control projects). To do so, however, the Bureau had to conduct range inventories determining if forage supplies on public lands were sufficient to support assigned grazing levels. If insufficient, the BLM could cut grazing permit allocations accordingly. Henceforth, under Martin, these decisions were premised on a new, relatively untested computer modeling system known as SVIM.

By 1980, Martin's initial enthusiasm in applying SVIM was surpassed only by the controversy, ill-will, and combativeness generated by the grazing decisions informed by the technique. Indeed, when several of the first 22 grazing environmental impact statements (EISs) premised on SVIM called for reducing ranchers' grazing rights by fully one-third, a distraught cattle industry sounded congressional fire alarms across the region. Their focus, not surprisingly, became Martin's vaunted SVIM computer modeling technique.

The scope and pace of the conflict rapidly spiraled.[5] Disgruntled ranchers, agricultural extension agents, and the New Mexico Cattle Growers Association contacted Republicans Domenici and Schmitt, as well as New Mexico Attorney General and Democrat, Jeff Binghaman. In turn, the senators held congressional hearings on BLM operations generally. Here, Western agricultural experts testified that the Bureau based its forage projections on one especially dry year, premised its grazing decisions on data collected by inexperienced BLMers, and calculated carrying capacity with misspecified quantitative models. Next, 33 poor and primarily Spanish-surnamed subsistence ranchers in Rio Puerco asked the Mountain States Legal Foundation to challenge in court the EIS and Grazing Management Program issued by BLM for their resource area (*Valdez v. Applegate*). In particular, they challenged BLM's use of "full force and effect" orders.[6] Finally, New Mexico officials refused to cooperate with BLM personnel seeking to cross state properties in order to conduct inventories on adjacent federal lands.

In the end, the congressional and judicial intervention spawned by fire alarm oversight resulted in a major retreat from Martin's policy reorientation efforts. First, the 10th Circuit—accepting James Watt's arguments as chief legal counsel for the Mountain States Legal Foundation—placed an injunction on BLM's implementation of grazing reductions in Rio Puerco. In brief, the ranchers' technical and due process arguments prevailed.[7] Second, Congress, in the so-called McClure Amendment, limited BLM grazing cuts across the West to ten percent per permit and narrowly circumscribed when cuts could take place. Finally, the Bureau abandoned SVIM and developed a new range monitoring process after consulting with ranchers, state officials, environmentalists, range scientists, and economists. That process involved more gradual grazing reductions, more government-subsidized range improvements, five-year plans for intermittent monitoring of rangeland, and periodic adjustment of grazing permits based on monitoring results. The Bureau also agreed to extend the concept of "consultation, cooperation, and coordination" with lessees, permittees, landowners, district grazing advisory boards, and any affected state agencies in "all phases of the grazing program."[8] Relatedly, and responding to ranchers' complaints about administrative costs overwhelming on-the-ground investments, the Bureau announced a $2 billion, five-year range improvement plan for the West.

Concessions like these, however, were too few, too little, and too late to assuage the Bureau's staunchest critics. Consequently, states like Nevada and New Mexico rushed pell-mell to enact Sagebrush Rebellion laws demanding that federal lands be turned over to them. Indeed, the Bureau's critics were beyond placating. In

Utah, for example, U.S. Senator Orin Hatch (R) spoke for those most viscerally disgruntled with the agency in the post-FLPMA era: "Where there used to be one BLM man per county, now there are sixty of them, stumbling over each other, acting like little gods. . . . They're being paid to cause trouble."⁹ To which environmentalists retorted, "If they [the Rebels] want government off their backs, they should get their hands out of its pockets!"

With the footsoldiers of the Reagan Revolution on their way to Washington, however, Rebels felt the time ripe for the Bureau's "unconditional surrender," with no prisoners taken, no compromises made. What is more, New Mexican rebels were particularly ebullient. After all, former Domenici protégés—Carruthers and DuBois—were slated to head the "revolution" in the Land and Water Resources Division at Interior. Regulatory relief and resource development on New Mexican rangelands could not be far behind—or could they?

BEYOND "COW WELFARE": BACKDOOR PRIVATIZATION IN NEW MEXICO

As advertised, the Reagan Administration unerringly promoted regulatory relief for its ranching constituency during its eight years in office. We have already seen how the President's deregulatory and pro-development ranching agendas were ratified dramatically over the years in the skill mix, staffing patterns, budgets, and structure of the BLM in New Mexico and the West. But to fully appreciate the dimensions of this effort, one has to understand as well Robert Burford's use of the Bureau's informal rule-making processes.

For many ranchers across the West, September 22, 1981 heralded the Reagan Administration's opening salvo against regulatory unreasonableness on the public rangelands. On that day, Burford administratively announced his interim Rangeland Improvement Policy (RIP). Designed to ensconce the Sagebrush Rebellion's four primary tenets in the hearts and minds of BLM personnel, the RIP (1) "privatized" the costs of rangeland maintenance by shifting them to users; (2) reduced the discretion of state

BLM directors (felt insufficiently sympathetic to rangeland development); (3) distributed Rangeland Betterment, or "8100" funds, on the basis of grazing fees paid rather than environmental need; and (4) limited the amount of funding allocated by the Bureau to administrative costs, as opposed to on-the-ground range improvements.[10]

Burford's privatization initiative had a threefold purpose: to reduce BLM overhead expenses, and thus increase funding for range improvements; to eliminate unwarranted subsidies to cattlemen (i.e., "cow welfare"); and to enhance the legal standing of ranchers claiming preferred access to the public lands over those not paying fees (e.g., recreationists and wildlife). Likewise, Burford wanted to redistribute 8100 funds in closer proportion to the grazing fees collected in each jurisdiction, rather than according to rangeland conditions. His goals? Emphasize productivity rather than actual environmental degradation; redistribute range improvement funds to larger, more productive, and more prosperous ranchers; and reduce the influence of ecologically minded state BLM directors and staff.

While the Bureau's generally less aggressive, less confrontational, and more consultative regulatory attitude defused the Sagebrush Rebellion, significant improvements in rangeland production failed to follow (see Table 3–9). Was Burford's agenda foiled by disagreeable weather conditions, market forces beyond anyone's control, or pockets of bureaucratic resistance?[11] All played a role, no doubt. But so too did the Reagan Administration's supply-side management agenda. Most illustrative is the fate of Burford's RIP in New Mexico. There, four primary issues had to be resolved, with substantial stakes for rangeland productivity. First, who would pay what and when for what types of improvements and maintenance on structural improvements? Second, would appeals to Secretary Watt and congressional patrons deter or alter the implementation of these decisions? Third, could the New Mexico Department of Agriculture effectively scuttle the Administration's plans? Finally, would the interaction of the Reagan Administration's privatization, range improvement, and supply-side management initiatives help or hinder its rangeland production goals in the long run?

The National Standards Issue

Divided into two programmatic thrusts, Burford's RIP dealt, first, with maintenance responsibilities for users. According to Burford, the logic behind this policy was fourfold. First, existing policy lacked clear definition and varied among BLM districts. Consequently, informed observers were unsure whether the BLM treated ranchers equitably or spent federal funds legally. Second, in an equitable system, those benefitting from range improvements should assume the costs of maintaining them. Third, ranchers were best able to maintain improvements in a timely manner, thus enhancing the "useful life" of government investments. And finally, the Washington Office had to standardize maintenance responsibilities, priority rankings, and specifications to avoid equity problems across BLM jurisdictions.

Under Burford's plan, permittees or leasees could either perform maintenance themselves, hire out or contract work to be done, or pay the Bureau to maintain their facility. Regardless of their choice, however, legally binding cooperative agreements documenting maintenance responsibilities became part of the leasee's grazing permit. Thus, failure to pay for or perform maintenance consonant with BLM standards terminated the rancher's grazing rights. Moreover, if cooperative arrangements proved nonnegotiable, BLM could assign maintenance responsibilities in any manner it chose. Lastly, and most critically for New Mexico, these tasks had to be assigned by the end of FY 1984.

Similar levels of specificity, standardization, and Rebellion fervor characterized the second component of Burford's Rangeland Improvement Policy: the distribution and use of Range Betterment (8100) funds. Indeed, the rationale for Burford's plan was threefold. First, because the Carter Administration had made minimal use of 8100 funds for on-the-ground improvements, it had ignored congressional intent. Specifically, Section 401 of FLPMA, along with the Public Rangeland Improvement Act (PRIA), charged the Bureau with improving forage conditions, not funding environmental assessments or research. Henceforth, the BLM would only fund overhead expenses of these sorts from specified Rangeland Management and PRIA funds. Second, because it had routinely flouted the "consultation, cooperation, and coordination" provisions in Section 8 of PRIA, BLM now had to consult grazing boards dominated by pro-development ranching interests before spending 8100 funds. Simultaneously, Burford stripped all review authority from Carter's multiple-use advisory boards. Finally, to counter excessive power of state directors, Burford placed spending of all 8100 funds at the discretion of district office managers.

As for distributing 8100 funds among the districts, each office would garner 50 percent of the grazing fees collected in its jurisdiction. True, state directors still could redistribute minor portions of Rangeland Betterment funds on the basis of prior commitments, resource conditions, or economic considerations. Nevertheless, an office's receipts averaged over a 5-year period had to equal its 50-percent-of-grazing-fee entitlement. Moreover, Burford personally had to approve yearly variations from that formula.

Even with their interests so well-protected, New Mexican cattlemen still balked at parts of Burford's RIP. In fact, many—such as the large-ranch-dominated New Mexico Cattle Growers Association—denounced the RIP as "arbitrary," impractical, and "detrimental to the intended purpose of range improvement."[12] According to Association members Phillip Bidegain, Bob Jones, and Phil Harvey, ranchers supported Burford's 50 percent formula for 8100 funds, as well as his proposal to make livestock owners responsible for rangeland improvements and maintenance. What they found offensive, however, were the decision-making process and substance of the national standards Burford wished to apply for constructing and maintaining these improvements.

As for the decision-making process, many saw the Bureau reneging on legally binding commitments. More precisely, ranchers operating under existing BLM cooperative agreements passed all maintenance costs on to the federal government. Thus, claimed Jones, Burford's plan summarily broke these agreements and ordered future range improvements and maintenance without any "coordination, consultation, and cooperation" with landholders or BLM grazing advisory boards. Thus, not only did range conditions vary so markedly that national standards were unfeasible, but a principle of fairness was at issue. Argued Phil Harvey, "I'm the one putting up the fence and it's my money. . . . I'm the one who will benefit from it, so it shouldn't matter to BLM how I do it, when I do it, or how I maintain it."[13]

Similarly disgruntled were smaller, less politically powerful ranchers in the Western states. To them, Burford was engineering a sizeable redistribution of federal dollars from smaller, more marginal operators to decidedly more powerful, less needy ranchers grazing greater numbers of cattle. A serious charge, indeed, but hardly a baseless one. For example, BLM careerists in New Mexico swore that "the larger operators in southern New Mexico were [the ones] pushing this policy."[14]

Thus, by mid-1982, both the Western livestock industry and Robert Burford were in a bind on the RIP. By then, most Sagebrush Rebels realized that turning over federal lands to the states was neither likely nor necessarily advantageous to the cattle industry. The federal government needed the grazing and mineral leasing revenues these properties generated as the economy slipped into a recession. Furthermore, "state officials [were] realizing how expensive it could be to manage the lands: why should we trade a rich landlord (the federal government) for a poor landlord."[15] Meanwhile, Burford's predicament was how to preserve the core of his "cow welfare" initiative while satisfying the disparate demands of small and large ranch operators. Witness, for example, the Administration's experience in New Mexico regarding the Rio Puerco pipeline.

The Rio Puerco Pipeline Exemption Issue

The Rio Puerco Resource Area (RPRA) lies roughly 40 miles northwest of Albuquerque in Sandoval and McKinley Counties. Containing over 800 square miles of semi-arid properties, three-quarters of which are managed by the BLM, Rio Puerco was plagued by the mixed pattern of ownership so common in the West and so deleterious to effective land management. Still, for nearly two hundred years the dominant use of these lands was grazing—or better put, over-grazing.

By the time Ronald Reagan assumed the presidency, the federal government already had mounted heroic efforts to address the watershed and erosion problems occasioned by over-grazing in the RPRA. During the 1930s, for instance, the Soil Conservation Service and Roosevelt's Civilian Conservation Corps constructed numerous watershed and erosion control devices throughout the area. Likewise, in the 1940s, the newly constituted BLM built several of its first intensive range and watershed facility projects in the RPRA. Efforts like these continued apace during the 1950s under the Bureau's "Frail Lands" program, with Rio Puerco cited as a priority area in the West. So designated, Rio Puerco absorbed a multi-million-dollar program of water facilities and land treatments, including hundreds of detention dams, reservoirs, dikes, and diversion structures. Then, dramatically, during the late 1960s and 1970s, the Bureau's perception of the problem shifted. Physical control of erosion was out; management of livestock distribution was in. Also planted, however, were the seeds of the Rio Puerco pipeline dispute of the 1980s.

The "New" Approach. As with most policy successes, the BLM's mitigation efforts in the RPRA had produced unintended and quite negative consequences. Specifically, in constructing the earthwork components of the "Frail Lands" project, the Bureau had drilled wells to provide water for earthfill detention dams. Each well had an open water pit next to it that, unintendedly, became a virtual oasis to thirsty livestock in a semi-arid land. Congregating near these pits, livestock severely over-grazed surrounding properties. This, in turn, prompted the agency to build extended water pipelines to disperse cattle over wider grazing areas. Initially, these efforts sought only to carry water to livestock drinking troughs a few miles away from the wells, troughs each capable of servicing the needs of a half-dozen or more allottees. Thus, by 1975 the entire Rio Puerco pipeline system consisted of some twenty miles of BLM-constructed and -maintained water pipelines.

In the immediate aftermath of *NRDC v. Morton* (see Chapter 1), however, the pace, scope, and complexity of the Bureau's pipeline construction effort spiraled in Rio Puerco. As noted, the court's verdict ultimately spawned a successful lawsuit filed by Rio Puerco ranchers challenging the way BLM implemented full-force-and-effect grazing cuts in their region. But Rio Puerco's EIS also contained a hefty range improvement program, one many ranchers embraced. Specifically approved, for example, were over 280 miles of water pipeline systems, including 180 miles of pipeline, 50 storage tanks, 152 cattle-watering troughs, and 49 wildlife watering ponds. Also scheduled on individual allotments were cattleguards, stock trails, vegetative manipulation, and over one thousand miles of fencing. Yet, these improvements could not proceed until the *Valdez* case was settled.

Still, by 1982 the major portion (more than 180 miles) of pipeline construction in the RPRA was complete. The result? An extremely complex, $2 million system of 10 interrelated—yet separate—facilities for several allotments, linking multiple and ethnically diverse grazing permittees. Individual pipeline facilities ranged geographically from the 95-mile Cabezon system to the 4.3-mile South Divide project. Levels of complexity also varied within the system. For instance, Cabezon consisted of 29 storage units, 59 water troughs, and 27 wildlife waters, while South Divide had only 4 troughs, 1 storage unit, and 3 wildlife waters. Most significantly, however, BLM district office officials felt that the government's $2 million investment was too technical, costly, and valuable to "hive-off" its maintenance to technologically unsophisticated allottees who could neither get along with each other nor afford its $80,000 to $90,000 annual costs.

Once in office, Secretary Watt ended the Rio Puerco stalemate for individual allottees by approving an out-of-court settlement of *Valdez* with the Rio Puerco ranchers he had previously represented! Not only did he vacate the Bureau's original full-force-and-effect orders, but he also prohibited any grazing cuts until the agency completed a five-year grassland monitoring program in the RPRA. To these ends, the agency launched an extremely difficult series of negotiations with individual allottees to craft legally binding grazing agreements with each, a task they completed by the end of 1981.

Moreover, each agreement stipulated that range improvements be completed over the next four years to offset the need for future grazing cuts by enhancing range quality. Yet these improvements required timely and adequate federal funding, a contingency now jeopardized ironically by the Reagan Administration's own supply-side management, 8100 funding, and privatization initiatives. Watt's own settlement now was hostage to his BLM Director's budget balancing, anti-environmental predilections.

The Administration's Dilemma. With parts of his Rangeland Im-

provement Policy ill-received by ranchers, Burford indicated flexibility on its particulars and solicited reactions from BLM careerists. Rio Puerco's reaction was quick, decisive, and worrisome
enough to get Deputy Assistant Secretary Frank DuBois involved,
prodded by both Senator Schmitt and BLM RPRA Manager Herrick (Rick) Hanks. "As a result of the recent [RIP] policy change,"
wrote Hanks, "funding constraints and the maintenance responsibility issue have now replaced the legal constraints [of the *Valdez*
injunction] as the primary factor affecting the implementation of
[the] Rio Puerco Livestock Grazing Management Program,"[16] as
well as Watt's settlement in *Valdez*. Averring that he and his staff
had "no problems" with the overall purposes, goals, and objectives of Burford's policy (viz., eliminating "cow welfare"), Hanks
noted how distraught they were at its "apparent lack of flexibility."
Most egregiously, the RIP "did not allow for differences in the
complexity of . . . pipeline system[s], the nature of the allottees,
[and] the historic practices of both the BLM and the ranchers."
Noting how "disastrous" this could be for ranchers, Hanks
claimed that the RIP would:

> have a social and economic effect on the majority of the Rio Puerco
> ranchers . . . [that] could be much greater than the effects of the
> implementation of the Rio Puerco grazing program as proposed in
> the ES . . . which resulted in [the *Valdez*] lawsuit and disrupted the
> orderly management of [Rio Puerco]. Many of the operators may be
> forced out of the livestock business, while the profits of others will be
> greatly reduced. Basically, the BLM will be imposing a rapid social
> and economic change on an area that cannot absorb the impact of
> such a change over such a relatively short time period [two fiscal
> years].[17]

To fully comprehend Hank's argument, one has to appreciate
the independent and interactive effects of Interior's efforts on BLM
and livestock operations in Rio Puerco. Independently, the effect of
shifting maintenance responsibility to allottees by the end of FY84
was formidable, indeed. As Jerry Schickedanz of the New Mexico
State University Range Improvement Task Force pointedly queried,
"Should permittees be required to be fully responsible for a
[pipeline] system that takes a hydraulic engineer to understand
and an unrecoverable sunken investment [by federal tax-

payers]?"[18] Bob Reed of BLM's Division of Operations in the Albuquerque District also worried about the RIP's legal implications: "Many ranchers are reluctant to do maintenance on simple projects and stagger at the thought of maintaining projects that are complex and expensive. . . . [And] since many ranchers will not be able to afford [maintenance responsibilities], this could lead to court cases and appeals."[19]

Severe, as well, were the interactive effects of Burford's new 8100 funding formula and the Reagan Administration's budget and personnel cuts in the Albuquerque District. Indeed, as Reed warned Hanks, the Bureau had "neither the funding nor the manpower to implement [Burford's policy]" during the time frame stipulated. Witness, for example, Reed's summary of the BLM's plight:

> In reference to the redistribution of the RB (8100) funds, it is proper [as Burford's RIP mandated] to return these funds to the areas from which they were collected. However, we must consider the result of this action. Frail lands that are not as productive, but in greater need of protection, will suffer due to the funding levels. [Moreover], no additional funds, but probable cuts are expected in the 4322, 4322 PRIA, 4340, and 4350 [funding accounts], so where will the funding come from to protect these lands? [Consequently,] *management objectives set by* [Valdez] *ESs are left without funding* [while] *those funds are allocated to areas that cannot use the extra funds due to lack of manpower, planning, and actual need.* Loss of manpower will be a great impact on districts that are funded at 25% of their traditional levels with no support from other range improvement activities such as 4322, 4340, 4350, etc.. The reason for this is the lack of funding created by the 5-year-pay-back policy . . . and the lack of stability in field expertise.[20]

In sum, most BLM officials felt that cuts of this magnitude could easily produce negative economic effects on the ranchers that were more severe than the original Rio Puerco grazing reduction orders Watt had challenged in court. In the short term, ranchers unable to pay their share of annual maintenance fees for the pipeline would have to absorb grazing reductions, while the marginal costs imposed by the additional fees would force some to go out of business altogether. Moreover, in the long term, funding and

work force cuts would force the postponement, if not the cancella-
tion, of range improvements desired by ranchers, stipulated in the
Valdez settlement approved by Watt, and anticipated by the Carter
Administration's five-year, $2-billion improvement plan.

The Administration's Response. Whether principled or the protectionist ploys of wily career bureaucrats, or both, the arguments of
Hanks, Reed, and others fell on somewhat sympathetic ears in the
person of Deputy Assistant Secretary DuBois. Indeed, DuBois candidly recalled years later that in helping to craft the RIP, he "hadn't
really thought about complex systems" such as Rio Puerco's. Thus,
the arguments advanced by careerists seemed compelling as long as
"it didn't appear that we [New Mexico appointees] were making
an exception for our own state."[21]

Consequently, DuBois, Burford, and other Administration officials began wrestling with Hanks and Reed's three suggestions for
altering policy: (1) extend the time frame for implementation and
allow the resource areas to implement the new policies "at a
schedule comparable to the extent of the problem"; (2) give the
BLM more flexibility in continuing to maintain the more complex
projects; and (3) provide additional funding and manpower "so
that the implementation can be done right the first time." Likewise, a plea by Jerry Schickedanz to reconsider the $3.44 per
animal-unit-month charge to ranchers drew the politically astute
DuBois' attention.[22]

Throughout the Rio Puerco controversy, Dubois suggested that
"we can work this out—they are in other places."[23] His reference
was to the way BLM officials in Idaho, Oregon, and Arizona were
handling similar situations in their states. Pressed by Dubois to
ensure that any compromise for Rio Puerco be consistent with
those crafted elsewhere, New Mexico's state BLM Director,
Charles W. Luscher, reported that the Vale and Burley Districts
offered allottees an option. Wrote Luscher to DuBois,

> Vale [, Oregon,] will not be in a situation to perform the maintenance
> without 8100 funds and other funding is not available to cover their
> $500,000 yearly maintenance costs. The District is providing the
> option of either the allottees providing contributed funds [to the
> BLM which then performed the maintenance] or the allottees form-
> ing associations and the associations performing the maintenance

under a cooperative agreement. . . . [Likewise], the Burley District began developing cooperative agreements which turn over the full maintenance responsibility to the associations. They started with the most cooperative associations first.[24]

But how applicable to Rio Puerco were such solutions, since historically its residents were ill-disposed toward cooperation? Witness, for example, how the various cultures—Pueblo Indian, Navajo, and Spanish-speaking—hid the location of religious shrines from each other, fearing desecration by their neighbors. Flaring alongside these religious differences were longstanding property feuds over ancient land claims. No, historical animosities among Rio Puerco communities did not bode well for implementing Burford's policy in a timely manner in the RPRA, especially when one considers how much cooperation was needed to effectively operate the highly independent, accident-prone 200-mile pipeline system. Indeed, Albuquerque District Manager Paul Applegate feared that assigning individual maintenance of segments of the pipeline systems to individual users could be an enforcement and administrative nightmare for BLM. Part of his worry: The slightest misadjustment (unintentional or deliberately sabotaged) of one of the pipeline's water-level adjustment valves could cause all the troughs down the line to overflow or not fill at all.

Animated by these concerns, Luscher asked BLM headquarters to exempt Rio Puerco from the pipeline provisions of Burford's RIP. Ever-sensitive, however, to charges of favoritism, Dubois and the Bureau's Assistant Director for Renewable Resources denied Luscher's request. Burford, however, did make one significant concession applicable to all states. Specifically, he relaxed by twelve months his original target date for transferring maintenance responsibilities to primary beneficiaries. Concomitantly, however, he also foreclosed further Rio Puerco appeals, and pressed BLM officials to meet with area ranchers and target group representatives (e.g., wildlife managers and hunters) to discuss their options.

With BLM's Washington Office foreclosing exemption, the issues now for area ranchers were (a) whether a direct appeal to Secretary Watt might reverse the DuBois-Burford ultimatum, and (b) if not, what the nature and appropriate share of their maintenance costs might be. As the FY82 and FY83 funding periods progressed, answers to the latter question typically took a circuitous path to resolution. In contrast, Watt's reaction to the ranchers' exemption request was straightforward. Although allottees such as Rudy Gutierrez of the Rio Puerco Grazing Association had felt that "the Secretary had acted in [our] behalf before, so perhaps [he] would again," Watt quickly quashed the idea in a meeting with five ranch representatives arranged by New Mexico congressman, William Richardson (D).[25] What is more, when additional opportunities to respond favorably arose after Watt's hasty exit from Interior, succeeding Secretaries Clark and Hodel similarly dismissed the entreaties of Rio Puerco ranchers.

Distinctly more tortuous, however, were the BLM's negotiations with various ranching cultures, communities, and families, as the agency sought to coax grudging compliance with Burford's privatization scheme. By the extended deadline, most allottees had entered into cooperative agreements with the agency to maintain the pipeline, but only after BLM had agreed to reduce maintenance fees anywhere from one-third to one-half of their original levels for individual ranchers. Getting to that point, however, tested the patience, commitment, and political savvy of the staunchest privatizers within the Reagan Administration.

Containing the Contagiousness of the Conflict. Between the fall of 1982 and the winter of 1983, the audience determining the outcome of the fight in Rio Puerco expanded. Yet it did so only in ways prescribed by law, without interbureaucratic rancor, and with lower-level officials resolving their differences without sustained macro- or micro-level political intervention. Pursuant to Section 8 of PRIA and the New Mexico–BLM Rangeland Consultation Memorandum of Understanding signed by President Carter's Interior Secretary, BLM district and resource area officials conducted a series of group meetings with New Mexico's Range Improvement Task Force, State Land Office, Department of Agriculture, Department of Game and Fish, Conservation Coordinating Council, Cattle Growers Association, Rio Puerco Livestock Association, Rio Puerco Grazing Association, and congressional staff.

These group meetings were supplemented by individual consultations with the 80 BLM grazing permittees served by the pipeline system. The consultations outlined maintenance options for the allottees and pressed BLM's preferred options upon them. Depending on area cultural and technological situations, there were two options: either (1) ranchers could pay the Bureau to maintain the system for an annual fee, or (2) they could sign a cooperative agreement to form a local organization responsible for operating and maintaining their part of the system. Under the second option, ranchers could either repair the system themselves or hire contractors to do the work, thus reducing their costs by eliminating government overhead expenses.

Initially, frustrated allottees used BLM's public meetings to vent their frustration with federal land policies generally, to chaff at the "burden" BLM asked them to assume, and to threaten careerists with a shutdown of the pipeline. Bristled defiant Rio Puerco ranchers Dickie Archuleta and Rusty Sandoval: "We have gotten along without BLM water before and we can do so again."[26] And lest anyone infer that only a few radical ranching elements held these sentiments, the Rio Puerco Livestock Association subsequently released a survey of area ranchers. Of the respondents, fully 95 percent wanted neither to assume maintenance responsibilities nor to pay maintenance fees to the Bureau for these services. Indeed, the same percentage favored abandoning the pipeline altogether, arguing that it was neither cost-effective nor practical for individual livestock use. Indeed, so undependable was the system that ranchers already had developed other water supplies.[27] Not so, retorted BLM officials: Alternative water supplies could never support existing grazing rates. Hence, if ranchers failed to cooperate, sizeable cuts in their grazing permits were in the offing.

Against this leitmotif, a second round of consultations proved equally futile until area ranchers realized how unsympathetic the New Mexico congressional delegation was to their cause. True, various members of the delegation routinely sent staff representatives to these meetings. Conspicuously absent, however, was the sustained, persistent, and vitriolic personal involvement and fire alarm oversight exhibited by the delegation during the Carter years.

Equally devastating to the allottees was a July 1983 resolution by the Albuquerque district grazing advisory board endorsing the assignment of maintenance responsibilities to ranchers.[28] Because the pipeline system served a small number of ranchers and less than three thousand cattle, the BLM should not be responsible for maintenance costs. Consequently, the large-operator-dominated Board advised all pipeline users to determine which sections of the pipeline system to abandon and which to maintain. Yes, BLM might have to continue maintaining the pipeline during a transition period when the impact on ranchers otherwise might be severe and cause "disruption of their operations." But BLM's long-term goal should be to "get entirely out of maintaining the system." Thus, with congressional redress unlikely, appeals to the Reagan Administration rejected, and local grazing boards unsympathetic to the ranchers' cause, pragmatism set in. Rio Puerco operators and their allies turned their attention to containing the economic impacts of Burford's RIP, whether those fell on users entering into BLM cooperative agreements or paying fees to the agency for maintenance services.

While the terms of debate varied among the ten systems within the RPRA, two issues related to the Bureau's projected maintenance fees stubbornly plagued the negotiations in each system. First, since wildlife benefited from the pipeline system, shouldn't part of the repair and maintenance fees be reduced accordingly for Rio Puerco ranchers? And second, how valid was BLM's formula for computing maintenance fees? Interestingly, on both points BLM technocrats made concessions, thus modifying Burford's original goal that primary users bear all maintenance costs.

Regarding wildlife, the New Mexico Department of Game and Fish (NMDG&F) enthusiastically corroborated the ranchers' claims and upped the ante by suggesting that even more wildlife support could be provided if adequate maintenance of the system occurred. In the Cuba, New Mexico area they argued, for example, that nearly half of all water systems were inoperative. In the end, the NMDG&F offered to partially fund maintenance of some of these systems—a move welcomed (if not encouraged) by many careerists in the BLM as a way to enhance the priority claims of wildlife populations to Rio Puerco water supplies. Thus, the ranchers' point had been made, but at a cost to their priority claims in the area. They intended for the BLM, not wildlife interests, to fund the difference in maintenance costs. Yes, their fees were reduced somewhat. But their "victory's" price came high: increased consideration for environmental values in the resource area.

In contrast, the ranchers enjoyed a more satisfying experience in their challenge to the way BLM computed its maintenance fee estimates. Specifically, while the Bureau originally computed this cost at $3.44 per animal-unit-month (AUM) in 1982, a study conducted by the New Mexico Range Improvement Task Force on actual repair and maintenance costs for improvements in northwest New Mexico projected that figure at $0.69 per animal-unit-month for Rio Puerco, or some 449 percent less than BLM's estimate.[29] While based only on experiences in other areas, the Task Force's finding significantly redefined the terms of debate regarding privatization of the Rio Puerco pipeline system. Indeed, after consulting with the Washington Office, the BLM conducted conferences with individual ranchers premised on substantially reduced maintenance costs. As noted, these ranged anywhere from one-third to one-half of the Bureau's original estimates, depending on which of the ten systems was involved. Importantly, however, the Bureau also turned the heat up on the allottees to enter into cooperative maintenance agreements. Indeed, in a meeting with Cuba area ranchers, a BLM spokesperson told them they "had no choice"; after Burford's deadline, BLM would have no funds to maintain improvements. "At that time," he admonished in tones reminiscent of the pre-*Valdez* era, "the electricity will be turned off if you haven't figured out a way to pay the bills."[30]

Certainly, in this instance, one might forgive Rio Puerco ranchers for finding it difficult to distinguish between the Carter Administration's "full-force-and-effect" orders and the "good neighbor" policy of the Reagan Revolution. Still, the ranchers had one last card to play, a wild card dealt by William Stephens, New Mexico's Secretary of Agriculture. Unfortunately for them, however, New Mexico's State Engineer, Steve Reynolds, trumped Stephen's card almost immediately.[31]

The Water Rights Exemption Question. Part of the Reagan Administration's "backdoor privatization" strategy was to reverse administratively BLM's longstanding policy precluding ranchers from applying to states for water rights on public lands. With water so scarce in the West, whoever controlled these rights—BLM or ranch operators—effectively controlled economic development as well. Before it could do so, however, those opposed to transferring pipeline maintenance responsibilities to Rio Puerco ranchers used BLM's ownership of these rights to stymie privatization. Their argument? BLM had either to perform its maintenance duties or forfeit its claims to "prior appropriation and beneficial yield."

In June and mid-August of 1983, New Mexico Agriculture Secretary Stephens wrote letters to BLM State Director Luscher outlining precisely such an argument. Stephens' logic was three-fold. First, the BLM has to comply with state water law when acquiring water rights anywhere in the United States. Second, New Mexico surface water law requires those filing for water rights to declare the beneficial use of the water taken. Third, the BLM had filed for Rio Puerco water rights with the State Engineer, thus setting forth the beneficial use for those waters. Therefore, under state law, the Bureau was itself the primary beneficial user. So, as primary beneficiary, the BLM—not allottees—had to maintain the Rio Puerco system. To do otherwise, Stephens argued, violated Burford's own Rangeland Improvement Policy.

Not surprisingly, Luscher challenged Stephens' argument, questioning especially his linking Burford's RIP and the Bureau's filing for groundwater rights with state agencies. In Luscher's view, state groundwater (not surface water) law should decide this issue; and in New Mexico, groundwater law allowed the BLM to file and obtain a water rights permit and then transfer the right to use the water to an allottee. In the process, the operator replaced the BLM as primary beneficiary. Moreover, state groundwater law did not define the phrases "beneficial user" or "primary beneficiary" at all, let alone in the manner Stephens suggested. Consequently, state law had "no relevance" to BLM's Rangeland Improvement Policy.

At loggerheads, Luscher and Stephens turned to State Engineer Reynolds to interpret New Mexico's water statute, to assess its relevance to the BLM's Rangeland Improvement Policy, and to ascertain whether or not BLM could transfer its water rights to individual livestock operators or pipeline associations in Rio Puerco. In short order, Reynold's responded to their inquiries in ways effectively proscribing further dilatory tactics by the allottees and their allies. Specifically, he agreed with Luscher that the groundwater statute was both operant and silent when it came to defining "beneficial user" and "primary beneficiary." Thus, Stephen's argument lacked a solid legal foundation. "What is more," wrote Reynolds, "the State Engineer is without authority to control BLM's assignment of primary responsibility for the operation and maintenance of facilities needed for the exercise of BLM water rights." With their last gambit aborted by Reynolds, holdout ranchers in Rio Puerco commenced and, for the most part, completed negotiations for assuming maintenance responsibilities by the Administration's amended deadline. In the process, Reagan's appointees conceded what Paul Sabatier calls "operating beliefs" (e.g., deadlines) in order to preserve their "core beliefs" (e.g., privatization and the redistribution of 8100 funds).[32]

The Southern New Mexico Experience

But what of the longer-term consequences of Burford's RIP for its presumed beneficiaries: the larger, more politically influential ranchers of southern New Mexico? Recall how these cattlemen lobbied for and enthusiastically embraced many aspects of Burford's RIP. Most cherished, of course, were the plan's redistribution of federal largess to their area, diminution of environmental emphasis, and limits on the discretion of state BLM directors. Still, words uttered in 1982 by one BLM district manager were the harbinger of even harder days ahead as the Reagan Revolution progressively took its toll on BLM's organizational capacity. Lamented Dan Rathbun, "The money [for improvements in southern New Mexico] is there, but the capability within the Bureau—those who actually survey, design, and build [these improvements]—that part has not been totally staffed."[33] Nor, as Chapter 3 demonstrated, were they ever sufficiently staffed during the Reagan years.

In truth, Burford's funding formula proved a mixed blessing for larger southern New Mexican ranches. Arguably, ranchers benefitted most from (1) the diminishing of the state BLM office's control over 8100 fund uses and distribution; (2) the shifting of available funds from administrative, planning, and environmental purposes to on-the-ground improvements; (3) the eclipse in influence of Carter's multiple-use advisory boards; and (4) the accompanying resurgence of rancher-dominated grazing advisory boards. Indeed, the Reagan Administration had decentralized funding authority to BLM district officials operating within a consciously renewed and crafted sociopolitical environment of dominant rather than multiple clientelism.

Still, for all concerned, the negative side effects of policy interaction were real, profound, and taxing. For example, with environmental studies and land use planning required before range improvements were possible, the decline in resource inventory and planning positions retarded Burford's reorientation efforts. Similarly, with Reagan appointees precluding BLM from spending 8100 funds on environmental inventories, BLM grazing administration accounts designated for range improvements and management remained underutilized. Indeed, work force shortages for project planning and contract supervision persistently plagued the range improvement process in New Mexico and throughout the West. In New Mexico, the minutes of district grazing advisory board meetings frequently refer to the dilemmas posed to development by the "turnover of BLM personnel"; the frequency of "carry-over" projects from year to year due to inadequate financing or labor; the inability of the Bureau to "promise anything" in the way of improvements given budget and personnel uncertainties; and the need to allow allottees "to contribute the amount necessary to cover the cost of preparing the environmental assessment and the necessary clearances if appropriated funds are not available to the Bureau."[34]

As for the West generally, a 1984 report by the Surveys and Investigations Staff of the House Committee on Appropriations documents vividly the self-defeating aspects of the Administration's rangeland and supply-side management policies. Indeed, this report—as well as congressional testimony provided by the Society for Range Management (SRM)—confirmed the prescience in 1981 of Guy Martin's critique of Reagan's policies:

> If I could make a central philosophical point today it is this: The lopsidedness of this budget, frankly, is likely to be counter-productive even to accomplish what the [Reagan] Administration most wants to

do. . . . Not only will it [Reagan's budget] penalize renewable resources [as intended], but it will wind up making it more difficult probably to achieve levels of development they would like to achieve on those public lands.[35]

By 1985, prognostication had become reality. Witness, for example, SRM's testimony at BLM appropriation hearings that year. A Denver-based organization counting ranchers and businesspersons as members, Society representatives pondered the consequences for public rangelands of Reagan's administrative presidency. Their conclusion:

> SRM is becoming increasingly concerned about the professional levels . . . of BLM range management activities. This is prompted by the significant reduction in their professional staffs. Minimum management levels are prompted by these reduced budgets as opposed to management directed to full potential of the range resource. . . . The Society is also concerned about the very limited recruitment of the range management and other professional graduates at the entry level needed to insure experienced replacements for the future. SRM believes . . . [the BLM is] to be congratulated for placing emphasis on the grazing permittees assuming more responsibility for all aspects of grazing management. However, [we] believe it is essential this be supplemented by increased levels of the Bureau's professional support.[36]

One might, of course, infer from these remarks that the Reagan Administration actually had succeeded in realizing a primary goal: a return at the BLM to those debilitating "minimalist management" days, where crippled agency budgets ensured regulatory relief. Too, one might interpret declines in recruiting professionals as deftly crafted to institutionalize the Administration's deregulatory agenda in the post-Reagan era of budget deficits, subterfuge, and accounting chicanery. Still, the paradox inherent in this "success" is striking. The more successful the Administration was in securing these "victories," the more threatened its overall pro-development agenda became.

In summarizing just how debilitating this situation became across the West, the Survey and Investigation staff reported:

> BLM [has] a backlog of about $26 million in range improvement projects. The backlog includes about 435 AMPs in the "improve" allotment category which have top priority for rangeland improve-

ment investments. These AMPs remain on the shelf with no improvement work initiated. For BLM to reduce the backlog over a four-year period would require additional funding of $6.5 million annually if no other additional improvement work were done. These figures represent construction dollars only and would require additional funds and personnel for project planning and contract supervision to enable the BLM to handle the increased workload above current levels.[37]

How had Reagan's BLM responded to this challenge? Again, the congressional staff report reveals how ill-suited the Administration's short-term actions were to the long-term range improvement productivity goals of its ranching constituency:

> Despite the backlog, BLM has requested less funds for grazing administration in each of the past three years. BLM also receives a range improvement appropriation for making on-the-ground improvements. [However,] the current situation of reduced grazing fee receipts [sparked by low grazing fee rates] coupled with the increased costs of range improvements from an average of $48,000 in FY 1982 to $60,000 per allotment in FY 1984 will reduce funding needed to make significant progress . . . on improving range conditions. [Likewise,] returning funds on the basis of where they were collected results in some districts making expenditures on allotments which provide a very limited return while other areas of the State have greater need.[38]

In sum, the Reagan Revolution had delivered less money for range improvements to ranchers by adding to backlogs of range improvement projects. These, in turn, were the product of (1) the excessively rigid budgeting categories noted in Chapter 4; (2) a refusal by appointees to move money when possible from accounts with excess resources to those less well-endowed; and (3) an undersupply of personnel in occupations denigrated by Reaganites, yet critical for improvements envisioned by the Public Rangeland Improvement Act.

CONCLUSION

The Reagan Administration's public rangeland experience in New Mexico exhibits many of the same managerial foibles and bureaupolitical dynamics reported previously in the BLM-MMS reorganization case. This time, however, the Administration's short-term tactics (supply-side management cuts in environmental protection budgets and positions, privatization of rangeland management costs, and decentralization of authority to district managers) meshed well with various sub-agendas (regulatory relief, reducing multiple clienteles in ways favoring production interests, and reducing "cow welfare"). Yet individually and collectively, they were ill-suited to the Administration's penultimate goal: dramatically escalating public rangeland production. In essence, if the Administration merely sought regulatory relief, the match between their tactics and that end made sense. Yet this was not the case; Reaganites were bent on both stopping things from happening (regulatory relief) *and* making things happen (rangeland development). Thus, paradoxically, their ideologically driven focus on the former helped dilute if not cripple their progress on the latter.

Concomitantly, the bureaupolitical dynamics of the Administration's rangeland experience in New Mexico were distinctly muted, with the scope of the conflict associated with policy reorientation quite circumscribed. Most likely, the nature of the policy initiatives proffered by Reagan appointees helps account for the limited scope, intensity, and contagiousness of the conflict experienced. Assigning maintenance costs to users, ending "cow welfare," and diminishing administrative overhead costs relative to range improvements were ideas that differed little from the status quo, did not represent abrupt changes from existing policies, and fitted well with the nation's emerging fiscal exigencies. In fact, their logic had informed small-scale "experimental stewardship" programs during the Carter years. Moreover, specialists across a range of disciplines, political persuasions, and presidencies had long advocated their implementation. Too, altering the 8100 fund formula represented a major step toward returning to pre-FLPMA days at the Bureau, with discretion maximized and ultimately "captured" by non-majoritarian interests at the district level. Finally, by working within the context of the administrative orthodoxy in making budget cuts and alterations, Reagan appointees preserved the power of program bureaucrats advantaged by fragmented, inflexible, and proliferating functional funding accounts.

To summarize, the gradualist nature of Burford's privatization agenda, while significant, offered little room to question the legitimacy and validity of their logic. Realizing how little fodder for challenge these initiatives afforded, and faced with the daunting political power of large-scale ranchers and their allies, those opposed (1) focused largely on technical questions (e.g., timing, pace, and cost), and (2) sought and acquired only limited support from macropolitical system actors. Keeping these patterns in mind, we next turn our attention in Chapter 6 to the Administration's plans to cut funding for public land acquisitions and to emphasize large-scale land exchanges involving nationally significant properties.

CHAPTER 6

Toward Becoming a "Good Urban Neighbor"? Or, "You're Not a Man Till You Do a Land Exchange"

Consistent with the President's production, economic development, and supply-side management goals, Reagan appointees vigorously pursued two prominent land exchange initiatives throughout the 1980s. The first afforded relief to "landlocked" urban areas where BLM property management complicated economic development. The second discouraged the purchase of additional wilderness, forest, and national park lands. To these ends, Interior Department officials sought to (1) solicit and aggressively expedite BLM land transfers to landlocked communities, (2) drastically cut Land and Water Conservation Fund expenditures for public land purchases, (3) limit acquisitions to nationally rather than locally significant properties, and (4) use massive land exchanges rather than cash purchases to acquire additional wilderness and park properties.[1]

This chapter reviews how the Reagan retrenchment necessitated a complex land swap in New Mexico known as the Las Cruces Industrial Park—Elena Gallegos land exchange. On the one hand, this trade threatened "landlocked" Las Cruces' ability to develop a long-coveted industrial park. On the other, it jeopardized Albuquerque's long-standing effort to expand the Cibola National Forest. Most significantly, however, this case illustrates how, in this instance, the Administration had to abandon one of its primary goals in order to placate powerful legislative sovereigns— precisely because of its supply-side management successes. An opportunity also arises to examine the bureaucratic politics of the administrative presidency as various statutes, federal and subnational bureaucracies, and diverse political agendas clashed within our Madisonian system.

THE PAST AS PROLOGUE; OR, "YOU'RE NOT A MAN TILL YOU DO A LAND EXCHANGE"

As discussed in Chapter 1, luring homesteaders to the West had by the 1980s rendered a "crazy-quilt pattern" of landownership in the region. Recall, for example, how the acquisition and disposal eras had begotten "balkanized" or "checkerboard" ownership patterns. More precisely, private, state, and local government properties nestled snugly amid lands managed by federal agencies. These lay in noncontiguous blocks with random sizes and patterns unamenable to efficient, effective, and apolitical land management. These ownership patterns, as well, too often stymied economic development on the fringes of Western cities. Thus, powerful banking, real estate, and Chamber of Commerce interests bayed relentlessly during the Carter years for the Administration to "unlock" urban areas by expediting federal land sales, transfers, and exchanges to "landlocked" localities. At the same time, however, the Administration faced formidable counterpressures during those years: the cries of environmentalists for federal acquisition of environmentally sensitive properties for preservation and protection. Since both pressures inform the Las Cruces Industrial Park–Elena Gallegos exchange, each merits further elaboration.

Trend I: Toward Public Land Disposal

The Bureau's disposal authority in the "lower 48" states stems largely from nine federal statutes. Two, however, were the most significant in the Las Cruces Industrial Park–Elena Gallegos case: the Federal Land Policy and Management Act (FLPMA) and the Recreation and Public Purposes Act (RPPA).[2] Given FLPMA's emphasis on land retention rather than disposal, Section 203 of the Act specifies what the Interior Secretary must consider in determining if land sales are "in the public interest." Specifically, after land use planning is completed, the Secretary must find that:

1. a tract, because of its location or other characteristics, is difficult or uneconomic to manage as part of the public lands and is not suitable for management by another Federal department or agency; or

2. the tract was acquired for a specific purpose and is no longer needed for that or any other federal purpose; or

3. disposal of the tract will serve important public objectives, such as expansion of communities or economic development, which cannot be achieved on other than public land. The objectives to be served by disposal must outweigh public objectives and values that would be served by retaining the tract in federal ownership.[3]

Likewise, under the RPPA, the Secretary can sell or lease lands to state or local governments, nonprofit corporations, or private associations. As amended, the Act imposes four criteria on such transactions. First, the "public purpose" involved must not be speculative; applicants must offer a detailed schedule for developing and managing the project. Second, while transferred public lands cannot be of national significance, their transfer and development have to "serve the national interest." Third, the property involved has to be "reasonably necessary" for the use proposed. And finally, developers have to apply local land use and zoning regulations on tracts over 640 acres in size.

But under what terms are lands legally conveyed? To delimit bureaucratic discretion, FLPMA provided precise financial standards for conveyances and priority rankings for conveyees. Specifically, transferees had to pay the equivalent of fair market value for the public lands, and federal agencies could not impose terms or conditions inconsistent with state or local land use plans. Moreover, priority was assigned to (a) applicants living in the state where the land was located, (b) local governments near the properties, (c) adjoining landowners, and (d) other interested individuals. In contrast, conveyances under the RPPA were permissible at less than fair market value to government entities and nonprofit corporations. In fact, local governments could acquire public lands for recreation purposes at no or nominal cost under certain conditions.

Finally, under FLPMA, the Secretary had to determine sale tract sizes based on land use capabilities and development requirements. Then competitive bidding had to take place, unless existing circumstances met narrowly defined criteria for noncompetitive leasing.[4]

Land sales and transfers, however, were not the only ways that federal agencies could rectify crazy-quilt ownership patterns in the West. Indeed, between 1970 and 1980, two-thirds of all public land conveyances in the region were exchanges, rather than sales or transfers. Again, FLPMA enumerated what the Interior Secretary had to consider before exchanging public lands. Would better federal land management result? Would the needs of state and local citizens be better met? Would acquired lands spur local economies, community expansion, recreation, or wildlife preservation? Were the purposes served by acquiring these lands at least equal to those fostered by the properties leaving federal ownership? And finally, were the values of the exchanged properties equal? If not, up to 25 percent of the total value of federal lands included in the exchange could be supplied in cash.

Typically, large-scale public land exchanges are complex, time-consuming, and fraught with trying, painstaking negotiation. As George Lea, Reagan's first Deputy Director for Lands and Resources at the BLM, summarized the process:

> In every exchange at least two properties must be appraised in each transaction. There must be voluntary agreement among the parties that values are equal. In addition, successful completion of an exchange requires input from many disciplines. The public and non-Federal lands in an exchange proposal are studied for their mineral potential, for cultural resource, plant, and wildlife values. The lands are also examined for potential flood hazards, [sic] and the [sic] socioeconomic impacts. When the studies are completed, the field manager weighs the public values that have been reported for the properties involved and makes a decision, subject to further public review, as to whether the exchange is in the public interest.[5]

Thus, despite trying during the Carter years to expedite exchanges as the Sagebrush embroglio grew, the BLM was able to complete only 62 small exchanges from FY78 through FY80, most of which merely rearranged marginal land tracts into more manageable blocks.

Trend II: Land Acquisition

What *had* spiraled during the 1970s, however, were federal efforts to acquire lands with amenity values deemed worthy of preserving or conserving. During fiscal years 1973 through 1977 alone, the Park, Forest, and Fish and Wildlife Services together purchased 2.2 million acres of land at a cost of $606 million.[6] In addition, a three-million-acre backlog remained of authorized but unacquired lands valued at over $3 billion.

Most critical in financing this expansion were the burgeoning coffers of the Land and Water Conservation Fund (L&WCF). Swollen by spiraling receipts from oil and gas leases, the L&WCF had 50 percent of expenditures earmarked to state and local governments for park acquisition. The balance funded land acquisitions by federal agencies. Flush with revenue between 1971 and 1982, the L&WCF financed a nearly threefold expansion (24.4 to 68.5 million acres) of the national park system.[7] Likewise, the Forest Service made frequent and dramatic use of L&WCF financing. Acquiring approximately 1.3 million acres of land for public recreation purposes, the Service expended approximately 21 percent of all L&WCF funds.[8]

The L&WCF was not without its critics, however. From across the political spectrum, those disgruntled attributed acquisition delays to its financing processes, criticized the inflationary impact these delays had on land values, and castigated the impact of land purchases on private property values both within and nearby the tracts involved. As William Reilly, then-president of the Conservation Foundation and later EPA Administrator in the Bush Administration, stated in 1981, the "very act of designating lands for acquisition drives up prices dramatically—on the order of nine hundred percent during the 1970s."[9]

Referred to as the "deep pockets" phenomenon, the financial dilemma confronting the federal government as Ronald Reagan assumed the presidency was put best at a congressional workshop on public land acquisition by conservationist Patrick Noonan:

> The very simple problem is this, [sic] there is an average 3-year time lag between the time lands are authorized and when the funds are appropriated. . . . This is a basic problem. What you have is specula-

tors playing off those values very quickly, [speculators] who love to sell to the Federal Government because it is an all-cash buyer. . . . In the private sector an exchange takes about six months. If DuPont can do it in six months to a year, we should be able to expedite some of our exchanges.[10]

In reality, however, there are a host of reasons why "DuPont can do it" more expeditiously and inexpensively than federal agencies can. Some are technical, some political, and some grounded in democratic theory. As Reagan's first Assistant Secretary for Natural Resources and Environment at the Department of Agriculture, John Crowell, testified and Senator Malcolm Wallop (R-WY) attested:

> The reason (for spiraling acquisition costs) is the problem of ascribing a value to the properties concerned. . . . It's a difficult thing to do. Those values tend to change . . . especially when we have an inflationary period. . . . [For example,] a land-locked city needs room to grow. The city goes to BLM, gets a price—a value. Then they must go through the state legislature, and the legislature doesn't meet until the end of the year. By that time the land value has changed, the process unravels, and it's necessary to start from point A again.[11]

Added Vernon Lindholm of the Forest Service when questioned directly about shortening the exchange process for his agency:

> If you are going to have public participation, the oversight by Congress, advertisements in the papers for four weeks, these take time. The assurance that we are not giving up lands with cultural resources or endangered species, especially in the West, unless they are protected, also takes time.[12]

In contrast, less charitable witnesses blamed mounting costs and delay on the Congress itself, with Secretary Watt the most belligerent proponent of this perspective. Focusing his attack on national parks, Watt mocked the acquisition process:

> Right now the . . . Congress proceeds in this fashion: They have their hearings. They go up and sometimes blind themselves and draw a circle on the map and say that will be a park. All of a sudden, the supply of land for that park is fixed—period. The demand for that land is unlimited because by statute of the U.S. Government we have determined that it is in the public [interest] to acquire everything

within that circle of land regardless of price over whatever time, so that the landowner only needs to sit tight.[13]

The acerbity of Watt's charges aside, his argument was well-taken and supported by more dispassionate observers. For example, a 1981 General Accounting Office (GAO) study found that federal agencies routinely ignored three highly negative impacts of land purchases on private owners and their communities: escalating prices of adjacent lands, the erosion of local tax bases, and the preclusion of agricultural uses. Indeed, the National Association of Realtors concluded that an "indirect condemnation" of private property without compensation typically resulted from the lengthy acquisition process. As spokesman Johnny W. McArthur argued, the existing system placed private owners "in limbo" once Congress identified their lands for acquisition. Specifically, a sometimes decades-long waiting period ensued before L&WCF appropriations were forthcoming. In the interim, "present and future uses and values [to the property owner were] frequently greatly diminished with no prospect of compensation. . . ."[14]

The Reagan Synthesis

Aside from the Reagan Administration's short-lived Asset Management Program, two of its more ballyhooed public land initiatives were (1) Interior's assault on the L&WCF and (2) Watt's pledge to use FLPMA and the RPPA to transfer public lands expeditiously to local officials once they identified them as important to economic development.[15] With their spirits buoyed, Western governors welcomed Watt's offer, identifying nearly 600,000 acres as necessary for community expansion within their borders. Decidedly unwelcome, however, were his attempts to, first, freeze and, then, dramatically cut L&WCF purchases of private lands.

Buttressed by GAO studies, Watt couched his assault on the L&WCF in terms of fiscal responsibility, protecting private property, and promoting cost-effectiveness.[16] Simultaneously, he mandated that acquired lands would have to be of national rather than local significance before an exchange could take place. What is more, to acquire them, federal agencies would have to eschew L&WCF purchases in favor of large-scale land exchanges.

Yet land exchanges of this scale are not without their problems, either. For example, as land exchange supporter Patrick Noonan pointed out during congressional hearings on the topic, large-scale exchanges necessarily involve transfers among a variety of federal, state, and private agencies. Unfortunately, each of these operate statutorily under numerous and overlapping exchange and transfer authorities. Consequently, a central mechanism is needed to coordinate the exchange process among government agencies. Likewise, both Noonan and William Reilly testified that large-scale exchanges of federal properties required a costly and time-consuming update of land inventories before they could legally proceed under FLPMA and other statutes. For example, the BLM's most comprehensive inventory to date had been done pursuant to the Classification and Multiple Use Act of 1964. As a consequence, that inventory sorely needed an update consonant with both FLPMA and NEPA, an update requiring two to three years to complete.[17] In addition, this update would be expensive: Federal agencies had to hire and train personnel skilled in exchange and valuation techniques. Yet knowledgeable observers already felt that poor staffing in BLM state and district offices was responsible for 10-to-12-year exchange delays in various parts of the West.

To these caveats, others added three additional impediments to success: agency turf battles, threats to personal bureaucratic sinecures, and technical disagreements over property evaluation. Regarding sources of bureaucratic resistance, a sympathetic Conservation Foundation official warned:

> Both state and federal agency personnel may use various means to discourage specific exchanges, out of concern for special land values, loss of job security, or threat of family relocation and other motives. . . . BLM staff members have reported problems of field-level opposition to disposal during the classification performed under the 1964 Classification and Multiple Use Act.[18]

Still, the most significant problem to overcome was the third and less Machiavellian source of delay: determining equal and fair market value for exchanges and disposals. Here, experts cited four primary difficulties. First, participants in large-scale exchanges typically want one side—presumably their own—to gain more in value from the transaction than the other side. Thus, getting participants to accept equal or fair market values has proven difficult, historically. Second, differences in evaluation methods exist among federal agencies. These often spawn disagreements over the value of specific tracts and therefore increase assessment delays and costs. Third, both these obstacles are especially trying in large-scale transactions, involved as they are typically with mineral, aesthetic, or amenity values. Finally, appraising mineral, aesthetic, and intangible values is exceptionally expensive, speculative, and controversial.

According to Christopher Duerkson, the Real Estate Appraisal Institute has yet to agree on a suitable, cost-effective mineral appraisal technique. True, drilling to ascertain mineral values has been a widely used method. But assessing mineral values in this fashion on 40,000 acres of land in the mid-1970s cost nearly $7 million. Thus, as Temple Reynolds of the Utah Department of Natural Resources and Energy warned, "there [was] simply not enough money . . . to do all the detailed valuation work in terms of drilling and other things" to effect exchanges on the scale promoted by the Reagan Administration.[19]

Unfazed, however, Watt and his successors proceeded persistently during the next eight years to proselytize the virtues of exchanges over purchases. They did so, initially, as recession plagued the economy, and later, as Reagan's "strategic deficits" wreaked havoc on discretionary domestic programs. In the end, however, neither the size, rate, nor frequency of land exchanges in the West exceeded rates generated by Reagan's immediate predecessors. This may not surprise some readers, especially those seeing Reagan's exchange strategy as designed purposely to stymie acquisitions. Yet neither did the pace of federal acquisitions slacken noticeably during his presidency. No, once again, the bureaupolitical dynamics of the administrative presidency combined with Reagan's own "supply-side management" philosophy to render his policies less effective than critics or supporters expected. To appreciate why, one has only to turn to the Las Cruces Industrial Park–Elena Gallegos experience in New Mexico.

THE LAND EXCHANGE DILEMMA IN THE
RIO GRANDE BASIN

Although the southern New Mexican city of Las Cruces had tried persistently since 1968 to obtain adjacent BLM properties for economic development, its efforts intensified during the Carter Administration. Specifically, local officials sought these tracts for two related purposes. First, 564 acres were needed to expand significantly Las Cruces' Crawford Municipal Airport. Second, 1000 acres were sought for a new industrial park south of and adjacent to the airport. Located in Dona Ana County, where 87 percent of all property belonged to either the BLM or the military, Las Cruces had an economy overly dependent on a single employer: the government. In fact, nearly one-half (46.9 percent) of those employed in Dona Ana County in 1981 worked in the public sector, a figure well above the nation's 15 percent average. Not surprisingly, then, county officials, bankers, and private developers saw the airport–industrial park project as a means for diversifying private investment, industry, jobs, and tax bases in the area.

Although the BLM in 1976 had identified these properties as suitable for sale, they still remained in federal hands on the eve of the Reagan presidency.[20] One recalls that under FLPMA, the Bureau could only sell them to Las Cruces on a competitive basis, at fair market value, and for uses consonant with the city's master plan. Unfortunately for Las Cruces, however, the city could not meet these conditions in the late 1970s. Pressed financially and lacking a master plan, city officials first sought congressional assistance and later Federal Aviation Administration (FAA) support for their acquisition bid. Their logic? Under the RPPA or the Surplus Airport Equipment Act (PL 80–289), the city could acquire the lands at either no cost or at less than market value. Because an industrial park qualified under the RPPA as a "public purpose," the Bureau could sell to Las Cruces lands so designated without competitive bids and significantly below fair market value. And because a thriving industrial park would generate lease and tax revenues earmarked for developing the adjacent municipal airport, the Surplus Airport Equipment Act allowed the BLM to donate industrial park properties to the city. This was true, proponents argued, as long as the revenue produced by the park was used for the improvement, operation, and maintenance of the city's public airport.

To the city's chagrin, these arguments proved unpersuasive to both the Carter and Reagan administrations. After BLM's district office in Las Cruces refused to conduct either "no cost" or "below-market-value" sales, New Mexico Congressman Harold Runnels (D) appealed the decision to the Interior Department in Washington. After investigations by the Interior Department's Field Solicitor in Santa Fe and the BLM Washington Office, Carter's Assistant BLM Director informed Runnels that the Bureau had "no sales authority which could convey this land at less than fair market" value.[21] Industrial parks, he averred, did not qualify as "public purposes." Thus, while BLM could transfer the lands for industrial park development, Las Cruces had to pay fair market value for the property.

Undaunted, Las Cruces later prevailed upon Senator Schmitt to seek the approval of Reagan's Interior Undersecretary, Donald Hodel, to transfer the properties at no cost under the Surplus Airport Equipment Act.[22] With their claims buttressed by an FAA district office opinion challenging the Bureau's interpretation of FLPMA and the RPPA, local officials hoped that Hodel might reverse lower-level decisions. The basis for their hopes? BLM officials had ignored a key phrase in FLPMA's requirement for fair market sales—viz., "unless otherwise provided for by statute."[23] In the FAA's opinion, the Surplus Airport Equipment Act provided precisely such an exception. Specifically, it considered "property needed to develop sources of revenue from nonaviation businesses at a public airport" as qualifying for no-cost transfers to municipalities.[24]

Under Senator Schmitt's plan, the BLM would declare the industrial park lands as surplus properties and transfer them to the General Services Administration (GSA). Then the GSA would transfer them to Las Cruces in a "no-cost" conveyance for airport development. In turn, Las Cruces would lease out this property for industrial development, earmarking the revenues they produced for operating and maintaining the Crawford Municipal Airport. Yet Schmitt was also a realist. In his letter to Hodel, the Senator added that he was willing to take a legislative route: "If, however, you still feel that the department is unable to accept such an arrangement, please have drafted the necessary legislation which would be required to transfer the land directly to the City of Las Cruces for municipal needs."[25]

With federal agencies split on the issue, with conveyance of the industrial park properties necessary before the state could begin building a much-heralded minimum security prison in Dona Ana County, and with a grant for planning and infrastructure development for the industrial park a victim of Reagan Administration budget cuts, proponents of the project were at their wit's end. Likewise, talk in Las Cruces of sales tax increases were already wearing thin the tolerance and patience of local citizens. Nonetheless, Interior's response to Schmitt's inquiry did little to assuage the community's distress. Wrote Hodel:

> Public Law 80–289 does not apply to the Las Cruces airport situation. . . . The public lands requested by the city of Las Cruces . . . are not part of a government surplus airport and thus, P.L. 80–289 is not applicable. FAA's *interpretation is in error* [emphasis added]. The reason for this is that the Federal Property and Administrative Services Act of 1949 . . . excepts public lands from its provisions *unless* they are withdrawn lands found to be not suitable for return to the public domain. . . . [Since this is not true in this instance,] BLM could not declare the lands surplus to GSA under this authority.[26]

Later, similar appeals by Senator Schmitt to Secretary Watt proved equally ineffectual. But this quickly became the least of Las Cruces' woes, as unexpected events in northern New Mexico involving Congressman Manuel Lujan (R), the Elena Gallegos Land Grant, and the U.S. Forest Service complicated the plight of the industrial park even further. To its surprise and anger, the city learned in June 1981 that the BLM had designated the industrial park properties as suitable for the Forest Service to exchange in a massive and complicated land swap involving the Elena Gallegos tract, an exchange engineered by Lujan to augment the Cibola National Forest near Albuquerque.

THE DISPUTE IS JOINED: OF APPRAISALS, REPRISALS, AND A RENITENT BUREAUCRACY

During the late 1970s, northern New Mexico's emerging preservationist community began to criticize Congressman Manuel Lujan. Critiquing his lackluster—some said, obstructionist— environmental voting record, this constituency garnered Lujan's attention once an electoral challenge loomed from Albuquerque's environmentally oriented Democratic mayor, David Rusk, or New Mexico newcomer, William Richardson (whom Lujan would eventually beat by only four percentage points). Thus, to combat his anti-environmental image at the local level, Lujan began promoting locally important environmental projects.

A centerpiece of Lujan's strategy was his successful sponsorship of the withdrawal of over 8100 wilderness acres near Albuquerque for incorporation into the Cibola National Forest.[27] Under the withdrawal's terms, the Forest Service had to purchase the Elena Gallegos Land Grant properties from the Albuquerque Boys Academy for nearly $20 million and place them within the Sandia Wilderness Area. However, for Lujan, a Republican, the rub was this. Since Congress had not yet appropriated funds for actual purchase of the Boys Academy's Elena Gallegos properties, the exchange became a victim of Reagan's budget assault on the L&WCF.

Initially, local Albuquerque officials blamed each other for appropriation delays, developed competing coping strategies, and jockeyed to claim credit for salvaging the project. This, of course, was not surprising, given the substantial economic and political stakes involved for all concerned. Under the original Forest Service–Boys Academy agreement, Mayor Rusk and the Albuquerque City Council had pledged three pieces of property valued at $4.7 million as an "option fee" or earnest deposit. If the deal failed to materialize, the city would forfeit these properties. With the $20 million purchase now nixed by the Reagan Administration from the L&WCF budget, Rusk and the Forest Service scrambled for a way to salvage both the deal and the city's property. Thus, after unsuccessfully lobbying for redress in Washington, Rusk returned to Albuquerque and tossed the political hot potato to the state's

Republican congressional delegation. Challenging their political "machismo," Rusk taunted, "It will be a real test of the influence of our delegation to see if they can pry loose $20 million from this Administration."[28]

Schmitt and Lujan, of course, lobbed salvos of their own back at the mayor. Schmitt, also perceiving Rusk a potentially formidable candidate for his own Senate seat, retorted caustically: "Since we had nothing to do with the [original] agreement . . . it can hardly be called a test of clout." To which Lujan added righteously, "We can't go and pork-barrel in our own backyard. . . . Acquiring land is not one of Congress' priorities when real services are being cut."[29] No, Lujan had a better idea. The then-ranking Republican on the House Insular and Interior Affairs Committee, he summoned Forest Service officials to a meeting.[30] There, according to interviewees, he suggested in the "strongest of terms" that the agency focus whatever organizational resources it took to cement the Elena Gallegos deal by implementing a massive land exchange with the Albuquerque Boys Academy. To consummate the exchange, the Academy, in return for the Elena Gallegos property, would receive federal lands of equal value scattered throughout New Mexico. So charged, the Forest Service asked other federal agencies to certify lands under their jurisdiction which were suitable for exchange. To this the BLM responded that the Las Cruces industrial park properties—as urban lands ripe for development—were among those most suitable for exchange.

Before resolving the Las Cruces Industrial Park–Elena Gallegos embroglio, the combatants had to address five primary issues. First, would the BLM and the Forest Service agree to drop the Las Cruces properties from the exchange? Second, if the properties were included, would their new owners guarantee to sell them back to Las Cruces at less than fair market value? Third, could the city of Las Cruces or private developers in Dona Ana County find alternative ways to acquire the lands before any exchange took place? Fourth, if the exchange proceeded, could the Forest Service and the BLM muster the intra- and interorganizational will, cooperation, and resources to perform a timely and mutually acceptable exchange? And finally, could New Mexico's congressional delegation persuade the Reagan Administration to approve a land deal funded partially with federal dollars and resembling only remotely a "nationally significant" acquisition?

The Land Inventory Question

Once the Forest Service's intentions reached a stunned Las Cruces, government and business leaders implored Senator Schmitt to bring the parties together, review options, and reverse a rapidly deteriorating situation. Since a clarification of the Forest Service's intentions was most needed, Schmitt first arranged a meeting between city staff, members of the BLM district office in Las Cruces, and the Forest Service. Most unclear were the specific lands targeted for transfer and what say, if any, Las Cruces had in the ultimate decision to release the properties to the Forest Service. Thus, a frustrated Raleigh Crausby, Las Cruces acting director of planning, complained:

> They're [the Forest Service] not being very up front about the land they're after. . . . There's a lot of contradictory information coming out of the Forest Service. First, the industrial park lands were involved; then it was [BLM] land also slated in the city's land use plan for development on the East Mesa [once the lands were transferred to Las Cruces]; today the Forest Service is talking about adding the industrial park land to the East Mesa properties.[31]

In response to Crausby, BLM District Manager Dan Rathbun offered little solace. "With the BLM, the Forest Service, Las Cruces, and the other interests involved, it is difficult to tell exactly how the exchange will end." He then added cryptically that the Forest Service would have to seek the city's input before an ultimate decision was made; but "getting their input is different than getting their concurrence."[32] Still, Forest Service Regional Forester, Jean Hassell, subsequently took the edge off this comment. He added that, "It was not, and is not, the intent [of the Forest Service] to move unilaterally on this matter, uncoordinated with the city of Las Cruces; nor to damage any needs of the city. . . ."[33]

Still, Las Cruscans in the interim took Hassell at his word, persuaded New Mexico's governor, Bruce King (D), to request that BLM transfer the lands to the city under Watt's Asset Management Program, and further pressed the New Mexico congressional delegation for assistance. Thus, as several companies indicated their interest in moving into the industrial park if completed, and as Reagan budget cuts eliminated grants for infrastructure development and planning for the park, Schmitt again brought the principals together for discussions in early July 1981.[34] Here, the parties reviewed the city's acquisition options and got reaction to them from the BLM, the Forest Service, the FAA, the New Mexico Department of Corrections, the Las Cruces City Commission, Senator Pete Domenici, and Congressman Joe Skeen (R-NM).

Not surprisingly, Forester Hassell favored the Forest Service's acquiring the properties and guaranteeing Las Cruces the right to buy them at fair market value. In the process, he argued, Las Cruces would get the lands it wanted, while the Forest Service would get the money it needed to purchase the Elena Gallegos lands from the Albuquerque Academy. Exasperated by the bind in which this and other options would place the city, Las Cruces property manager, Ed Garland, asked if the Forest Service "would back off [the industrial park properties] if the city asked them to."[35] Hassell's response: A "reluctant 'yes,'" a public commitment that later came to haunt him.

Each of the remaining options depended directly upon the parties' arriving at a mutually acceptable price for the industrial park properties. This, however, was no mean task. Indeed, substantial disagreement reigned, with appraisals ranging from Garland's $500,000 "guesstimate" to Hassell's projection "at somewhere between a half million and two million" dollars. Thus, with Schmitt's legislative option a "last resort" and "most uncertain," with fair-market-value purchases "beyond the city's resources," and with the BLM's option to lease the lands to the city "pretty steep" at 5 to 7 percent of fair market value per year, Las Cruces pressed Hassell to live up to his "commitment" to "back off" if asked by the city.

Claiming that Senator Domenici, among others, was "very supportive" of the Las Cruces position and pledged to "doing everything he could to get us approval" of the park, Mayor Joseph Camunez was confident that Las Cruces' problems were over. Proclaimed the mayor, "I don't think there is anything to worry about; the Forest Service will remove the industrial park lands from the exchange list."[36] Yet, as the expiration of Albuquerque's option to purchase the Elena Gallegos lands drew nearer, and as Albuquerqueans grew impatient to complete the exchange, removing the Las Cruces properties became a nonviable option.

Most telling in fostering this situation were three factors. First, because trustees of the Albuquerque Academy didn't want to manage lands scattered all over the state, they insisted that any land exchanged with them be highly marketable. There goal was to sell off these properties as quickly as possible. Thus, as was typical of exchanges across the West, urban properties—such as Las Cruces' West and East Mesas—were among the most coveted for their high resale value. Second, as the Forest Service and the BLM performed environmental, archaeological, and paleontological inventories of tradeable federal lands around the state, the stock of land available for the exchange shrank drastically. Indeed, acreage contracted so sharply that the Las Cruces properties were either part of the deal, or the deal was off. As summarized by Forester Fred Galley, "We originally started with 42,000 acres for the land exchange, but we have steadily lost land to Indian, mining, and archaeology claims." Thus, according to Galley, the Forest Service could not "afford to lose any more land earmarked for the trade and still have enough with which to negotiate."[37] Lastly, initiatives by Congressman Lujan and Senator Schmitt to convey the lands to Las Cruces by a "direct congressional transfer" failed. Only lands for public purposes could be conveyed this way, and industrial parks did not qualify as public purposes. Thus, the Forest Service informed angry Las Cruces officials that both the East and West Mesa properties had to remain in play. Hassell's earlier assurances were operative no longer. But neither was Las Cruces' cooperation guaranteed.

With the Forest Service's announcement nonnegotiable, Las Cruces' only hope was to persuade BLM officials to withdraw the industrial park properties from the exchange. After all, they too had promised to do so if the city so desired. Indeed, BLM district officials had given the city three options: (1) refuse to allow the Bureau to release the land for trade and pursue other options, such as private purchase by interested investors; (2) allow the land to be traded to the Albuquerque Academy, and then buy it back from the trustees; or (3) if unable to obtain a right of first refusal to repurchase the lands from the Academy, take them out of the trade and buy them directly from the BLM at fair market value.

Much to the city's disappointment, however, options one and three soon became moot. Reagan's budget cuts and alterations of skill mix at the BLM interacted with pressing time deadlines to render them unrealistic. Specifically, as BLM District Manager Dan Rathbun, seconded by Schmitt staffer Tom Baca, pointed out:

> Withdrawal and sale of the industrial park lands by the BLM meant that all Forest Service appraisal, as well as environmental, paleontological, and archaeological inventorying would cease. Yet, because by law these activities had to be completed prior to any sale, the Bureau would have to incur these costs itself. Thus, the city had little choice but to leave the lands in the exchange once BLM officials indicated that budget and staff cuts meant that nothing would happen for 18 to 24 months. . . . Moreover, by the time appraisals and competitive sale procedures could be arranged with a reduced staff, another 18 to 24 months could pass.[38]

Las Cruscans, of course, could ill-afford such a delay. First, Department of Corrections officials in New Mexico required immediate commitments from the city for the delivery and cost of utility services to their new prison. Yet financially strapped city officials couldn't give these commitments until they were sure that the industrial park could proceed. Specifically, the city could minimize construction costs if infrastructure needs were known in advance and tailored to meet various exigencies—viz., whether a prison and an industrial park, or just a prison would hook up to the system. Second, during the 18-to-24-month hiatus needed for inventories, the purchase price of the land would spiral after the city installed utilities for the adjoining prison site. Finally, in the interim, potential park tenants—already chaffing under delays and looking elsewhere to relocate—might bolt altogether. Thus, city officials "granted graciously that which they could no longer withhold": They left the West and East Mesa lands in the proposed exchange until further notice.

The Preference Sale Issue

Although Las Cruces was, in effect, compelled to leave the industrial park lands in the exchange, no guarantee existed that the

Albuquerque Academy would accept the land package offered by the Forest Service. Indeed, by late 1981, Academy trustees—stressing that cash flow and maximization, not property management, animated their concerns—grew anxious over the exchange's pace, parameters, and possibilities. You will recall how federal law required that exchanged properties be of equal value, with no more than 25 percent of the total price payable in cash. And, of course, logic dictates that the lands offered in an exchange be acceptable to all parties. Unfortunately, both requirements become major obstacles in large-scale exchanges involving the federal government; properties typically remain in federal stewardship precisely because they are unattractive to private developers. Moreover, because those seeking large-scale exchanges have to cobble together scattered, relatively small, intermingled tracts, management difficulties further diminish their allure to investors. Thus, when the parties recognized that an "equal value" exchange for the 8,000-acre Elena Gallegos tract required the Forest Service to offer approximately 40,000 acres scattered statewide to the Academy, the trustees' dismay was understandable and difficult to assuage.

While awaiting the Academy's decision, however, neither the Forest Service, the cities of Albuquerque and Las Cruces, nor the New Mexican congressional delegation stood pat. Indeed, with congressional fire alarms sounding, Domenici and Lujan each launched an initiative, one legislative and the other mediative. Thus, in early 1982 the Senator introduced a bill in Congress to circumvent both the Reagan freeze on land purchases and the Academy's qualms about the land exchange. In announcing his action, Domenici explained:

> The Forest Service has already identified some parcels of land they would like to [apply] toward the purchase price of Elena Gallegos, but the Academy has found [that] these lands do not meet its needs. This bill allows other interested parties in New Mexico to purchase these and other parcels they may be interested in at public auction with all of the money being applied to Elena Gallegos.[39]

In the process, of course, Domenici's initiative gave Las Cruces a back-up option for acquiring the industrial park lands. The city, too, could attempt to directly purchase the properties from the BLM should the Boys Academy demure. Then, just four days after

Rusk left office, Lujan announced that the Albuquerque Academy, the Forest Service, and Rusk's Republican successor had—with the congressman's intervention—struck a deal "unlocking this lengthy stalemate."[40]

Subject to approval by Academy trustees and the Albuquerque City Council, Lujan's pact reduced to approximately 30,000 acres the amount of federal property needed to complete the exchange by cutting the amount to be acquired by the Forest Service. In the process, the Las Cruces properties could be dropped from the exchange. For Lujan, "it was the only logical suggestion—if you don't have enough money, you buy less land."[41] Perhaps. But a coalition of environmental, business, and "good government" groups in Albuquerque were unpersuaded. For them, political will, not fiscal stress, was the primary obstacle to making the full 8,000 acre addition to Sandia a reality.

Known as the Elena Gallegos Trust Fund Committee, this 25-member task force mounted a full-bore campaign to persuade the Albuquerque City Council to raise temporarily its gross receipts tax by one-quarter cent and to earmark the proceeds for the Elena Gallegos purchase.[42] According to Committee estimates, Albuquerque could raise nearly $30 million over a three-year period, with approximately $25 million going to fund the purchase. The city thus would acquire the whole tract, designate 640 acres of it for open spaces, and exchange the rest with the Forest Service for approximately 33,000 acres scattered statewide. In turn, these acquired federal lands could be sold to buyers in ways calculated to realize a total profit of about $24 million for Albuquerque. In the end, this option prevailed—the epitome of Reagan's philosophy that if locals truly wanted to acquire lands for preservation, they should raise their own taxes to pay for them. In the interim, however, the plan only muddied the waters further for Las Cruces. Unclear to that city was from whom, at what price, and if at all they could purchase the industrial park properties.

With inventory work delayed largely by Reagan cutbacks, Congressman Lujan again met with Forest Service officials in 1981. There, in a penultimate exercise of fire alarm oversight, Lujan pressed the Forest Service to reallocate to New Mexico every ounce of available manpower in the multi-state Southwest region. Las

Cruces, however, did not have the luxury of awaiting the outcome of this process. Thus, as appraisals continued, city officials sought with abandon to obtain a right-of-first-refusal commitment from the three potential "owners" of the industrial park properties: the Albuquerque Academy, the Forest Service, and the City of Albuquerque. Ideally, Las Cruces would obtain the right to purchase these lands at a pre-agreed price *before* the owner entertained other bids or inflation raised their market values.

Rebuffed, first, by the Academy, Las Cruscans were impaled on the horns of a dilemma exacerbated by Reagan's supply-side management successes. Speaking for Academy trustees, President Richard Elkins denied the city's offer to purchase the industrial park lands for $557,000, a figure based on an appraisal financed by Las Cruces. Wrote Elkins to Mayor Camunez:

> The Board is sympathetic with your needs, but feels that inasmuch as no agreement [with the Forest Service] has been consummated which would provide the Academy a deed to the 1,900 acres, that we are not now in a position to provide you with a right of first refusal. . . . No formal proposal has been presented to us for consideration. When, and if, such a proposal is provided . . . we will be pleased to discuss with the City of Las Cruces our mutual needs and to work towards a solution . . . with each party's best interest in mind.[43]

Similarly throttled were Camunez' entreaties to the Forest Service for guarantees. Like Elkins, the Service's regional director of lands and minerals, Dick Harris, also expressed "sympathy" for Las Cruces' concerns. However, from his perspective, the Service lacked jurisdiction to intervene in Albuquerque Academy decisions. Neither could the Forest Service itself guarantee anything until massive appraisal discrepancies on the parcels were reconciled. More precisely, the Forest Service had to receive both an agency and an independent appraisal before an exchange could take place. And once they had been carried out, these two appraisals not only differed substantially, but also were two to three times higher than Las Cruces' offer. Thus, for the Service to commit itself to Las Cruces' roughly half million dollar bid would have been initially quite foolhardy and eventually quite illegal.

Forester Harris then proceeded to turn up the heat on Las Cruces. The city, he argued, had to decide either to withdraw formally the industrial park lands from the exchange, or forever leave them in. "We need the city's [final] decision," he remarked, "before we can complete the federal requirements for including the land in the swap and before completing the approximately $60,000 worth of assessment and mitigation work necessary before the lands are ready for exchange."[44] Thus, an agonizing choice confronted Las Cruces. Its leadership could leave the lands in the exchange to expedite Forest Service appraisal work, avoid lengthy delays should a resource-short BLM have to complete these tasks, and more quickly resolve the ownership and appraisal issues. The risk, of course, was that the eventual owner would not sell the lands to the city. Alternatively, Las Cruces could formally request withdrawal of the lands from the exchange, but only at the risk of inordinate appraisal, negotiation, and mitigation delays scaring off potential industrial park tenants and jeopardizing Dona Ana County's minimum security prison.

Initially, Mayor Camunez' staff opted for a "hard line" approach by formally requesting the Forest Service to withdraw the industrial park properties from the exchange. Setting aside this letter, however, Las Cruces' City Commission (with Camunez and one other commissioner dissenting) approved and sent to Jean Hassell a substitute document giving the city an "escape clause" crafted to entice negotiation. Like Camunez' letter, the city asked the Forest Service to withdraw the properties. However, the Commission added the following codicil:

> If during ensuing negotiations between the Forest Service and the Academy, it were mutually agreed that the City of Las Cruces be granted [first] option to purchase the approximately 1,900 acres *at the agency* [i.e., Forest Service] *approved value* [emphasis added] . . . the City Commission of the City of Las Cruces . . . would be willing to have the parcel again included in the exchange.[45]

In sponsoring this initiative, commissioner Ron Hudson explained the Commission's logic:

> We're not locked into anything with this letter. With the [Camunez] letter, all negotiations were off. We have preliminary indications it would take 12 to 18 months just to negotiate with the BLM for the land [if withdrawn from the exchange]. By that time, the value would

have substantially increased because of the installation of utilities to the adjoining prison.[46]

Still, critics—including the city's legal staff—viewed the clause as imprudent, if not illegal.

Prudential and legal merits aside, however, the Forest Service's "startling" retort to Las Cruces in March of 1982 rendered them moot. True, few were shocked when Forester Harris testily nixed the proposal as unrealistic and more: "You can't just . . . say the deal is dead, and then say go ahead and consider it anyway. . . . It's asinine to try to do both." What *did* startle and irritate many, however, was his acerbic denial of Las Cruces' right to withdraw the properties altogether. Scolded Harris:

> [Some city commissioners] haven't been able to gain a full under-standing of what's involved in an exchange of U.S. government land. There are many considerations required by federal regulations—ranging from archaeological values and floodplain studies . . . [to] land titles and possible endangered species. If the land is withdrawn now, [these] processes will have to start all over, including appraisals. The city will end up paying more for the land. You just can't take it [the industrial park lands] out and continue negotiations.[47]

Thus, in one fell swoop, Harris effectively neutralized Las Cruces' "bargaining chip." In the process, he left new Las Cruces mayor, David Steinborn, three options: (1) appeal to Congress the Forest Service's decision to go ahead with the swap; (2) ask Senator Schmitt to expedite a congressional transfer of the land to the city; and (3) request the Forest Service to find other lands to trade. To Mayor Steinborn's dismay, however, the first two options were bleak. Lujan, dean of the New Mexico congressional delegation and originator of the land exchange scheme, could stymie any legislative proposal that might threaten it. As for the third option, the pool of available federal properties consistently shrank as land inventories eliminated ecologically fragile or culturally rich tracts.

Frustrated, Las Cruscans and their congressional allies charged the Forest Service with foot-dragging during the inventory and appraisal process, thus unnecessarily sacrificing the city's develop-ment needs. Yet, as the following section documents, the more likely culprits were the Reagan Administration's supply-side man-agement philosophy and its failure to heed earlier warnings about the pitfalls of large-scale land exchanges absent radical reform of intra- and interbureaucratic processes.

The Land Appraisal Issue

Recall how even supporters of large-scale land exchanges questioned their feasibility during 1981 congressional hearings in Washington. Indeed, most foresaw their futility without additional resources, strong mechanisms for interbureaucratic coordination, and adequate training for appropriate skill mixes of professionals. Animated partially by visions of underfunding, personnel deskilling, and insensitivity to environmental values by the Reagan Administration, their concerns stemmed as well from more prosaic concerns. Specifically, they appreciated the internecine bureaucratic rigidities, ideologies, and turf battles awaiting implementors in enterprises so costly, complex, and combative as land exchanges. Just how prescient their concerns were is apparent in the denouement of the Las Cruces Industrial Park–Elena Gallegos experience.

As documented above, several of the most critical junctures in this case were either occasioned, conditioned, or determined by the federal government's land appraisal and inventory process. For example, the Forest Service's dissatisfaction with Elena Gallegos appraisals in the late 1970s rendered the exchange vulnerable to Reagan's policy and budget juggernaut in the early 1980s. Likewise, early in the controversy, Las Cruces' inability to get a right of first refusal stemmed largely from the Forest Service's difficulties in completing its own, and reconciling divergent, appraisals. And because the BLM had to restart these processes if industrial park tracts were withdrawn from the exchange, Las Cruces nixed this option.

To fully understand the knotty appraisal problems proffered by this case, one first has to appreciate the Olympian nature of the enterprise. Knowing that the exchange initially involved 42,000 acres scattered across New Mexico is a start, but does not do justice to its magnitude. As Robert Armstrong of the Forest Service recalls proudly, the exchange's size was unprecedented for his agency: "This [the exchange] was a fluke with a million ways to fail—most of which are human and not maliciously intended . . . yet we succeeded."[48] To this his colleague, Eric Johanson, added, this was the "first and largest instance where BLM and the Forest Service—with their ancient antagonisms—had to cooperate."[49]

Further complicating the matter, according to Armstrong, was the penurious attitude of the Reagan Administration: "It couldn't afford the luxury of speeding more money into the project," given the President's rhetoric, a disintegrating economy, and OMB's budget-cutting penchant. Yet if the exchange—overseen by Lujan and Domenici and pitting them against Schmitt—was to proceed apace, additional funds were mandatory. Thus, under Lujan's prodding, "at least a couple of million dollars [was] diverted from an already tight Forest Service budget for the big ticket items of archaeological and mitigation reviews."[50] Referred to by some of the careerists interviewed as among "the hardest, most horrible, most expensive damn processes" involved in the exchange, the Forest Service had to hire field crews, temporaries, archaeologists, and anthropologists to augment those previously scheduled for release under Reagan's spartan budget. Too, the project's opportunity costs were significant; staff and materials went to New Mexico and away from formerly ranked "priority projects"in other states.[51]

Yet, a full appreciation of the exchange's costs is impossible until one understands the bureaucratic and political stakes involved. As characterized aptly by Armstrong, the Forest Service was "beginning to undergo the stress of declining budgets," while the BLM was "having its cookie jar raided [by the Forest Service], since the best of its properties [i.e., near San Juan and Las Cruces] were the core of the exchange."[52] Moreover, all this coincided with the BLM-MMS reorganization, an exercise already halving the Bureau's budget and removing its off-shore leasing functions. Thus, as one veteran BLM careerist candidly conceded, "The bureaucratic empire of the BLM [in New Mexico] was under attack and it responded. . . . The Forest Service was gaining and we were losing."[53]

To no one's surprise, then, "plenty of bad blood" developed between the agencies. Basically, the Forest Service viewed the BLM district office's incessant reminders to Las Cruces that it could "withdraw lands at any time" from the exchange as attempts to "submarine" the deal. Indeed, according to Johanson, BLM careerists kept "throwing sand in the works" during the whole exchange process.[54] Here, "really serious" interagency problems got resolved only when Lujan pressed Hassell and state BLM director, Charles Luscher, to "step in and impose orders [that] 'this is the way its got to be!'" True, Forest Service representatives understood the resistance mounted by BLM careerists. Yet their frustration with these antics was evident even years later in their references to the Bureau's "footdragging," to "beating heads" with BLM careerists, and to the "incorrigible" attitudes displayed by the agency.

Even under the most tranquil of relationships, however, the legal, procedural, and political labyrinth that implementors must navigate in large-scale exchanges taxes their patience, stamina, and legerdemain. Witness, for example, the reminiscences of various BLM and Forest Service employees.[55] Their comments crisply convey the disparate institutional cultures, procedures, and professional worldviews that negotiators had to overcome to complete the Elena Gallegos exchange. All noted that while the Forest Service technically was the "lead agency" on the appraisals, the BLM could not abdicate its legal responsibility to sign off on appraisals over $15,000 in value. The rub, of course, was this: The Forest Service and the Bureau operated under different statutes with disparate administrative requirements for doing appraisals. As Johanson, Armstrong, and Rathbun noted, these diverged so pronouncedly that "tunnel vision" plagued each agency, a bureaucratic pathology that ultimately led to the protracted, trying, and confrontational negotiations between the parties over property values.

As the following collage of comments attests, however, the sources of this conflict were both administrative and political:

> Each agency operated under different advertising requirements, different ways to assess mineral values, and different methods for determining ownership rights regarding grazing, archaeological finds, and permittee-owned rights . . . with the major problem coming on BLM land. . . . Legally, two teams of surveyors with significantly different perspectives and criteria . . . had to approve any appraisal. . . . Yet BLM had a much more rigid, stylized process—they went much more "by the book," while the Forest Service applied "looser" standards. . . . Also, while the Bureau assessed mineral values by looking

only at whether minerals existed or not, the Forest Service assessed whether or not a market or need existed for the minerals. . . . When the BLM's computer inventory of [among other things] ownership rights broke down, the Forest Service had to go back to square one in determining these rights . . . and throughout, the political spectrum kept falling in . . . this was a battle pitting Lujan and Domenici in the north against Schmitt in the south.[56]

Thus, whether principled or obstructionist—incidental, accidental, or contrived—this bureaupolitical imbroglio combined with Reagan's supply-side management philosophy and Congress' fire alarm oversight to persistently narrow the options of Las Cruces, the Boys Academy, Albuquerque, and the Forest Service. What is more, these factors combined to abort a private-sector effort to purchase and develop the industrial park properties, an initiative endorsed by Las Cruces as a way out of its financial dilemma and a scheme suffused with Reagan's free-market approach to community development.

The Private-Sector Development Issue

Late in the summer of 1981, local Las Cruces developer Klaus Wittern provided the city with another option for developing the industrial park properties.[57] At a special meeting of the City Commission, Wittern asked the commissioners to approve a proposal whereby a private corporation—the Greater Las Cruces Industrial Development Authority—chartered by him would purchase the lands and develop the park. Most important, the city would become one of the corporation's stockholders. Sounding quintessentially Reaganesque, Wittern argued that "the private development of this land is more suitable and inherently better for the overall development of the area than a government approach; private industry can do the job faster—governments should govern and private business should do business."[58]

Under Wittern's plan, the Greater Las Cruces Industrial Development Authority would sell stock worth $7 million at $10 per share. To assure local ownership of the park, rather than "foreign control" by El Paso or Albuquerque, Wittern limited initial sales solely to the Las Cruces area. After ninety days, however, stock sales could go national. Ultimately, Wittern envisioned Las Cruces and Dona Ana County purchasing 15 and 5 percent of the stock, respectively. The remainder, he assumed, would fall to individuals (30 percent), as well as firms, financial institutions, and business groups (50 percent).

Not everyone embraced Wittern's logic, however, and some were wary of the wily developer's intentions. However, with Schmitt eliminating all hopes for a below-market-value transfer to the city, and with preliminary Forest Service appraisal estimates indicating the likely purchase price was beyond its means, the Commission gave Wittern 60 days to put together the investment package. At the end of that time, the city stood ready to resume its own acquisition efforts. As Senator Schmitt noted at the time, "The big question is, can the money be raised?" To which Wittern, backed by the Chamber of Commerce, retorted with a hubris that soon haunted him: "Bankers are skeptical about raising $7 million. . . . They are conservative by nature. . . . Actually, I think we could have [the investment package] ready in a week!"[59] The sixty days came and went, however, with Wittern returning to the Commission railing against "federal government inactivity" and petitioning for a time extension.

The essence of Wittern's argument in mid-October was simple, if distinctly impolitic: "If they [the City Commission] don't extend the deadline, they're wacko. . . . As far as I'm concerned the 60 days haven't started yet."[60] His logic? Delays by the Forest Service and the BLM in appraising the park land properties meant that the Albuquerque Academy could not approve the trade. In turn, without knowing if they were in the exchange, the Academy could not commit itself to selling the lands to Wittern's group. His group, said Wittern, had "gone as far as we can go" until details of the exchange are known:

> We can't raise money until we have something to purchase. We don't know what we're buying or how much it will cost. We want to buy the land, but we have nothing that anyone wants to sell. . . . They haven't set a price, and they haven't said we could buy it. . . . The Forest Service promised to have the land appraised by September 1, but that appraisal has not been made.[61]

Wittern, too, had also received pledges for stock purchases in the corporation, but the federal Security and Exchange Commission

(SEC) refused to certify the corporation until it held tangible assets. Yet, in classic Catch-22 fashion, without a commitment from either the Forest Service, the Boys Academy, or the City of Albuquerque to sell the land to Wittern's Industrial Development Authority, the corporation had no assets!

At this point, the plot thickened. Wittern announced that he was about to sign a contract with the Crowder Investment Company that could provide him with the assets needed by the Authority to satisfy potential investors and the SEC. Crowder, with a proven track record in working with the BLM in land exchanges, proposed to enter into a memorandum of understanding with the Authority. Therein, the investment company guaranteed to sell the industrial park properties to Wittern's group once it acquired them from the BLM in exchange for other properties Crowder owned. The advantages, insisted Wittern, were substantial: "This would be an intra-agency exchange and it could be expeditiously handled [by the BLM]."[62] In the end, the Commission approved both of Wittern's requests. Indeed, a 30-day extension seemed the only prudent thing to do once the city learned that the Forest Service's preliminary appraisal of the industrial park lands ($1.1 million) was double its own appraisal.

In approving Wittern's extension, Mayor Camunez remarked sternly to the developer, "If [at that time] you can't do it [raise sufficient money to purchase the land], get out of the way and let the government do it."[63] And step aside Wittern had to—at least temporarily. His extension expired without BLM "being willing to swap the lands to Las Cruces, Crowder, or anybody else," and without Wittern or the city able to get an official sale price, purchase agreement, or date of transfer from any of their northern neighbors. Thus, with Lujan and Schmitt at odds over pursuing a congressional statute exempting the industrial park lands from the strictures of the Recreation and Public Purposes Act, Las Cruces rejoined the fray.

Unbeknownst to the city, however, events in Albuquerque were about to take a new twist, one which gave a "third life" to Wittern's private sector initiative. In March 1982, the Albuquerque City Council approved the proposal proffered earlier by the Elena Gallegos Trust Fund Committee. You will recall that under that proposal, Albuquerque would purchase the entire land grant from the Boys Academy by temporarily raising its sales tax by one-quarter cent. After keeping the land it wanted for open spaces, the city would exchange the rest with the Forest Service for nearly 33,000 acres of property scattered around the state. Then Albuquerque could sell these surplus properties for a sizeable profit. In the end, this approach carried the day. After negotiations with the Academy, Albuquerque purchased the Elena Gallegos properties and successfully completed the exchange with the Forest Service.

Certainly, the good news in all this for Las Cruces was that an owner with whom it might deal for the industrial park property was at hand at last. The bad news was that purchasing the lands at Albuquerque's $1.1 million asking price was impossible. Purchasing the lands in total at that price meant that the city could not meet the matching fund requirements of a waste treatment grant necessary for further economic development and diversification in Las Cruces. Ironically, of course, these were matching requirements made more stringent for localities by the Reagan Administration. Thus, in desperation, city commissioners turned again to Klaus Wittern, giving him 60 days to reach a purchase agreement with Albuquerque.

Once again, however, Wittern's efforts stalled. First, Albuquerque—fearing he was attempting to undermine Las Cruces—refused to deal with Wittern. Next, after Las Cruces disabused Albuquerque of this notion, Mayor Kinney concluded that state law required the city to hold a competitive sale wherein neither the Forest Service's appraised price nor Las Cruces' chosen buyer (Wittern's group) could be given priority. Then Wittern refused to sign a memorandum of understanding with Las Cruces stipulating that his Industrial Development Authority pay for the oversized pipes needed to bring utilities to the park.

Finally, afraid that no one would purchase the land, Albuquerque offered to sell it directly to Las Cruces for $1.1 million, but with more affordable installment payments, over a 3-year period. Thus, with direct purchase now an affordable option, Las Cruces accepted Albuquerque's offer.[64] The only obstacles then remaining for the city were the approval of the Elena Gallegos exchange by Ronald Reagan and the U.S. Congress. Yet approval by these actors was hardly routine, especially when it violated every one of the Reagan Administration's preconditions for federal land acquisition.

The Exchange Approval Issue

As noted, the Reagan Administration did not favor federal land acquisitions if they lacked national significance or were targeted for single- rather than multiple-use purposes. The Elena Gallegos exchange was clearly a single-use purpose (wilderness and open space preservation), and careerists within the Forest Service candidly conceded that the acquisition was clearly of local rather than national significance. Indeed, in Forester Johanson's words, "This [Domenici's] bill was purely a local interest [exchange] since the land was not of national interest—national environmentalists could care less—it only helped Albuquerque."[65]

What is more, in mid-1982, the Administration announced its controversial Asset Management Program. Heeding the call of privatization zealots within its ranks, the Administration—and a reluctant James Watt—announced a sell-off of "surplus" federal properties, with proceeds earmarked to lower the federal debt. Granted, the Administration eventually scuttled the program; Western ranchers, real estate interests, and politicos within the Interior Department ultimately scotched the revenue projections and goals of the privatizers as naive, unrealistic, and undermining pro-development interests. Yet before its demise, talk of surplus land sales was real, high on the Administration's agenda, and diametrically opposed to the Forest Service's use of such properties in New Mexico to close the Elena Gallegos deal.

Nevertheless, during congressional hearings on the exchange, chaired by Domenici, the Administration made an exception for Elena Gallegos. The Administration's rationale, explained by Deputy Chief Raymond Housely of the Forest Service, placed its angst in perspective and sought to dissuade others from using a similar approach in the future. Spoke Housely:

> The Administration supports the exchange reluctantly, since these are the types of land [we] would likely be considering for sale [under the Asset Management Program]. President Reagan's program of disposal of federal land would generally preclude an exchange such as

this set up by a [state congressional] delegation bill. The Administration is backing it only because the proposal has been under development for several years and substantial commitments have been made. . . . We would not expect to support . . . [such a] proposal in the future.[66]

The fact that the bill's sponsor, Pete Domenici, was a senatorial steward of Reagan's budget juggernaut in the U.S. Congress didn't hurt either! Thus, in October 1982, Congress passed and the President "reluctantly" signed Domenici's bill authorizing the exchange that so fundamentally violated major planks in the natural resource platform of the Reagan Revolution.

As for the Las Cruces Industrial Park, had the city failed to exercise any of its three purchase options in a timely fashion, Albuquerque could have sold the remaining property to the highest bidder. True, Las Cruces eventually obtained the full industrial park site. Yet the price it paid was double the city's appraised value, and Albuquerque temporarily replaced the BLM as steward for lands sought by Las Cruces for economic development.

Neither did all proceed as planned for Albuquerque. Ultimately, the city did obtain clear title to the open-space properties it had so long coveted. It did so, however, at a rather steep price: The overwhelming majority of scattered, unattractive properties received from the Forest Service remained unsold well into the late 1980s. In fact, the only lands sold during this period were the Las Cruces properties, along with certain mineral-rich tracts in the San Juan Basin in northwestern New Mexico. In sum, the promise of great profits from land sales never materialized for the Albuquerqueans. Indeed, they were later asked to approve a second tax increase for land maintenance and acquisition. Likewise, the bottom line was no less bittersweet for the Reagan Administration. Reagan appointees left the experience with little more intact than their growing image as "pragmatists"—the "P-word" so offensive to the ideological footsoldiers of the Reagan Revolution.

CONCLUSION

The Reagan Administration's experience in the Las Cruces Industrial Park–Elena Gallegos case exhibits many of the same complications reported in the previous two chapters, but with quite different bureaupolitical dynamics, results, and consequences. First, the managerial complications. Once again, we see how the Reagan Administration's supply-side management successes (viz., cuts in federal grants for economic development, funding restrictions on the Land and Water Conservation Fund, and BLM personnel cuts and alterations in agency skill mixes) seriously hampered its ability to realize primary strategic goals (viz., expediting land exchanges, such as Elena Gallegos; unlocking "landlocked" urban areas, such as Las Cruces; and discouraging land acquisitions of only local significance, such as Albuquerque's proposal).

In contrast to the previous two cases, however, the bureaupolitical dynamics of the Industrial Park—Elena Gallegos experience were decidedly more contentious, broader in scope, and contagious in conflict. However, as the reader will witness in the next two chapters, these dynamics were nowhere near as volatile as they can become when presidents seek to reorient policy administratively. What accounts for the way this case differs from its predecessors? Arguably, the most apparent distinction between them lies in the nature of the policy initiatives pursued.

Unlike the rangeland and management reform cases, large-scale land exchanges were not widely accepted, long-debated, marginal extensions of existing policies. Indeed, the unprecedented scale of the operation envisioned made it a qualitatively different initiative from its more widely accepted kin, the small-scale land exchange. What is more, Reaganites launched this initiative amid great controversy over its feasibility in the absence of significant reform and capacity building within and among implementing agencies. During the Reagan years, however, these reforms took a back seat to supply-side cuts operationalized ideologically within a framework of the administrative orthodoxy. Thus, as expected, BLM careerists balked at this "assault" on their territory, finding ample grist and opportunity for doing so.

What is more, the novelty, complexity, and uncertainty surrounding large-scale exchanges provoked frustration, provided grounds for intervention by interested parties, and offered multiple access points for fire alarm oversight. Most important, these consequences dwarfed those in the rangeland management case. Note, for example, how Lujan and Schmitt effectively defined the contours, stated the terms, and wrestled grudging support from the Reagan Administration for the settlement they helped craft. Yet never did the disputants try to expand the scope of the conflict to full-scale judicial or congressional arenas. None wished outside actors to intervene, and none could afford to see delay scotch aspects of the deal dear to their hearts.

It is important to note, however, that this predisposition to limit the scope of the conflict also strengthened the hand of those politically advantaged in the dispute. For example, crafty old hands like Lujan and Domenici pummeled Schmitt, the neophyte, on critical issues (e.g., stopping the exchange and pulling Las Cruces' lands out of the exchange). Likewise, populous Albuquerque did the same to tiny Las Cruces, while the powerful Forest Service dominated the decidedly less potent BLM. Indeed, the Bureau was reduced to "guerilla warfare" tactics versus its "superstar" adversary, the Forest Service. Thus, arguably, a more biased pluralism dominated resolution of the controversy.

As noted, however, containing the conflict is not the only option open to those affected by the administrative presidency. Nor does biased pluralism of the kind witnessed here necessarily determine the result—as Chapters 7 and 8 will vividly illustrate. Thus, we turn next to the way the Reagan Administration's efforts to revamp Western water policy interacted with evolving case law to drive the bureaupolitical dynamics of groundwater regulation in New Mexico.

CHAPTER 7

Thou Shalt Not Covet Thy Neighbor's Water

Referring to the spiraling complexity of our federal system, Catherine Lovell observes that intergovernmental relationships are "complicated by a pervasive tension between strong centralizing forces and equally strong decentralizing forces."[1] Our nation's interest in securing adequate water supplies in an era of scarcity profoundly demonstrates this inherent tension. With water demand burgeoning nationally, water supplies precarious in many regions, and federal water project assistance assaulted by both the Carter and Reagan administrations, water-deficient states increasingly covet the supplies of their more fortunate neighbors. Moreover, those states that are vulnerable to these demands seek to impose or preserve statutory barriers to water export.

During the 1980 presidential campaign, Ronald Reagan seized upon these states' rights tensions to solidify his electoral support in the West. This chapter focuses on New Mexico's experience within this context as it sought first to deny and later to place strict limits on groundwater exports to El Paso, Texas. The events preceding and subsequent to the *El Paso v. Reynolds* decision demonstrate how retrenchment, cost-sharing of water development projects, and the Administration's reaction to evolving case law interacted to threaten New Mexico's ability to regulate and protect water supplies within its borders from out-of-state exporters. At a time when disparate elements within the Reagan Administration sought simultaneously to protect state control over groundwater, to create markets in water rights, and to dramatically cut federal funding for water research, evolving case law required timely, extensive, and expensive hydrological data from the states to protect their supplies from covetous neighbors or to acquire more from them.

163

THE PAST AS PROLOGUE: TOWARD A DEMAND-MANAGEMENT ERA?

The epitome of pork-barrel politics, federal water project programs had become by the mid-seventies the bane of environmentalists, the scourge of efficiency-minded economists, and the targets of federal deficit cutters.[2] Historically, of course, this was not the case; federal water programs grew proportionate to Congress' desire to supply cheap water and hydroelectric power to develop the West. Thus, as Jimmy Carter took office, Bureau of Recreation (BuRec) water projects alone irrigated acreage in the West equal to nearly one-sixth of the nation's cropland. Moreover, between 1965 and 1980, Congress authorized $52 billion in water projects nationally.

Most disturbing to its critics, however, Congress had authorized many water projects without rigorous tests for economic, environmental, or aesthetic impact. Not only did the Reclamation Act provide irrigation water to farmers at rates considerably below cost, but Congress incorrigibly subsidized water projects benefitting ranchers, municipalities, and private industry. Thus, while subsidies varied from project to project, researchers calculated that irrigation farmers repaid only 3.3 percent of BuRec's original capital costs. Similarly distorted were municipal water rates, with water-short El Pasoans charged only 53 cents per 1000 gallons in 1983, while water-abundant Philadelphians paid $1.73 per 1000 gallons.

Taking office, the Carter Administration sought to curb federal water subsidies and to develop a national water strategy. To the astonishment of outraged Western users, the Administration planned to cut out of its budget 18 partially completed water projects judged economically and environmentally unwarranted. Quickly, a second "hit list" followed, targeting 277 additional water projects. Stymied in his plans by Western senators led by New Mexico's Domenici, President Carter still threw down the gauntlet to Western congressmembers, their constituents, and pro-development advocates: An era of demand management rather than supply management was upon them. And while popularly pilloried as quixotically tilting against congressional windmills, Carter's thrusts and parries set well into the 1980s the substance, tone, and agenda for water policy debate in the West.

As Thomas Arrandale reports, the pace of federal project construction slowed demonstrably by the late 1970s amid soaring budget deficits, environmental activism, and diminishing quantities of unappropriated surface water.[3] Indeed, Congress didn't authorize any new water projects in the West between 1977 and 1984, while slowing to a trickle appropriations for ongoing projects. Thus, while Ronald Reagan's victory promised a welcome respite from Carter's assault, critics by 1986 chided Reagan appointees as well for "waging water war on the West." Indeed, while Watt and his successors dismissed off-handedly the idea that all water projects worth building had been built, they coyly offered two formidable prerequisites for renewed support: (1) national economic recovery had to foil budget deficits, and (2) the states had to agree to a new cost-sharing policy that upped their contribution to project financing.

The Reagan Administration began catching flak in 1981 once its uniform cost-sharing policy became public. Therein, appointees tagged states, municipalities, industries, and farmers with an even larger share of multipurpose project costs (those providing flood control, electric power, irrigation water storage, and water transportation) than even President Carter had proposed (viz., ten percent of construction costs). As initially envisioned, power companies, as well as states and localities, had to pay 100 percent of any hydroelectric generating costs associated with a project. Beneficiaries, too, would pay 50 and 35 percent of recreation and irrigation and flood costs, respectively. Most significantly, users had to pay these levies up-front, before construction began.

So shrilly did Western senators react to this proposal, and so compelling were fears of electoral retribution, that Assistant Secretary Carruthers substituted a "case-by-case" approach in its stead. Designed to assuage Western concerns, Carruthers' plan was to look at each individual project, assess the local economic situation, ascertain the likelihood and extent of state or local contributions, and calibrate benefits accruing to the private sector. Still, he insisted on private-sector participation; Interior could not build additional water projects without "new partners."

In turn, Reagan appointees persistently reworked cost-sharing proposals throughout the President's second term, offering more flexible payment ratios and schedules. Nonetheless, the Administration's message was clear, consistent, and distressing to those benefitting from the status quo: supply augmentation in the West was "out"; demand reduction was "in." Altered as well were the scope, focus, and intensity of Western water politics, with redistributive conflict replacing distributive consensus. In addition, with most surface water already appropriated in the West, redistributive conflict now included groundwater supplies as well.

When Jimmy Carter assumed the presidency, the ratio of groundwater to total water use in the 11 contiguous Western states ranged widely, from a high of 62 percent in Arizona to a low of two percent in Montana.[4] Over the next decade, however, pressures spiraled to manage groundwater more stringently to cope with regional population growth, mineral development, legal requirements to maintain in-stream water flows, maintenance requirements, and water-based recreational pursuits. Thus, by the end of Reagan's first term, almost one-quarter of the nation's fresh water supply and three-quarters of its drinking water sprang from groundwater aquifers. Moreover, in the West, nearly one-quarter of all groundwater withdrawals were overdrafts (i.e., withdrawn in excess of annual rates of precipitation and natural recharge). Indeed, so desperate did things seem that some observers prophesied a veritable "rural-urban war" over scarce water supplies.

As intrastate demand for nonagricultural uses quickened, as the availability of and funding for acceptable projects dwindled, and as reallocating water among existing users grew more likely, state officials looked for help outside their borders. Here, New Mexico's situation on the eve of the Reagan presidency is illustrative. Having already appropriated most of their surface water, New Mexicans looked, first, to the state's underground aquifers for respite, and later, to water supplies in Texas, Arizona, the Great Lakes, and the Pacific Northwest. Strapped as well, however, neighboring states, in turn, eyed New Mexico's supplies. Thus, by 1990, Texans expected water shortfalls that were four times as large as what New Mexico already diverted in supplies from the Rio Grande River! Moreover, in those parts of Texas, Arizona, Colorado, and Oklahoma closest to the state, experts projected water deficits quenchable only by importing the equivalent of 50 to 63 percent of New Mexico's then-current supply.

Obviously, areas of New Mexico ripe for water export varied according to the projected costs of transfer. But as costs increased for augmenting dwindling water supplies in other states, importing water from New Mexico became more politically attractive and economically viable for its neighbors. Still, New Mexicans failed to appreciate how precarious their water situation was until the city of El Paso, Texas tried to tap groundwater supplies underlying New Mexico during the first term of the Reagan Administration.

THE REGULATORY DILEMMA IN THE RIO GRANDE BASIN

Prior to the 1980s, Texas and New Mexico shared uneventfully a common border, a strong commitment to economic development, diminishing water supplies, and claims to groundwater in the Mesilla and Hueco bolsons of southern New Mexico. But then a dramatic focusing event occurred in the lower Rio Grande Basin (RGB): El Paso officials petitioned New Mexico for 326 drilling permits to export 246,000 acre-feet of water per year from the state. Expecting New Mexico to reject its petition, El Paso also filed a suit alleging that a 1953 New Mexico statute banning water exports violated the commerce, privileges and immunities, and equal protection clauses of the U.S. Constitution. New Mexico quickly rejected El Paso's applications and closed both bolsons to further drilling by anyone—including New Mexicans—until the suit was decided.

With El Paso seizing the initiative, the scope of the conflict quickly expanded in both states. Local water managers in New Mexico (especially in Las Cruces and Albuquerque) urged city officials to intervene in the suit against El Paso to protect urban interests. Simultaneously, New Mexico's irrigated farming interests did so, and launched a provocative, anti-El Paso media campaign. Therein, Las Cruscans chided their neighbor's "nefarious lawsuit," urged citizens to "rise up against those who would rob us of our water," and hyped an economic boycott of El Paso businesses to combat El Paso's "water grab." Everyone, it seems, had a formal position except the Reagan Administration. The Interior Department, fully aware that drilling ultimately could take place on BLM properties if approved, averred that the federal government "ought not [yet] take a position on the question."[5] Still, Watt and Carruthers routinely waxed Reaganesque, emphasizing the Administration's sympathy for a state's right and responsibility to control its own water.

From El Paso's perspective, tapping New Mexico's groundwater was the "cheapest and environmentally soundest" alternative to fueling the city's economic development. Consequently, even though New Mexico argued adamantly that conservation, recycling sewage water, and retiring agricultural water rights were the keys to sustaining El Paso's growth, Texans remained unpersuaded. Their argument? Approaches like these cost $1 to $5 billion more than pumping water from New Mexico and were too politically explosive to implement. Equally unpersuaded, New Mexicans replied that El Paso unfairly envisioned their state's water supplies as a "panacea for the city's [El Paso's] failure to plan . . . refusal to institute basic water management regulation . . . and desire to continue to promote growth and water usage," rather than conservation.[6]

Thus, at the heart of the dispute as Reagan assumed the presidency were two quite disparate regulatory philosophies. As noted in Chapter 1, the doctrine of prior appropriation and beneficial use underpins water regulation in the West. By the early 1980s, New Mexico's water statutes reflected this tradition, but within one of the West's most progressive regulatory frameworks. Individual users did not own water rights. Instead, the state engineer regulated the appropriation, transfer, and distribution of water for the beneficial use of all state citizens.

Most notably for the RGB dispute, scholars applauded New Mexico's innovative groundwater policies.[7] Among the first Western states to recognize by statute that surface and groundwater supplies are linked hydrologically, New Mexico made prospective groundwater users apply to the state engineer for drilling permits. In turn, existing users could file protests with the state engineer to deny an applicant's permit. If unappropriated water were available, if existing water rights were not permanently impaired, or if existing uses were retired to offset new ones, the state engineer could issue new drilling permits. After acquiring them, permittees could sell their rights to fellow New Mexicans for use within the state's borders. Sales for exports to neighboring states, however, were expressly forbidden by statute.

In contrast to the respect they held for New Mexico's regulatory regime, scholars viewed Texas' groundwater law as rife with serious and glaring shortcomings. Those most salient to the RGB dispute involved the ownership of groundwater, the decentralized nature of the Texas regulatory framework, and the state's failure to recognize the hydrological link between ground and surface water. Regarding ownership, Texas saw groundwater as the private property of surface owners. Virtually free to "intercept, impede, and appropriate" groundwater, surface owners had only to be sure they did not maliciously injure their neighbor or "wantonly waste" groundwater supplies. Likewise, the decentralized Texas system meant that no conservation district had jurisdiction over an entire aquifer. Consequently, individual districts had no incentive to restrict withdrawals, since those outside their jurisdictions might preempt "conserved" supplies. Lastly, critics decried Texas' failure to integrate surface and groundwater rights and to provide a permit system for groundwater extraction. Moreover, the state's courts consistently ruled that the doctrine of private ownership superceded any claim that depleting groundwater compromised surface water quantity and quality.

THE LOWER RIO GRANDE BASIN DISPUTE: OF CASES, COMPACTS, AND CONSTITUTIONALISM

Before the federal courts rendered a series of judgements in the RGB dispute, the combatants clashed over three primary issues. First, how would projected groundwater needs affect the quantity and quality of groundwater supplies in the RGB? Second, did El Paso's claim to groundwater underlying New Mexico violate the Rio Grande Compact of 1938? Finally, could New Mexico embargo groundwater exports without violating the commerce clause of the U.S. Constitution? Certainly, one cannot appreciate the regulatory dilemma in the RGB without understanding these issues. Nor can one ignore how the supply-side management philosophy of the

Reagan Administration helped frame, inflame, and complicate their resolution.

The Groundwater Supply Issue

As Ronald Reagan assumed the presidency, uncertainty abounded over the quantity, quality, and perennial yield of groundwater supplies should El Paso export groundwater from New Mexico. Yet determining this impact with sound hydrological data was critical since New Mexico's state engineer had to demonstrate that El Paso's water diversion would permanently injure existing uses and users in the RGB. Indeed, the stakes surrounding these calculations were quite high for Dona Ana County, New Mexico, and El Paso County, Texas.[8]

In Dona Ana County, irrigated agriculture dominated water consumption, accounting for fully 95 percent of all water demand. Of this, groundwater supplies accounted for nearly 20 percent. What is more, over the next 20 years, planners expected municipal needs to expand persistently as population grew annually by three percent, noncommercial water use grew apace, and supply pressures spiraled to accommodate a new industrial park, a medium-security prison, and an expanded airport facility (see Chapter 6).

The water situation in El Paso County was more precarious yet, and likely to grow acutely worse over the next fifty years. Agriculture used nearly 85 percent of all allocated water, with nearly 61 percent of that total provided by groundwater. In contrast, water for cities and industries accounted for only 11 percent of all withdrawals, but groundwater provided nearly 71 percent of that total. Moreover, precipitous increases in water demand were likely as the population doubled or tripled by the year 2020, and as cities and factories quenched their thirsts with approximately 132,500 acre-feet annually over the next twenty years.

Decidedly less understood, however, was the water supply situation facing the RGB. In denying El Paso's drilling permits, the New Mexico state engineer, Steve Reynolds, concluded that the city's proposed wells "would virtually create an impact of no surface flows in the Rio Grande [River] . . . a decline of the water table in the floodplain aquifer," and a gradual increase in the salinity of regional groundwater supplies.[9] However, with the state engineer's data bases so inadequate, his ability to finance additional studies so limited, and the time constraints under which he labored so pressing, El Paso's lawsuit offered hydrological models of the Rio Grande Basin that directly contradicted Reynold's. Specifically, the city's expert witnesses testified that the Mesilla Bolson alone contained enough water to make reducing surface flow unnecessary for at least 170 years, even with exports. In contrast, New Mexico's experts predicted an ebb in surface flow within 50 years, if the state's embargo failed. Still, all conceded that pumping groundwater to the surface differs considerably in practice from theory: actual appropriation typically yields "far less [water] than what is theoretically possible."[10] As a consequence, costly investments in deep-well drilling had to follow if El Paso's arguments prevailed.

With debate joined in this fashion, New Mexicans quickly realized that their compatriots at Interior were ill-disposed toward providing federal assistance for groundwater research in the RGB. Instead, Reagan's appointees tried to: (1) eliminate the federal Office of Water Research and Technology (OWRT), water desalting research, and other water research and development (R&D) efforts; (2) abolish the Water Resources Council (WRC), a national panel that coordinated water programs and made grants to states for water planning; (3) assign the WRC's tasks to the Cabinet Council on Natural Resources and the Environment; (4) cut completely all Interior Department research grants to state water resource institutes; (5) abolish six river basin commissions engaged in water resource planning; (6) scuttle a congressional proposal to create a Commission on Federal Water Policy; and (7) trim Interior's overall R&D budget by $52 million. Their logic? "High priority [research] activities [had] been completed, and remaining [federal] programs are carried out ineffectively."[11]

Simultaneously, Reagan's appointees took actions that made state regulators' control of water resources decidedly more difficult.[12] Most critically, they failed to offset cuts in state research grants by increasing research funding for Interior's U.S. Geological Survey. For example, the Administration tried deferring $6 million from the revamped FY81 Geological Survey budget for surveys, investigations, and research. Likewise, they budgetted only nominal increases in FY82, FY83, and FY84 for the Geological Survey's national program of water research. Most notably for New Mexico, of course, these patterns prevailed even though the most recent Geological Survey studies on Great Plains groundwater conditions failed to assess the hydrology of aquifer recharge.[13] True, Assistant Secretary Carruthers promised federal funding for hydrological studies to the disputants. But his promise had one catch: Funding for studying the hydrological recharge issue was impossible until the federal courts resolved the RGB dispute. How soon might this be? At the time, most predicted a decade at least for the case to wend its tortuous way to the U.S. Supreme Court.

The Rio Grande Compact Issue

In 1905, Congress authorized the Bureau of Reclamation to construct the Elephant Butte Dam on the Rio Grande River, about one hundred miles north of the New Mexico–Texas border. Its purpose was to foster irrigated agriculture in the Elephant Butte and El Paso irrigation districts. During the 1920s, however, Colorado diverted river flow so seriously that Elephant Butte residents suffered intolerable shortfalls. In response, Congress created the Rio Grande Commission to "equitably apportion" the river's bounty. Comprised of representatives from Colorado, New Mexico, Texas, and the federal government, the Commission developed over the next decade a complex water delivery schedule premised on surface flows above the Elephant Butte Dam. The agreement—known as the Rio Grande Compact of 1938—called for Colorado to deliver stipulated amounts of water at the New Mexico–Colorado border, and for New Mexico to do the same at the Elephant Butte Dam (rather than the New Mexico–Texas border). Subsequently, contracts let to irrigate nearly 155,000 acres of prime farmland produced an allocation ratio between Texas and New Mexico of 43% and 57%, respectively.

Hotly debated during the RGB controversy were two fundamental elements of the Rio Grande Compact.[14] First, did the Compact specifically appropriate Rio Grande surface water below Elephant Butte to Texas and New Mexico? Second, would diverting groundwater to El Paso unlawfully reapportion Rio Grande surface waters that the Compact had already allocated? New Mexicans used the Compact to try and dismiss El Paso's suit entirely. The constitutionality of the state's export embargo was not the real issue, they contended. The Compact, approved by Congress and superceding state statutes, precluded the state engineer from approving El Paso's water claims. Their logic? Because the Rio Grande River was hydrologically linked to the Mesilla and Hueco bolsons, appropriating groundwater in amounts and at rates envisioned by El Paso could deplete not only the aquifers, but also the river's surface flow. This, they argued, constituted a de facto reapportionment of interstate water supplies, a reapportionment requiring approval by all parties to the original Compact or by the Supreme Court.

Countering, El Paso dismissed the "Rio Grande Defense" as "frivolous." Not only did Texas law not recognize the hydrological link between ground and surface flows, but the Compact also specified delivery one hundred miles north of the New Mexico-Texas border. Thus, it did not allocate water to Texas alone, but collectively to New Mexican, Texan, and Mexican appropriators. El Pasoans also claimed that the Rio Grande Compact did not refer specifically to groundwater allocations, that New Mexico's state engineer had previously taken the legal position that the Compact failed to apportion the river between the two states, and that retiring water rights was not necessary, since nearly 10,000 acres of irrigated land could be retired instead.

As noted, Interior officials repeatedly expressed their opinion that the federal government should remain neutral in interstate disputes of this kind. Said Carruthers, "I view [the suit] as a states' rights problem; we would prefer that the federal government . . . stay out of it [since our participation] would be an interference . . . [with] states' rights." Moreover, both Carruthers and Watt made clear their preference for a mutually negotiated interstate groundwater compact approved by Congress. Yet compacts, too, need extensive, accurate, and trusted data to inform the compromises buttressing successful negotiations. Where were these data to come from? Certainly not from the federal government if Reaganites had their way in persistently whittling water research and development funds from agency budgets.

The Dormant Commerce Clause Issue

While the U.S. Constitution allows Congress to regulate interstate commerce, the "dormant commerce clause" clouds somewhat its authority to regulate interstate groundwater transfers. Specifically, the states' authority in such matters is ambiguous; Congress has neither assumed responsibility for itself, nor explicitly granted regulatory authority to the states. Neither had the federal courts shed much light on the issue prior to the RGB dispute. Indeed, as Jolene Crane puts it, the courts had addressed the issue only on a "groping, case-by-case basis."[15]

Nonetheless, one could decipher a fairly clear four-pronged test for the constitutionality of state groundwater embargoes from cases involving other natural resources.[16] Thus, to defend the constitutionality of its export ban, New Mexico most likely had to show that its statute (1) was not discriminatory on the face of it; (2) did not impose excessive burdens on interstate commerce relative to the local benefits it delivered; (3) was "narrowly tailored" (i.e., drafted in ways directly related) to realize those benefits (viz., the conservation and protection of natural resources); and (4) was the least burdensome, discriminatory, and drastic alternative available for accomplishing its ends. Even more fundamentally, however, New Mexico had to prove that groundwater is different from other natural resources, and hence not an article of commerce.

With battlelines clear in the RGB dispute, New Mexico officials began proselytizing others about water's unique status as a publicly owned natural resource, a status they claimed Congress implicitly agreed to when it granted statehood to the territory. Recognizing this uniqueness, they suggested, effectively excluded water as an article of commerce. Anyway, hadn't Congress authorized arid Western states to impose "otherwise impermissible burdens" on water use? And couldn't arid states exercise plenary regulatory powers over groundwater, given its immunity historically from commerce clause scrutiny? In rebuttal, El Paso's attorneys argued that deferring to state water regulators hardly implied that Congress tolerated state-imposed discriminatory barriers to interstate commerce.

In sum, El Paso's attorneys wanted to focus debate in their

lawsuit on a single, profound, and narrow issue: whether state water managers could "absolutely embargo" groundwater from out-of-state use. In contrast, New Mexico's Attorney General, Paul Bardacke, wished to frame the issue quite differently: "The question is not whether El Paso can [import] New Mexico groundwater, but whether the Texas method of treating groundwater as private property can be exported to New Mexico."[17] Permitting groundwater exports against state wishes, Bardacke contended, emasculated New Mexico's regulatory regime. State regulators "would be unable to effectively control [their] water resources for the social, health, and economic needs of [their] citizens."[18]

As the RGB dispute evolved, the U.S. Supreme Court's leading case involving interstate groundwater and the commerce clause was *Sporhase v. Nebraska, ex. rel. Douglas.* The Court held that a Nebraska water export ban unconstitutionally hindered interstate commerce because (a) water is an article of commerce, and (b) the drafters had insufficiently tailored the statute to conserve and protect diminishing groundwater resources. Importantly, however, the Court also ruled that "there are legitimate reasons for special treatment accorded requests to transport groundwater across state lines," and that "the existence of unexercised federal regulatory power does not foreclose state regulation."[19]

Then what *is* determinative in deciding the constitutionality of state water embargoes? For the Justices, only those laws targeted narrowly to protect public health and safety were legitimate. Those designed for or resulting in economic protectionism did not pass constitutional muster. Moreover, those states wishing either to pursue or to thwart protectionist claims must do battle armed with compelling hydrological data, comprehensive water plans, and assessments of how realistic water projects might be that proposed diverting supplies to needy intrastate areas.

Quite naturally, El Pasoans heralded *Sporhase*'s warning against protectionism: "A core element of [a state's] police power is equitable regulation for the 'protection of the residents'" welfare, not simply the health of the economy. To wit, they labeled New Mexico's embargo "inequitable and clearly excessive in relation to . . . [its] putative local [health and safety] benefits."[20] Their justification was twofold. First, New Mexico failed to place comparable intrastate restrictions on its own citizens. And second, an interstate embargo was (a) discriminatory and (b) ill-suited to ensure groundwater to New Mexicans. New Mexico had no realistic plan or means in place to transfer water to arid areas within its borders. Of course, New Mexicans countered by hyping those parts of the majority opinion allowing arid states to justify groundwater export bans as conservation measures: Since water is essential to human survival, designing water rules to further commerce must be done cautiously, if at all.[21]

The Reagan Administration gave its most studied response to *Sporhase* during congressional hearings on the coal slurry pipeline.[22] In mid-1983, an epic struggle ensued in Washington over the merits and implications of this project for state water regulation. At issue was how best to protect the states' primacy in water regulation. One widely touted proposal sponsored by then-Congressman Richard Cheney (R-WY) allowed Congress to overturn *Sporhase*—a sentiment gaining momentum as its threat to state regulators became clearer.[23] To many, *Sporhase* seemed to create an interstate market for water supplies, if it did not actually federalize groundwater reserves.

On behalf of Reagan's Justice Department, Carol Dinkins— Assistant Attorney General, Division of Land and Water Resources—testified before Congress that *Sporhase* directly threatened the states' abilities to regulate water within their borders. Especially imperiled, she admonished, were the regulatory regimes of those thirteen Western and Midwestern states with reciprocity requirements or total water export bans. Sill, *Sporhase* did permit the states to impose otherwise unconstitutional barriers on water use, if Congress explicitly allowed them to.

But how broadly or narrowly should Congress stipulate these terms, if at all? To Dinkins, a narrowly drawn statute recognizing state primacy only over coal slurry pipelines was infinitely more prudent than a broad-based one attempting to resolve the entire dormant commerce clause issue. Testified Dinkins:

> It may be advisable for Congress to avoid enacting any "across the board" remedial legislation. Congressional self-restraint leaves open the possibility that states individually will be able to satisfy *Sporhase* simply by recasting their existing export restrictions or enacting new,

nearly equivalent restrictions which demonstrate a close nexus to the conservation and preservation of water. Even more fundamentally, the mere attempt by Congress to define which types of state restrictions are proper and which are not, would amount, ironically, to the very type of federal legislation which proponents of state water rights have historically opposed. And it certainly would be no easy task to develop comprehensive guidelines defining the scope of permissible state restrictions. Such an effort may lead to a result that is more problematic from the point of view of the states than the *Sporhase* decision itself, and undermine, not promote, the goal of the Administration and this Congress to maintain the historic primacy of state regulation of water.[24]

In contrast, New Mexican water experts such as Tom Bahr, then director of the state's Water Resources Research Institute and later director of Reagan's Office of Water Policy, urged Congress to address directly the larger dormant commerce clause issue. Congress, wrote Bahr, should "say loudly and clearly enough for the lawyers to hear" that the Commerce Clause "is a good tool for some jobs, but not for apportioning water in water-scarce states."[25]

The Reagan Administration ultimately took a compromise position on the coal slurry legislation, one reflecting a growing internecine rift between proponents of states' rights and the New Resource Economics. For New Mexicans, however, the news was bad: The Administration reiterated its support for letting water flow to its highest economic use, regardless of state boundaries. What is more, it refused to support or sponsor legislation that more broadly resolved the dormant commerce clause issue. Still, to assuage states' righters, the Administration said the states could impose conditions on the use of water in slurry pipelines that might preempt federal concerns.

Not surprisingly, many New Mexicans were quite cynical about the Justice Department's position on the dormant commerce clause issue, given Dinkins' background.[26] Before joining the Reagan Administration, she worked at the Houston law firm of Vinson & Elkins—the same firm representing El Paso in its lawsuit against New Mexico! Too, Vinson & Elkins represented such energy titans as Gulf Resources & Chemical, Houston Natural Gas, Superior

Oil, and Texas Eastern. With many New Mexicans seeing the *El Paso* case as a stalking horse for energy companies developing a slurry pipeline out of the state's San Juan Basin, Dinkins' ties were troublesome. Even more so was her close relationship to Texas Governor William Clements, an advocate of interstate water transfers into Texas from the Great Lakes, the Ogallala Aquifer, and the Missouri River basin. And most vexing of all, many expected Dinkins to run for Texas Attorney General after leaving Washington.

About this time, however, New Mexicans became even more alarmed about another connection to the Vinson & Elkins law firm: former Texas governor, John Connally.[27] After his aborted 1980 presidential bid, Connally returned to Texas as a senior partner at Vinson & Elkins. There, many New Mexicans speculated that his clout in Washington was one of the primary reasons why El Paso retained Vinson & Elkins as counsel. With most of the wells El Paso intended to drill accessible from BLM lands, New Mexico editorialists warned their congressmen to be wary of—and to head off—the "possibility of any backdoor dealings going on already between El Paso, its lawyers, BLM, and Department of Interior officials." Connally's lobbying, they feared, might persuade Interior officials to lease BLM land west of Mesilla Valley to El Paso. Then the *Bureau* could issue drilling permits to Texans without New Mexico's approval.

Whether real or imagined, this "threat" never materialized. Certainly, the bad press didn't help. Moreover, any compact so conceived would have sorely jeopardized Carruthers' chances to become governor of New Mexico. Finally, the Administration had bigger fish to fry. Specifically, concern over the El Paso dispute paled compared to Reagan's pledge to reverse the Carter Administration's policy on federal nonreserved water rights such as those attached to the BLM lands in question.

Designed by the Carter Administration to circumvent the Supreme Court's decision in *U.S. v. New Mexico*, the "infamous" Kurlitz opinion on nonreserved water rights decreed that federal agencies had a priority claim over other users. Therefore, federal agencies could use any unappropriated water they needed to manage public land programs, even if these programs were not the primary purposes of the properties.[28] In contrast, the Reagan Administration pledged in early 1982 to stand in line like any other applicant for a state water permit: Federal agencies did not have priority over other users. Hailed by Senator Domenici as a major victory for state water regulators, the Administration's decision prompted Carruthers to announce that the BLM would apply for water permits to the New Mexico state engineer, regardless of the outcome of El Paso's lawsuit.

THE COURT'S DECISION AND ITS UNRAVELING

Federal District Judge Howard Bratton issued his initial decision in the RGB dispute in early 1983 (*City of El Paso v. S. E. Reynolds,* D.N.M. Civ. No. 80–730-HB). In declaring New Mexico's export statute unconstitutional, Bratton reasoned that (1) water is an article of commerce subject to commerce clause analysis; (2) New Mexico's export statute facially discriminated against El Paso by placing more stringent transfer requirements on nonresidents than on citizens of the state; (3) the embargo served no legitimate local purpose; and (4) the statute failed to narrowly tailor the embargo to address the health and safety concerns of southern New Mexicans.

Judge Bratton also dismissed New Mexico's arguments concerning the Rio Grande Compact and the water supply situation in the RGB. Wrote Bratton, neither the "history of Compact negotiations, the ultimate terms of the Compact, nor the defendant's subsequent interpretations and actions" indicate that de facto reapportionment would occur if groundwater from New Mexico was exported to El Paso. Because the Compact had not authorized allocating water to New Mexicans through user contracts, those contracts were not binding. Thus, exporting these waters to Texans did not "reallocate" supplies already allocated under the pact. What is more, in challenging New Mexico's data, Bratton accepted El Paso's position; New Mexicans could impose less discriminatory measures than an embargo to conserve their water supplies. These might include tightening intrastate regulations and retiring water permits in other parts of the state.

To best ascertain the Reagan Administration's response to Bratton's decision, one has to revisit Carol Dinkins' congressional testimony.[29] Asked to assess *El Paso's* impact on various coal slurry bills, Dinkins indirectly comforted both Texans and New Mexicans. Consonant with the Texan position, she saw two appropriate extensions of *Sporhase:* those aspects of his ruling emphasizing how New Mexico's embargo was discriminatory on its face, and the fact that the embargo's provisions were not "narrowly tailored." In Dinkins' view, New Mexico's statute did not ensure the conservation of embargoed water. Neither did the state convincingly demonstrate that intrastate transfers to water-short areas of the state were imminent. New Mexico had shown that transport was technically feasible, but it had not demonstrated persuasively that intrastate transfers were economically feasible, likely, or necessary in terms of health and safety.

Still, Dinkins' testimony buoyed New Mexican spirits in two ways. First, the Justice Department felt that *Sporhase* had not compelled Bratton to distinguish between economic considerations and promoting "health or safety." Granted, health and safety were paramount concerns, but they were not mutually exclusive from economic ones. Thus, facing water shortages, an arid state could give a preference to its own citizens, even though its water needs stemmed partly from economic activities (i.e., industry, agriculture, energy production, fish and wildlife, and recreation). Second, the Department felt that Bratton went far beyond *Sporhase* in asking the state to justify its export ban in terms of immediate needs in specific locations. In Dinkins' words, if "the water shortage, though distant in time, is actual and foreseeable and the State's plan for intrastate transportation sufficiently concrete, the existence of a time lag should not by itself render it infirm under the Commerce Clause."

In sum, as the federal courts threw Western water law into a tizzy by apparently "regionalizing" (some said "federalizing") state water supplies, the philosophically diverse Reagan Administration seemed to "feel strongly both ways." On the one hand, the Administration aggressively discouraged Congress from imposing a broad-based federal solution to the water export question, one precluding interstate transport of groundwater. On the other, the Administration stood foursquare behind state control of water resources by (1) disavowing nonreserved federal water rights, (2) supporting a state's right to give "limited preferences" to its own citizens in allocating water, and (3) questioning why Bratton interpreted the dormant commerce clause issue more rigidly than *Sporhase* required. Nonetheless, even though the courts and certain Administration officials recognized that funding for water research, comprehensive state planning, and water diversion facilities were the price for state primacy, Reagan's Office of Management and Budget continued its budgetary assault on precisely these items.

The Administration's sentiments aside, New Mexico steadfastly pursued judicial and legislative redress for its now-compromised water regulatory regime. Appealing the *El Paso* decision, the state argued that Bratton defined "human survival" too narrowly. It meant more than "water sufficient for drinking, cooking, bathing, and fire protection." *Sporhase*, they contended, also permitted arid states to favor their own citizens in limited ways to ensure environmental, economic, and agricultural protection.[30]

Simultaneously, New Mexicans revised their export statute in ways imposing substantial and costly additional data analyses on both potential exporters and state regulators. Henceforth, New Mexico's state engineer had to consider the following before issuing permits for groundwater exports: (1) New Mexico's available water supply, (2) state demands on these supplies, (3) existing water shortages, (4) whether targeted supplies could alleviate water shortages in other parts of New Mexico, (5) what supplies were available to the applicant in his or her own state, and (6) the demands placed on water supplies in the applicant's home state. Predictably, El Paso countered that the "clear intent and effect" of the new law was economic protectionism. Its provisions were not narrowly tailored to protect the health and safety of New Mexicans, but instead to limit "exports to keep water within the state for irrigation agriculture."[31]

With $500,000 in legal and hydrological study fees already incurred by El Paso, and with fellow Texans pledging further financial support, the New Mexico legislature appropriated an additional $250,000 to continue the state's defense effort. It also commissioned a Water Law Study Committee to assess the policy and administrative implications of El Paso's legal victory. Ultimately, that Committee recommended: (1) imposing a five-year moratorium on groundwater drilling in the Mesilla and Hueco bolsons; (2) appropriating $500,000 for badly needed hydrological studies in that region; (3) negotiating an interstate compact with Texas to divide surface waters south of Elephant Butte Dam; and (4) initiating a two-year study to see if the state should appropriate to itself all or part of its unappropriated groundwater.[32]

Judge Bratton's eagerly awaited ruling in mid-1984 on New Mexico's appeal allowed each litigant to "declare victory and retreat." More important, however, it settled the lawsuit. Both El Paso and New Mexico—staggering under economic downturns and Reagan's devolution of federal responsibilities to the states— waived their rights to appeal.[33] While Bratton declared constitutional New Mexico's revised export statute as it applied to new wells, he ruled it unconstitutional to apply the criteria to the transfer or sale of existing water rights. The latter, he maintained, could hinder interstate commerce. Thus, a window of opportunity, albeit slight, still remained for El Paso. Current users could sell their existing water rights to Texans if they desired. Moreover, Bratton left the door further ajar for El Paso by declaring New Mexico's moratorium unconstitutional. Wrote Bratton, its "illegitimate protectionist purpose" rendered the moratorium prima facie discriminatory.

Even with New Mexico's right established to restrict groundwater exports, the state engineer's implementation of the new law still had to pass constitutional muster. Plainly, Reynolds could not discriminate against El Paso's applications when applying the six criteria.[34] This process, of course, promised to be a long one; intervenors already had filed over twenty-seven hundred challenges to El Paso's applications. To facilitate this process, the disputants agreed to hold hearings in two phases: one, on the 60 Hueco Bolson permits, was to begin in 18 months (May 1986), and a second, on the remaining 266 applications in the Mesilla Bolson, was scheduled for three years hence (November 1987). These delays, it seems, were unavoidable; attorneys could not prepare their cases adequately until the U.S. Geological Survey completed Carruthers' long-promised hydrological studies. In turn, most predicted that these hearings were preliminaries to the main event:

losers challenging the state engineer's decisions in court. Thus, by mid-1986, a backlog of applications existed for the two bolsons totaling 1,473 permits, or a total of 858,581 acre-feet of water per year. Frustrated, New Mexico expanded the scope of the conflict, mounting a second, two-front assault before the U.S. Congress and its own state legislature.

FROM MARKET REGULATOR TO MARKET PARTICIPANT?

The Congressional Front

Over the years, Congress periodically had grown impatient with the states' inability or unwillingness to resolve interstate ground-water disputes among themselves. And prompted by decisions like *Sporhase,* the coal slurry pipeline, and the RGB dispute, the issue resurfaced in the early 1980s with New Mexican politicos leading the fray. Their argument was that *Sporhase* ensured that immediate water demands by covetous neighbors would stymie state efforts to plan for the future needs of their citizenry. In Domenici's words, "If someone can prove a present need in another state, they can take your water."[35] Likewise, Senator Schmitt maintained that: "The proven interrelationship between some groundwater and surface water in situations like . . . the Mesilla Bolson is too important an issue for the Congress to continue to ignore, particularly when an interstate river is involved."[36] The congressional delegation's proposal: federal legislation to prohibit all groundwater exports in the absence of an interstate compact, an act of Congress, or a Supreme Court decision.

As noted, Reagan's appointees at the Justice and Interior Departments saw the risks of federal legislation ultimately outweighing the benefits. Pleaded Carruthers, "We don't want to have a federal water law in the western states. . . . Think about it, when you lean on the federal government to solve your problems, they usually pass one law that affects everybody equally," regardless of circumstances.[37] In contrast, Lujan and several Western governors portrayed the New Mexico congressional delegation's bill as only an extension of present law: Since interstate compacts, Supreme Court orders, and congressional designations already drive surface water issues, "We are not doing anything new except expanding from surface water to include underground water. . . . Legislative action is the best way to handle the dispute."[38] Unpersuaded, however, the Reagan Administration offered no formal support for Lujan's bill.

Thus, in the end, New Mexico's hopes for congressional redress were dashed. New Mexicans, it seemed, could rely only on their own wits, ingenuity, and finances to thwart water raids by their neighbors. Thus, with interstate water negotiations with Texas stalemated, and with stopgap measures instituted, New Mexico turned to developing more long-term solutions to its groundwater problems.

The State Legislative Front

As Stephen Williams has argued, by the 1980s the doctrine of beneficial use was a major cause of waste in water resource management: "One [could] acquire a property right in water only by applying it to a 'beneficial use,' and in no state [did] reservation of water for future use qualify as a beneficial use."[39] Certainly, early developments in the RGB dispute vividly illustrated the agenda-setting, economic, and environmental consequences of this regulatory philosophy. Because existing water doctrine, in effect, considered storage "wasteful," most states defined groundwater issues in terms of augmenting supplies and maximizing use, not controlling demand.

In the wake of El Paso, New Mexico swiftly amended state law to allow municipalities to set water aside for future use. In response, of course, El Paso threatened a lawsuit challenging the law's constitutionality as a "legal fiction," one designed solely to thwart water exports to Texas. Clearly, a comprehensive and less legally assailable approach was needed lest economic development in the lower RGB atrophy for years to come.

In 1983, you will recall, the New Mexico Water Law Study Committee decided to evaluate the pros and cons of the state's becoming a water market participant rather than a regulator. By 1986, the results were in. The Committee concluded that state appropriation of unappropriated groundwater "could ensure a water future for New Mexico by assisting the various regions of the state to plan and control their water futures."[40] The Committee's reasoning was that no "trick legislation" was possible to protect New Mexico's groundwater from interstate water markets created by *Sporhase*. But a state legitimately could enter that market as a participant by appropriating and developing its own groundwater supplies. To do so, of course, New Mexico would have to make long-term, substantial, and coordinated investments in water studies, extraction, and diversion equipment. But because the state was no longer a market regulator, the U.S. Constitution's commerce clause did not apply. New Mexico could decide like any other seller if, to whom, and on what terms it might sell its groundwater.

The Committee also noted a variety of other benefits from appropriating groundwater, most especially the revenue produced by water sales or leases. Indeed, some saw in appropriating the water an antidote for Reagan's relentless assault on funding for water research and development projects in the West. For example, the value of New Mexico's unappropriated groundwater supplies was between $33 and $38 billion (compared to the $22.7 billion value of its oil reserves).[41] Consequently, sales or leases could help fund engineering assistance, water rights acquisition, and distribution systems for the state's financially strapped areas. Besides, New Mexicans might better afford badly needed and extremely expensive hydrological studies, research otherwise jeopardized by the U.S. Geological Survey's expecting "major financial [and manpower] constraints on its [research] activities in the future" from the Reagan Administration.[42]

Let us be clear, however. Entering the market as a participant was neither routine, inexpensive, nor guaranteed to squelch cries of "economic protectionism." Evolving case law, for instance, established four constitutional criteria for adequately demonstrating state ownership: A state had to (1) formally decide to purchase unappropriated groundwater rights; (2) be willing to spend its own money to do so; (3) develop a concrete, long-range plan or plans for using these supplies beneficially over a specific time period; and (4) demonstrate that state appropriation was not a ruse or "legal fiction" intended to regulate groundwater indirectly. Fundamentally, appropriation statutes had to pass constitutional muster on criteria designed to prevent states from using their power as water participants as a "disguise" for economic protectionism.[43]

These caveats aside, in 1986 the New Mexico legislature adopted in principle the concept of state appropriation of groundwater. Actual funding, however, was provided only for regional groups to begin groundwater planning in their areas. In essence, New Mexico's legislature embraced the idea of a "state partnership" in regional planning financed by water marketing, but failed to finance regional water development or diversion systems. True, it initiated regional planning processes, which continue to function today. However, little else occurred during the Reagan years to advance New Mexico's shift from market regulator to market participant.

Four factors helped stall this initiative. First, expenses associated with state purchase of existing water rights proved exorbitant. Second, key actors feared an inordinate centralization of state bureaucratic power in central planning units. Third, officials disagreed over which administrative unit should serve this powerful function. And finally, spasms of serious "rural-urban warfare" surfaced over intrastate water transfers. Thus, with the planning, feasibility, and political plausibility of interbasin transfers critical to state groundwater appropriation, intrastate opposition to water transfers was debilitating. Likewise, it boded ill for the state's ability to meet *Sporhase* criteria in future court battles over water exports. In particular, New Mexico would be challenged to demonstrate that it was serious about supplying "conserved" groundwater to water-parched areas within its borders.

As the Reagan Administration prepared to leave office in 1988, the RGB disputants were back in federal district court. This time, however, El Paso was challenging New Mexico State Engineer Reynolds' decision in 1987 to deny groundwater export permits to the city. Reynolds' rationale against El Paso was that the city had inadequately demonstrated that its projected shortages over the next 40 years were sufficiently severe to warrant interstate water transfers.

Ironically, this latest stalemate arose only after internecine rifts among New Mexicans dashed hopes for a negotiated interstate settlement. Specifically, the year before, New Mexico Attorney General Bardacke, lawyers for Las Cruces, and elements of New Mexico's irrigated agriculture industry began conciliatory talks with El Paso's legal staff. Even pecan magnate William Stahmann, an early, fervent, and vocal opponent of negotiation as the decade began, had agreed the time for compromise had arrived. His group had concluded that evolving water law ensured to some degree the inevitable success of El Paso's water requests. Thus, negotiation, not judicial fiat, could best assure New Mexicans a say in how much groundwater El Paso received. In Stahmann's words, "If we go to hearings, we don't know what we'll get. . . . El Paso may be able to get enough water to impair our water rights and put us out of business."[44]

Alas for conciliation, not all New Mexicans shared Stahmann's sentiments. When reports surfaced that "secret" interstate negotiations might allow El Paso to receive barely one-fifth of its original water demands, Governor Anaya, Dona Ana County, and the Elephant Butte Irrigation District (EBID) loudly balked. Proposing that "New Mexico . . . fight El Paso water well applications all the way to the Supreme Court, if necessary," EBID officials maintained that negotiations "mean compromise and compromise means surrender—El Paso has nothing to give."[45]

Postscript

If the regulatory conundrum in the RGB looked depressingly familiar upon the eve of the Bush Administration, one could not say the same about federal water policy in the West generally. Its metes and bounds were shifting profoundly—and rapidly. In 1986, the Western Governors Association (WGA) called for drastic changes in the region's water policy, changes purported to "fine-tune" for efficiency the West's water laws, policies, and management. A free-market approach, by promoting intrastate and interbasin water transfers, could eliminate policies discouraging conservation and efficient use.[46] To these ends, the governors proposed a task force of WGA members, the Western States Water Council, and the Interior Department. Their proposal: to develop and implement critical, market-based water policy changes at federal, state, and local government levels.

As Interior Undersecretary Ann McLaughlin put it, those changes shifted policy in a way that shook "older Reclamation hands (the dam builders) down to their 'water boots'." Noting the acceptability of using water markets to encourage the transfer or exchange of water supplies both within and across state boundaries, McLaughlin outlined Interior's "new" role as water manager, rather than provider. Her comments were indicative of how the Reagan Administration now recognized the historical error of its supply-side management ways:

> Although some developable water supplies can still be tapped for the next decade or two, it is obvious that presently available supplies will need to be reallocated to accommodate new needs. Allowing market forces to influence that allocation has many advantages. . . . One of the ways that the market can work most effectively is through voluntary water exchanges. Where willing buyers and sellers of developed water desire Interior's assistance, we are available to assist. . . . We in the Department are aware of the complexities voluntary water exchanges present, particularly given state water rights primacy and the body of Federal and State law which exists. However, our aim is *partnership*—to be a part of the solution, not the problem. . . . Reclamation, the Geological Survey, and the Fish and Wildlife Service [will] assist in providing data on the potential for an impact of voluntary water exchanges. . . . Interior would be pleased to provide the level of support which is envisioned [in the governors'resolution].[47]

To sum up, the states' rights rhetoric proffered by the "first generation" of Reagan appointees at Interior (Watt, Carruthers, and Clark)—while still bandied about—had in fact taken a back seat to the "second generation's" (Hodel, McLaughlin) emphasis on market-based solutions to Western water problems. In effect, the second generation tacitly acknowledged the changing water regulatory realities of the West. These were important realities that both generations had intentionally or unintentionally abetted with their supply-side management philosophy. For southern New Mexicans, fears enunciated in the early 1980s were disastrously prescient: Western governors and the Interior Department were on the verge of "exporting" to New Mexico both the Texas regulatory regime and its water priorities (i.e., giving preference to those uses and users that procure the highest economic return). Rather than protecting, nurturing, or bolstering the state's primacy in water regulation, the Administration's policies had combined with evolving case law to—wittingly or unwittingly—maintain New Mexico and other states' vulnerability to water raids by their neighbors.

With evolving case law making costly water research critical, with economic reasons alone insufficient for justifying groundwater transfer restrictions, and with scant hope for financial backing from the Reagan Administration, states such as New Mexico turned to the market for long-term solutions. Some, such as Wyoming and Montana, appropriated all unappropriated water within their boundaries. Others, like South Dakota, declared water exports for coal slurry pipelines a "beneficial use." In return, slurry developers promised to pay nearly $9 million in fees, all earmarked for state water development projects. Yet, in doing so, each state had to make substantial capital investments in water planning, extraction, and distribution systems. Put bluntly by critics, each state joined the "race to the bottom of the aquifer" in order to "protect" their water from premature depletion by outsiders.

CONCLUSION

How well were the Administration's short-term supply-side management tactics linked to its strategic goals in groundwater resource policy? Not well at all, if the goals of states' rights advocates within the Administration are the criteria. OMB cutbacks, deferrals, and rescissions in federal funding for water development and research, as well as the Administration's position on *Sporhase*, spawned two primary responses by the states. First, they embraced both intra- and interstate market reallocations of existing supplies. Second, they sought alternative market-based ways to finance water transfers, research, planning, and development projects. These, in turn, made participating in markets eminently more attractive to beleaguered state officials than regulating them.

Theoretically, of course, states adopting this approach could deflect commerce clause scrutiny, while using market proceeds to finance water development and research projects. In the process, water could flow unfettered by regional and state boundaries to its "highest economic use." Moreover, possibilities arose of overcoming the dysfunctional aspects of a prior appropriation system geared more toward rural than urban and industrial use. Yet as the sun set on the Reagan era, formidable political, social, and economic obstacles to state appropriation and water markets prevailed. Put simply, states were as vulnerable as ever to water raids by their neighbors. In fact, their position had deteriorated some-what: Reagan's legacy of water research and development cuts left them distinctly vulnerable to commerce clause challenge.

But what if one takes the Administration's strategic goal to be water marketing as proposed by devotees of the New Resource Economics? How well linked were its actions to that goal? Again, the analysis is unflattering. A glance at evolving case law reveals that to survive judicial scrutiny, funding for state water plans had to precede, not follow, groundwater appropriation schemes. Sim-ilarly, according to "second-generation" appointees like Ann McLaughlin, the Administration neglected at its peril federal fund-ing for accurate, timely, and unbiased hydrological research. One could not expect state officials to act without assessing the poten-tial for, impact of, and mitigation efforts required by water market transfers on the scale envisioned for the West.

Turning to the bureaupolitical dynamics of this case, one is struck by how closely the scope, intensity, and contagiousness of the conflict resemble the virulence occasioned by the Carter Ad-ministration's efforts to cut drastically the number of cattle grazed on public lands (see Chapter 5). What is more, these dynamics dwarf those exhibited in the BLM-MMS, Elena-Gallegos, and Rangeland Improvement Policy experiences. True, the cases offer different perspectives on the administrative presidency. Grazing cuts directly sparked the Rio Puerco imbroglio. In contrast, Rea-gan's water policies framed the decision-making context for dispu-tants grappling with *Sporhase's* implications for state regulation. Still, in both instances, the combat grew so nonnegotiable that the disputants willingly turned to the courts and Congress to settle *aspects* of the conflict (e.g., the constitutionality of statutes and the state engineer's handling of permit applications). Nevertheless, while individual actors spoke of doing so, all could not agree on persistently pushing for ultimate judicial or congressional resolu-tion of the crux of the debate: the dormant commerce clause issue. All ultimately feared losing control of the issue to outsiders or opponents.

What accounts for these bureaupolitical dynamics? Again, the Rio Puerco and Rio Grande Basin disputes have one thing in com-mon. Both involved policy initiatives premised on "technological breakthroughs" (SVIM and state market participation, rather than regulation). Significantly, while long-debated among specialists, these initiatives were launched abruptly without consensus within relevant policy communities on their legitimacy. What is more, public disagreement over the RGB dispute paralleled private schisms within the Reagan Administration itself. Fueled by the diverse perspectives of and bureaucratic politics occasioned by states' righters, New Resource economists, and politicos within the Justice and Interior Departments, these divisions highlight a persistent constraint on the administrative presidency. Specifically, attaining either ideological purity or policy consensus among appointees is nowhere as simple or as threatening as either proponents or critics of the administrative presidency imply.

At this point, we have witnessed the disparate dynamics of four separate Reagan Administration experiences in New Mexico. Yet we still have not exhausted the types of bureaupolitical dynamics and paradoxes wrought by Reaganites using the administrative presidency to reorient natural resource policy. To see how and why this is true, we turn next to the debilitating conflict aroused by the Reagan Administration's efforts to drastically accelerate coal leasing in New Mexico's San Juan Basin.

CHAPTER 8

Wilderness, King Coal, and the San Juan Basin

As John Leshy suggests, three primary wilderness issues faced pro-energy development Reaganites when they took office.[1] First, to what extent would they allow new mineral leasing activities in existing areas of the National Wilderness Preservation System (NWPS)? Second, what kinds of intrusions—timber harvesting, road building, mineral development—would they permit in areas Congress was considering for wilderness designation? And finally, what recommendations would they make to Congress in the way of including new wilderness areas in the NWPS?

Angered, primed for combat, and ready for redress, the energy industry rejoiced at the prospect of a Reagan presidency. And if judged solely on effort, the Reagan Administration did little to disappoint developers. Upon taking office, Reagan appointees wielded with dispatch the tools of the administrative presidency in ways designed to satisfy the most virulent anti-preservationist or most fervent energy developer. As with Reagan's energy policy generally, however, the results of this effort were lilliputian compared to the sound and fury which attended them.

This chapter suggests why this happened by examining the Reagan Administration's attempt to increase coal leasing dramatically in the San Juan Basin (SJB) of northwestern New Mexico. With the SJB rich in coal, wilderness study areas, paleontological treasure, and disputed Navajo Indian land claims, this case well-illustrates the dilemmas posed to policy reorientation by BLM's multiple-use mandate under the Federal Land Policy and Management Act (FLPMA). It affords as well a propitious window for observing the bureaucratic politics of the administrative presiden-

193

cy, and for seeing how well- or ill-suited the Administration's tactics were to its strategic goals.

THE PAST AS PROLOGUE, OR, "THERE'S BLACK GOLD IN THEM THAR HILLS!"

To paraphrase Thomas Hobbes, the politics of federal coal leasing over the past two decades has been "nasty, brutish, and short" on compromise. Given Interior's essentially reactive posture prior to 1970, however, this was not always true. Granted, the Mineral Leasing Act of 1920 stemmed from controversy over illicit and speculative mining practices. As such, it replaced land sales with tract leasing as the primary conveyance vehicle for public land exploration. Yet Interior still processed lease applications routinely and noncontroversially until the 1970s. This, of course, was true because the Department paid little attention to the amount of coal reserves leased or to the environmental consequences of leasing.

All this changed, however, in the 1970s. As noted in Chapter 1, coal demand burgeoned during the 1960s and 1970s. With the most readily recoverable coal supplies on private properties tapped already, and with low-sulfur Western coal seen as more environmentally benign, pressures to lease coal-rich federal lands in the region blossomed accordingly. Initially, Interior's response was generous, increasing the amount of federal acreage under lease by tenfold between 1945 and 1970. By 1971, however, critics reproached leasees as animated more by greed than any desire to increase energy supplies. They argued that while the amount of federal lands open to coal leasing grew tenfold in the postwar decades, annual coal production actually fell, from 10 million to 7.4 million tons. What is more, an astounding 90 percent of those lands produced no coal whatsoever.[2]

Persuaded that leasees were taking advantage of lax federal enforcement of "due diligence" standards (i.e., standards requiring that coal be mined in a timely fashion), President Nixon's Interior Secretary, Rogers Morton, imposed a moratorium on all nonemergency coal lease sales. He also barred new prospecting permits and limited new leasing to areas adjacent to existing mines and necessary to keep them operating. Conceived originally as a two-year hiatus for crafting a long-term coal-leasing strategy, Morton's moratorium ultimately survived for ten years as both the Ford and Carter administrations tried to draft plans acceptable to environmental and industry interests. Indeed, during the Nixon-Ford years, Interior issued just ten leases covering approximately 30,000 acres, only seven of which had produced coal by the end of 1976.[3]

At the same time, energy developers criticized the informal understanding throughout the Nixon, Ford, and Carter presidencies that coal exploration and leasing were inimical to wilderness values and unnecessary given alternative supplies. Operationally, this understanding meant that Interior Secretaries in each administration eschewed leasing not only in designated wilderness areas, but also in wilderness study areas. Thus, the rub for the energy industry. While the Wilderness Act of 1964 allowed restricted leasing activity to continue in designated wilderness areas, it stipulated that Interior could recognize no new mining rights after December 1983. In effect, Congress had created a twenty-year window of opportunity for new mineral development, after which no new leasing could proceed. Thus, by eschewing wilderness exploration during the twenty-year window, prior administrations were effectively precluding it forever on nearly 25 million acres of public lands. Distraught, energy producers and their allies routinely alleged that Interior was violating congressional intent. The Wilderness Act, they maintained, required the Department to encourage vigorous exploration on federal lands before the window closed in late 1983. Interior officials countered, however, that leasing was a discretionary option, one the Department chose not to exercise under the circumstances.

Likewise, tensions also grew as Interior implemented a third, more long-term component of Morton's initiative. Synoptic in design and largely abandoning the government's reactive posture to market forces, Morton's policy was twofold. First, Interior had to develop a comprehensive planning system for ascertaining the location, size, and timing of future coal leases. Second, careerists had to prepare a programmatic environmental impact statement (EIS) for Interior's national coal-leasing plan. So charged, Interior released in 1974 a draft EIS for a new coal-leasing system, the Energy Minerals Allocation Recommendation System. Known as EMARS I, Morton's system pleased neither friend nor foe of coal leasing. Environmentalists saw EMARS I as too sketchy and ambiguous, and too focused on new leasing when many existing tracts lay undeveloped. By contrast, Interior's emphasis on government planning rather than industry initiative most animated the concerns of energy companies.

Trying to address these disparate complaints, Interior issued its final programmatic EIS for coal leasing in 1975. A consensus-building effort, the report tried to navigate the Scylla of ecological destruction and the Charybdis of bureaucratic torpor in a new plan, EMARS II. Thus, to placate industry, EMARS II gave more weight to the companies' proposals for site leasing. Simultaneously, to placate environmentalists, the plan enhanced ways for citizens to weigh more systematically into the decision-making process. Henceforth, Interior would entertain lease proposals, with industry giving supporting documentation as to where, when, and how much it proposed to lease. Then Department analysts would develop land-use plans and perform environmental analyses, resolve resource conflicts (e.g., leasing versus habitat or ranching uses), and proceed to lease environmentally suitable tracts.

To its chagrin, however, the Ford Administration found itself in court that same year defending EMARS II. In *NRDC v. Hughes,* environmentalists charged that Interior's final EIS on coal leasing failed to do three things: (1) describe EMARS II adequately, (2) fully consider more environmentally benign alternatives to energy leasing, and (3) sufficiently assess if additional leasing were necessary. Persuaded, the D.C. District Court remanded the EIS to Interior for reformulation with this proviso: The Department could not in the meantime "take any steps whatsoever, directly or indirectly" to implement the Secretary's coal-leasing plan. By then, however, the Carter Administration was in office and began a *de novo* review of the issues at hand.

Chastened already by an activist judiciary dissecting its leasing procedures, Interior next found its culture, procedures, and planning capabilities the subject of both congressional and presidential scrutiny. Specifically, in 1977 Congress reformulated in more environmentally sensitive ways the statutory base for federal coal leasing, enacting the Federal Coal Leasing Amendments Act (FCLAA) of 1976, the Surface Mining Control and Reclamation Act (SMCRA) of 1977, the Department of Energy Reorganization Act of 1977, and the 1977 Clean Air Act Amendments. Simultaneously, President Carter took a series of executive actions to promote further the "greening" of Interior. For example, in his 1977 National Energy Plan, in his subsequent Environmental Message, and in instructions to Secretary of Interior Andrus that same year, Carter stressed that the rush to "energy independence" did not mean sacrificing environmental values. Wrote Carter to Andrus, "manage the coal-leasing program to assure that it can respond to reasonable production goals by leasing only those areas where mining is environmentally acceptable and compatible with other land uses."[4] Likewise, he ordered the Secretary to apply the same criteria before increasing production at existing leases, including applications for Preference Right Leases (or PRLAs).[5]

In response, Andrus ordered a full-scale interagency review of federal coal policy, set up a review committee consisting of all Interior Assistant Secretaries and the Department's Solicitor General, and created the Office of Coal, Planning, and Coordination at the department level to coordinate the task. The Committee proposed scrapping EMARS II and its projections as incompatible with President Carter's goals, indefensible in court, and outdated by new statutes. But what to offer in its place? After two years of analysis, circumspection, and consensus building, Interior released in 1979 a Coal Management Plan (CMP) which served during the first term of the Reagan presidency as the basis for the first coal lease sales in over a decade.

As the left side of Table 8–1 reveals, Andrus' CMP offered a comprehensive, elaborate, and time-consuming leasing process, one premised on complex planning systems, market analyses, National Environmental Protection Act procedures, and Regional Coal Teams (RCTs). At its heart was a three-tiered analysis of current and projected market conditions, with the RCTs a vehicle for consulting, coordinating, and balancing the perspectives on these issues of the Interior Department, other federal agencies, state governments, and Native American tribes.

Before deciding to engage these actors in negotiations, the Bu-

TABLE 8–1
Comparison of Andrus (1979) and Watt (1982/83)
Coal-Leasing Regulations

1979 Rules	1982/1983 Rules

A. *Land-Use Planning*

No special call for coal resource information issued during land-use planning.

BLM will issue a call for coal resource information during land-use planning to aid in early consideration of lands with coal potential.

Leasing considerations confined to areas with high or moderate coal development potential.

The restriction to considering only lands with high or moderate development potential is removed, allowing all areas with coal development potential to be considered.

Purpose: To obtain more and better coal resource data earlier in the planning process and to attain the flexibility to meet the coal production needs of a region.

B. *Leasing Levels*

Leasing targets based on Department of Energy projections of national energy needs (demand for production and other factors) in a target year approximately 10 years later.

Leasing levels will be based on various factors that may include land-use planning data, regional and national market information, coal resource information, and advice from affected state governors.

The Regional Coal Team (RCT) recommends to the Secretary a single leasing target, usually within a narrow range.

After receiving alternative leasing levels and a recommended leasing level from a Regional Coal Team, Secretary will set a leasing level in a broadly defined range.

Purpose: Leasing levels represent a more market-oriented approach to approximating need for leasing than the leasing target approach with its attempt to closely match coal lease supply to projected demand for coal production for the target year approximately 10 years later.

(continued)

TABLE 8–1 (*Continued*)

1979 Rules	1982/1983 Rules

C. *Presale Consultation*

The Secretary consulted in writing with governors in states where lease sales were proposed before making a coal lease sale decision.

The Secretary will consult in writing as before but also publish in the Federal Register his reasons for accepting or rejecting governor recommendations.

Purpose: To show the Department's commitment to coordination and consultation with the states that bear the impact and obtain much of the financial benefits of federal coal leasing.

D. *Unsuitability Criteria*

The rules established a series of 20 unsuitability criteria to be applied to lands being considered for leasing, to PRLAs, and to existing leases.

Unsuitability criteria will no longer be applied to existing leases during land-use planning, but the mandatory criteria under SMCRA will still be applied to these leases during mine plan review.

The leasing of federally owned coal for surface mining prohibited if coal overlain by districts, sites, buildings, structures, or objects included or eligible for inclusion on the National Register of Historic Places.

Automatic prohibition against coal leasing removed for eligible properties. National Register sites are still protected.

Purpose: To eliminate an unneeded regulation, because the application on existing leases nearly always postponed until mine plan review. The criterion conforms with Office of Surface Mining Reclamation and Enforcement criteria for designation of lands as unsuitable during mine plan review and reflects court decisions on SMCRA.

(*continued*)

TABLE 8–1 (*Continued*)

1979 Rules	1982/1983 Rules
E. *Emergency Leasing*	
Lease applicants meet certain criteria before bidding at emergency lease sales.	Requirements eliminated that (a) lease applicant have a mine in production 2 years before filing an application; (b) lessee be restricted to one emergency lease per operation; (c) competition for leases sold under the emergency criteria be limited only to bidders meeting those criteria.
State governors notified through the RCT of pending applications for coal lease sales.	State governors doubly notified of pending lease-by-application actions, through the RCT and separately.

Purpose: To follow the intent of Congress that all coal be leased competitively and to present more evidence of the Department's commitment to work with the states.

F. *Surface Owner's Consent*	
Regular appeal channel through Interior Board of Land Appeals (IBLA) used by surface owners determined to be unqualified under section 714 of SMCRA.	Surface owner appeals go to the BLM state director and then to the BLM Director; surface owners cannot appeal to IBLA.

Purpose: To speed up the decision process.

G. *Alluvial Valley Floor Exchanges*	
Alluvial valley floor fee coal exchanges discretionary.	Alluvial valley floor fee coal exchanges mandatory rather than discretionary.

Purpose: To provide stronger recognition of the rights of lessees and owners of alluvial valley floors. The changes make the regulations consistent with the court's decision in *Texaco and NCA v. Andrus.*

(*continued*)

TABLE 8–1 (*Continued*)

1979 Rules	1982/1983 Rules

H. *Lease Sales*

Competitive lease sales held by sealed bid only or sealed bid followed by oral auction.	All competitive lease sales held by sealed bid only.
Minimum acceptable bid $25 per acre.	Minimum acceptable bid $100 per acre.

Purpose: To provide more assurance of the public's receipt of fair market value for the coal resource.

I. *Diligence*

All nonproducing coal leases issued before August 4, 1976, the effective date of Federal Coal Leasing Amendments Act (FCLAA) had to be producing coal in commercial quantities by June 1, 1986.	Pre-FCLAA lessees will have 10 years from the date of the first lease readjustment after August 4, 1976, to be producing coal in commercial quantities.

Purpose: To address concerns that the 1979 rule making was a unilateral adverse change in fundamental lease terms (diligent development obligations) and had a poor legal basis to be enforceable before readjusting those leases. The 1986 deadline set forth in the 1976 regulations as the time requiring production for all pre-FCLAA leases may have resulted in many leases failing to meet diligence simply because the market could not absorb that much production by 1986. The Department would be left in the situation of cancelling leases that could not meet diligence in 1986 and then face a shortfall in federal lease development in the early 1990s. Now, all leases will not be due to produce by 1986, but will be spread out between 1986 and 2005.

reau of Land Management had to complete its own Resource Management Plan listing acceptable resource uses. To qualify as such, coal leasing had to satisfy four criteria: (1) coal reserves in the area were economically promising; (2) the tracts met all 20 environmental protection criteria identified by the Secretary as rendering a site suitable for development; (3) other resource uses (e.g., recreation or ranching) were inferior in value to coal mining; and (4) insignificant numbers of qualified surface owners opposed coal mining.

Passing muster on these dimensions, regional activity planning then could commence. First, Interior issued calls to developers to nominate tracts for leasing. Next, BLM established leasing levels; delineated tracts for leasing; and ranked, selected, and scheduled them for sale. Informing these decisions, of course, were the decision-making processes of the Regional Coal Teams. In that process, the RCTs considered long-range market analyses for the nation to see if supply and demand justified new leasing. Next, they assessed regional market analyses to determine alternative leasing levels and their consequences. Then the RCTs used current tract-marketability analyses to see if potential leasees were still likely to purchase leases if offered. Finally, the RCTs recommended which tracts should be offered and when, with the final decision left to the Interior Secretary. Informed in this fashion, the Final Environmental Statement issued by Andrus offered six preferred leasing levels and locations, listing Powder River Basin first and New Mexico's San Juan Basin second, in priority. Incorporating a 25 percent "fudge factor" as a hedge against unexpectedly high demand, Andrus then proceeded to schedule 1981–1982 sales totaling 1.5 billion tons of coal.

While ostensibly reconciling the competing claims of disparate public interest groups, the energy industry, and affected state governments, Andrus' program was much more. More precisely, it reflected Interior's herculean effort to reconcile a series of statutory initiatives crafted to dampen the environmental impact of coal development across the country. Not the least of these were the Federal Coal Leasing Amendments Act of 1976, the Federal Land Policy and Management Act, and the Surface Mining Control and

Reclamation Act of 1977. In the process, however, Andrus' effort resulted in a complex, computer-model-driven, command-control regulatory structure, one which contrasted starkly with Ronald Reagan's proposed market-driven agenda for natural resources.

Computer forecasts, of course, are only as good as the assumptions underlying their calculations. Thus, Andrus' initial goals had but a brief half-life. Indeed, as Interior economist Robert Nelson caustically put it, "It is fair to say that central planning in this case turned out to be more like writing fiction than real planning."[6] Unstable market conditions quickly undermined Interior's assumptions, producing in their wake equally unstable production goals. In fact, before leasing actually resumed in 1981, Interior switched its targets at least three times to accommodate OPEC oil price increases, reduced electricity demand, natural gas price shifts, and diminished prospects for synthetic fuels. Thus, by mid-1982, Interior had managed to lease only about one-third (473 million tons) of Andrus' original 1.5-billion-ton target.

Likewise, Andrus' approach to coal leasing on surrounding wilderness lands struck pro-development interests as positive, but too little and too late. As mentioned, the Interior Department, the Forest Service, the Defense Department, and other agencies implemented the Wilderness Act of 1964 in ways barring or heavily restricting leasing—be it oil, gas, coal, strategic mineral, or hard rock mining in nature. Indeed, during the first ten years of the 20-year window afforded by the Wilderness Act, they declared nearly two-thirds of all public lands off-limits to mining and mineral exploration and leasing. Thus, early moves by the Carter Administration significantly buoyed industry spirits. For example, under FLPMA's charge to review existing wilderness study areas, BLM released sizeable amounts of roadless area from wilderness designation. In fact, so controversial were many of these decisions that environmentalists repeatedly attacked the Bureau for selling out to the energy industry.

Still, in the longer term, the Carter Administration reaped its full share of opprobrium from energy developers. Most of them felt that a president unabashedly courting environmentalist support could not be trusted, whatever his words or short-term actions. More trustworthy was Ronald Reagan, a fellow Westerner running on an energy platform touting "production, production, production."

Obviously, the supply-side management machinations of Reagan's appointees recounted in Chapters 3 and 4 did much to please energy developers and arouse the ire of environmentalists, Western politicians, and Native American tribes. So too did Secretary Watt's efforts to amend administratively the substance of Andrus' Coal Management Plan. (The right side of Table 8–1 compares these amendments to Andrus' 1979 Plan.) Announced in 1983, after an 18-month internal review, Watt's new rules for leasing (1) substantially downgraded the status of the Regional Coal Teams, (2) based Interior's selection of coal tracts primarily on industry preferences, (3) deferred BLM land-use planning to later in the leasing process, and (4) amended Interior's twenty "unsuitability" criteria to decrease the likelihood that tracts might automatically disqualify for leasing. Outraged, environmental groups challenged Watt and Burford in court, claiming the new rules violated FCLAA, FLPMA, and SMCRA.[7] Similarly, in Congress, a shift to "police patrol" oversight rapidly ensued amid Watt's caustic comments, documented charges of "fire-sale" leasing in the Powder River Basin, and softening markets for the region's "black gold."

However, even after Watt's hasty exit in 1983, congressional and judicial scrutiny of the Interior Department's coal-leasing activities dissipated not a wit. For their part, Watt's successors— William Clark and Donald Hodel—continued to press a robust pro-development agenda upon the nation, albeit one less massive in scale, less confrontational in style, and less ideological in approach. Too, both incorporated within their initiatives most of the Linowes Commission's more environmentally oriented recommendations. Nevertheless, the legacy of distrust and supply-side management Watt bequeathed his successors ultimately helped foil coal leasing throughout Reagan's tenure in Washington.

According to a 1986 report prepared for Secretary Hodel, the time required to complete planning and environmental analyses deferred by his predecessors precluded new coal sales until late 1987, at the earliest. Moreover, for those tracts farthest behind in the process, leasing was unlikely until 1989. In turn, and under the best of circumstances, these would not be productive leases until after the year 2000. To understand why this happened, the Reagan Administration's coal-leasing experience in the San Juan Basin is most instructive.

THE DEREGULATORY PARADOX IN THE SAN JUAN BASIN, OR, "KEEP YOUR GREED-INFESTED CLAWS OUT OF THE BISTI"

The San Juan Basin (SJB) encompasses 1.9 million acres of land and mineral resources nestled snugly within the northwest corner of New Mexico.[8] Known popularly as the "checkerboard lands" for its complex ownership patterns, the SJB is a unique cornucopia of natural, cultural, and recreational resources. Most significant among these for the Reagan Administration's initiatives were the region's (1) semi-arid climate, (2) internationally renowned cache of 600-million-year-old paleontological treasure, (3) uniquely rich Anasazi and Navajo cultural artifacts dating back ten thousand years or more, (4) disputed Navajo Indian claims to over two million acres of SJB land, (5) undisputed tribal claims to 35,000 acres in the state under the Navajo-Hopi Relocation Act, and (6) three wilderness study areas—the Bisti Badlands, De-na-zin, and Ah-shi-sle-pah wilderness study areas (WSAs).

As Ronald Reagan assumed the presidency, an equally formidable array of energy development projects awaited fruition in the SJB. First, nearly 75,000 acres of coal-rich Preference Right Lease Applications (PRLAs) awaited noncompetitive leasing, with nearly 60 percent of Ah-shi-sle-pah included in two PRLAs. Second, 24 tracts with approximately 1.32 billion tons of federal in-place reserves awaited competitive lease sales. Finally, the Public Service Company of New Mexico sought state approval to construct a 2,000 megawatt, coal-fired electric generating plant on land claimed by the Navajos in the Navajo–Hopi Relocation project. Thus, BLM careerists in New Mexico viewed the environmental, economic, and social stakes of coal leasing in the SJB as real, substantial, and conflict-ridden.

Before the Bureau could resolve the coal-leasing dispute in the SJB, four primary issues begged resolution. First, could the Reagan Administration administratively drop the Bisti Badlands and Ah-shi-sle-pah from wilderness consideration? Second, could the Interior Department's computer projections and environmental assessments justify satisfactorily the competitive and noncompetitive coal-leasing targets it set for the region? Third, could the BLM successfully navigate the Navajo's recognized and disputed claims in the SJB? And finally, what effect might the New Mexico congressional delegation have on the ultimate parameters of a San Juan Wilderness Bill?

The Wilderness Exclusion Issue

As noted, the BLM was considering three WSAs in the San Juan Basin for permanent designation (i.e., protection) under the Wilderness Act. Encompassing nearly 24,000 acres, all three were located in and adjacent to PRLAs near the proposed site of the New Mexico Generating Station (NMGS). Furthermore, the Dena-zin and Ah-shi-sle-pah WSAs directly overlapped portions of PRLAs in the region. Thus, coal leasing in the area posed profound threats to both the ecological integrity and human enjoyment of its environs. For example, both extracting coal and operating the NMGS would be noisy enterprises capable of diminishing one's image of solitude, a central tenet of wilderness values. In turn, developing the region would stimulate additional traffic, further diminishing wilderness solitude and increasing noxious air pollutants. Likewise, with mining features (i.e., strip mines) and operations (e.g., transmission lines and railroads) visible in many directions from the WSAs, scenic vistas were similarly threatened. Add to these the already exorbitant demands placed on regional water supplies and recreation areas, and one has a blueprint for ecostress in the SJB. At issue, of course, was just how severe these impacts might be, how facilely mitigation might handle them, and whether marketable coal reserves in the SJB justified the ecological disruption its mining entailed.

In announcing its plans for coal leasing late in 1981, however, Interior officials deftly ducked these issues. Their highest priorities were lease sales in the Powder River and San Juan basins, with sales in the former projected to double Andrus' 1979 sale targets. As for the SJB, Interior slated it to become the site of the second largest coal sale in U.S. history. Scheduled for September 1983, the SJB's leasing target for competitive tracts was 1.2 to 1.5 billion tons, with an additional 2.3 billion tons of coal available once BLM processed 26 noncompetitive PRLA properties.

BLM careerists in New Mexico, however, were much less sanguine about the environmental implications of these targets. Indeed, the *Cumulative Overview* they wrote for the SJB documented the devastating consequences of leasing on the Ah-shi-sle-pah area. To be sure, denying wilderness status to Ah-shi-sle-pah released 270 million tons of strippable coal for lease. However, wilderness preservation values would be lost, recreation-use values diminished, most archaeological sites destroyed, and paleontological resources nearly eliminated. Faring poorly, as well, were threatened and endangered flora and fauna awaiting landscape reclamation under SMCRA.

Unpersuaded, unsympathetic, and unbridled in their zeal to break leasing logjams, Reagan's appointees, first, proposed that only the Bisti and the De-na-zin be designated permanent wilderness areas. Dropped entirely for consideration as a wilderness area was Ah-shi-sle-pah.[9] Yet hardly was the ink dry on this proposal when Watt took actions administratively which imperiled wilderness designation for even Bisti and De-na-zin. Specifically, after soliciting ways from subordinates to "open wilderness areas" for development, Watt announced that he was dropping from wilderness consideration all WSAs under 5,000 acres in size.[10] Following this, he placed "split estates" off-limits for wilderness designation.[11]

With the Bisti only 3,500 acres in size, and with all three WSAs incorporating a number of split estates, Watt's actions immediately roused the ire of environmentalists, the New Mexico congressional delegation, and state government officials. For the state at large, the split-estate ruling placed nearly one-fifth of its 44 WSAs in jeopardy. What is more, it wreaked havoc with virtually the entire system by making it impossible to assemble manageable chunks of wilderness in many wilderness study areas. Thus, aside from becoming a rallying cry nationally for environmentalists sounding fire alarms in Congress, Watt's actions aroused so potent a coalition of interests in New Mexico that he exempted the Bisti from his ruling within 24 hours of his announcement. As a precaution, however, against further backsliding on the Bisti by Watt and his successors, Senator Domenici introduced a bill to designate the Bisti as a permanent wilderness area.

Likewise heated was the controversy attending the Administration's recommendation for Ah-shi-sle-pah to be dropped from wilderness consideration, despite its aesthetic and cultural riches. In doing so, the Bureau offered the following rationale:

> Although it [Ah-shi-sle-pah] contains outstanding opportunities for solitude, primitive and unconfined recreation, and special features, and [sic] has good characteristics of naturalness, the conflicts with other resource values offset the advantages of wilderness designation. . . . In addition, the Ah-shi-sle-pah WSA duplicates many of the characteristics of solitude, recreation, naturalness and special features found in the other two WSAs. Wilderness designation of the Bisti and De-na-zin WSAs would not significantly affect other resource uses; however, designation of the Ah-shi-sle-pah WSA would result in significant impacts on mineral resources, while not providing diversity in the National Wilderness Preservation System beyond that offered by the Bisti and De-na-zin WSAs.[12]

Not surprisingly, those wishing to have Ah-shi-sle-pah permanently designated a WA labeled the Bureau's judgement "misguided." To them, the 380 million tons of strippable coal, including portions of three PRLAs located within the WSA, constituted only 0.9 percent of the estimated federal coal reserves in the SJB. Thus, the area's reserves would hardly be missed and would not provide benefits anywhere near the environmental and social costs incurred by leasing and developing them. Leasing proponents, however, took a long-range economic view: mining over a 40-year period would generate approximately two thousand jobs with an annual income of $45 million to local residents. Too, Ah-shi-sle-pah's recoverable coal reserves promised to generate up to $288 million in severance tax revenues for the state of New Mexico, along with nearly $700 million in royalties shared equally between New Mexico and the federal government. Still, debate on these issues was speculative and driven by one overriding concern: Given soft energy markets, how prudent was leasing of *any* new reserves—in WSAs or anywhere?

The Leasing Target, Timeliness, and Appropriateness Issue

Recall how Secretary Andrus envisioned the Regional Coal Teams as the linchpin of the intergovernmental coal-leasing process. Comprised of public- and private-sector representatives, these bodies were to distill federal, state, and local interests into recommendations to the Interior Secretary regarding leasing locales, levels, and limitations. Nevertheless, when the BLM initially announced its coal-leasing targets for the SJB, it did so in ways stressing Secretary Watt's predilections, not RCT-informed objectives. This approach rapidly unraveled, however, once public comment began on BLM's draft EIS for the San Juan Basin.

Fifteen months after its original proposal, BLM felt compelled to reduce its competitive leasing target in the SJB by a whopping 40 percent (800–900 million tons) and pledged to select for development those tracts with the least social, environmental, and economic costs. Recanted as well were its earlier intentions to maintain PRLA leasing on 26 tracts without performing environmental impact assessments. In essence, the Administration's initiatives "beached" on two primary shoals: (1) the problematic premises of and inferences drawn from BLM's coal market projections, and (2) BLM's failure to sufficiently address PRLAs in the draft EIS for the region. What is more, the Reaganites' troubles were abetted by the President's "top-down," ideologically driven supply-side management philosophy.

"In God We Trust—All Others Must Have Credible Data." The reaction of opponents of the BLM's original 1982 EIS for coal leasing in the SJB was swift, formidable, and calculated to derail the Bureau's plans. In fairness, perhaps no less could have been expected—San Juan was the first large-scale lease proposal after Interior's debacle in the Powder River Basin. As Chapter 4 summarized, Interior's unorthodox bidding procedures at Powder River ignited full-scale oversight hearings on the Department's coal-leasing program.[13] Previously, Interior had published its estimates of tract values in its notice of lease sale. However, for Powder River, Carruthers introduced a new system. Interior published only minimum acceptable entry-level bids, ones far below what critics felt were the tracts' fair market value. Thus, when Interior leased reserves in Powder River at 4.3 cents per ton—far below the 20-to-30 cents per ton obtained in recent smaller sales—all hell broke loose.

To Carruthers, nothing was amiss in his approach. Given the nation's 10-year moratorium on coal leasing, he averred, "fair market values" were no more than bureaucrats' "best guesses" of what markets might bring. Thus, if set too high, they inordinately discouraged bids, jeopardized future energy supplies, and diminished needed state and federal revenues. Moreover, to those chastising him for coal leasing in "soft" markets, Carruthers demurred that long and ever-lengthening time periods between coal leasing and production precluded further delays. Failing to lease now meant exorbitantly high energy costs and foreign oil dependence ten years down the line.

Interior's critics, however, bought none of this. To them, Carruthers was only further lowering coal prices, revenue in state coffers, and ecosystem quality. Thus, in the short term, the Assistant Secretary's initiative sounded congressional fire alarms that stalled the acceleration of coal leasing. And in the long term, his actions helped diminish the perceived integrity of the coal-leasing program so badly that the Reagan Administration never recovered, despite Clark and Hodel's efforts to have smaller, more frequent sales under revamped procedures.

Equally devastating was a Natural Resources Defense Council (NRDC) lawsuit filed against Watt for flouting NEPA requirements when issuing his 1982 amendments to Andrus' Coal Management Plan. Here, plaintiffs charged successfully that a new EIS should have accompanied Watt's amendments because these changes were not covered in the 1979 environmental impact statement. As NRDC spokesperson Laura King put it, "Every single time Interior has come up with a new program, they have claimed it's not a new program, [and] we've [had] to sue and convince them it is."[14] Thus, once Watt left Interior, Secretary Clark felt compelled to announce a halt to coal leasing until the Department developed a new and acceptable EIS for the lease program. Still, in 1982, the pending suit only afforded additional grist to leasing opponents in the SJB. To them, this was but further evidence that Watt and New Mexico's Carruthers were remiss in assessing the implications of leasing in the state's fragile badlands.

Against this leitmotif, BLM and the RCT held a series of open meetings in the SJB from 1983 through 1985.[15] Their purpose was to gauge public reaction to Interior's proposed leasing programs, both regionally and nationally. The verdict? Back to the drawing board! Most notably, critics excoriated the first *draft EIS* for the SJB for failing to treat PRLAs as a separate issue (see below). Indeed, so devastating were these complaints that the BLM had to produce a *second draft EIS* for public comment, presaging a similar fate for each Programmatic EIS proffered by Interior during the Reagan years. True, local governments and other federal agencies responded quite positively to the Administration's plan for the SJB. Stridently opposed, however, were state government agencies and environmental groups who attacked the Bureau's supply and demand projections, its procedures for deducing fair market value, and its computer modeling techniques for assessing paleontological losses in the SJB. Each of these concerns merits separate attention.

As a key member of the RCT planning process, former New Mexico Governor Bruce King (D) had agreed to Interior's original coal-leasing targets. In fact, these were especially appealing to this pro-development governor after 14 years of no competitive leasing in his state. However, King's successor, Toney Anaya, harbored both a conservationist ethos and strong aspirations for national office as the only Hispanic governor in the United States. While no doubt principled in wanting to mesh environmental protection and energy leasing in ways maximizing New Mexico's tax coffers, Anaya found attractive as well the national political exposure he garnered by jousting with Watt.

Anaya, along with the state's Attorney General, Bardacke, and Public Land Commissioner, Jim Baca, pleaded successfully with Carruthers to reduce competitive coal leasing in the SJB by one-half, to 800 or 900 million tons. In addition, they urged him to postpone immediate leasing in favor of a phased offering of specific tracts once markets grew less slack and EISs were redone. Their logic:

> Due to numerous and very significant deficiencies found in the [EISs] by various state agencies, we strongly recommend issuance of supplemental draft environmental impact statements for all three documents [EISs for the wilderness study areas, the New Mexico Generating Station, and the San Juan Regional Coal Leasing Program]. We

feel our recommendation is substantiated by the fact that [these] documents are not of NEPA quality, thus making them legally deficient and potentially subject to challenges via litigation.[16]

Anaya and company then outlined how inadequate was the data base supporting BLM's leasing recommendations. They wrote:

The State of New Mexico has been made aware of the fact that the [electricity] load forecasts utilized in the DEIS [for the NM Generating Station] are now inaccurate. [Moreover,] . . . treatment of the impact upon the State (in *every* respect) from the development of the PRLAs was totally deficient in the [PRLA] DEIS. . . .

We feel [our] . . . recommendation is further substantiated by additional factors. For example, the uncertainties surrounding construction of a railroad in the San Juan Basin and the litigation undertaken by the Navajos certainly contribute to reducing the value and true economic potential for competitive leasing . . . [yet] BLM has not discounted its coal-leasing values accordingly.[17]

Accompanying these critiques, environmentalists charged the Bureau with (1) failing to adequately consider water supplies in the region, (2) inadequately assessing the cumulative impact of projects in the SJB, (3) manipulating data, (4) premising its conclusions on faulty assumptions, and (5) making inferences that contradicted its own calculations. Witness, for example, the Environmental Defense Fund's (EDF) blistering assessment of the *draft EIS* for the San Juan Basin. Pulling no punches, the EDF alleged duplicity:

The BLM's own methodology for setting both preliminary and final leasing target[s] indicates, when current data are used, that *no* coal should be leased. BLM's response to this has been to ignore more recent data, and to disavow its own methodology. BLM's methodology made explicit assumptions with regard to demand, coal mine life, baseline production, and recovery factors. . . . As early as February 1982 the BLM was informed that its methodology implied, given current data, that no coal should be leased. [Nevertheless,] BLM continued to use the same leasing target, based on obsolete data. Later, internal agency BLM memoranda [among Burford, Carruthers, and Luscher] . . . show that BLM used a specific quantitative formula to produce very precise [target] numbers, a formula which it never published, never admitted to in writing, and tried to claim was proposed by others.[18]

In fairness, kudos from other quarters countered allegations of BLM chicanery by the EDF and others. Yet the latter doggedly rebuked the Reagan Administration and consistently delayed its policy reorientation efforts. Indeed, these charges led, initially, to congressional moratoria on leasing and, eventually, to Secretary Clark suspending all competitive coal lease sales until the Bureau could develop a legally unassailable EIS for the lease program. Yet, in "successfully" understaffing and deskilling precisely those environmental and planning positions necessary to produce such a document, the President's supply-side management tactics undercut the agency's ability to meet this challenge. Moreover, energy developers were less likely to bid on tracts with insufficient, untrustworthy, or legally challengeable EISs. Ironies all, these shortcomings posed long-term problems for Reagan's pro-development agenda. "Strategic" budget deficits chronically impoverished the BLM, its data bases, and its analytical expertise, rendering even Secretary Hodel's revamped EIS vulnerable to legal assault in the late 1980s.

Preference Right Lease Applications. With its competitive lease plans stalled and scaled back nearly 40 percent in the SJB, Interior's hopes now hinged on leasing noncompetitively nearly 2.3 billion tons of coal on 26 Preference Right Lease Applications in the region. To proceed, however, Reagan's appointees had to address two interrelated sub-issues. First, could the Administration legally exclude PRLAs from EIS requirements and revamped market analyses? And second, was the Bureau's leasing of PRLAs truly a nondiscretionary duty, as Burford claimed?

On these issues, the Administration made its position crystal clear in its first draft environmental impact statement for the San Juan Basin. Bureau officials argued that the Federal Coal Leasing Amendments Act (FCLAA) gave them no choice but to exclude the PRLAs from environmental analyses. They argued that FCLAA required federal regulators to issue noncompetitive coal leases automatically to PRLA applicants who had discovered commercial quantities of coal while holding their prospecting permits. Thus,

PRLAs were exempt from any EIS or economic analyses beyond what little was required when they obtained their initial prospecting permits years, if not decades, before.

Since twice the amount of coal on competitive leases was at stake on PRLAs, jeremiads swiftly followed from opponents who impugned the Administration's logic, prudence, and motives. For example, David Glowka of the Sierra Club bridled at the time, "If they proceed with the [PRLA] applications, there's not much significance at all in [Secretary Clark's] delaying the competitive leasing."[19] Likewise, environmentalist Jonathan Teague spoke in 1984 for all leasing opponents in skewering the Bureau's position on PRLA leasing:

> We wish to observe that the various San Juan Basin PRLAs must still meet strict tests of commercial quantities of coal, subject to appropriate environmental protection and surface occupancy stipulations, before any actual rights of lease ownership [shall] be forthcoming from the federal government. Moreover, the PRLAs have yet to withstand thorough scrutiny regarding the validity of the prospecting permits from which they originated.[20]

Lastly, all critiqued the Bureau's environmental impact analyses for the PRLAs. BLM, they alleged, had relied on pre-field work predictive modeling techniques of dubious validity. Specifically, instead of conducting on-the-ground surveys of paleontological and archaeological resources in the region, BLM used overviews of existing site records to build computer models "predicting" how significant the tracts' artifacts might be. Appalled, New Mexico's Cultural Properties Review Committee labeled Interior's approach patently illegal:

> State-of-the-art, on-the-ground, systematic inventory surveys are required in all surface coal mine impact areas. . . . Pre-field work research designs have been required by our state guidelines since 1980 as a means to adequately identify resources that are likely to be in an area. However, this initial overview can by no means be allowed to replace the actual on-the-ground survey [as Interior proposed]. . . . The development of an overview [alone] . . . cannot possibly take into account the wide variety and significance of the cultural properties that are likely to be on the ground.[21]

Similarly, State Archaeologist Curtis Schaafsma was even more blunt: "It is *patently absurd* to believe that a predictive model based on an overview can satisfactorily locate and evaluate all cultural properties that are likely to be present in a given area." Continued Schaafsma, "If implemented as proposed . . . [this inventory procedure] would result in increased costs to any company attempting to utilize it inasmuch as it would require constant revisions and double-checking. . . . It is far more cost-effective and efficient to perform a complete survey at the earliest possible stage of a project so that everybody knows what is present in an area."[22]

Ultimately, the federal courts resolved the PRLA issue in New Mexico. In the process, the Bureau had to concede that PRLA leasing affected the environment so significantly that an EIS was necessary to comply with NEPA. To do otherwise violated two major court decisions now ensconced in Council of Environmental Quality regulations regarding EIS preparation: *NRDC v. Morton* and *NRDC v. Berglund*.[23] Thus, one sees again the folly of undermining BLM's planning and environmental capabilities without first being sure that regulations and procedures requiring these skills were relaxed as well. Supply-side management cannot summarily repeal the statutory bounds within which appointees must labor when trying to reorient policy administratively. Nor can implementors facilely dissuade, deter, or dismantle coalitions of affected, vigilant, and litigious political actors determined to amend or thwart policy reforms. This becomes readily apparent when one examines the third primary issue driving the SJB dispute: contested Navajo land claims in the region.

Cattle, Coal, and Checkerboard Lands in the SJB

That sordid bit of Cherokee Indian history known as the Trail of Tears has long haunted America. Yet similar, if less publicized, travails also dispirited the Native American inhabitants of the desert Southwest, most notably the Hopi, Navajo, and Ute nations. Indeed, so effectively dispossessed were these people that by 1876 only 10 percent of their original land was still in Native American hands. By 1976, only three percent remained.[24]

But rapacious Anglo settlers were not the only problems confronting Native Americans in the Southwest.[25] As frequent intertribal conflicts well attest, the Navajo and Hopi since the seventeenth century have spent much of their time worrying about each other's close proximity, disparate lifestyles, and intense territoriality. The Hopi are a pueblo people residing primarily in tightly clustered villages organized primarily around agricultural pursuits. In contrast, the Navajo are a pastoral, nomadic people residing in hogans or other types of dwellings widely scattered near individual grazing spots. With tribal lifestyles so incongruent, with Navajo population growth so pronounced, and with tribesmembers insatiable in their thirst for more grazing lands to nurture ever-expanding cattle herds, intertribe rivalry was inevitable. Perhaps unavoidable, as well, was the twentieth century's version of the Cherokee's "Trail of Tears": the Navajo–Hopi Settlement Act of 1974.[26]

To understand how this statute affected the coal-leasing controversy in the SJB, one first has to place the Act in proper context. Congress had established the Navajo Indian Reservation in 1868 with 3.3 million acres, an area totally inadequate to handle the tribe's nomadic grazing needs. Indeed, so miserly were its confines in terms of the tribe's traditional lifestyle that by 1880 nearly half of all Navajos lived off the Reservation. This, in turn, provoked the animosity of the Hopi, Anglos, and New Mexican Pueblos in their path. In fact, so heated did these rivalries become that President Chester Arthur had to intervene in 1882 to bring a modicum of peace to the area. His plan was to establish by executive order the Hopi Indian Reservation, thus formally establishing the two tribes on their own separate sovereign land.

Over the next 75 years, however, the Interior Department and its Bureau of Indian Affairs virtually erased the Reservation's boundaries by ignoring and implicitly ratifying Navajo incursions on Hopi lands. Thus, by 1958, the Hopi Reservation had shrunk to approximately one-tenth of its original size, with the Navajo and Hopi jointly using approximately 1.8 million acres of disputed lands in northeastern Arizona.

To rectify this situation, Congress created a three-member tribunal to resolve competing tribal claims. Their decision, affirmed in 1963 by the U.S. Supreme Court, satisfied no one.[27] Because the panel had no jurisdiction to partition the lands jointly used by tribesmembers, the two tribes had to share title to both surface and subsurface mineral rights within the Navajo-Hopi Joint Use Area (JUA). Thus, rather than diminishing, intertribal rivalries escalated over grazing rights and new construction in the JUA. Ultimately the Hopi obtained court injunctions restricting Navajo activities in the area, restrictions that led the Navajo to appeal for congressional redress. That redress purportedly came in the form of the Navajo-Hopi Settlement Act of 1974.

Under the Settlement Act, Congress assigned 900,000 of the disputed acres to each tribe, charging the federal courts with equally partitioning the JUA between the two combatants. Importantly, the courts were to ignore current settlement patterns in partitioning these properties. Once the courts decided the partition issue, a three-member Relocation Commission was to oversee resettlement of uprooted tribesmembers (mostly Navajo). Voluntary relocations began in 1977 once a Federal District Court in Tucson issued its first Act of Partition. Therein, the court ruled that 3,000 acres occupied by Navajos in the JUA belonged rightfully to the Hopi Tribe. Consequently, the ten thousand Navajos living there had to evacuate and resettle elsewhere by 1986. Within one year, however, the Ninth Circuit Court of Appeals vacated that partition order, citing faulty surveying of the southern and western boundaries of the JUA.

Over the next five years, the court announced a second partition line, the Relocation Commission tried to overcome massive Navajo resistance to relocations, and a trickle of voluntary Hopi and Navajo relocations resumed. So stalemated grew negotiations, so costly grew relocation costs ($88,000 per family), and so horrendous grew the tales of relocatees swindled by real estate agents that U.S. Senators Domenici and DeConcini (D-Ariz.) called in 1982 for outright repeal of the 1974 Settlement Act. Nonetheless, the Commission eventually coined a viable land exchange settlement with the two tribes, with profound implications for the Reagan Administration's coal-leasing plans for the SJB. For abandoning their property claims in the Joint Use Area, the Navajos got to select 35,000 acres in New Mexico for resettling displaced tribesmembers. Only one stipulation applied: Navajo could only select public lands within 18 miles of their Reservation in New Mexico.

Thus did the plot thicken in the SJB. In a move designed partially to scuttle the new agreement, Navajo Chairman Peter MacDonald selected one-half of an area known as Paragon Ranch, 35,000 acres of the most coal-rich property in the San Juan Basin. As such, of course, Paragon had many suitors ready to do battle with the Navajo: The Public Service Company of New Mexico wanted to build a new power-generating station there; environmentalists saw Paragon as a buffer against polluting the Bisti Badlands; and the Reagan Administration wanted it for coal leasing.

Into this cauldron the Navajo also tossed a second issue of significance to New Mexicans and to the Reagan Revolution: the tribe's strident, litigious, and controversial claims to nearly two million acres of land in the SJB. Indeed, spokespersons for the interests of traditional Navajo (i.e., those wanting to maintain traditional agrarian lifestyles, customs, and mores) reacted with outrage to the Bureau's draft (1982) and revised (1983) EISs; these plans targeted for relocation all tribesmembers residing on lands the government said was not theirs, or those living on split estates. All told, according to Navajos John Redhouse and Paul Fyfe, three thousand tribesmembers with primordial claims to those properties would have to relocate. Added Redhouse, he and other Navajo favoring traditional lifestyles were prepared to go to jail to prevent relocation: "We are a land-based people. . . . The land is a living being—its our mother. . . . To destroy the land is also to destroy the people."[28] Other, more cynical observers, saw less noble motives. Less traditional Navajo, they assumed, sought to leverage their position when bargaining with energy companies, the state of New Mexico, and the federal government for mineral bonuses, royalties, and Native American employment guarantees.

How likely was the Reagan Administration to support Indian claims? In some ways, early indications from Interior—particularly at the Bureau of Indian Affairs (BIA)—somewhat encouraged Native Americans. For example, BIA's Deputy Solicitor, Moody Tidwell, proclaimed that the Reagan Administration believed in Indian "self-determination" and wished to pursue a "new direction" in Indian affairs. Likewise, Interior's Assistant Secretary for Indian Affairs, Kenneth Smith, a Wasco Indian, stated that his department "wants done with natural resources that Indians own, what the Indians want done with them."[29] What is more, Interior officials emphasized that Watt was determined to resolve amicably outstanding Indian claims involving water rights and surface occupancy issues.

Yet in the minds of many Indians, the way Reagan's appointees wielded the administrative presidency was a more accurate and distressing indicator of the Administration's intentions. Not only did the BIA absorb massive budget cuts, but the D.C. Circuit Court of Appeals ruled that the Reagan Administration had not litigated aggressively enough the seventeen thousand outstanding Indian damage claims pending in federal courts.[30] Moreover, the Interior Department fired its only Native American field solicitor in early 1982, along with a sixteen-year Interior attorney known for advocating Native American causes. The former, a Navajo, claimed she lost her job by insisting that energy resources on reservations were a tribal, not a national, resource. The latter, "convinced that [Native Americans] hadn't gotten a fair shake [from Interior] in the past," was more stoic about his fate: "They want to change the direction of things, and I think they have a right to." Still, this "new" direction dismayed many others, including the Native American Rights Fund. Referring to the two firings, its legislative liaison, Susan Harjo, noted that similar cases elsewhere revealed a clear pattern: "It does seem that many of those people who have been most vigorous in pursuit of benefits for the Indian people are the ones being moved out or moving themselves out."[31] Moreover, she claimed that while state courts traditionally were hostile to Native American lawsuits, that was where the Reaganites urged tribal councils to turn for redress.

Against this leitmotif, the Navajo adopted a legal strategy which further clouded the Administration's coal-leasing agenda in the SJB. Specifically, the Navajo Nation filed suit, claiming it owned nearly 2 million acres in the "checkerboard area" of the SJB, including all of Ah-shi-sle-pah and parts of the Bisti Badlands.[32] Navajo Chairman Peter MacDonald claimed the tribe had no other way to win back territories illegally seized by the federal government. An election ploy by MacDonald, as some claimed, or principled defiance? To Reagan's Interior Department, the consequences were the same: Contested title claims doused hopes of expeditiously developing coal supplies in the region. Without knowing who owned the properties, Interior could not get permission for leasing to proceed.

To the Navajo's anger, however, no one ever got to argue their case on its merits. In early 1984, U.S. District Judge Juan Burciaga dismissed it on procedural grounds. The Navajo, he ruled, had waived their right to appeal over thirty years ago by not petitioning the Indian Claims Commission for redress. Frustrated, the Navajo Nation's Justice Department vowed to appeal the decision, and immediately filed a second suit. This time the tribe claimed that the Navajo had the right to control coal leasing: They were the de facto landowners since they had occupied the lands for at least one hundred years with the Interior Department's tacit approval. Thus, as the BLM title-clearing process plodded slowly along in the wake of Reagan's budget and personnel cuts, even those Navajo with clear titles refused to lease their allotments to coal developers.

Still, Judge Burciaga's decision buoyed the spirits of both Interior officials and New Mexicans now excused from nearly $2 billion in Navajo reparation payments. Their exuberance, however, was tempered by a third litigation front opened up by the Navajo: a lawsuit claiming tribal ownership of 35,000 acres on the Paragon Ranch. As noted, the Navajo had selected these coal-abundant properties for their recompense in New Mexico under the 1974 Navajo-Hopi Settlement Act. Technically, the BLM "owned" the property, but the Public Service Company of New Mexico (PNM) and its subsidiaries had long held leases on it. What immediately provoked the Navajo's suit, however, was a 1982 action taken by Secretary Watt at BLM's request, and unbeknownst to the tribe.[33] Under a land swap planned prior to the Navajo selection, PNM was to acquire 8,400 Paragon acres for its power plant, while the Bureau received 10,000 acres of aesthetically valuable property north of Taos, New Mexico. To protect that exchange, Watt formally withdrew the Paragon acres from consideration under the Navajo-Hopi Settlement Act.

Outraged, Chairman MacDonald went to court challenging Watt's decision for violating both the 1974 Settlement Act and the federal government's responsibility to act as trustee for the Navajo

Nation. Citing the socioeconomic hardships already suffered by relocated Navajo in the Southwest, the tribe's attorney, Don Wharton, pleaded for an injunction against further relocation of his clients.[34] He argued that since the Paragon lands were within the eighteen-mile limit set by the Settlement Act, Interior had to give priority to the tribe's selection. The Navajo's not-so-hidden agenda in filing the suit? If the tribe could acquire ownership, it would have an important bargaining chip against PNM in its ongoing negotiations for a joint venture in developing the power plant, one guaranteeing Navajo profits, jobs, and input into the region's energy development.

As John Kingdon argues so compellingly, however, nonincremental shifts in policy agendas can occur quite rapidly as changes occur in political actors.[35] Thus, Peterson Zah's stunning victory in 1983 over Peter MacDonald as Navajo Chairman presaged a distinct agenda shift in the region. Empowered presumably was a leader with a more flexible, conciliatory position—a leader emphasizing joint development projects, Navajo–Hopi joint ventures, and resettlement based on selecting the best available properties for relocatees.[36]

While Zah's election was perceived positively by the Interior Department, New Mexico officials, and private landholders in the SJB, environmentalists were much less sanguine. In fact, they grew distraught when Zah tried to cut a deal with PNM for joint development of the Paragon Ranch project. They feared that the lure of two thousand Indian jobs and $15 billion in royalties to the tri-state Navajo Tribe over the project's 40-year time span might be too attractive for the tribe's less traditional leaders to turn down. This, they feared, even though the seven Navajo chapters closest to the area favored traditional agrarian lifestyles over Zah's modernist alternatives. Put less tactfully by some interviewees, environmentalists feared a sell-out of local Navajo by the Arizona-based Zah.[37] In the process, they envisioned the Bisti, De-na-zin, and Ah-shi-sle-pah WSAs sold out as well.

As unsettling as Zah's election was to some, other changes in political actors soon occurred to bolster the spirits of environmentalists and local, more traditional Navajo. Specifically, freshman U.S. Senator Jeff Bingaman (D-NM) and first-term Congressman

Bill Richardson (D-NM) joined the fray, jousting aggressively with their senior Republican counterparts, Domenici and Lujan. With the administrative presidency a victim of fire alarm oversight both nationally and in New Mexico, congressional power politics at the grassroots had to salvage what it could of Reagan's energy agenda in the SJB.

The Wilderness Designation Issue Revisited

As noted, Reagan's appointees at the BLM originally recommended excluding Ah-shi-sle-pah from wilderness designation, but designating the Bisti and De-na-zin as permanent wilderness areas (WAs) in the National Wilderness Preservation System. Yet subsequent actions revealed their true preferences. Note, for example, how Senator Domenici and Congressman Lujan had to get the Bisti exempted when Watt tried to drop from wilderness consideration all WSAs of less than 5,000 acres. Remember, as well, the implications for the SJB of Watt's split-estate initiative. Unsated, in 1983 the Administration next tried to postpone permanent wilderness designation for both Ah-shi-sle-pah *and* De-na-zin, only this time with Domenici and Lujan's assistance. Indeed, both solons introduced bills to foster the Administration's ends, albeit with significant differences in approach.[38] Domenici's bill, co-sponsored initially by Senator Bingaman and endorsed by Carruthers, permanently designated the Bisti as a wilderness area, but only included De-na-zin as a WSA. Moreover, Ah-shi-sle-pah received no protection at all. In contrast, Lujan's bill—distinctly less preferred, but not formally opposed by the Administration—designated Bisti as a WA, but included *both* De-na-zin and Ah-shi-sle-pah as WSAs.

During legislative hearings on these bills, both Domenici and Carruthers urged upon the Congress patience, prudence, and restraint in light of formidable environmentalist pressure to designate all three as wilderness areas. Now even backing away from the Bureau's earlier recommendation to designate De-na-zin a wilderness area (WA), Carruthers testified in support of Domenici's proposal to designate only the Bisti as a WA at that point. In Domenici's words, "There are problems in the De-na-zin area with split estates, valid oil and gas leases, and private estates." To which Carruthers added, "Legislators should not rush to designate additional areas prior to completion of the wilderness study process and the opportunity to review its findings."[39]

Nonetheless, their pleas went unheeded among Democratic members of the New Mexican delegation: Representative Richardson and Senator Bingaman (deserting Domenici) introduced legislation designating all three WSAs as wilderness areas. Their proposal also set aside over 6,000 more acres for wilderness designation than the Reagan Administration had under wilderness study. And if this weren't disturbing enough for the Reaganites, imagine their chagrin in late 1983 when fellow-Republican Lujan agreed to support permanent wilderness designation for *both* the Bisti and De-na-zin areas, as in the Richardson-Bingaman bill. Indeed, Lujan's bill even upped the ante; he joined with Richardson to seek "special protection" for a fourth area in the SJB, the so-called "Fossil Forest."[40]

The last thing the Administration needed now were justiciable claims to these areas by the Navajo Nation, claims it will be remembered that actually arose in late 1983 when the tribe selected portions of De-na-zin, Ah-shi-sle-pah, and the Fossil Forest as part of the 1974 Settlement Act. Once the Relocation Commission approved these selections, regulatory authority under the Surface Mining Control and Reclamation Act (SMCRA) would pass to the tribe or its members. It would, that is, unless Reagan appointees—using the administrative presidency—amended existing regulations. With SMCRA silent on the matter, the Interior Department historically had recognized the Navajo's regulatory authority on reservation lands. Left unclear, however, was the tribe's authority over off-reservation lands such as De-na-zin and Ah-shi-sle-pah. Thus, seeking to cauterize the hemorrhaging of its control over the situation, the Reagan Administration's response was predictable. The Bureau ruled that the tribe was a "nonqualified owner," lacking regulatory authority: It received an insufficient share of its income from off-reservation lands to qualify.[41]

Significantly, the Navajo's land selections were just as perplexing to the New Mexico congressional delegation. For Richardson and Bingaman, the tribe had tossed a monkey wrench into their wilderness designation plans. Specifically, the Navajo's selections overlapped 8,000 acres that both members of Congress wanted to include in the San Juan Wilderness bill. Moreover, when asked to select comparable properties instead, the tribe declined, stating that none existed within 18 miles of the Reservation. Consequently, Richardson amended his bill to allow the tribe to select New Mexican lands up to 36 miles from reservation borders, rather than 18 miles.[42] His logic was that an exchange could take place, with the Navajo swapping the 8,000 acres they selected in Paragon for mineral-rich properties of comparable value beyond the present 18-mile radius stipulated in the 1974 Settlement Act.

Informed of Richardson's amendment, both Domenici and Lujan erupted. Said Domenici, "The original Navajo-Hopi relocation plan [which he had helped develop] was carefully crafted . . . and it would not be right to significantly alter it in a circuitous way such as has been proposed."[43] Also, Domenici and Lujan noted that a 36-mile limit allowed the tribe to select and control New Mexican oil and gas fields near Farmington. This, they railed, was not only intolerable, but also distorted the purposes of the 1974 Act. Argued Lujan, "It was intended that they be given new lands for residences to replace the land they lost so they could continue their same [nomadic, cattle-raising] life-style. . . . [Instead,] Navajo leaders have selected lands with mineral deposits."[44]

Needless to say, with the most senior and powerful members of the New Mexico delegation opposing it, Richardson's amendment was dead on arrival. Still, its demise did little to advance the Reagan Administration's agenda in the SJB. Reagan's appointees had played their last administrative card when BLM narrowly interpreted the Navajo's leasing authority on off-reservation lands. It was, in any case, a card trumped later by legal realities: BLM's position was indefensible in court. Thus, for all intents and purposes, the Administration's last hope of promoting its agenda was Republican Senator Pete Domenici.

Publicly, Domenici remained firm: "We see no need to short-circuit [BLM's wilderness] study, which is costing millions."[45] Privately, however, this astute tactician knew that the political "train" was leaving the station, especially when Richardson agreed to back Lujan's bill. The time for credit claiming had arrived. Not only did the House of Representatives unanimously vote to pass the Lujan-Richardson compromise in June 1984, but Governor Anaya's support for the bill was assured once it was amended to protect New Mexico's six percent share of coal royalties on lands selected under the Navajo-Hopi Settlement. Too, the Navajo Nation climbed aboard once Lujan agreed that the tribe could control all surface and subsurface mineral rights in the An-shi-sle-pah if it ceded the Paragon properties to the Public Service Company of New Mexico. Declaring "victory," Domenici now hailed the Lujan-Richardson bill as "the best opportunity we will have for decades to develop the rich coal resources of the San Juan Basin, while at the same time preserving important wilderness areas for our future generations of New Mexicans to enjoy."[46]

The San Juan Wilderness Act of 1984 bore scant resemblance to the Administration's goals as expressed by Carruthers in congressional testimony.[47] Indeed, the Act was distinctly less presidentialist than legislative in its contours. To recap, President Reagan had just signed a bill designating both Bisti and De-na-zin as permanent wilderness areas, with Ah-shi-sle-pah remaining a WSA. Moreover, because surface and subsurface mineral rights to Ah-shi-sle-pah and approximately 29,000 additional acres in the SJB now belonged to the Navajo, no one was sure if, to what extent, or on what terms coal mining might occur. Most ironically for the Reagan Administration, these and other regulatory decisions now rested with the Navajo Nation—a tribe whose wrath it had routinely aroused. If traditional Indians won out, development was unlikely. If less traditional elements and their patrons prevailed, coal leasing was likely, but only on Navajo terms. True, environmentalists were uncomfortable about the arrangement: Leasing regulations typically were more lax on reservation properties. Thus, some saw the Reagan Administration's hand strengthened in the deal. This seemed unlikely, however, given the Administration's earlier attempt to prevent the Navajo from regulating off-reservation lands under the Surface Mining Control and Reclamation Act.

CONCLUSION

This discussion of the Reagan Administration's efforts to accelerate coal production in the San Juan Basin once again portrays a process of paradox and bureaupolitical angst at both the macro- (national) and micro-implementation (SJB) levels. As in previous chapters, we see how the Administration's supply-side management successes sorely strained Interior's ability to attain its pro-development energy agenda. However, in this instance, the ramifications were more dire still: a series of congressional moratoria which nearly crippled the Administration's ambitious agenda well into the Bush Administration.

The "recipe" for these moratoria? First, add personnel and budget cuts in environmental planning, EIS, and title-processing activities within the Interior Department (for BLM and the Bureau of Indian Affairs). These prevented timely and legally unassailable completion of statutorily mandated tasks (e.g., EIS preparation). To this base, mix in Watt's attempts to administratively amend the Andrus CMP, to drop split estates and public land parcels smaller than 5,000 acres from wilderness protection, and to render wilderness areas vulnerable to exploration until the year 2000. Together, these set off congressional fire alarms and emotions that Watt's successors could never quell, either nationally or in the SJB. Finally, stir in the Powder River Basin scandal, Watt's doubling of Andrus' leasing targets, and the Administration's dubious computer modeling formulae and projections. Certainly, no more volatile a brew existed for rapidly turning fire alarm into police patrol oversight by Congress and an aroused, litigious, and unyielding environmental community flushed with past courtroom success.

Obviously, it is impossible in this case to separate national from subnational politics in the SJB: The former affected and were affected by the latter. What *is* possible to discern, however, is how the disintegration of comity, civility, and trust went far beyond the bureaupolitical dynamics of the cases reported in earlier chapters. What accounts for this? Certainly Watt's confrontational, arrogant, and badgering style fanned the flames of conflict with congressional oversight committees, state RCTs, and the environmental community. Too, the missteps outlined above surely incited many of the Administration's problems. Still, Watt's abrasive style was not peculiar to energy leasing; it cut across each of the other policy arenas covered in this book. Moreover, while the national response to Watt's style and initiatives framed events in the SJB, several of the bureaupolitical obstacles to policy reorientation at that micro-level had other, more administrative (e.g., problematic EIS assumptions) or site-specific sources (e.g., the Navajo-Hopi Settlement Act). In sum, coal leasing held no monopoly on Watt's pugnacity, boorishness, or political missteps. Yet only in the SJB case was Interior's policy agenda (as opposed to its operations, as in the Elena Gallegos experience) thrown virtually into receivership. The trustees of that "bankruptcy": nationally, the United States Congress; in northwest New Mexico, the state's congressional delegation.

What differences from the other cases, then, do exist in the SJB experience that might help account for its peculiar dynamics? Most striking are the differences in the nature, scope, and pace of this initiative relative to the others. Specifically, in contrast to their actions in other cases, Reagan's appointees rushed pell-mell into a radical departure from existing policy (doubling coal leasing and mining wilderness areas) without attempting to craft consensus among strategic actors (Andrus' fragile state-industry-environmental coalition, as well as the Navajo Nation).

Taking this view, one sees Watt's style and missteps as contributing but hardly sufficient factors in the donnybrook. Arguably, the more encompassing and telling intervening variable lies in the initiative itself. Thus, non-negotiable positions at the macropolitical (or national) level were functions of an unprecedented, nonincremental, abruptly announced, and procedurally flawed energy policy. In effect, Reaganites offered a policy that struck many in relevant issue networks as lacking three things: (1) legitimacy (because of its unprecedented scale, timing, and pace); (2) a compelling rationale (why accelerate leasing with coal markets already soft?); and (3) a broad-based political coalition for reversing two decades of bipartisan wilderness leasing policy. Consequently, at the macro-level, stymieing Watt and his successors took on symbolic, even moral overtones unconducive to compromise on Congress' part. Meanwhile, at the micro-level in the SJB, Reagan appointees realized how prepared, well-armed, and potent were their aroused, litigious opponents. Compromise there became a necessity lest court suits halted coal leasing altogether in the region.

PART III

Beyond Fear or Favor:
Lessons for Theory
and Practice

CHAPTER 9

Missing Links, Links Gone Missing, and Natural Resource Management

Over a decade and a half has elapsed since Erwin Hargrove issued his clarion call for researchers to explore the "missing link" in policy analysis: the implementation process.[1] Since then, a multidisciplinary rush heeding Hargrove's advice has ensued in both national and crossnational contexts.[2] Yet despite its substantive breadth, and the heuristic value of its conceptual frameworks, propositions, and models, this literature has its shortcomings. Indeed, one of the field's leading scholars, Benny Hjern, has observed that an important link toward understanding implementation is still "gone missing": a theoretically grounded, empirically based study of interorganizational dynamics.[3]

Certainly, one might say the same thing today about our understanding of the administrative presidency. Indeed, to paraphrase Schattschneider, there exists a growing "mountain of data surrounding a vacuum of theory" on the topic. Moreover, that data base consists primarily of information on the policy formulation and legitimation aspects of the administrative presidency in Washington. Its "missing link" is a focus on the bureaucratic politics of the administrative presidency in the field during implementation. Its "link gone missing"? Much of the popular and academic debate surrounding the promise, performance, and normative implications of the administrative presidency is short-circuited by the triumph of ideology over objective inquiry.

With the "missing link" issue addressed in Parts I and II of this book, we turn in Part III to the "link gone missing" issue as it applies to natural resource policy, in particular, and to the administrative presidency, more generally. Assessed are the practical and theoretical lessons proffered by the Reagan Administration's experiences in New Mexico. To these ends, this chapter focuses on three questions relating exclusively to public lands policy. First, what do the cases reveal about what can happen, and why, when appointees use the administrative presidency to reorient public lands policy? Second, under what conditions and using what implementation strategies will the administrative presidency prove most successful in this policy arena? And third, what do the cases suggest about the efficacy of traditional administrative and market-oriented reforms for designing effective public land policies for the 1990s and beyond? Chapter 10 then pitches the discussion at a broader, more abstract level. Conceptual frameworks and implementation strategies are offered applicable to the administrative presidency across different policy domains (domestic, foreign, and defense), arenas, and goals.

In essence, the arguments proffered in this chapter are three-fold. First, while the administrative presidency connotes a managerial enterprise, its implementation at the grassroots produces different types of bureaupolitical dynamics. In turn, these dynamics are functions of the nature, mode, and tempo of the types of policy initiatives pursued. Second, given the ultimately political nature of the administrative presidency, neither a "top-down" nor a "bottom-up" implementation perspective is adequate for successful policy reorientation. Rather, a "reversible logic" strategy combining both is most likely to succeed. Finally, those seeking policy direction and effectiveness should rethink the prescriptions of both the administrative orthodoxy and the New Resource Economics. Each is disastrously incomplete. The former focuses on control rather than accomplishment; the latter typically exhibits a debilitating naiveté. Instead, a middle-ground alternative— organization by task or work flow rather than function—seems most capable of fostering both realism and accomplishment in the contemporary administrative state.

THE POLITICAL MORPHOLOGY OF THE ADMINISTRATIVE PRESIDENCY

As noted in Chapter 1, the administrative presidency has its supporters as well as its detractors. To some, the strategy affords an

overdue dose of presidential leadership, purposiveness, and prerogative. To others it is an untoward assault on congressional intent, the U.S. Constitution, and neutral competence. Thus, partisans clearly differ over the consequences of the administrative
presidency for the Republic. Nonetheless, all persistently debate its
merits as if the administrative presidency clearly attenuates, copes
more readily with, or avoids altogether the vigilance of macropolitical system actors.

But how valid is this assumption? Does the administrative presidency really advantage chief executives to the extent contemplated
by its most unabashed supporters or critics? With the last five
presidents—and particularly Ronald Reagan—devotees of the
strategy, protean anecdotal evidence now exists which renders this
conclusion dubious.[4] In fact, as the cases in this book illustrate,
administrative strategies frequently appear no more nor less dependent on political prowess than most legislative strategies.

Whither the Politics of the Administrative Presidency?

Why, then, has debate over the administrative presidency often
proceeded as if presidents wielding its tools reap decisive advantages at the macropolitical system level? At least four reasons seem
plausible. First, those debating tend to overestimate the ability of
political appointees to strike summarily, quickly, and quietly. Put
differently, disputants reason as if presidential appointees in Washington can stealthily change arcane administrative rules, budgets,
personnel, and intraorganizational structures relatively unfettered
by micro- or macropolitical system actors.[5] Hindsight now tells us,
however, that the courts, the Congress, federal bureaucrats, interest groups, and state and local politicos are formidable, patient,
and principled overseers of the administrative presidency.[6]

Recall, for example, how the federal courts helped stymie the
Carter Administration's EMARs and SVIM initiatives in New
Mexico. Quashed as well were the Reagan Administration's efforts
to accelerate both off-shore oil leasing and mineral leasing within
wilderness areas. Likewise, note how New Mexico's congressional
delegation set bounds on coal leasing in the San Juan Basin (SJB);
helped amend Burford's rangeland privatization strategy; got an
exemption for the Bisti from Watt's anti-wilderness policy; and

helped acquire the Elena Gallegos tract, despite its local rather than national significance. In effect, then, inadequate recognition is given to the bureaucratic politics of the administrative presidency as its initiatives wend tortuously through the channels of our Madisonian system. Thus, in practice, the administrative presidency is nowhere near as potent, unruly, and constitutionally mischievous as some of its opponents fear.

A second, rather cynical possibility, of course, is that opponents really don't believe that presidents are asymmetrically advantaged by the administrative presidency. Instead, raising the spectre of an "imperial presidency" is a political tactic masking less noble motives. In this view, opponents worry not about the strategy itself, but about the policy goals sought by those wielding it. Put most plainly, opponents of Nixon and Reagan's (and to an extent Carter's) deregulatory agenda scurried to the "moral high ground," couching their partisan assaults in lofty constitutional arguments. Thus, the administrative presidency was okay, as long as the policy swath cut by its scepter displayed the liberal, positive state goals of a Roosevelt, Kennedy, or Johnson. Indeed, how curious that the symbiotic relationship of the field of public administration with the American presidency grew tepid once Republicans seemingly gained an electoral lock on that post in the 1980s.

A third, less cynical reason why the relative prowess of the administrative presidency is overestimated involves the conventional wisdom surrounding congressional oversight of the bureaucracy. Indeed, classics in the field by Scher, Bibby, and Ogul stress the institutional disincentives for comprehensive or police patrol oversight.[7] Specifically, so fleeting are its political rewards, so impenetrable are the maze of agency activities that solons must oversee, and so stingy are the resources allocated to legislators for these purposes that oversight has low priority on Capitol Hill. Concomitantly, other scholars chronicle how agencies enjoy an asymmetrical power advantage over macropolitical actors during implementation, shaping policy to their own tastes.[8] With these conceptions, scholars logically concluded that the administrative presidency inordinately advantaged presidents and their emissaries. After all, hadn't Congress abandoned the playing field to presidentialists recognizing the wisdom of Nathan's now (in?)famous encomium: Operations constitute policy?

Yet more recently rational choice theorists have challenged traditional notions of congressional oversight. Instead, they portray a process much akin to the Reagan Administration's experiences in New Mexico. Not only do scholars now recognize how formidable fire alarm oversight can be, but some now claim that even police patrol oversight has increased dramatically since the mid-1970s.[9] As noted, in contrast to police patrol oversight, fire alarm oversight is less formal, ongoing, and systematic. Decidedly more episodic, fire alarm oversight results from the entreaties of constituents disgruntled with bureaucratic failings—be they real, imagined, or contrived. As McCubbins and Schwartz discuss, legislators exercising fire alarm oversight wish credit for satisfying constituent demands without engaging in comprehensive, time-consuming, and low-profile police patrol oversight. To wit, they quite rationally await outcries of bureaucratic malfeasance, misfeasance, or nonfeasance before initiating more formalized, focused reviews of agency behavior. In turn, this approach renders macropolitical oversight a more important, extensive, and effective check on the executive branch than previous research concedes. To this, Joel Aberbach's research adds an additional twist. His comprehensive analysis of congressional oversight suggests that both traditionalists *and* rational choice theorists insufficiently consider changes in congressional incentives since 1975. Chronicling longitudinally a dramatic increase in police patrol activities since that year, Aberbach demonstrates impressively how changing institutional structures and political environments have dramatically increased the rewards to congressmembers of police patrol oversight.

One possibility is that the use of the administrative presidency by recent incumbents is responsible to an extent for the oversight trends noted by Aberbach as well as by McCubbins and Schwartz. Indeed, the time periods covered by these scholars coincide directly with the wide-scale introduction of administrative strategies by President Nixon and his successors. But regardless of whether the strategy is cause, consequence, or merely coincident with these patterns, the implications of more aggressive congressional oversight are clear for the administrative presidency. Moreover, they reveal the first of several paradoxes prompted by the Reagan Administration's use of the administrative presidency to reorient public lands policy. Namely, the more Chief Executives and their appointees pursue policy reorientation administratively, the more likely they are to "set off" fire alarms prompting resistance from Congress, disgruntled clienteles, unsympathetic agency careerists, and aroused, litigious publics. Yet, if they don't pursue aggressive and skillful administrative strategies, their agendas are distinctly vulnerable to congressmembers "micromanaging" agency operations in pursuit of their own agendas in an era of divided government.

Witness, for example, the New Mexico congressional delegation's persistent intervention in the Elena Gallegos land exchange and the Bisti Badlands wilderness leasing issue. Likewise, recall how various politicians pursued a legislative strategy to affirm New Mexico's right to deny water exports to El Paso. Illustrative as well are Governor Anaya's success in altering Interior's coal-leasing schedules in the SJB, the oil and gas industry's lobbying for regulatory relief from the Bureau of Land Management after the Federal Oil and Gas Royalty Management Act, and the series of congressional moratoria on coal and leasing on the Outer Continental Shelf during the Reagan years.

The final reason why many overestimate the capacity of the administrative presidency is their focus on its ability to *stop* rather than to make things happen. For example, this perspective led most to conclude correctly that Reagan's supply-side management successes would significantly compromise or cripple certain regulatory activities. What it ignored, however, was this: The Reagan Revolution was not just about stopping things from happening (e.g., regulatory enforcement and environmental planning), but also about *making* things happen (e.g., promoting land exchanges rather than purchases, increasing the states' ability to plan for and control their own water futures, increasing rangeland improvements to avoid grazing reductions, and boosting energy production in the West). Thus, early assessments of Reagan's supply-side management strategy erred much like the appointees did who wielded the administrative presidency. First, they underestimated how predisposed and capable Congress was of attenuating budget cuts in key areas (e.g., the phasing out of funding for state water resource institutes). Second, they failed to anticipate how poorly Reagan's appointees often linked these tactics to the President's long-term strategic goals requiring positive actions.

Applying the latter linkage as a "competent process standard" for assessing the Administration's efforts provides an unflattering picture. Indeed, the New Mexico experiences demonstrate how inadequate linkage among the Administration's goals, objectives, and operational tactics regularly, but avoidably, compromised the President's natural resource agenda. In the process, the cases reveal a second implementation paradox of the Reagan Revolution: The more Reagan's appointees successfully used the administrative presidency to pursue regulatory relief, the more difficult it became for them to meet their resource production goals in New Mexico.

Clearly, the Administration's efforts to "unlock" urban areas for economic development, decelerate public land purchases and acquisition, and accelerate range improvements were sorely complicated by failing to link budget and personnel commitments with these strategic choices. Similarly, although appointees allocated resources in the Bureau of Land Management-Minerals Management Service (BLM-MMS) case in ways consistent with accelerating and deregulating energy production, the effort initially went awry. Why so? They were assigned to an organization more comfortable with, and culturally predisposed toward, multiple-use surface management than dominant-use subsurface energy production.

Finally, Reagan's administrative strategy no doubt brought regulatory relief to ranchers by slashing budgets and personnel for planning and for protecting the environment. Indeed, these actions rapidly helped defuse the Sagebrush Rebellion. Yet the Administration's unflagging zeal to retrench eventually jeopardized BLM's ability to perform statutory obligations in timely ways so that ranch improvements, monitoring, and production could expeditiously, confidently, and legally proceed in the long run.

Toward a Conceptual Framework

Following this argument, the administrative presidency is no more or less dependent on political and strategic prowess than are legislative strategies. Still, the bureaucratic politics of the administrative presidency are not uniform across disparate cases. Indeed, even a cursory review of the evidence amassed since Nathan's classic reveals just how variable these conflicts are in terms of scope, level, intensity, and outcome. But what accounts for these disparities? Again, the New Mexico cases are instructive. As noted in Part II, their bureaupolitical dynamics varied with changes in two critical policy characteristics: (1) the extent to which actors viewed the policy's core concepts, axioms, and deductive premises as incremental and valid;[10] and (2) how widely, persistently, and successfully "softened" the policy was before its inauguration.[11] For convenience, one might label these "policy validity" and "policy softening," respectively.[12]

In essence, political appointees using the administrative presidency to reorient policy are trying to alter bureaucratic agendas substantially. In doing so, they are unlikely to find an agency's "dominant coalition" predisposed to change. Coalition members are prone to buffer organizational cores from such "turbulence" and to protect their organization's fragile political economy. Equally unsympathetic to change are clienteles accustomed to existing agency rules, relationships, and largesse. This, in turn, makes policy initiatives distinctly vulnerable to fire alarm oversight, with the type of agenda item pursued by appointees conditioning the nature, scope, and intensity of resistance mounted by opponents.

The first policy characteristic—validity—requires one to view the initiatives pursued as "hypotheses" or "idea sets" that are more or less accepted as valid.[13] Policy implementation theorists term this the "validity of the causal theory." One also has to conceptualize the means for implementing a policy's goal as part of that hypothesis or idea set. Here, the logic is straightforward. Policy ends and means are inseparable; one cannot know if an end is worthy of pursuit without knowing how valid, ethical, and costly are the means for attaining it. True, the validity of the causal theory underlying a policy initiative varies, perhaps dramatically, over time. Thus the shifting assessment of a policy's validity will condition its bureaupolitical dynamics during implementation. Generally, the more novel the policy initiative, the less valid or widely accepted the components of a policy's idea set, and the more intensive bureaupolitical resistance will be to its implementation.

The second policy characteristic—softening—stems from

John Kingdon's work on agenda setting. Kingdon maintains that policy alternatives—whether incremental or nonincremental—must be considered, regularly discussed, and routinely debated over the years to be legitimate options when opportunities for policy choice arise. To Kingdon, an alternative not yet softened in this way lacks credibility and staying power. He writes that policy entrepreneurs:

> push their ideas in many different forums. [They] attempt to "soften up" both policy communities, which tend to be inertia-bound and resistant to major changes, and larger publics, getting them used to new ideas and building acceptance for their proposals. Then when a short-run opportunity to push their proposals comes, the way has been paved, the important people softened up. Without this preliminary work, a proposal sprung even at a propitious time is likely to fall on deaf ears. . . .There are many common language expressions of the same idea, phrases like "greasing the skids" and getting your ducks in a row.[14]

Thus, based on Kingdon's logic, the following proposition holds: The less a policy initiative is previously well, persistently, and effectively softened over time, the less likely is successful implementation.

In the real world, of course, these two variables can interact to produce distinct bureaupolitical dynamics. Take note, however: The bureaucratic politics occasioned are not "caused" by the interaction of the two variables, validity and softening. Rather, their interaction either affords or constrains opportunities for challenge to those opposed to drastic policy reorientation. Whether or not opponents will seize these opportunities—and hence initiate the bureaupolitical dynamics described—depends on other factors discussed later in Chapter 10. To see how and why this is true, we turn next to the four types of agenda items and bureaupolitical dynamics culled from the New Mexico experiences.

Type I. At one extreme, the first type of agenda item—high validity, high softening—and its consequences are exhibited in the decidedly modulated bureaupolitical dynamics of the Rio Puerco pipeline case. There, the ideas of assigning maintenance costs to rangeland users, ending "cow welfare," and decreasing the proportion of BLM funding for administration relative to range improvements enjoyed wide support and validity after years of persistent and effective softening. Indeed, economists in the Carter Administration, as well as many BLM careerists, wanted to wean ranchers from the federal dole and to emphasize on-the-ground improvements now that preparing EISs was well along. Recall, as well, how the Carter Administration left office proposing a massive range improvement program. Thus, when the Reagan Administration proposed such initiatives, they were neither novel, unsoftened, or abrupt departures from ongoing trends. In fact, specialists across a range of disciplines had developed and persistently offered them for debate over the years. Too, they had broad-based support across a macropolitical system weary of federally subsidized overgrazing of the public lands. Finally, they seemed to be ideas whose time had come, given the nation's fiscal stress and its receptivity to user fees in other policy contexts.

So conceived, the Administration's Rangeland Improvement Policy dismayed some parties, but offered little fodder for debating the legitimacy of its idea sets. Thus, while attitudes among the parties—ranchers, state BLMers, and BLM's Washington Office— were sometimes competitive, mutual respect and trust largely colored their exchanges. Moreover, because the validity of the idea set was not an issue, BLM's Washington Office communications were specific, relatively consistent, and well-understood in the field. To the extent to which controversy arose, the most salient issues involved timing, pace, costs, and scope of implementation, not whether privatization should occur at all. Thus, once DuBois, Burford, and Watt realized that its pace placed inordinate burdens on smaller, marginal, and less well-heeled ranchers like those in Rio Puerco, they did not feel compelled to junk the policy. Rather, they slowed its implementation to accommodate the concerns of state BLM officials. In sum, a pattern of mutual accommodation characterized the dispute.

Likewise, while previously litigious Rio Puerco ranchers appealed for redress to Watt, local congressmen, and New Mexico's Secretary of Agriculture, the scope, intensity, and contagiousness of the conflict never reached the epic proportions witnessed elsewhere in Part II. Instead, lower levels of BLM's hierarchy essentially resolved the dispute, with upper-level Interior officials, such as DuBois, occasionally setting the parameters of the settlement. Why was this true, even though ranchers and state BLM directors were uncomfortable with Burford's initiatives? Arguably, the legitimacy of privatization and of political appointees shifting expenditure decisions to district office managers was unquestioned, well-softened, and politically sexy. Consequently, had opponents tried to mobilize external political resources extensively, their actions were unlikely to succeed and very likely to be labeled illegitimate and obstructionist.

Type II. In contrast, the second agenda type—moderate validity, low softening—and its consequences are exhibited in the somewhat more contentious bureaupolitical dynamics of the Las Cruces Industrial Park–Elena Gallegos Land Exchange. Here, sociopolitical and economic events converged to propel rapidly a decidedly less tested and more precarious idea set than privatizing rangeland costs (viz., large-scale land exchanges) to the center of Reagan's land acquisition agenda. Recall how land exchange was a time-worn, routinely practiced, and widely appreciated method for acquiring federal properties. Indeed, most natural resource agencies acquired land exchange authority over the years. What troubled many, however, was the unprecedented scale of the land exchange task envisioned by Reagan's appointees. In essence, the "marginal" validity of the causal theory underlying large-scale land exchanges was sorely in doubt, although the "generic" validity of exchanges as a tool of land management had high validity.

To see why this was true, one has only to remember the concerns expressed during the 1981 Workshop on Public Land Exchanges. Witnesses worried, for example, that techniques for assessing fair market values were too primitive, that staffing for exchanges was too minimal, and that incentives to speculate were too overpowering to render large-scale exchanges viable unless major reforms occurred. Two key reforms proposed were (1) increasing staffing and training for exchange personnel and (2) creating a process to coordinate exchange procedures among state, federal, and local governments. In sum, subsystem actors and portions of the larger macropolitical system viewed land exchanges as a valid, long-softened approach to land acquisition. Yet Reagan's precipitous rush to propel large-scale exchanges occurred without persistent softening of significant actors, in the absence of consensus over techniques, amid supply-side management cuts, and with powerful concerns over its negative consequences for acquiring public lands.

Against this backdrop, BLM careerists in New Mexico perceived the initiative as decidedly less legitimate than Burford's more softened, widely established rangeland initiatives. Moreover, their resistance heightened once the territorial stakes of the exchange were clear for the BLM and the Forest Service. Still, the Reagan Administration's premature foisting of the exchange initiative on Interior's policy agenda drove the bureaupolitical dynamics of the land exchange significantly. How so? With assessment procedures and market values so problematic and contentious, with interagency bureaucratic routines so inimical, and with transfer authority so complex and debatable, communications among the parties were often unspecific, inconsistent, and misunderstood. These, in turn, aroused competitive, less respectful, and more inflexible negotiating patterns among the parties, especially when compared to the Rio Puerco case. Note, for example, how strained negotiations were between Albuquerque, Las Cruces, the Boys Academy, and the Forest Service. Most ascribed this situation to inadequate staffing, uncertainty over land transfer authorities, untimely delays occasioned by assessment difficulties, and doubts about giving preference to Las Cruces in any subsequent sale of the properties.

For the disputants, the uncertainty and ambiguity surrounding this rapidly softened policy initiative meant that success was attainable only by expanding the scope, level, and intensity of the conflict. Moreover, these same characteristics made it distinctly possible for them to do so. Recall, for instance, how the parties repeatedly and successfully recruited Schmitt and Lujan as "fixers" during implementation. Indeed, Lujan figuratively placed the southwest region of the Forest Service in his "receivership" until the exchange occurred. Likewise, when "ancient antagonisms" twixt the BLM and the Forest Service threatened to derail the exchange, Schmitt and Lujan pressured upper-level managers such as Jean Hassell and state BLM Director Luscher to resolve the disputes. Forthwith, land appraisals proceeded expeditiously and logjams over conflicting agency standard operating procedures broke. Finally, recall how Senator Domenici cajoled the Reagan Administration into swallowing a "local" land exchange, one inimical to its "national priority" criterion and nascent Asset Management Program.

Certainly, the efforts to arouse micro- and macropolitical intervention in the Industrial Park–Elena Gallegos case were more substantial in scope and successful in application than in the Rio Puerco case. Not only did the uncertainty, novelty, and complexity surrounding large-scale exchanges make them possible, but these same characteristics fell on sympathetic ears, provided grounds for intervention, and multiplied access points for fire alarm oversight. Still, the scope and intensity of the conflict—while greater than the mutual accommodation patterns that accompanied the Rio Puerco experience—were substantially less broad, adversarial, or sustained than in either the Rio Grande Basin or the Bisti Badlands cases. In these, the disputants sought, obtained, and benefitted from full-scale congressional oversight and judicial appeals.

Instead, the Elena Gallegos experience offers a pattern of conflict wherein the disputants tried to manipulate or maneuver each other into agreement. They did so fully cognizant that a linear sequential pattern of interdependence structured their relationships: The actions of each actor were inputs to at least one of the others.[15] All, except for elements within the BLM, wished some form of land exchange to take place. And all realized that others had to take certain actions sequentially in order for Las Cruces, Albuquerque, and the Forest Service to complete the exchange. Acting in ways reminiscent of Eugene Bardach's "odd-man-out" implementation game,[16] participants in this "assembly-line" process often withheld their necessary contributions. They did so until (1) they were sure that others would contribute and (2) they were able to contribute on their own terms.

Yet never did the disputants try to expand the conflict to full-scale judicial or congressional arenas. To do so might jeopardize tight timetables or the conditional cooperation of the others. Delay—always an inflationary nemesis in real estate transactions—already plagued the appraisal process, given the Administration's budget and personnel cuts. It also took its toll on

Wittern's private-sector industrial park initiative, and threatened Las Cruces' prison and airport expansion.

Most common, instead, were attempts to "maneuver" cooperation from others by "seizing the moral high ground" (e.g., Democratic Mayor Rusk's goading of Republicans Schmitt and Lujan) or brief episodes of fire alarm oversight by congressional fixers. But a full-tilt assault on the "idea" of exchanges itself (in favor of fully restoring Land and Water Conservation Fund appropriations) by the disputants never occurred. It was precluded at both the national and subnational levels by the moderate validity of the technique (i.e., of land exchanges generally), the need to avoid acquisition delay, and the Reagan Administration's strategic budget deficits. For those pushing land acquisition, exchanges became one of the few games in town. Meanwhile, exempting Elena Gallegos from their "national priority" policy to placate Domenici and Lujan was worth it to the Reaganites to salvage other parts of their agenda where the two legislators were influential.

Type III. The third type of agenda item—low validity, high softening—and its consequences are exhibited in the distinctly more adversarial bureaucratic politics of (1) the Carter Administration's SVIM computer modeling experience, and (2) the Reagan Administration's response to the Rio Grande Basin water dispute. Recall how the inventory of public rangelands to determine carrying capacity was a long-standing, well-softened, yet conspicuously underfunded activity throughout BLM's history. Equally discussed and underfunded was creating an accurate data base for assessing the quantity, quality, perennial yield, and hydrological relationships between surface and groundwater supplies in the Southwest. In the late 1970s and early 1980s, both the Carter and Reagan administrations had to address these issues, as overgrazing became a dire threat and *Sporhase* menaced state control of groundwater supplies.

In both instances, these ideologically disparate administrations proffered quite novel, untried, and controversial "policy fixes" or idea sets. In the rangeland case, the environmentally oriented Carter Administration took advantage of new, relatively untested computer modeling methods to mathematically project diminished carrying capacity. Based on these projections, the BLM reduced grazing permits accordingly. In the process, the Bureau produced a qualitatively different type of grazing reduction policy, shifting from on-the-ground monitoring to stochastic modeling techniques. Similarly, when Reagan's Interior Department eschewed solving by statute the dormant commerce clause issue, and when it cut groundwater research funding, it effectively opted for a novel states' rights policy. In essence, states like New Mexico had to consider participating in rather than directly regulating water markets.

Both policy initiatives—one deliberate and the other a logical consequence of inaction—were significant breaks with the past in one important sense. Specifically, the "technical means" (viz., SVIM, water export restrictions, and water market participation) to accomplish their long-softened goals (viz., grazing reductions and the protection of state water rights) were quite novel and unsoftened. Thus, as key technical changes in policy, they qualitatively altered their respective idea sets as well. In the process, the novelty of each provided opponents (on whatever other grounds) with credible grist for principled, bitter, and prolonged conflict.

In reality, of course, the cases also differed somewhat. Carter's SVIM initiative was central to the fight engulfing grazing reductions in New Mexico. In contrast, Reagan's emergent water market initiative, research cutbacks, and cost-sharing proposals afforded only a backdrop to the El Paso–New Mexico dispute. Still, actors in the latter largely predicated their actions on either actual or anticipated Administration policies. What is more, both disputes shared many of the same characteristics. For instance, both "technological breakthroughs" (SVIM and water markets) were ideas well-incubated (or softened) by specialists within relevant policy communities, but relatively unknown to nonspecialists. Finally, both of them sparked among the parties (1) high levels of skepticism and distrust, (2) spiraling and contagious conflict, (3) persistent and overt ally mobilization, and (4) periodic intervention by Congress and the courts over elements of the dispute. Thus, in both instances, the combat grew so non-negotiable that the parties willingly let the courts and/or Congress settle aspects of their disagreement.

To appreciate these points, one needs only to recall the specifics of the SVIM case. As reported, the first three SVIM-based EISs cut grazing capacity sharply, thus prompting disgruntled ranchers and agricultural extension agents to expand the scope of the conflict initially by contacting Domenici and Schmitt. Engaging in fire alarm oversight, both in turn held congressional hearings on general BLM operations. Here, critics feasted on the vulnerability to challenge of emergent policy initiatives like SVIM. Thus, to thwart grazing reductions, most persuasively alleged that the data informing and assumptions underlying SVIM's carrying-capacity models were unsound.

Simultaneously, as contentiousness grew and stalemate ensued, the combatants expanded aspects of the conflict to the courts and to Congress. Ranchers, for example, turned successfully to the courts to contest successfully the technical and due process aspects of the Carter Administration's actions. Likewise effective were their entreaties to Congress to limit the magnitude of grazing cuts (viz., the McClure Amendment). Still, the parties studiously avoided an externally imposed settlement of the larger issue—viz., crafting a range-monitoring and carrying capacity process capable of satisfying ranchers, state officials, environmentalists, range scientists, and economists. The result of this strategy was the model memorandum of understanding between the BLM and the State of New Mexico institutionalizing consultation among all the parties in future grazing decisions.

Type IV. The final agenda type—low validity, low softening—and its consequences are illustrated by the bureaupolitical dynamics of the San Juan Basin case in particular, as well as Secretary Watt's energy program generally. As reported in Chapter 8, the idea of coal leasing in wilderness areas and wilderness study areas was one that Democratic *and* Republican administrations had eschewed as misguided since passage of the 1964 Wilderness Act. Likewise, while even the Carter Administration had planned to increase coal leasing in the Powder River and San Juan basins, the Reagan Administration's wide-open leasing plan nearly doubled the Carter Administration's production goals. This, in turn, changed qualitatively a familiar idea with widespread consensus into an unsoftened, radical one lacking face validity. Lastly, and likewise unsoftened and untenable, was the Reagan Administration's plan to allow the free market rather than Regional Coal Teams (RCTs) to determine production levels. Once again, Reagan's appointees rapidly cast each idea upon the political agenda without sustained, persistent softening up of key actors in Andrus' fragile state-industry-environmental coalition.

Just how much "quantum" changes like these can disintegrate comity and civility among the parties is clear from a national perspective. With coal markets, prices, and demand "soft," the Reagan Administration's "unsoftened," vastly accelerated program provided leasing opponents with credible and persuasive grist for political challenge. For example, Reagan's appointees failed to prove compellingly that circumstances leading previous administrations to nix coal leasing in WAs and WSAs were operative no longer. Neither did they demonstrate compellingly why the industry had to explore these fragile lands first, given how little they could contribute to regional supplies. Likewise, how could anyone justify severely disrupting traditional Navajo when energy demand was declining? In sum, softening of these issues never had high priority for the Administration, an attitude that played directly into the hands of leasing opponents who rapidly expanded the scope, level, and intensity of the conflict in receptive congressional and judicial arenas.

Initially, and with great success in the wake of the Powder River sale, opponents raised the issue of procedural legitimacy. True, charges of illegality never stuck to the Administration. Nevertheless, the Linowes Commission and Office of Technology Assessment studies so tellingly impugned the Administration's judgement and motives that major Republican oil, gas, and coal-leasing initiatives were effectively dead until the first term of the Bush Administration. Even then, Bush appointees had to scale back considerably their initial proposals. In sum, this quantum change in policy wrought rigid, non-negotiable demands, hostile attitudes among the disputants, broken communications, and overall settlements imposed by macropolitical actors.

Within the SJB, bureaupolitical dynamics were somewhat different, yet conditioned directly by national forces, factors, and actors. Specifically, the way parties interacted was distinctly less rigid and demands were significantly more negotiable. Of course, actors there did not have to wrestle directly with the non-negotiable issues resolved at the macropolitical level by congressional moratoria, appropriation bill riders, annual authorizing amendments, and federal judges. But the nature, scale, and timing of the Reagan Administration's initiatives in the Basin evoked similar feelings of illegitimacy, hostility, and appeals to macropolitical sovereigns for an imposed settlement. Recall, for example, Governor Anaya's ultimatum regarding leasing levels, his acerbic exchanges with Secretary Watt, and his state's direct challenges to the Administration's projections concerning appropriate leasing targets, projected energy demands, and state royalty payments. Equally illustrative was the fire alarm oversight exercised by Lujan, Richardson, and Domenici who effectively cobbled together the particulars of the San Juan Basin Wilderness Bill to their liking, rather than the Administration's.

Summing Up

The preceding suggests two things. First, disparate types of bureaupolitical behavior characterized the Reagan Administration's experiences in New Mexico. Second, these disparate patterns are associated largely with the interaction patterns of two key variables. These are: (1) the established validity of the idea set underlying the policy initiative pursued, and (2) how persistently and effectively softened the policy was prior to joining the Administration's agenda. Are these two variables equally important for understanding the dynamics of the administrative presidency in other policy arenas, or are they merely peculiar to natural resource policy? Later, in Chapter 10, a framework incorporating these two variables is elaborated and extended across a range of domestic and foreign policy initiatives. At present, however, the task of assessing the implications of the New Mexico cases for natural resource policy is unfinished. Thus, we turn next to the implementation lessons they afford those using the administrative presidency as a tool for substantially reorienting policy at the grassroots.

BEYOND FORWARD MAPPING: TOWARD A STRATEGIC PERSPECTIVE

In recounting her days as a speechwriter in the Reagan White House, Peggy Noonan notes that "Soldier On!" was a common greeting among the footsoldiers of the Reagan Revolution.[17] And soldier on they did, in a supply-side management mode, throughout the President's two terms in office. The New Mexico experiences, however, imply that the supply-side management zeal of key Reagan appointees had three shortcomings. First, it was not always linked well to the president's substantive policy goals. Second, the strategy took a decidedly top-down or hierarchical perspective on implementation. Finally, the strategy's purveyors failed to entertain sufficiently how implementing any single initiative affects ongoing policy efforts in related areas, given the polycentric nature of most public problems. These lessons, in turn, alert us to how important it is for appointees and scholars to conceptualize policy reorientation as a process pursued strategically within two realms: the "governance structures" of individual organizations and the "governance networks" of specific policy arenas.[18]

As posited by Karen Hult and Charles Walcott, a governance perspective views organizations as political systems, political arenas, or polities "that develop structures for channeling political dynamics and performing political tasks."[19] Moreover, these scholars view this model as a more apt metaphor for organizational behavior than three popular alternatives: the "mechanistic" (or "control system"), biological (or "natural system"), or "political arena" models. These three, they aver, are not so much wrong as they are incomplete models of organizational phenomena.

To Hult and Walcott, the mechanistic model understates the importance of human psychology, organizational environments, and goal ambiguity in understanding why public agencies act the way they do. Similarly, the biological model understates how much disharmony typically exists within organizations, while the political arena model overstates the competitive, pluralistic, and combative aspects of organizational life. Thus, Hult and Walcott laud at length the superiority of the governance metaphor.

> The model posits uncertainty and controversy [over policy ends and means], located both inside and outside of organizations. It also assumes that organizations actively seek to cope with these circumstances: they take what measures they can to reduce uncertainty and to keep controversy within manageable bounds, leading ultimately to an organizationally acceptable decision. In addition, the governance model anticipates that an organization's approaches to handling

problems involving uncertainty or controversy become more stan-
dardized as the problems recur. The resulting decision-making
routines are what we call "governance structures" . . . interlocking series of processes that require the input and acquiescence of
a number of people and that permit outside influence to affect the
outcome. . . . This is not an improvised power struggle, but a re-
curring cycle of decision making and influence, some of it formally prescribed by agency procedures, some informally added on in
practice.[20]

The concept of governance networks is similar to Hjern and
Porter's notion of "implementation structures." These scholars
warn us not to conceptualize implementation as the activity of a
single, unified department or agency formally charged with effecting policy (the "lonely organization syndrome"). Instead, they
portray a more robust intra- and interorganizational process. In
their words, programs "are implemented by clusters [or 'subsets']
of parts of public and private organizations" which are "more
likely to be self-selected than designed through authoritative
relationships."[21]

So conceived, implementation is understood best and its travails anticipated most readily by: (1) identifying the pool of organizations which must contribute to successful implementation; (2)
defining the subunits within and across these organizations which
must cooperate for implementation to succeed; (3) appreciating
how decisions to contribute to implementation within the matrix
of this implementation structure are based on consent and negotiation; and (4) understanding that administrative priorities (i.e., organizational imperatives) must be synchronized across organizations (i.e., program imperatives) for policy implementation to
proceed effectually.

But how does all this relate to Reagan's use of the administrative presidency to reorient natural resource policy in the West? Put
most simply, the New Mexico cases portray an Administration
that, to its peril, largely eschewed the governance model in favor of
a top-down, control-oriented, mechanistic one. This approach, in
turn, drastically complicated and compromised the President's
pro-development agenda for natural resources. Recall, for example, how ignoring the administrative imperative within organiza-

tions proved costly when appointees assigned on-shore energy leasing and regulatory responsibilities to the BLM. Similarly frustrating was how appointees failed, despite adequate warnings, to provide mechanisms for meshing disparate SOPs, institutional cultures, and territorial rivalries among land exchange agents. Finally, the Administration's leasing efforts in the Powder River Basin and the SJB floundered fatally when appointees tried either to "end-run" (e.g., the RCT) or to steamroll (e.g., the Navajo) members of the energy leasing network.

This, of course, is not to suggest that Reagan's policies "failed" in the traditional sense of the term. In fact, Reagan's appointees made some progress toward the President's goals in each case. But, as Aberbach suggests, theirs was more of an "imprint than a revolution."[22] What is more, their failure to link short-term supply-side management tactics to Reagan's long-term strategic goals is directly responsible for this outcome.

This tendency to take a mechanistic rather than a governance approach to applying the administrative presidency broke two cardinal rules of policy implementation. The first is Landau and Stout's now-classic warning to administrators: "To manage is not to control."[23] The second is Richard Elmore's sage advice to eschew both "forward" and "backward" mapping implementation styles in favor of a "reversible logic" approach.[24] Taking Landau's missive first, he attached importance to both goal and technical uncertainty. Specifically, Type II errors are exacerbated by control-oriented strategies. These close prematurely an agency's ability to "learn" by demanding rigid adherence to rules, regulations, and other standard operating procedures. Extending Landau's thinking, other scholars have suggested matches between levels of policy uncertainty, controversy, and governance structures (see Table 9–1).

While hardly exhaustive, exclusive, or immutable, the matches portrayed do place the Reagan Administration's natural resource fortunes in New Mexico in perspective. Most especially, they highlight how mismatched their top-down approach was to the decision settings they encountered. Indeed, trolling the organizational theory literature reveals a common theme: control-oriented, bureaucratic approaches like the Administration's are most appropri-

TABLE 9–1   Decision Settings and Appropriate
Governance Networks

Technical	Goal		
	Uncertainty	Consensus	Controversy
Uncertainty	1 Decentralized	2 Team	3 Confrontational Bargaining
Certainty	4 Team	5 Bureaucratic	6 Confrontational Bargaining
Controversy	7 Consultative Confrontational	8 Consultative Confrontational Appeals	9 Indeterminate

Source: Karen Hult and Charles Walcott, *Governing Public Organizations* (Pacific Grove, CA: Brooks/Cole Publishing Company, 1990), p. 105.

ate when consensus exists over policy ends and means. Yet in the New Mexico cases, this was the exception, not the rule.

Witness, for example, the Elena Gallegos–Industrial Park case. While consensus existed nationally that exchanges were promising, the technical aspects of *large-scale* exchanges were distinctly uncertain. Under these circumstances, the literature calls for a team rather than a bureaucratic approach to decision making and implementation. Yet, Reagan's appointees summarily instituted their plans without prolonged softening or consensus-building in relevant governance networks. A similar critique applies to the San Juan Basin (goal controversy, technical certainty), the Rio Grande Basin (goal controversy, technical uncertainty), and rangeland privatization (goal consensus, technical controversy) disputes. Thus, instead of the administrative orthodoxy, these cases seem better suited to confrontational bargaining (the SJB and RGB disputes) and consultative decision styles (rangeland privatization). Indeed, all three wound up being resolved in one of these fashions anyway.

In essence, not only were the Administration's short-term supply-side management tactics poorly linked to Reagan's pro-development goals, but its decision styles were equally ill-matched to their particular decision settings.

Turning to Elmore's advice, a reversible logic approach to policy design seems distinctly more likely to craft policy change under fiscal stress than Reagan's forward-mapping strategy. The latter implicitly admonishes policy formulators to frame solutions incorporating those implements over which they have the greatest control. Then evaluators measure how closely the implemented policy resembles original design intentions. Deviations mean that hierarchical control was applied ineffectively, while prescriptions call for tighter controls on implementors' discretion. Thus, policy makers begin with the implements (e.g., budgets, rules, structure, and personnel decisions) they can control. Next, they (1) assess the parameters (i.e., the sociopolitical environment) within which these actions will occur, (2) identify implementing agencies and the target groups affected by them, and (3) hypothesize the effect of agency actions. Here, "the important strategic decision is how much vertical control to exercise on what subjects."[25] Unfortunately, however, a focus on how well implementors and targets comply with national policy in specific ways through vertical lines of authority creates a kind of Gresham's Law of policy implementation. Specifically, focusing on compliance renders tangential or ancillary a more appropriate focus: How well did the policy accomplish what it set out to do, and what can be learned from this?

The New Mexico cases offered several examples of precisely this dysfunction. As noted, both the industrial park and rangeland management cases demonstrate how Secretary Watt's anti-environmental retrenchment crusade in Washington negatively affected the Administration's production goals in the field. Most striking, however, was how the Administration persisted in its supply-side vendetta—long after its counterproductive aspects were clear. For example, regulations proscribing the expenditure of certain funds for administration, environmental assessments, and planning remained in force, despite the bottlenecks these regulations produced for range improvements and monitoring. Thus, by not seeing implementation as "an interlocking system of parochial decisions," Reagan's appointees ideologically and tirelessly bashed certain aspects of the implementation process, seeming to dismiss how vital these were to their production plans. Likewise, by focusing only on what they could directly "control," Reagan's appointees compromised their ability to anticipate and cope with the actions and responses of subnational actors within the Madisonian federal system. Witness, for example, DuBois candidly revealing that the Administration didn't anticipate the problems Burford's privatization program might pose for less affluent ranchers and for monitoring multi-million dollar, technologically complex federal projects.

Finally, the Administration's top-down perspective emphasized control over specific budget accounts, personnel allocations, and rule-making exercises in specific agencies and policy areas. This focus, however, ignores the nature of public problems in contemporary America: Because they are polycentric in nature (i.e., they cut across different policy areas), a change in policy in one arena most likely has ramifications in others. Recall, for example, how the Navajo-Hopi Relocation Program and the Administration's coal-leasing agenda clashed fractiously in the crowded "policy space" of northwestern New Mexico. In sum, those wishing to reorient policy must adopt a strategic perspective, one capable of viewing their actions within a matrix of ongoing policy efforts. Then, they must assess how each initiative affects the other. Finally, they must determine where, when, and how best to apply the tools of the administrative presidency to create a "policy bias" favoring their goals. In effect, appointees have to view implementation as a "trading among objectives," an enterprise that requires more emphasis on lateral relationships among organizations within implementation structures. So informed, vertical control of federal bureaucrats becomes more tactical than strategic.

But what would such a perspective look like in practice? One option, less promising, is to take solely a backward-mapping approach to implementation analysis. As sketched by Elmore, this approach begins at the last stage of the implementation process: realizing goals in the field. Policy makers identify tasks that different administrative levels must perform to reach that goal. Then they ensure that these organizations are sufficiently equipped with "men, money, and materiel" to perform these duties. More precisely, policy makers identify the targets of a policy initiative (e.g., ranchers or energy companies) and assess the nature and direction of the behavior they wish to effect in them. Next, they specify which organizations (public or private) can affect most immediately the behavioral choices these targets make. Finally, they ascertain which implements (i.e., methods or tools) will most effectively persuade targets to make behavioral choices in the desired direction. To do so, however, federal policy makers give those actors closest to the problem the discretion to select which combination of implements should be applied to it.

Coincident with this analysis, policy makers also ask what tasks various organizational units have to complete, what human and capital resources they need to do so, what policy predilections or biases implementors hold, and where internal or external veto points or bottlenecks might occur. To take one example, once presidential appointees selected urban economic development and public land exchanges as objectives, a backward-mapping process would have identified as essential the need to complete timely planning and environmental inventories to comply with the law. Then, policy makers would have adequately funded these activities—regardless of the philosophical angst they experienced in doing so.

Such an approach, taken within the governance structure of the BLM, would involve two things: (1) examining the funding and structural needs of the agency's overall management system, and (2) recognizing the legal and operational relationships among management activities. So, rather than maintain a budgetary perspective focusing exclusively on individual programs, funds, or issues, policy makers would consider what resource levels are needed to manage complex, natural resource systems on the ground for multiple-use purposes. In the process, they would consider how changing priorities (e.g., emphasizing oil and gas production) affect the financial and personnel needs of other programs.

All this is acutely necessary in the natural resource arena. Note, for example, how the statutory components of the BLM land management process support and depend upon each other. To increase natural resource production, the Bureau has to complete management plans for specific activities (e.g., ranching or recreation). These rely on comprehensive resource management plans that, in turn, piggyback on substantively precise and legally adequate resource inventories. Undergirding everything, of course, is a sufficiently staffed, trained, and funded personnel system with requisite resource production and protection skills. To discount, dismiss, or ignore these interdependencies—or to make funding and staffing decisions predicated on summarily "repealing" them—is folly and hazardous to one's production goals.

But does backward mapping alone really offer sufficient counsel to those wielding the tools of the administrative presidency in the natural resource policy arena? More recent scholarship by Elmore suggests not. He suggests that forward and backward mapping are each disastrously incomplete if used without the other. Likening implementation analysis to a decision tree, Elmore advises policy makers to work their way mentally through the process in an interactive fashion, using both top-down and bottom-up perspectives. He writes:

> To construct a decision tree, we first break a complex problem into a series of choices (decision nodes) and uncertain events (chance nodes). We then arrange those choices and events in sequence from the first possible choice to all possible outcomes or end values. The branches of the decision tree describe alternative paths to a variety of end values.

But how does one choose which path to take? Elmore continues:

> To use a decision tree for this purpose, we must assign values to the pay-offs associated with each node on each path. We do this by "folding-back" or "flipping" the tree. Folding-back or flipping involves using the values at the ends of various branches to assign values to specific nodes along each path. The model works, first, by laying out sequences of choices and events, and then by using end results to assign values along each path.[26]

Be advised, however, that reversible logic can be as quantitative, impressionistic, or intuitive as the situation or skills of policy makers allow. Elmore uses decision analysis to convey only the thought processes involved in reversible logic. The message for policy makers? Applying solely a forward-mapping perspective focuses one exclusively on those implements that decision makers can control, their costs, and their effects on policy goals. True, in the process they will assess the critical cause-effect aspects of an idea set: What is the relationship between an implement, or bundle of implements, and an expected outcome? But this ignores the equally critical bottom-up or backward-mapping perspective. Hence, policy makers must simultaneously "reverse the logic and assess the cause-effect relationship from the point of view of [target populations] or the implementing agencies, asking what [behavioral] options they face."[27] Put differently, how are these targets likely to react to the initiative? With what intensity? With what resources? With how much success?

To summarize, the reversible logic approach does three things: (1) allows policy makers to identify key actors, behavioral responses, and coping strategies that elude forward mappers; (2) lets them realize how heterogeneous their target populations are and how varied the responses to their initiative will be; and (3) displaces their mechanistic models of implementation with governance models. Thus informed, policy makers can adjust accordingly the mix of policy implements they apply to best advance their policy agenda.

Linking reversible logic to the administrative presidency certainly does not preclude retrenchment efforts like the Reagan Administration's. But it could help avert the self-frustrating cuts and initiatives that plagued its experiences in New Mexico. Granted, reversible logic might have spawned less political symbolism and fewer references to a "Reagan Revolution." Yet achieving the President's long-term natural resource goals more robustly might have been less problematic as well. Environmentalists might have eschewed the sustained vigilance and ire provoked by these same symbols and rhetoric. Too, the institutional capacity and political savvy for effectively reorienting policy might have been in place when needed.

Thus, the problems which plagued policy reorientation in New Mexico are indeed noteworthy. However, they only reflect problems in the Reagan Administration's approach to the strategy, not in the strategy itself. Collectively using budgets, personnel policies, agency rule making, and reorganization to energize one's agenda is a time-worn, increasingly vital, and effective presidential strategy. Yet a necessary albeit insufficient condition for success is an adroit meshing of strategic, operational, and political choices. Note, for example, how Reagan's appointees failed to satisfy this condition in the BLM-MMS case. Assigning responsibility for on-shore minerals to the BLM was politically appealing to the President's ranching constituency, to ambitious politicos seeking rancher support in future electoral ventures, and to BLM careerists long coveting these tasks. Yet operationally, it was patently unsuited to Reagan's energy production goals, given BLM's dominant subculture and multiple-use, surface management mandate. Without a firm political hand to the contrary, a reorganization reaffirming BLM's traditional values was inevitable.

Without question, presidents seeking policy dominance are doomed to failure in the American political system of checks and balances, issue networks, and judicialized administration. Thus, they will find any administrative strategy wanting, no matter how well conceived and executed. Those who only seek, however, to marshal a policy bias favoring their agenda within that system should not dismiss hastily an administrative strategy linked tautly to a reversible logic implementation style.

Truly, reorienting policy administratively is a formidable task, as the New Mexico cases detail so poignantly. Yet, as Ronald Reagan poetically put it, "History is as heroic as you want it to be, as heroic as you are."[28] In this spirit, Chapter 10 will offer academics and practitioners a framework for understanding, evaluating, and pursuing this "heroic" task across a variety of policy domains. Before leaving this chapter, however, a final lesson of the New Mexico cases deserves attention. Here, the focus is on the formidable final obstacle to reorienting policy administratively within the natural resource policy arena: the stubborn persistence of administrative orthodoxy as the pillar of organizational reform in the contemporary administrative state.

TWIXT MARKETS, HIERARCHIES, AND CLANS

Thus far, this chapter has treated the implementation conundrum of the Reagan Administration in New Mexico as the product of (1) bureaupolitical dynamics and (2) appointees failing to link wisely their short-term actions to the President's avowed long-term goals. To these, however, one must add a third conditioning factor: the tendency for Reagan's appointees to apply the administrative presidency in ways consistent with the traditional administrative orthodoxy. Yet the problem runs deeper still. At its heart is our predilection in a democracy to structure public organizations for control and accountability rather than accomplishment.

Nonmarket Failures and "Simplistic Sovereignty"

As discussed in Chapter 2, Golembiewski cogently argues that bureaucratic "reform," as most often practiced, involves only fine-tuning structures and procedures to fit better the conventional tenets of bureaucracy. Thus, the solution to bureaupathologies becomes *more* bureaucracy more adroitly applied. Ironically, however the bureaucratic model—characterized by strict division of labor, hierarchical control, and procedural regulations—produces "functional fiefdoms," "rational ignorance," and organizational rigidity rather than Weber's smoothly functioning, highly rational bureaucratic machine. Writes Golembiewski, "Departmentation below the chief executive by separate 'functions' at the highest levels, and by 'processes' or 'tasks' at lower levels . . . commonly fragment[s] a flow of work so as to preclude any agent or agency from handling a 'complete transaction'."[29]

Likewise, procedural rules reinforce the insularity of each program, unit, and person within the public agency. This does two things. First, it pits subunits against each other in a zero-sum struggle for autonomy, resources, and program priority. Second, it creates perverse incentive structures in which rational individuals produce collective irrationality. Specifically, everyone pursues his narrow self-interest while remaining "rationally ignorant" of the need to cooperate to achieve overarching policy goals.

In light of these pathologies, why does the administrative orthodoxy dominate popular, presidential, and media prescriptions for handling the "bureaucracy problem"? Applying a neoinstitutionalist perspective, Jack Knott and Gary Miller suggest that the fragmentation the administrative orthodoxy produces redounds to the benefit of interest groups, members of Congress, and the professional-bureaucratic complex.[30] Fragmenting bureaucracy and making it more complex afford access and autonomy to well-heeled, well-organized, and well-educated elites. Similarly, Terry Moe alleges that public agencies are intentionally designed around functions or programs for political advantage.[31] Specifically, winners and losers in the policy debate purposely structure agencies to be ineffective when staffed by the other. Finally, neo-Marxists suggest that the administrative orthodoxy prevails because it maintains control over a passive work force "deskilled" by fragmenting work flow.

These pejorative interpretations notwithstanding, a more noble reason for the resiliency of the administrative orthodoxy lies in our democratic values. Most telling are those that Rosenbloom associates with the political tradition of public administration: accountability, responsiveness, and representativeness. Again, the link between structure and democratic values is put best by Golembiewski when he writes of "safeguarding sovereignty in simplistic ways":

> What accounts for this curious imbalance of relinquishing the bureaucratic model in many [private sector] areas and yet clinging to it in the public sector? Consider the notion of "unity of command" central in the bureaucratic model. At the broadest level, the concept provides perhaps *the* central linkage in democratic political philosophy, albeit simplistically. Unity of command in the office of the presidency suggests a kind of "direct-line democracy," with the electors/people choosing a president who serves as the "head" of the plural executive, whose officials are in turn the bodily appendages serving his directing will. This primitive ideation still provides the major linkage between those doing the public's work and the publics constituting the republic, a vexatious problem in political philosophy.[32]

Equally simplistic is the American propensity to use rules and fixed operating procedures as guides to agency success and as guarantors of accountability. As Donald Warwick suggests, doing so in the public sector is quite understandable, with goals ambiguous, agreed-upon performance criteria elusive, and market discipline typically absent.[33] Thus, imposing and complying with rules "remains the most direct and reassuring sign of a job well done," despite the goal displacement, rigidity, and insularity these rules produce. Indeed, Anthony Down's law of increasing bureaucratization finds few challengers among students of the administrative state.[34]

Today, however, many are abandoning the Panglosian view that this is the best of all possible worlds. In fact, so debilitating to effective public management has this complex web become that even Reagan stalwarts have called for "deregulating the public sector." The comments of Constance Horner, former director of Reagan's Office of Personnel Management, are illustrative:

> Conservatives have been much less enthusiastic about removing paperwork and regulatory burdens from the civil service than they have about deregulating the private sector. Some have even supported highly centralized new controls on the bureaucracy, despite their opposition to *dirigisme* everywhere else. . . . But deregulation of the public sector is as important as deregulation of the private sector . . . to liberate the entrepreneurial energies of Americans at work. . . . A crisp, decisive, lean, productive civil service, able to decide and act, rather than wait and see, would lead to smaller, more accountable government . . . and improve the quality of government services.[35]

Similarly, outcries against "personnel overregulation" and "micro-management" of agencies by Congress grow daily more common. Included in this chorus are such disparate voices as David Packard, Chairman of President Reagan's Blue Ribbon Commission on Defense Management; Richard Cheney, President Bush's Secretary of Defense; and U.S. Senator Sam Nunn (D-GA), Chairman of the Senate Armed Services Committee.[36] Echoing more general concerns expressed by the National Academy of Public Administration, the Packard Commission complained:

> Program managers have in effect been deprived of control over programs. They are confronted instead by never-ending bureaucratic obligations for making reports and gaining approvals that bear no relation to program success. The nation's defense programs lose far more to inefficient procedures than to fraud and dishonesty. The truly costly problems are those of overcomplicated organization and rigid procedure, not avarice or connivance.[37]

Cheney and Nunn also rued the "duplication, complexity, and lack of coordination" wrought by a congressional oversight process animated less by broad policy concerns than by micromanaging details. In the process, a power asymmetry arises favor-

ing program managers over generalists, line administrators, and—
ironically—political appointees. Thus, a third paradox arises
when one applies the administrative presidency within the framework of the administrative orthodoxy. Namely, the more successful
one is in applying the administrative orthodoxy for accountability
purposes to agency operations, the less successful one is in assuring
accountability to society's majoritarian rather than parochial
interests.

For evidence of this paradox, and to see the perverse consequences of the simplistic sovereignty model, look no further
than the BLM's budgetary framework in New Mexico. As a product partially of this orgy of accountability, that system produced
forty-plus subactivity funds, each subdivided into a plethora of
program elements and "condensed" into 2,500 pages of multi-year
revenue printouts per office. Inflexible and unassimilable by gener-
alist managers, the document was left for formulation, interpretation, and implementation in the willing hands of program managers. The latter gladly delved into the arcane details of the
process—with this effort came decision-making authority as well.
As Middaugh suggests, the result strikes many as pernicious. BLM
program staffs in Washington gain "vertical control over their programs and exert vertical program control over states." Coinciden-
tally, neither state BLM line managers nor political appointees can
exert the "horizontal control" across these subactivities, programs,
and BLM divisions needed to coordinate a coherent land use plan
or policy initiative.

But redistributing power to program managers at the expense
of line managers and political appointees was not the only consequence of this byzantine budget system. Most tellingly, rigid sub-
categories and atomized program elements scattered across different subactivities often precluded the funding and coordination of
comprehensive land-use plans or initiatives. Thus, political appointees funded or defunded individual program parts, but the
parts often failed to fit a comprehensive program whole. Again,
Middaugh best summarizes the political economy of the dilemma:

> The matter at hand, for managers, is the day-to-day decisions involv-
> ing multiple-use resource management. These are not decisions that
> always maximize individual program objectives [yet this is precisely

what program managers try to do]. . . . There is tremendous organizational inertia to perpetuate this system since [BLM's Washington Office] program staffs can operate in their organization vacuums and only have to nurture their congressional contacts to perpetuate their jobs.[38]

In essence, what Middaugh and others describe is the fourth paradox of the administrative presidency revealed by the New Mexico experience: The greater the success of appointees operating within and strengthening vertical control systems, the greater the power of program bureaucrats, and the less influential political appointees. But how can this "simplistic" and self-deluding penchant for accountability through overhead control be overcome in natural resource agencies such as the BLM? To proponents of the New Resource Economics (NRE), the solution lies in getting beyond the bureaucratic model and returning for accountability to the discipline of private markets.

Market Failures and the New Resource Economics

As noted in Chapter 3, devotees of the NRE champion market processes and private property rights as the only realistic escape from public-sector bureaucratic pathologies. As described by Andrew Dana and John Baden, the NRE proponents see efficiency as fostered only when resource managers consider and personally suffer the opportunity costs of their actions.[39] This, in turn, cannot occur until property rights are well-defined, enforceable, and transferable. Moreover, since government resource agencies manage public property largely unfettered by market discipline, they inevitably are inefficient and unaccountable to majoritarian rather than parochial political interests.

In contrast, when property owners or bureaucrats holding "de facto" property rights expect personal gains or losses from their actions, the reverse is true. Markets most clearly, swiftly, and effectively signal through prices what the consequences of actions are. What is more, they allocate those costs directly and unforgivingly to those most responsible for any negative externalities produced. Put differently, markets, not hierarchies, foster accountability best in the natural resource arena. Having concluded this, New Resource economists see a twofold role for government in natural resource management. First, it should help define and enforce property rights. Second, "when beneficial on the margin," government should regulate private resource use to minimize negative externalities.

But how does one operationalize this philosophy? NRE devotees embrace privatizing as their preferred alternative, but concede it is not always feasible or wise. Indeed, selling off public lands should occur only when property rights to resources can be well-defined, enforced without exorbitant costs or difficulties, and transferred among owners. Also, markets are dysfunctional when transaction costs are inordinately high, information is imperfect, public goods are undersupplied, or negative external consequences are unacceptable. Finally, even when private owners and government agencies have adequate price information, faulty resource decisions still may ensue.

So what, then, for those resources or properties plagued by one or more of these difficulties (e.g., airsheds and fugitive wildlife resources)? Public agencies, they say, must continue to manage and regulate their use. Moreover, agency experts must still compute resource values scientifically with the most sophisticated computer modeling techniques available (e.g., the Forest Service's FORPLAN model). However, what has to change is the context within which these technocratic decisions are made. Dana and Baden write, "If a bureaucrat understood that he could lose his job for an economically irresponsible or environmentally insensitive decision, as he would in the private sector, accountability and responsibility would be furthered."[40]

After years of "softening" within policy communities by the Reagan and Bush administrations, the New Resource Economics now has a certain degree of credibility and legitimacy. Witness, for example, how environmentalists and fiscal conservatives are now frequent allies pursuing market solutions to Western water woes.[41] Still, as a general remedy for the pathologies occasioned by our "simplistic quest for direct-line democracy," the approach of the New Resource Economics alone is wanting. How so? First, and as conceded by its supporters, it is not applicable in many situations. Second, the primacy it assigns efficiency is woefully inadequate and impractical in light of competing democratic values. Thus, as

Lee Brown and Helen Ingram ask, what gives efficiency an inherent claim to priority over the damage a market in water rights would impose on Native American lifestyles and cultures in the Southwest?[42] Similarly, as New Mexico's Attorney General warned so bluntly during the RGB water dispute, "Water runs uphill toward money." What happens to equity in such cases?

While NRE advocates offer answers to questions such as these, the potent political hostility these raise in many Western states indicates that change will not come easily. Yet NRE economists are strangely silent on how one might enact their property rights framework given the formidable bureaupolitical obstacles to change. Recall, for example, how efficiency values ran pell-mell into political realities during the Reagan Administration's ill-fated Asset Management Plan. Here, both ranchers and local governments demanded preference or priority in land sales, thus defeating the purpose of letting markets rather than bureaucrats set property values.

Of Clans, Cultures, and Control

With the paradoxes of hierarchy so disturbing and rampant, and with the political shortcomings and consequences of the NRE so often dysfunctional, do other options exist for reforming natural resource management? William Ouchi has described one increasingly heralded alternative for attaining efficiency, effectiveness, and accountability: the development of "clans." As Ouchi describes, clans use socialization as a means of unobtrusive control in organizations. Thus, despite their genesis in the private sector, clans will sound familiar to students of the Forest Service, the U.S. Public Health Service, the Army Corps of Engineers, or the U.S. Foreign Service. Writes Ouchi:

> Industrial organizations can, in some instances, rely to a great extent on socialization as the principal mechanism of mediation or control. . . . It is not necessary for these organizations to measure performance to control or direct their employees, since the employees' natural [socialized] inclination is to do what is best for the firm.[43]

Not unlike markets and hierarchies, however, clans are inappropriate, unlikely to form, or ineffective under certain circumstances. As Ouchi contends, employees must share three primary norms before clans become vehicles for accountability: reciprocity, legitimate authority, and common values and beliefs. What is more, goal incongruence among organizational members has to be low and be accompanied by high performance ambiguity. Thus, for example, the BLM seems decidedly less suited for this approach than the Forest Service. What is more, the recent revolt of forester dissidents within the Forest Service itself indicates that necessary preconditions for clans may be dissolving as well in that agency.[44]

As Herbert Kaufman chronicled so brilliantly, the Forest Service has traditionally relied on schools of forestry to inculcate common pro-development, multiple-use, and sustained-yield norms among their students.[45] The Service then reinforces these norms, while bolstering employees' vertical allegiance, through value-affirming personnel, reward, operating, and assignment procedures. In contrast, by the end of the Reagan presidency the Bureau of Land Management exhibited far less of the normative coherence necessary for clans to develop and be effective mechanisms for bureaucratic mediation, control, and accountability. The influx of disparate professions in the late 1970s, the absence of a common pre-service socializing experience, chronic underfunding and staffing, and the tardiness of its "organic statute" made the BLM an organization lacking esprit de corps, rife with professional antagonisms and worldviews, and driven by horizontal (i.e., clientele) rather than vertical loyalties.

Markets, hierarchies, and clans. Of these three conventional responses to "reforming" public agencies in the contemporary administrative state, each has serious shortcomings. Still, three things are clear. First, even if privatization of public lands is executed to the maximum extent feasible, and even if socialization is applied in all agencies ripe for clans, conventional bureaucracies will still remain. Second, to succeed within this context, presidents and their appointees will have to wield the administrative presidency in ways overcoming the common pitfalls of the administrative orthodoxy. And third, citizens and their elected representatives will have to revamp their simplistic notions of direct-line democracy to accommodate the implementation realities of the 1990s and beyond. The heart of the matter? How best to organize, evaluate, and hold accountable natural resource agencies so that agency accomplishment replaces control as the primary focus of policy makers.

A Fourth, Less-Traveled Road

Can a democracy such as ours accomplish such an end in ways that maximize the strengths and attenuate the weaknesses of markets, hierarchies, and clans? Arguably, Golembiewski's work offers the rudiments of a promising general approach to this task. Focusing on the intraorganizational dimension of the problem, he advises reformers to focus more on "integrative wholes" rather than "parts" of organizations. Golembiewski writes, "Observers typically use similar terms to characterize public-sector management: 'piecemeal,' 'balkanized,' 'fragmented,' 'substantially autonomous policy communities,' 'partitioned,' and so on."[46] Recall, for example, how BLM's balkanized, program-based budgeting system made holistic perspectives on policy problems unlikely since the problems did not adhere to single program categories. Thus, instead of generalists or political appointees checking bureaucratic power, this system actually enhanced the power of career program specialists. Or as Golembiewski perceptively summarizes, "It complicates management problems, trivializes legislative oversight and often misdirects it, precludes power-checking, and exacerbates the problems of popular control" rather than diminishes them.[47]

How best to integrate rather than fragment public agencies? Experts offer two basic and complementary methods for restructuring organizations for purpose rather than control. First, impose "value overlays" to cope normatively with the pathological features of function and process structures. And second, impose parallel or collateral organization structures to cope instrumentally with the same. Thus, political appointees might consciously replace dysfunctional "administrative" cultures which are "rule and role-bound" by suffusing their organizations with an ethos valuing accomplishment. Or, as Tom Peters suggests, they might alter their agency by "modeling nonbureaucratic behavior."[48] Yet, as even Golembiewski concedes, value overlays "may exact a substantial human toll"; they place trying cross-pressures on employees when reformers leave conventional bureaucratic structures intact. To remedy this, he counsels structural renovation as well, offering four basic ways to de-emphasize departmentation by function or process: collateral or parallel structures, project management, the mature matrix, and flow-of-work structures.[49]

Of these approaches, only one—project management—has garnered much attention from reformers in natural resource agencies. You will recall, for example, the prescriptions of the BLM Management Study Team: use project teams as collateral structures for circumventing bureaucratic pathologies, and promote participative management. Yet reorganizing functionally and clarifying roles were the most prevalent "reforms" mentioned, two prescriptions for continued rule- and role-boundedness. Likewise, while the BMT encouraged participative management, this philosophy was not a value overlay capable of overriding parochial allegiances to organizational sub-units, professions, or programs. Finally, although the Bureau exhibited a divisional structure conducive presumably to vertical flow-of-work departmentation, mid-management levels within these divisions typically were organized by functions or programs. Thus, as several interviewees noted, coaxing cooperation across divisional sub-units is often the most vexing problem confronting those attempting to manage Resource Management Plans rather than discrete program elements.

Under these circumstances, making the horizontal flow of work a basis for departmentation seems especially promising. But how would this work? According to Golembiewski, one begins at lower organizational levels. There, one identifies "discrete sub-assemblies charting the incidence and significance of [horizontal] interactions between specific people, skills, or whatever, and departmentalizing around the more dense clusters of interaction."[50] This approach recognizes explicitly that some clusters are more persistent and significant than others. Then, more distal activities are grouped into staff units that support divisions at higher levels (see Figure 9–1).

How might this approach have informed the Reagan Administration's energy or rangeland production agendas? At the micro- or intraorganizational level, appointees would have (1) identified those sub-assemblies of program elements necessary to complete management plans expeditiously; (2) restructured sub-units around these horizontal clusters rather than around discrete functions, processes, and decisions; (3) reduced rather than merely

Figure 9–1   Traditional and Alternative Production Structures

Traditional Structure: Departmentation by Function

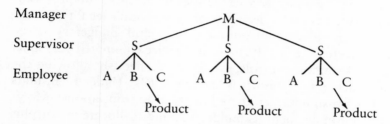

Alternative Structure: Departmentation by Horizontal Flow of Work

Reprinted by permission of Greenwood Publishing Group, Inc., Westport, CT, from Glenn W. Rainey, Jr., "Implementation and Managerial Creativity: A Study of the Development of Client-Centered Units in Human Service Programs," in *Implementation and the Policy Process*, edited by Dennis J. Palumbo and Donald J. Calista. Copyright © 1990 by the Policy Studies Organization. Adapted from Robert Golembiewski, *Men, Management, and Morality* (New York: McGraw-Hill, 1965), by permission of Robert Golembiewski.

defunded the number of budget subcategories to overcome program parochialisms and rigidity; and (4) let line managers (rather than ideologically motivated political appointees) identify and relax self-imposed procedural rules and regulations hindering productivity and effectiveness. Likewise, at the meso- or interorganizational level, political appointees, first, would have identified the "meso-sub-assembly lines" engaged by their policy reorientation efforts. Then, they would have targeted for waivers and/or deregulation disparate BLM and Forest Service procedures for assessing fair market value.[51]

Far fetched? Perhaps. But consider the Forest Service's recent experiment in public-sector deregulation. Interestingly enough, this experiment occurred during the second term of the Reagan Administration.[52] In 1985, an internal Forest Service study blamed red tape within and outside the agency for a dearth of entrepreneurship and creativity at the agency. In response, Forest Service Chief F. Dale Robertson, a career civil servant, selected four experimental field units to participate in a pilot study designed to cut through the procedural morass in their units.

Employees first identified barriers to productivity that were both within and beyond the Forest Service's authority to change. Next, a steering committee selected specific deregulation proposals to implement, basing its decisions on a proposal's legality, consonance with basic Administration policy, and budgetary costs. Then, to sweeten the deal further, the Service eliminated personnel ceilings and staffing controls, while simultaneously allowing the units to practice End Results Budgeting (ERB). Under ERB, units received lump-sum rather than line-item appropriations. Moreover, if a unit underspent its budget, it could reallocate the surplus to higher priority projects or give bonuses to employees. Finally, for procedures outside its authority to change, the Forest Service asked Congress and other resource agencies for waivers. In exchange, each unit had to specify more clearly and precisely its priorities, objectives, and output targets.

Clearly, these pilot studies did not deregulate or restructure the Forest Service to the extent advocated by Golembiewski, Peters, and others. Still, they (1) represent a major step toward reform; (2) suggest that more extensive efforts might further enhance bureaucratic efficiency, responsiveness, and accountability; and (3) offer insight into the bureaucratic politics of deregulating the public sector for accomplishment rather than control. By April 1987, pilot units had increased their productivity an average of 15 percent. Too, evaluators reported sizeable savings in the Ochoco and Gallatin National Forests, unprecedented levels of productivity gain in California's Pacific Southwest Station, and improvements in consumer satisfaction across all units. Moreover, in the Mark Twain National Forest alone, the Forest Service adopted 106 new ideas suggested by careerists for improving management. Most important, however, a surprising finding emerged concerning the sources of bureaucratic rigidity in public organizations. While most might predict that Congress was the major source of procedural "kudzu" in the agency, the Forest Service had itself imposed 70 to 80 percent of the identified barriers to productivity. Quipped Robertson, "We had assumed, wrongly, that we were the victims of bureaucratic circumstances largely beyond our control."[53]

Naturally, not everyone in the Forest Service embraced Robertson's experiment. For example, roughly half of all middle managers in the pilot units felt that deregulation threatened their jobs and power bases within the organization. That is, by effectively decentralizing authority to lower organizational levels, the experiment threatened to make mid-level managers superfluous. Thus, even granting the overall success of Robertson's initiative, his pilot studies uncovered formidable barriers to reform consonant with those identified by interviewees at the BLM. Witness, for example, Geoff Middaugh's prescription for compressing BLM funding sub-categories into half as many—and the realpolitik of such an endeavor given organizational inertia to perpetuate the power of program bureaucrats and their congressional patrons:

> I would not advocate total dismantling of the program structure. I *would* advocate a clearing-house/coordination approach to Bureau budgeting and priority setting. This requires *muscle*. This requires someone in the [Washington Office] to assure that programs are coordinated across [BLM] Divisions and territories. At the present time, we send program packages to the WO, and they are never seen again until the June or July prior to the budget year. Then we find out about all the surprises made through the political process on workloads and priorities.[54]

While Middaugh did not gear his advice to political appointees using the administrative presidency to reorient policy, his description of bureaupolitical resistance and his advice for creating and applying "muscle" speak to their needs as well.

Is the effort worth it to restructure organizations for accomplishment rather than control? Mounting evidence suggests it is, and that this approach offers the advantages of markets, hierarchies, and clans while considerably diminishing their shortcomings. As Golembiewski predicts, and the Forest Service experience confirms, an element of market competition and cooperation can be introduced into conventional bureaucratic structures when departmentation by task or work flow replaces functional or programmatic bases of organization. He writes:

> The model raises the probability that socioemotional attachments between sub-unit members will reinforce the technical contributions necessary for the flow of work. Moreover, the basic structural reorientation has significant implications for power dynamics. The comparative measurement of sub-unit performance will inhibit such socio-emotional attachments from resulting in the kind of high cohesiveness that is sometimes reflected in low productivity among mono-specialized work units, for example. In addition, *the subunits can compete in terms of more efficient performance on comparable flows of work, which encourages a useful discipline unlike the win/lose dynamics associated with the separate functions or processes of the bureaucratic model* [emphasis added].[55]

In sum, appointees can change strategically the perverse, zero-sum incentive structures of the administrative orthodoxy to stress accomplishment, not control. To do otherwise is to lose control *and* to diminish effectiveness. How ironic that support for this claim arose during the tenure of a president bent single-mindedly on top-down control of the bureaucracy. And how appropriate that these initiatives were pioneered by a careerist within the Forest Service, an organizational gemstone of the Progressive Era with its focus on scientific management, professionalism, and the administrative orthodoxy!

But under what conditions can appointees use this information to reorient public policies administratively across a variety of domains and arenas? Absent empirical research across a range of contexts, one can only speculate about factors that might limit the generalizability of deregulatory reforms and purpose-oriented nontraditional structures. As the Forest Service experience suggests, however, structural reforms of this nature probably require contexts suffused with entrepreneurial leadership, slack resources, a threshold level of internal support for change, and relatively long time frames for implementation. One might also speculate that the applicability and feasibility of both structural and deregulatory reforms varies with (1) how encapsulable (or how isolatable) is the service or product affected; (2) whether single- or multi-attribute problems or values are involved; (3) the number, density, and importance of contextual goals that must be satisfied; (4) whether the desired values are measurable or not; (5) how observable the outcomes are of the products or services involved; (6) whether decision-making situations are permeable, operating cores are buffered, and task environments are turbulent; and (7) how well agency personnel incorporate—or can be induced to include— larger democratic and societal values in their professional world views and everyday decisions.

Are there strategies more or less useful for applying these reforms in other policy arenas and domains? Lessons suitable for application and for testing in future research must await Chapter 10. For now, one thing is clear in the natural resource arena. Structural reform predicated on accomplishment rather than control and informed by "reversible logic" appears promising, timely, and challenging. As well, it offers a middle-ground complement to markets, hierarchies, and clans by emphasizing their strengths while attenuating their shortcomings.

As noted, implementing these reforms is not easy. Nor is it a task for the meek, impatient, or politically unastute. Those trying to enhance the efficiency and effectiveness of natural resource management must become more skeptical of the administrative orthodoxy. Likewise, Congress and the American public have to become more skeptical of "safeguarding sovereignty in simplistic ways." Finally, presidents bent on affecting natural resource policy have to appreciate how imperiled their agendas can become if pursued solely within the framework of the administrative orthodoxy.

CHAPTER 10

"Fire Alarms," "Garbage Cans," and the Administrative Presidency

Having reviewed the natural resource implications of the New Mexico cases, this chapter shifts to the theoretical, strategic, and normative implications of the administrative presidency as a generic approach to executive leadership across various policy arenas. Three basic questions frame the analysis. First, does research suggest a conceptual framework by which scholars and practitioners can understand, apply, and assess the administrative presidency? Second, under what conditions and using what implementation strategies will the administrative presidency most likely succeed? And third, what are some implications of the administrative presidency for democratic values in the contemporary administrative state? Ideally, this focus should accomplish three things: (1) provide "middle-ground" alternatives to presently polarized debates about the administrative presidency; (2) offer "competent process standards" for honing and assessing future administrative strategies; and (3) help develop an empirically based and theoretically grounded understanding of the processes of the administrative presidency.

AGENDAS, ALTERNATIVES, AND THE ADMINISTRATIVE PRESIDENCY

As discussed in Chapter 9, the New Mexico experiences suggest that one profitably views the bureaucratic politics of the administrative presidency as byproducts of agenda processes.[1] Most telling were the validity of the policy's "idea set" and how well and persistently "softened" it was prior to appearing on an administration's agenda. The questions of how, when, and why disparate issues achieve decision-agenda status have long intrigued students of the public policy process.[2] Similarly, scholars have long applied extended metaphors—whether of the biological, game theory, or cybernetic variety—to enhance our understanding of otherwise nebulous social, political, and organizational concepts and processes.[3] Only recently, however, has John Kingdon used extended metaphors to describe and explain the dynamics of agenda processes in the United States, an exercise rife with implications for appreciating the political dynamics of the administrative presidency.

Kingdon conceptualizes agenda setting as independent streams of problems, policies, and politics awaiting periodic, albeit fleeting, opportunities for policy choice. Within this "organized anarchy," solutions largely—but not exclusively—chase problems rather than vice versa. The availability and popularity of particular solutions—not any inherent priority or urgency of public problems—frequently determine which subjects achieve decision-agenda status. The likelihood of a particular condition becoming a public problem deemed actionable, and for one "solution" to prevail amid all possible alternatives in the "primeval soup," soars if there is a coupling of the problem, the policy, and the political streams. To happen, however, "policy windows" occasioned by problem opportunities must open, viable solutions must exist and be "linked" to the problem by entrepreneurs operating within specialized policy communities, and the political environment (e.g., the national mood or partisan predispositions in Congress) must be amenable to policy change. Thus, unlike traditional incremental models of policy making, this adaptation of Cohen, March, and Olsen's garbage can model of organizational decision processes accommodates both gradual and nonincremental changes in agenda setting. Prior research on the administrative presidency suggests that such a conceptualization is useful as well for understanding how the bureaupolitical environment helps set presidential agendas.

Less common, however, are analyses of how different types of presidential initiatives affect the post-decision policy process when pursued administratively. Applying extended biological metaphors and concepts in a manner analogous to Kingdon's study of agenda processes, this chapter argues that it is useful to view presidential policy alternatives along two discrete continua used by natural scientists to describe evolutionary patterns: mode and tempo. Respectively, these terms elaborate and extend Chapter 9's two primary conditioners of bureaucratic politics: validity and softening. The interaction of these two factors yields at least four analytically distinct types of presidential agenda items: Quantum, Emergent, Convergent, and Gradualist initiatives. Each, in turn, spawns its own peculiar political dynamics (see Figure 10–1).

Before discussing each ideal type of policy initiative, the logic of the typology should be explained. As discussed in Chapter 9, it assumes that anticipating and understanding the political dynamics of the administrative presidency require one to view the policy initiatives pursued as hypotheses or "idea sets" that are more or less accepted as valid. Recall that the validity of the causal theory underlying a policy initiative can vary—perhaps dramatically—over time. Key determinants here are (a) how widely, persistently, and successfully softened it has been; and (b) if perceptible changes have occurred in the validity of its core concepts, axioms, and deductive premises. For instance, in deciding to use pollution fees to curb ecological damage, the core concept of "marginal utility" is coupled with the axiomatic premise that "polluters act rationally to maximize their profits," to produce the deductive proposition that "pollution fees are the most economically efficient way to reduce environmental degradation." Thus, as Paul Schulman contends, a policy (or idea set) "offers a causal explanation for a given social condition or problem 'state,' a forecast regarding future states, and a prescriptive inference for policy intervention on behalf of a desired outcome."[4]

Turning to key terms, "mode" refers to the character of the presidential policy initiative.[5] Here, policy initiatives range along a continuum from "pure mutations" to "gradualist transformations." For evolution theorists, pure mutations are totally new proposals, akin to what Charles Lindblom terms "fundamental" or "root decisions." In contrast, gradualist alternatives (technically referred to as "phyletic transformations") are the product of cumulative marginal extensions of existing policies and are analogous to Lindblom's branch alterations to initial root decisions.

The second evolutionary continuum—"tempo"—refers to the

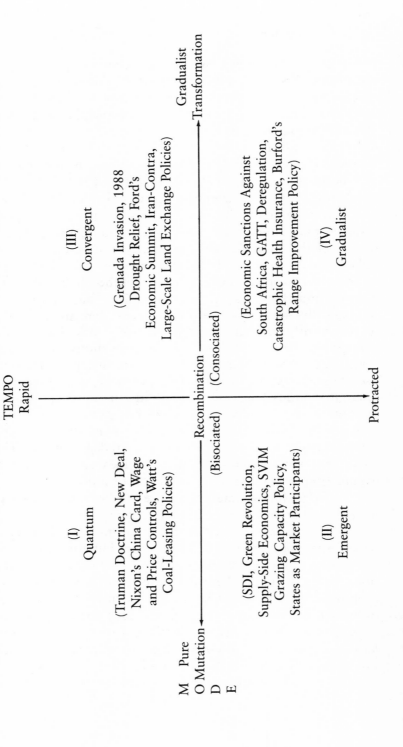

Figure 10–1
A Typology of Agenda Items

gestation period of agenda alternatives, with initiatives classified along a continuum of incubation periods ranging from rapid (i.e., moving swiftly from conception to a prominent position in the policy stream without persistent and prolonged softening of extended policy communities) to protracted (i.e., moving glacially from the initial conceptualization, with extensive and persistent softening within advocacy coalitions and issue networks).[6]

Since most presidential agenda items are not totally new to the policy process, nor bypass the softening process completely, most initiatives belong near the intersection of the axes rather than at the extreme reaches of mode and of tempo. These "recombinations," in turn, consist of two subcategories: consociated (the recasting or repackaging of diverse, but familiar elements to produce an alternative different in degree rather than kind), and bisociated (the creative recombining of the same, but in ways producing a qualitatively different alternative). Here, Christopher Hood's work on the "tools" of government is instructive.[7] He notes that recombining familiar ideas can produce qualitatively different (i.e., new or novel) agenda types. More precisely, fundamental or bisociated qualitative changes (differing in kind rather than degree) can occur when one applies old policy instruments in new or different ways or contexts (e.g., educational vouchers suggest housing vouchers), when technological change transforms old instruments (e.g., the Strategic Defense Initiative relative to Antiballistic Missile Systems), and when the "mix" of instruments is different from what existed before (e.g., altering the mix of regulatory tools from process to performance measures).

Each of the four types of presidential policy initiatives has its own specific parameters (see Table 10–1). To frame the analysis, the discussion here employs the decision parameters labeled critical by Cohen, March, and Olsen in their "garbage can" model of decision making. These include: (1) decision structures, (2) access structures, (3) entry times (for choices and problems), and (4) energy loads and distribution among decision makers. The first two parameters represent who can participate legitimately in various choices and how open choice opportunities are to having problems linked to them, respectively. Thus, one can classify both types of structures as either unsegmented (choice opportunities open to

TABLE 10–1
Decision Parameters of Different Types of Presidential Agenda Items

Types	Decision Parameters
Gradualist	Unsegmented access structures
	Specialized decision structures
	Low energy distributions with energy loads favoring careerists and subsystem actors
	Periodicity of entry times
	Well-softened initiatives
	Use in other policy arenas
Convergent	Unsegmented access and decision structures
	Highly concentrated energy distributions
	Negligible or rapid softening
	Energy loads favoring presidential appointees
	Cascading policy effects
	Random entry times
	Exploiting new possibilities
Emergent	Hierarchical access structures
	Specialized decision structures
	Energy loads favoring careerists and issue network members
	Unstable entry times
	Protracted or persistent softening needed for idea-set breakthrough
Quantum	Hierarchical access and decision structures
	Asymmetrical energy distribution favoring presidential advisors and appointees
	Negligible or rapid softening
	Sudden and unanticipated entry times
	Demand for swift action

all problems and actors), hierarchical (the most important actors and problems having access to many more choices), or specialized (each problem and actor with access to only one decision choice). Entry times refer to the pace at which problems and choice opportunities confront decision makers, while energy loads (light, moderate, and heavy) refer to the total amount of energy (time, expertise, budgets, etc.) available to the organization for solving all problems during the policy-relevant time period. Finally, energy distribution refers to how much attention various actors can afford or are allowed to give particular problems, given the opportunity costs involved with foregoing other opportunities for policy choice.

Before proceeding, three points are noteworthy. First, decisions to place specific policy initiatives in particular quadrants as illustrations reflect an assessment of their development at the time they first became viable alternatives for selection (see Figure 10–1). Second, with the exception of policies associated with the New Mexico cases, the illustrations used were not necessarily products of an administrative strategy. This in no way detracts, however, from their ability to convey key points about the quadrant under analysis. Finally, the discussion focuses on nonroutine rather than routine policy initiatives, whether successfully implemented or not.

Quadrant I: Quantum

The Quantum quadrant consists of policy initiatives pursued administratively that demonstrate "Eureka" or breakthrough qualities, short lapses between idea formation and decision-agenda status, little research within or involvement by extended policy communities or issue networks, and negligible softening. Yet they frequently involve topics related directly to what Sabatier terms the "normative" and "policy" cores of belief systems.[8] The former refers to fundamental normative or ontological axioms (e.g., basic criteria of distributive justice). The latter refers to fundamental policy positions concerning the basic strategies for achieving those axioms of the normative core (e.g., basic choices about policy instruments, such as coercion versus inducements versus persuasion). Importantly, while the elements comprising these types of initiatives may not be "new," their combination is synergistic; the policy that results is qualitatively different from its predecessors (i.e., it represents a bisociated recombination).

In the policy formulation stages, both decision and access structures are quite hierarchical, with resources (i.e., energy loads) distributed disproportionately to limited numbers of privileged presidential advisors or appointees. Here, the entry times of the issues that these policy initiatives "chase" are quite sudden and unanticipated. Typically, these initiatives are in response to crises demanding swift, decisive, or even secretive presidential action (e.g., the Cuban Missile crisis, British withdrawal from Greece after World War II, the Great Depression), or to instances of "doctrinal shock" when events rapidly overtake existing policies (e.g., the demise of Eisenhower's massive retaliation doctrine or stagflation causing Nixon's unprecedented use of wage and price controls in peacetime).

Two varieties of policy initiative inhabit this quadrant. First, many of those policies associated with the "megapolicies" of foreign and domestic politics (e.g., epoch-defining doctrines of domestic and foreign policy, such as Roosevelt's New Deal and the Reagan and Truman Doctrines) often arrive suddenly on the decision agenda without widespread, persistent, or prolonged softening within policy communities. True, debate may have previously developed over the individual parts of these synergistic or bisociated recombinations. Yet the qualitatively different alternative that emerges from this recombination escapes prolonged, sustained scrutiny de novo.

Likewise, a second type of less overarching policy initiative also produces quantum shifts that are equally abrupt, marked, and unsoftened in periods of doctrinal shock or crisis (e.g., the Brady Commission recommendations on stock market controls after "Black Monday," or the use of the U.S. military in combating narco-terrorism). In both instances, however, the predecision policy process is dominated by relatively small and isolated groups of presidential advisors operating in "counterbureaucracies" on the periphery of congressional and bureaucratic oversight and accountability.[9] As a result, these initiatives can be and often are launched quickly without lengthy softening, lest they be "diluted" or aborted by the sheer bulk of bureaucratic and congressional actors with legitimate claims to participation. Here, Nixon's China initiative and Roosevelt's "first hundred days" are especially illustrative.

What are the implications of Quantum policy shifts for the administrative presidency? Given the low validity, low softening nature of Watt's coal-leasing policy, the Reagan Administration's experiences in the San Juan Basin are most illustrative of a Quantum agenda item (novel in mode, rapid in tempo). This case suggests that with the magnitude of the policy change involved and the rapidity of the gestation process, rather traumatic disruption is inevitable in long-standing rules, regulations, and routines throughout the Madisonian system. Similarly challenged are cherished philosophical beliefs and worldviews concerning the proper nature, role, and scope of the federal government. True, access structures tend to be hierarchical in the pre-decision phase of the process. Yet precisely because of this, operationalizing administratively the components of the initiative in the post-decision process—whether in agency rule making, budgets, personnel decisions, or reorganizations—is destined most likely for strong intra- and intergovernmental conflict in both the micro- and macropolitical systems. Precisely what these bureaupolitical dynamics will look like follows in the next section of this chapter. Before getting to that, however, it is important to outline the remaining three types of initiatives.

Quadrant II: Emergent

Presidential initiatives characteristic of the Emergent quadrant also have a synergistic quality, but they rely for their novelty mostly on rapid conceptual breakthroughs (or "mutations") in the components of their idea sets within relatively segmented policy communities. Here, secondary aspects of a belief system are most likely involved. These are "instrumental decisions and information searches necessary to implement core policy positions."[10] Consequently, the entry times and the energy loads associated with them are random and unpredictable, with accompanying energy distributions highly concentrated within policy communities. As such, their viability when implemented administratively depends acutely on sustaining favorable and widely accepted forecasts of technological workability over the short-to-medium term.

Simultaneous and persistent softening throughout policy communities and issue networks by policy entrepreneurs—most likely the president and his close advisors—is vital once the policy initiative is announced and pursued administratively. Thus, the half-life of policies premised on such breakthroughs can be extremely brief and fraught with implementation difficulty. In fact, they are distinctly vulnerable to empirical challenge over the validity of their causal theories. Specifically, the technological breakthroughs (social, economic, or scientific) supporting these initiatives usually are amenable to testing by specialists within relevant policy communities using either sophisticated computer modeling (e.g., simulations of strategic nuclear exchanges or acid rain dispersion), experiential feedback, or divergent epistemologies. Potentially debilitating as well are actual performance data from the field (e.g., the green revolution, monthly trade figures on the effect of letting the dollar fall to correct trade deficits, and rural-urban warfare over water rights), or the questioning of model specification and data bases informing policy prescriptions.

What are the implications of this bisociated type of policy initiative for the administrative presidency? Given the low validity, high softening nature of its computer-based grazing reduction policies, the Carter Administration's experience in implementing SVIM in Rio Puerco is most illustrative of an Emergent agenda item (novel in mode, protracted in tempo). So, too, are policies making states participants in, rather than regulators of, water markets. These cases suggest that with (1) the critical role played by specialized decision structures (policy communities), (2) the significance of unpredictable "technological" breakthroughs (natural or social scientific) in idea sets, and hence (3) the randomness of entry times, administrative strategies effecting Emergent agenda items typically experience moderate to high levels of political conflict over particular aspects of the policy's idea set. To begin with, policy softening that is sustained, persistent, and effective is critical within relevant issue networks once such policies are announced. More precisely, administration officials must demonstrate persuasively the workability of the breakthrough (e.g., "maximum feasible participation" or the EMARS computer modeling method for projecting coal supply and demand).

To their chagrin, and as the SVIM case illustrates, political appointees frequently become embroiled in controversy in the post-decision process; demonstrating workability pits competing components of policy sectors and issue networks against each other. In turn, disputes among techno- and socioscientific elites undermine the public's confidence in the policy initiative, thus jeopardizing expeditious or uneventful implementation. Equally destabilizing to the administrative presidency are the random entry times that accompany policy initiatives in this quadrant. This occurs as the advantages of initiative and energy distribution shift predominantly away from political appointees and toward career bureaucrats, technocrats, and their legislative patrons within the micropolitical system.

Federal courts, too, can derail an administrative strategy premised on agency rule making or adjudication should the initiative rest inordinately on precarious computer modeling techniques, sociological theories, or data collection methods. Here, judges may stymie policy reorientation by ruling exercises of bureaucratic discretion "arbitrary and capricious" or incapable of meeting "substantial evidence" tests. Again, it is possible to delve more deeply into the bureaupolitical dynamics of Emergent agenda items, painting their subtleties with much more precision. Before doing so, however, the remaining two agenda types—Convergent and Gradualist—must be outlined in terms of their decision parameters.

Quadrant III: Convergent

Policy initiatives characteristic of the Convergent quadrant reach decision agendas quite rapidly as circumstances "converge" at unanticipated entry times to propel their salience or viability as issues. As such, the decision and access parameters associated with them during the predecision process are relatively unsegmented; actors and policy entrepreneurs from a variety of issue networks strive to link their definitions of problems and preferred solutions to "windows" of choice opportunities. Concerned largely with secondary (i.e., instrumental) aspects of belief systems, they can be or can produce a consociated recombination, inversion, or extension of persistently softened ideas that gain either notoriety or obscurity within the press, policy communities, or the court of world opinion.

Two varieties of presidential policy initiatives inhabit this quadrant: (1) foreign policy initiatives pursued covertly (e.g., the Iran-Contra Affair) and (2) those geared toward the rapid exploitation of new possibilities in either the domestic or foreign policy arena (e.g., Carter's Camp David summitry, or EPA's initiatives after Times Beach, Love Canal, and the Superfund scandals). In the first instance, presidents or their appointees cast covert operations rapidly upon the decision agenda (in either overt or covert policy streams) once threats (real, imagined, or contrived) to national security arise. In the second, they pursue opportunistic initiatives when propitious changes occur in the social, economic, or ideational context of a policy problem. Here, long dormant yet well-softened policy alternatives—or those not applied in this policy arena before—are thrust quickly to the forefront of presidential or agency agendas (e.g., stricter controls on the nuclear power industry after Three Mile Island). Significantly, friends and foes expect such initiatives to produce either positive or negative consequences that will cascade throughout an issue arena in unpredictable ways—thus raising immeasurably the political stakes. Energy distributions, too, will differ depending on whether operations are overt (widely distributed) or covert (asymmetrically favoring low-level bureaucrats, mercenaries, and hierarchical superiors).

What are the consequences of this type of policy initiative for the administrative presidency? Given the moderate to high validity, low softening nature of large-scale land exchange policies, the Reagan Administration's experience in the Las Cruces Industrial Park-Elena Gallegos case is most illustrative of a Convergent agenda item (incremental in mode, rapid in tempo). As reported in this case, these agenda items can spawn moderate levels of difficulty for those implementing them administratively as fire alarm oversight is triggered by disgruntled clienteles. Thus, with appointees perceiving windows of opportunity as fleeting, they act quickly and perhaps summarily (i.e., without consulting affected and influential members of Congress). This strategy, in turn, tends to provoke congressional hostility from those not consulted (e.g., congressional reaction to the Reagan Administration's efforts to summarily implement the Forest Service–BLM Land Exchange or President Bush's decision to reopen talks with the People's Republic of China in the post–Tienanmen Square era). At the same time, opponents try to delay swift action by "throwing sand in the works." Again, a more precise account of the bureaupolitical dynamics of this type is possible, but must await a description of the parameters of our final agenda type: the Gradualist initiative.

Quadrant IV: Gradualist

One best conceptualizes policy initiatives in the Gradualist quadrant as "branch" or incremental agenda items that differ only marginally from existing policy. Hence, they tend to be old, established policy alternatives that have experienced persistent softening over the years within relevant policy communities. Put differently, they are known best for their merely transforming, recombining, or inverting of familiar elements. What is more, choice opportunities for these consociated initiatives tend to have more unsegmented access structures, more specialized decision structures, and more regularity (periodicity) in entry times (e.g., budgetary and reauthorization cycles). Finally, their consequences are well-researched and regularly debated. Thus, as Kingdon notes, policy initiatives such as health maintenance organizations (HMOs) and deregulation of the surface transportation industry are especially illustrative of those in this quadrant. There is an apparent tendency as well for alternatives to move from the other three categories over time into this one; the reverse of this directional movement seems to be relatively uncommon, yet possible, given changes in key concepts, axioms, and deductive propositions.

What are the implications of Gradualist types of agenda items for the administrative presidency? Given the high validity, high softening nature of Burford's Rangeland Improvement Policy, the Reagan Administration's experiences in Rio Puerco and southern New Mexico are most illustrative of a Gradualist agenda item (incremental in mode, protracted in tempo). These experiences suggest that congressional fire alarms are more difficult to sound given the validity of the causal theory underlying this agenda type. Similarly calming, consociated initiatives such as those in the Rio Puerco case typically require only marginal changes in an agency's historical base of expenditures, skill mixes, rules, and structures. Solons, as well, tend to rely more on the police patrol oversight afforded by the periodicity of entry times and constituent case work, with fire alarms sounded only if glitches occur in bargaining among lower-level specialists. Here, courts become a factor only in protecting the substantive and procedural due process rights of program beneficiaries and restricted clients.

BUREAUCRACY, POLITICS, AND THE ADMINISTRATIVE PRESIDENCY

As these four types suggest, substantial variation exists in the nature, scope, and intensity of the bureaupolitical responses mounted against the administrative presidency. In some instances, acquiescence is rather routine while in others it comes—if at all—after prolonged, bitter intransigence. Indeed, at least four analytically distinct patterns of bureaupolitical response are most prevalent in the literature (see Table 10–2).[12] Progressing from least to most conflictual, these are: (1) mutual accommodation, (2) manipulated agreement, (3) adversarial engagement, and (4) disintegrative conflict. In turn, these implementation scenarios vary across six characteristics: (1) the clarity of communications among the participants, (2) the structure of interaction among the actors, (3) the attitudes of the participants, (4) the degree of perceived policy legitimacy, (5) the intensity of implementation conflict mounted, and (6) the need for external political support.

Not Going Gently into That Good Night

Mutual accommodation scenarios involve explicit yet relatively minor and short-term disputes that require formal resolution by lower-level technicians and bureaucrats. Of the Reagan Administration's experiences in New Mexico, the case most illustrating these dynamics is the Rio Puerco pipeline dispute. Recall how the high validity, high softening character of this Gradualist initiative (Burford's Rangeland Improvement Policy) helped limit the contagiousness of the conflict (e.g., full-bore fire alarm oversight never occurred); wrought competitive but respectful professional exchanges among appointees and careerists at BLM (e.g., DuBois' concession about unforeseen consequences for complex projects); produced flexibility in negotiating patterns given the perceived legitimacy of privatization (e.g., because most at BLM agreed that "cow welfare" needed ending, appointees made concessions on deadlines for implementing the RIP); and evinced only limited appeals to and intervention by upper management and political appointees (e.g., the abbreviated appeals to New Mexico's Secretary of Agriculture).

In contrast, manipulated agreement scenarios arise when one of the parties to the dispute initially and determinedly refuses to concede the others' demands. Here, attempts are made to coax acquiescence through "moral persuasion" or the manipulation of rewards and punishments. Most illustrative of these bureaucratic politics are the Reagan Administration's experience in New Mexico during the Las Cruces Industrial Park–Elena Gallegos case. Recall how the moderate validity, low softening character of this Convergent initiative (i.e., large-scale land exchanges) helped spawn significantly more resistance than Burford's rangeland policy did in Rio Puerco. Moreover, less flexibility and precision characterized discussions (e.g., the Forest Service's ultimata to Las Cruces); less respect and more competitiveness characterized their attitudes (e.g., BLM's "sand-in-the-works" tactics); micro- and macropolitical intervention was sought by parties and proffered willingly (e.g., Lujan's intercession with the Forest Service); and the direct intervention of upper management at both the BLM and the Forest Service was necessary to resolve interagency conflict (e.g., Hassell and Luscher ordering their careerists to cooperate). Moreover, some tried to manipulate the acquiescence of the other parties by seizing the moral high ground through appeals to the public interest or adverse publicity (e.g., Mayor Rusk framing the issue in terms of the "influence" of the Republican congressional delegation with Reagan).

The third type of implementation scenario—adversarial engagement—represents a significant escalation of the intensity, length, and scope of the conflict. These dynamics can result in temporary

TABLE 10–2

Bureaupolitical Dynamics of the Administrative Presidency by Type of Agenda Item

Characteristics	Gradualist	Convergent	Emergent	Quantum
Decision parameters	Unsegmented access structures; specialized decision structures; low energy distributions with energy loads favoring careerists and subsystem actors; periodicity of entry times; well-softened initiatives; use in other context	Unsegmented access and decision structures; highly concentrated energy distributions; energy loads favoring presidential appointees; cascading policy effects; random entry times; exploiting new possibilities	Hierarchical access structures; specialized decision structures; energy loads favoring careerists and issue network members; unstable entry times; persistent softening need for idea-set breakthrough	Hierarchical access and decision structures; asymmetrical energy distribution favoring presidential advisors and appointees; negligible softening; sudden and unanticipated entry times; demand for swift action
Type of conflict	Mutual accommodation	Manipulated agreement	Adversarial engagement	Disintegrative conflict
Nature of communications (cues & information concerning directives, rewards, & penalties)	Specific; consistent; understood	Less precise	Vague; ambiguous	Broken down
Structure of interaction	Moderate; flexibility with negotiated bargaining	Less flexibility, with negotiated & non-negotiated bargaining	Somewhat rigid; possible stalemate; non-negotiated bargaining, followed by negotiation	Rigid; non-negotiable demands

(continued)

TABLE 10–2 (Continued)

Characteristics	Gradualist	Convergent	Emergent	Quantum
Attitudes between or among the parties	Competitive; mutual trust & respect in professional exchanges	Competitive with less respect	Defensiveness; growing distrust & skepticism about motives; spiraling contentiousness	Antagonistic to hostile
Perceived legitimacy	High; preimposed and generally accepted procedures	Moderate	Low	Extremely low
Scope, level, & intensity of conflict	Low two-party conflict; functional hierarchy & some upper management involvement	Moderate with unilateral attempt by appointees to mobilize ally allies; greater upper-management involvement	High; mutual attempt to ally mobilization; subsystems with periodic macropolitical intervention involving aspects of dispute only	Extremely high; macropolitical system involvement to resolve total dispute
Mobilization of political resources	Minimal	Moderate	High; actors still desirous of managing overall conflict themselves	Appeals to sovereigns for imposed settlement
Case illustration	Rio Puerco pipeline (Burford's Rangeland Improvement Policy)	Las Cruces Industrial Park, Elena Gallegos	El Paso-New Mexico water dispute, SVIM	San Juan Basin coal leasing

bargaining stalemates. Most illustrative among the New Mexico experiences covered in this book are the bureaupolitical dynamics of the RGB groundwater and the SVIM modeling disputes. Again, recall from Chapter 9 how the low validity, high softening nature of these Emergent agenda items wrought spiraling defensiveness, skepticism, and hostility among the parties. As these mounted, the antagonists mobilized allies capable of supporting their cause within legislative, executive, and judicial arenas. Still, the parties continued to negotiate over the larger issues (e.g., the model BLM–New Mexico memorandum of understanding), leaving the courts and other macropolitical actors to resolve discrete aspects of the cases (e.g., the McClure Amendment). What is more, intransigence for the parties has definite time limits. Indeed, one factor is most compelling in bringing these disputes to an end: the fear of losing total control of conflict management to external actors—the Congress or the courts—whose policy preferences are unknown or presumed to be unsympathetic (e.g., the decision by New Mexico and El Paso to forego appeals of *El Paso v. Reynolds II*).

Finally, disintegrative conflict represents the most formidable and deteriorated circumstance that can confront those wielding the administrative presidency. Indeed, such conflict provides the most acerbic, prolonged, and difficult implementation experience and is most likely to provoke settlements imposed by macropolitical actors. The most illustrative of this type among the New Mexico experiences treated in Part II is the Reagan Administration's experience in the San Juan Basin case. As Chapter 8 chronicles and Chapter 9 summarizes, implementing this low validity, low softening, Quantum agenda item—calling as it did for leasing in previously pristine wilderness areas and for unprecedented levels of general coal leasing—fell to the Congress (with Lujan and Domenici acting as brokers among the parties). Indeed, the Administration became more of a bystander than a player as Domenici and Lujan tried to save as much of Reagan's agenda as was politically feasible. In the interim, and as a three-tiered backdrop, (1) the legitimacy of Reagan's coal-leasing program plummeted, given its magnitude and questionable need; (2) increasingly hostile, distrustful, and resentful parties took non-negotiable positions (e.g., repeated congressional moratoria on its funding for leasing activities); and (3) appeals to Congress and the courts imposed over-all settlements on the controversy.

In sum, and typical of disintegrative conflicts, both the SJB and Reagan's national coal-leasing program took on less tangible, more symbolic, and broader meaning for the disputants. Thus, for the Reagan Administration, the issue pitted free-market versus Eurosocialistic planning philosophies. For wilderness preservationists, the issue pitted biocentric versus anthropocentric perspectives on the environment. And for conservationists, the issue pitted the sustained-yield, scientific management philosophies of the Progressive conservationists against the rapaciousness and greed of developers. Disputes of this kind, as Austin Sarat and Joel Grossman suggest, "tend to be less conducive to negotiations [because] the currency of easy compromise is often lacking and the psychic costs of compromising 'principles' is much greater than that of a satisfactory mutual adjustment of other types of interest."[13]

Arguably, then, at least four patterns of bureaupolitical response exist (mutual accommodation, manipulated agreement, adversarial bargaining, and disintegrative conflict) and are illustrated within the natural resource cases examined in this study. Moreover, these patterns (as summarized in Table 10–2) are linked directly with the four types of agenda items (Gradualist, Convergent, Emergent, and Quantum) typically pursued by presidents. Beware, however. This is not to suggest that agenda types will automatically spawn commensurate types of bureaupolitical dynamics. Instead, disparate agenda types afford an *opportunity* for bureaupolitical challenges. To anticipate the likelihood of these challenges developing, we must turn next to identifying and understanding a most critical intervening variable in this process.

Anticipating Bureaucratic Resistance

Under what conditions will each of these four patterns of bureaupolitical response to administrative strategies emerge? Of importance, of course, are such factors as (1) the extent to which careerists positively identify with existing agency or program missions, (2) the political clout of their allies, (3) their possession of expertise valued by appointees, and (4) the political prowess which they attribute to those appointees. Yet arguably the most critical intervening variable conditioning bureaupolitical response is an adaptation of what elsewhere has been termed the "non-compliance delay effect."[14] This is a function of the interaction patterns of two factors: (1) the degree to which a policy initiative applies directly to activities central to a target agency or program's mission or culture, and (2) the extent to which the time delay and angst inherent in challenging that initiative is perceived by the agency or program's dominant coalition to adversely affect its ability to define or realize that mission.[15] Both factors range along a continuum from minor to major effects. Combinations of these two factors yield a typology of bureaupolitical response (see Figure 10–2) that corresponds to the four types identified above: mutual accommodation, manipulated agreement, adversarial bargaining, and disintegrative conflict.

Mutual Accommodation. Policy initiatives in Quadrant I are likely to provoke a mutual accommodation pattern of bureaupolitical response. That is, despite a perception that significant and perhaps costly changes in preferred practices and procedures are required by careerists, sustained resistance—even if likely to succeed—could spawn mission-threatening delay. Consequently, dominant agency coalitions and their allies—even if they could marshal formidable political resources (e.g., powerful interest groups or legislators)—are likely to forego escalating the scope, intensity, and visibility of appointee-careerist disagreement. In such a situation, lower-level staff and political appointees mostly handle their differences dispassionately and professionally, although abbreviated, quiet, and rather limited appeals to legislative sovereigns may occur simultaneously. To avoid debilitating delay, however, affected careerists try to resolve their differences with appointees through informal settlement processes (low-key discussions). Throughout this joint problem-solving effort, communications between the parties remain clear and consistent, flexibility characterizes discussions, and competitiveness is leveled by mutual trust.

In addition to the Rio Puerco privatization case, Secretary of Defense Casper Weinberger's attempt to eliminate strategic planning uncertainties at the Defense Department is an excellent example of a mutual accommodation pattern of bureaupolitical re-

Figure 10–2

Bureaupolitical Response as a Function of the Noncompliance Delay Effect (NDE)

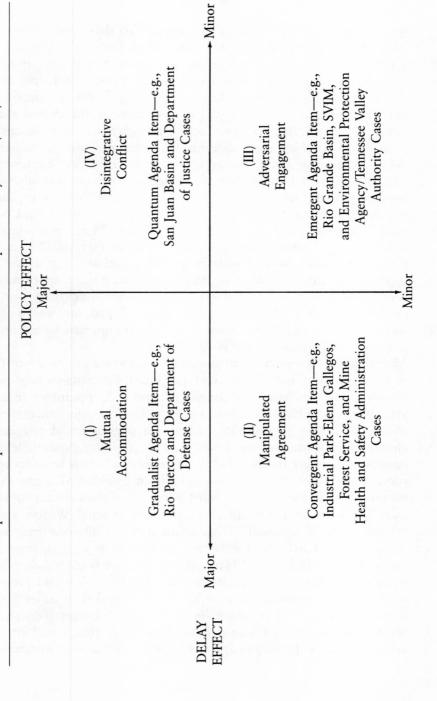

sponse to a Gradualist policy initiative.[16] To these ends, one of Weinberger's principal objectives was to move from a single-year to a multi-year weapons procurement policy—a policy directly related to the Reagan Defense Department's core or mission activities. Thus, inordinate resistance or prolonged delay in carrying out the Secretary's initiative could have directly threatened the ability of careerists to perform activities (weapons procurement) centrally related to their mission (strategic defense planning). When a question arose, however, over how multi-year contracts should be financed, disagreements ensued between (among others) presidential appointees and career bureaucrats. At issue was whether "full" or "incremental" funding mechanisms should be used. Careerists understandably worried that "full" multi-year funding might harm their established program budgets. As Laurence Lynn notes, while low-level specialists debated, upper-level supervisors and political appointees remained passive spectators venting only "an occasional opinion." Rather quickly, a compromise involving "almost-full" funding developed, one which assured careerists and their allies that multi-year contracts would not jeopardize historical agency budgets.

Manipulated Agreement. Bureaupolitical response in Quadrant II is typically (but not exclusively) produced by cross-cutting or cross-over policy initiatives sought by political appointees (e.g., veterans' preferences or environmental protection requirements).[17] Here, the agency or program's dominant coalition and relevant clientele anticipate only moderate changes in policy. Nonetheless, coalition members try to avoid these "nuisance" costs in order to prevent diversion of scarce resources from established organizational tasks. These situations mostly involve appointees trying to gain the acquiescence of affected careerists to what Wilson and Rachal term "contextual" (e.g., affirmative action measures) as opposed to "active" or substantive policy goals (e.g., operating public housing facilities).[18] Here, more resistance is offered than in mutual accommodation situations, and less flexibility and precision characterize discussions. Still, careerists and their allies fear that prolonged, concerted challenges might occasion increased scrutiny of the agency's core activities by outside groups and interests, as political appointees appeal to macropolitical system actors.

Consequently, even if they could marshal the political wherewithal to contest appointees' initiatives aggressively, they tend not to do so.

In these instances, political appointees often try to manipulate the acquiescence of careerists by seizing the "moral high ground" through appeals to the public interest and by the use of adverse publicity—tactics which threaten to mobilize agency or program friends and foes alike. If effectively isolated in this manner, careerists and their allies make a tactical decision not to expand the scope of the conflict, thus preventing it from spilling over into future interactions with appointees over other policy issues. After a brief period of continued bargaining, careerists acquiesce amid some "face saving" proffered by the appointees in the form of information exchange, endorsement of some other undisputed policy proposal, the promise of future cooperation, or negotiated concessions to key agency or program clientele.

In addition to the Las Cruces Industrial Park–Elena Gallegos case, two excellent examples of manipulated agreement responses to a Convergent policy initiative are John Crowell's and Ford B. Ford's efforts to reorient management emphases at the Forest Service and the Mine Health and Safety Administration (MHSA), respectively.[19] In pursuing the Reagan Administration's agenda for enhancing government-industry cooperation (Ford) and market-based solutions to public policy problems (Crowell), both appointees stressed a range of reorientation objectives. Among those high validity, low softening, Convergent initiatives perceived as less directly threatening to established core activities in the Forest Service was Crowell's effort to incorporate economic analysis into the national forest planning process. Similarly less direct, but greeted with dismay by careerists at MHSA for disrupting established behavioral patterns, was Ford's policy of requiring pre-citation conferences between inspectors and mining officials.

In both instances, careerist cooperation occurred without protracted or vociferous appeals to micro- or macropolitical sovereigns; careerists anticipated that delays eventually could affect other cherished programs, processes, or lifestyles should the scope of the conflict expand substantially. Moreover, both of these appointees manipulated symbols to seize the moral high ground and crafted face-saving compromise resolutions for careerists and their allies. Ford effectively portrayed his actions in the media as embodying Reagan's popular "regulatory unreasonableness" campaign, a rallying theme that threatened to activate the President's deregulatory allies on Capitol Hill had careerists intensified their resistance. Likewise, Crowell met little serious opposition once Bush's Task Force on Regulatory Relief elevated the public visibility and status of his efforts. Also critical in this instance were the "face-saving" policy concessions he made to the Forest Service's environmental constituency.

Adversarial Engagement. A substantial escalation of bureaupolitical resistance occurs in situations falling into Quadrant III. Here, program careerists and their allies perceive the expected degree of behavioral change sought by appointees as extensive, costly (in terms of program, policy, or psychic costs), and illegitimate—an unwarranted intrusion on bureaucratic expertise or subsystem autonomy. Nonetheless, they do not perceive these initiatives as directly affecting their agency or program's core activities. Equally nonthreatening to them is the delay involved in challenging these policy initiatives; their ability to realize their agency or program's existing mission is undiminished. Instead, the longer the delay spawned by their resistance, the more likely an appointee's initiatives can be avoided, as agendas shift, priorities change, policy enthusiasm wanes, and turnover in elected and appointed sovereigns occurs. Thus, careerists try (or welcome efforts by others) to expand dramatically the scope, intensity, and duration of the challenge by rallying extra-agency allies among sympathetic legislative, executive, and judicial sovereigns. Mobilized, too, are constituents and clienteles ill-disposed toward, uncomfortable with, or diametrically opposed to policy implementation.

While careerists and their allies may persistently seek to widen the scope of the conflict to a point of decisive advantage or to seek delay for its own sake, the nature and duration of their intransigence have definite limits. Indeed, a "negotiated" settlement eventually becomes attractive to them as they begin to worry about long-term, negative agency or program implications. Two factors are especially compelling in this decision. First, careerists fear totally losing control of conflict management to external actors whose policy preferences are unknown, unreliable, or potentially unsympathetic. Thus they seek external support for their position on discrete aspects of the dispute, but they do not try to resolve the conflict in its entirety. Second, they worry should agency capacity to pursue related policies atrophy or if changes occur in the relationship between their agency or program's mission and the appointee's objectives. Here, the need arises among agency careerists and their allies "to get this issue behind us" as shifts in core technology and affected activities take on a new, more critical role in mission realization.

In addition to the Carter Administration's experience with SVIM recounted earlier, an excellent example of an adversarial engagement response to an Emergent agenda item is President Carter's attempts to bring the Tennessee Valley Authority into compliance with sulfur dioxide (SO_2) regulations promulgated by the Environmental Protection Agency during the 1970s.[20] Careerists at TVA wanted to meet federal regulations by diluting SO_2 emissions from their power plants in a tried-and-true fashion: building significantly less expensive taller smokestacks to disperse emissions over wider areas. In contrast, Carter's appointees wanted actual reduction of these emissions by employing an expensive and then relatively untested technological breakthrough: electrostatic scrubbers (low validity, high softening). With TVA planning to rely in the future on nuclear power, SO_2 standards affected a power source—coal-fired power plants—that the agency's dominant coalition thought increasingly less important to the agency's long-term power production mission. Hence, rather than perceiving Carter's regulatory initiatives as mission-threatening, disgruntled TVA careerists saw prolonged, obstreperous compliance delay an eminently rational and affordable strategy to take. To wit, TVA officials carried their anti-emission-reduction, anti-scrubber message to state regulatory bodies, federal courts, the press, and the U.S. Congress for resolution of discrete aspects of the dispute. In contrast, the same officials strongly *discouraged* their allies from doing the same when EPA applied thermal pollution regulations to its nuclear power plants. In that instance, the delay in licensing and constructing nuclear facilities such challenges would occasion was thought to jeopardize TVA's power production mission.

Eventually, it became clear that TVA would have to rely on coal rather than nuclear power plants to meet the energy demands of Valley consumers. At that point, TVA careerists implored Carter's appointees to "find someone we can surrender to." Subsequently, EPA and TVA officials (both careerists and appointees) hammered out in highly adversarial negotiations a settlement to the controversy, thus avoiding a court-imposed judgment.

Disintegrative Conflict. Situations involving disintegrative conflict are most likely when political appointees pursue initiatives administratively that apply directly to activities central to or especially symbolic of their agency or program's mission. Simultaneously, careerists and their allies must view the lengthy delay and high-profile recalcitrance they display in this stalemate as nonthreatening to or even enhancing their mission. Only under these conditions can these actors conceive and take advantage of the long-term benefits of "principled," confrontational, and uncompromising resistance. And only here are they willing to allow external actors to impose an overall settlement to the conflict. Thus, disintegrative conflict spawns the most acerbic, prolonged, and demoralizing implementation experiences for political appointees wielding the tools of the administrative presidency. What is more, it is most likely to require macropolitical actors (e.g., Congress or the courts) to impose a resolution to the dispute once patterns of civility disintegrate irreparably.

In addition to the San Juan Basin case, a particularly good example of a disintegrative conflict response to a Quantum policy initiative that took on symbolic overtones was the reaction of civil rights attorneys at the Justice Department to the school desegregation initiatives of the Nixon Administration.[21] After years of federal school desegregation orders mandating the busing of school children, Nixon appointees announced that they would no longer initiate court suits challenging neighborhood schools—a literal symbol of racial segregation in the South (a low validity, unsoftened initiative). Thus, as a series of frustrating, conflictual, and intrigue-provoking meetings proceeded with Nixon appointees, careerists in the civil rights division continued to file lawsuits against neighborhood school plans. In fact, several even called a press conference to denounce the Administration's policies and to announce their intention to proceed apace with lawsuits. Eventually, Nixon and his appointees retreated from this policy in the face of vocal careerist intransigence and ensuing Supreme Court decisions.

A second illustration of these dynamics is Alfred Regnery's effort during the Reagan Administration to reorient policy at the Office of Juvenile Justice and Delinquency Prevention (OJJDP).[22] Prior to Regnery's arrival at OJJDP, agency officials pursued three fundamental purposes: freeing juvenile offenders from adult jails, removing all "status offenders" (e.g., runaways, truants, incorrigibles) from juvenile correction facilities, and funding research grants and projects promoting children's legal rights. In contrast, Regnery introduced Quantum-type policies (low validity and unsoftened) premised on a decidedly different idea set: (1) crime does not stem from social factors that are beyond the control of perpetrators; (2) children are responsible for their misdeeds and should be held accountable for them; (3) punishment, not rehabilitation, should inform juvenile justice policy; and (4) children should not have the same legal rights as adults. To these ends, Regnery summarily developed and pursued plans (without sustained, prolonged, and extensive softening within established juvenile justice system networks) to reprogram research funding priorities from delinquency prevention to punishment of chronic juvenile offenders. He did so, first, by administratively terminating funding for $67 million worth of grants declared inconsistent with the Reagan Administration's goals. Then he used administrative discretion to award certain grants on a noncompetitive, sole-source basis for projects focusing on punishing juveniles engaged in serious crimes (rape, murder, robbery, child abuse, and crime in schools).

In response, an iron triangle of grant recipients, OJJDP careerists, and congressional sovereigns such as U.S. Senators Arlen Specter (R-PA) and Howard Metzenbaum (D-OH) expanded the scope of the conflict outside of the juvenile justice policy community into sympathetic extended issue networks (e.g., the Legal Services Corporation), liberal advocacy coalition members (e.g., the National Juvenile Law Center), and ultimately into the arena of judicial scrutiny for imposed court settlements. For his part, Regnery cultivated the active support of the conservative advocacy coalition associated with juvenile justice issues (e.g., the National Center for Neighborhood Enterprise), "street-level" criminal justice professionals (e.g., the National District Attorney Association), and conservative academics (e.g., Harvard professor Glenn Lowry). Ultimately, Congress eliminated the noncompetitive, sole-source grant procedures from OJJDP's organic statute and abolished the agency's National Advisory Committee after Reagan appointed all 15 of its members. Meanwhile, Specter and Metzenbaum episodically ordered General Accounting Office studies of the effectiveness or legality of Regnery's administrative actions (e.g, the awarding of grants, and the existence of a "hit list" of Regnery's bureaucratic opponents at OJJDP). In the end, however, several of Regnery's most controversial programs—viewed as nonnegotiable by both he and his opponents—wound up in federal court.

TWIXT BUREAUPHOBES AND BUREAUPHILES: TOWARD A PUBLIC SERVICE MODEL OF APPOINTEE-CAREERIST RELATIONS

While presidents and their appointees expect macropolitical resistance to their agendas, bureaucratic resistance to their initiatives engenders feelings of betrayal, outrage, and even vindictiveness. Especially galling are perceptions that careerists have subverted presidential agendas, seemingly interested more in pursuing their own rather than an administration's policy preferences. Indeed, precisely these fears helped launch the administrative presidency as a tool for executive leadership.

Certainly, Aaron Wildavsky is correct in noting how many novice, reform-minded political appointees among Reagan's "true believers" tended to experience an epiphany of sorts once in office. Writes Wildavsky:

> After the identification of 'the bureaucracy' with all their [i.e., appointees'] troubles wears off . . . [they] begin to realize that the disagreement on policies they once thought they were supposed to be carrying out against bureaucratic opposition has causes much closer to home. . . . Indeed, it would be fair to say that [Reagan's more

ideological appointees] had more difficulty in persuading the Republican Administration to steer in the direction they thought had been agreed upon than in getting the bureaucracy to follow a clear command.[23]

Witness, for example, how the diverse philosophies, policy agendas, and political ambitions of Reagan's appointees—budget-balancing conservatives, free-marketeers, states' righters, and politicos—influenced many of the cases and illustrations reported in earlier chapters.

Nonetheless, Ronald Reagan and his most recent predecessors viewed the bureaucracy as largely unsympathetic at best, and at worst, hostile to policy reorientation. As such, they took the view that loyal political appointees had to control bureaucratic operations and actors hierarchically, closely, and from a top-down perspective. This presidential paranoia, of course, reached its apex during the Reagan Administration. Indeed, this book has chronicled its manifestation and consequences for reorienting natural resource policy in the West. Yet it has also revealed (1) how internal divisions over policy goals among political appointees are often the most serious obstacles to policy reorientation, (2) how bureaupolitical resistance can vary across different types of agenda items, and (3) how these variations in resistance are products of the noncompliance delay effect.

So is there a better way for presidents and their emissaries to approach the federal bureaucracy when seeking policy change or redirection? Among those distressed by President Reagan's use of the administrative presidency, Patricia Ingraham and Carolyn Ban have argued most compellingly for a public service model of political appointee–careerist relations, one premised on mutual responsibility and respect, joint tempering, and concern for the public interest. They write:

> The concept of the public interest does not mandate that there be perfect agreement between political appointees and careerists about either ends or means. It only ensures that the dialogue is carried out with the intent of achieving some larger, broader public good. Neither political control nor career expertise and objectivity are superior; both are simply component parts of a necessary process. Each is, therefore, seasoned and tempered by the other.[24]

Left unclear, however, is how best to nurture the values treasured in this model, after years of shrill and polarizing "bureaucrat bashing."

Premised on the preceding analysis, the remainder of this chapter argues that altering appointee-careerist attitudes in ways advancing the values espoused by the public service model requires an approach to executive branch relationships that is more "conditionally cooperative," yet more well-grounded in notions of shared responsibility for lawful governance, than those models which have dominated the debate over the past decade. Moreover, to be successful, this hybrid contingency-based approach requires three things. First, political appointees must acquire more sophisticated, realistic, and less polarized expectations about the nature and legitimacy of careerist behavior and dissent than those typically informing the present debate. Second, they must be afforded the heuristic tools and strategies necessary for anticipating, understanding, and constructively engaging careerists responding disparately to their initiatives. And third, careerists must appreciate what presidentialists already understand and what ample empirical evidence over the past five presidencies readily supports: If political direction and career expertise are to "season and temper" each other effectively, appointees must increasingly wield the tools of the administrative presidency with political and strategic finesse.

Thus far, this chapter has used the noncompliance delay effect to identify when political appointees can expect various types of bureaupolitical reactions to major and disparate types of agenda items. Thus, it has addressed several of the above-mentioned needs directly. Still lacking, however, are strategies for appointees to emphasize when pursuing policy goals likely to ignite one of the four types of implementation scenarios discussed. To identify strategies worthy of advancing the values espoused by the public service model, we turn next for guidance to prior research on leadership, organizational behavior, and executive branch politics. The analysis begins by critiquing the two most popular and polarizing perspectives on the administrative presidency as it relates to appointee-careerist relations. Following this, a contingency strategy elaborating and extending the work of Hugh Heclo on this topic is offered. Premised on the noncompliance delay effect, as well as on the scholarship of Paul Hersey and Kenneth Blanchard, this strategy is designed to foster both accomplishment and a public service ethos within the executive branch.

Before proceeding with the analysis, however, three points of clarification are necessary. First, while appointee-careerist relationships typically are interactions in which both sides are reacting simultaneously to each other's cues, this chapter provides a strategic perspective to appointees only. The logic of this focus is quite straightforward. If relationships within the executive branch are to be crafted in ways fostering the normative ends of the public service model, the initiative must come largely from political appointees. It is they who effectively set the bounds and tone of appointee-careerist relations.

Second, while some might find the administrative presidency a strange if not inappropriate vehicle for realizing the less presidentialist and more cooperative values of the public service model, this need not be the case. As Richard Waterman and others chronicle, incumbents have wielded the tools of the administrative presidency with varying degrees of malice, malfeasance, and passion to dominate careerists.[25] For example, the Reagan Administration's early use of the administrative presidency at the Environmental Protection Agency was largely confrontational and control-oriented. In contrast, the Carter Administration's efforts to reorient regulatory policy at the Interstate Commerce Commission were decidedly more cooperationist and persuasion-oriented. Thus, while some have applied malevolently the tools of the administrative presidency to the career service, Woodrow Wilson's advice in a different context seems prudent here as well: "If I see a murderous fellow sharpening a knife cleverly, I can borrow his way of sharpening the knife without borrowing his probable intention to commit murder with it."[26]

Finally, the strategic perspective offered here is designed for the overwhelming majority of situations wherein appointees are lawfully pursuing legal, constitutional, and ethical policy ends. Still, the potential for a "lawless presidency" is real, formidable, and intolerable. Thus, one should not construe the strategic approach offered as diminishing either the responsibility or the capacity of careerists "running a constitution" to instigate fire alarm or police patrol oversight in defense of lawful government.[27]

With this said, we turn now for context to those "ideal types" of views that have dominated academic, practitioner, and popular discourse on appointee-careerist relationships during the 1980s: the "bureauphilic," "bureauphobic," and "realpolitik" perspectives.

The Bureauphilic Perspective

Those taking a bureauphilic perspective on appointee-careerist relations condemn the administrative presidency as an untoward assault on the neutral competence of the career bureaucracy.[28] This is not to suggest that bureauphiles are apologists for bureaucracy; they, too, lament bureaucratic imperialism, inertia, capture, and biased pluralism. Indeed, they readily concede that careerists engage in policy making, are intimately involved in policy networks, and are motivated by agency, professional, and personal interests that may not coincide with a president's agenda. Still, they argue, appointees routinely can expect and craft with careerists cooperative working relationships that respect bureaucratic prerogatives, professionalism, expertise, and autonomy. To do otherwise, some suggest, is fraught with hazard; careerists are so expert, politically adroit, and well-connected that presidential agendas are largely doomed or ill-advised in the absence of careerists' approval or uninformed by their expertise and institutional memory. Others contend that politicization is a dubious strategy anyway; most appointees are in-and-outers with horizontal loyalties to issue networks rather than vertical loyalties to presidents.[29]

For harried, accomplishment-oriented, short-term political appointees, the advice proffered by bureauphiles flies in the face of popular (mis?)perceptions that cooperative strategies have derailed the agendas or wrought the demise of naive political appointees. Consequently, many are skeptical of "Theory Y" advice that effectively states, "If you will only trust and involve careerists in agenda and policy formulation, they will at worst offer 'loyalty that argues back' and at best faithfully carry out your initiatives."[30] Equally distressing, bureauphiles tend largely to discount or disparage evidence demonstrating how President Reagan's top-down, control-oriented politicizing strategy was quite effective at times and in the long run—whether or not careerists approved or cooperated. Thus, as Lynn warns Reagan's critics:

> Failure to understand the Reagan experiment in public management will mean that a valuable lesson for future administrations— administrations that have a more positive view of government—will be lost. That lesson is that loyal and competent supporters in key executive branch positions can be a potent tool of administrative leadership.[31]

For Lynn and others, one cannot overstate the value of political appointees' tethering tautly a coherent presidential vision to aggressive implementation, especially when they establish "understandable premises for their organization's [mission], . . . identify [their] organization's core activities, and engage the informal organization that supports and justifies them."[32] Inestimable, too, are the Office of Management and Budget's efforts to give "operational meaning" to the President's agenda, efforts supplemented by close Executive Office of the President oversight of political appointees effecting these changes. To do otherwise, many charge, is to opt essentially for a fragmented, decentralized, and hyperpluralistic model of "congressional bureaucracy."[33] What *is* possible to overestimate, however, is the applicability of a politicized, "top-down," Theory X management control strategy in all situations. Unfortunately, devotees of such a "bureauphobic" perspective have often captured popular and presidential imaginations with just such a fallacious prescription.

The Bureauphobic Perspective

In contrast to cooperationists, those exhibiting a bureauphobic perspective are distinctly more distrustful of the career bureaucracy and typically advocate a significantly more confrontational "Theory X" approach to appointee-careerist relationships.[34] They argue that the federal bureaucracy has become an independent political actor sapping constitutional powers that belong most appropriately to elected officials. To many bureauphobes, the solution to this problem is a "jigsaw puzzle" management philosophy that strictly isolates careerists from policy formulation and advocacy. Thus, bureauphobes also acknowledge the demise of the politics-administration dichotomy. But most viscerally eschew accommodations with careerists in favor of direct frontal assaults when it comes to agenda setting and policy formulation. In Michael Sanera's words, when appointees are "inundated by the bureaucratic perspective," risk-averse careerists can dissuade, disarm, or disrupt presidential priorities.[35] In addition, many bureauphobes dismiss as ingenuous the claims of cooperationists that presidentializing the bureaucracy is an assault on neutral competence. How so, they ask, when bureauphiles, too, portray careerists as flush with political philosophies, agendas, and acumen? For them, only a wary, more control-oriented, and exclusionary strategy is sufficient for success.

Just as generic prescriptions for cooperation are disastrously shortsighted, so are calls for indiscriminately applying "supply-side," "jigsaw puzzle," or "mushroom" management. Such a philosophy ignores substantial empirical evidence which suggests (1) how infrequently political appointees can "maintain full control of policy processes and decisions" and (2) how vulnerable appointees' agendas are when uninformed by or incompatible with careerist expertise, predispositions, or political skills.[36] Arguably, then, a more contingency-based approach to appointee-careerist relations is needed, one that is grounded in the values of the public service model. Fortunately, the rudiments of such an approach are offered by proponents of a "realpolitik" perspective on appointee-careerist relations.

The Realpolitik Perspective

Theorists and practitioners unpersuaded by blanket characterizations of bureaucrats have taken modest yet important steps toward developing a "realpolitik" model of executive branch relationships. To date, Heclo provides the most developed framework for making behaviorally based distinctions among, and prescriptions for dealing with, federal careerists.[37] Premised on exchange theory, Heclo's pathbreaking work is important in (1) helping appointees and bureaucrats to understand their different motivations, (2) demonstrating that the bureaucracy is not monolithic, and (3) suggesting how appointees can use this knowledge to advance their political agendas.

Heclo suggests an alternative, "conditional cooperation," to preconceived Theory X or Theory Y approaches to appointee-careerist relations. After identifying four different types of bureaucrats (program, staff, reformers, and institutionalists) with four different types of reactions to appointee initiatives (opponents, reluctants, critics, and forgottens), Heclo explains how political appointees might employ this diversity to foster cooperation. Conditional cooperation, he writes, emphasizes:

> the need [for] executives [appointees] and bureaucrats to work at relationships that depend on the contingencies of one another's actions, not on preconceived ideas of strict supervision or harmonious goodwill. . . . By making their reactions conditional on the performance of subordinates, political appointees create latitude for choice—possibilities for various types of exchanges with different [types] of bureaucrats. The basis for executives' leadership becomes strategic rather than 'take it or leave it.' . . . The real basis of conditional cooperation lies in making bureaucrats creditors rather than debtors to the political executives: that is, giving them a stake in his [the appointee's] future performance.[38]

Heclo's insights, however, require further elaboration and extension to realize markedly and prudently the values cherished in a public service model of executive branch relations. Conspicuously underdeveloped, for example, are robust contingency strategies for anticipating and reacting to the disparate bureaucratic responses outlined. As noted, the noncompliance delay effect has sought to more systematically address how appointees might anticipate these different dynamics. The remainder of this chapter provides the rudiments of strategies designed to cope with each.

The logic of the "realpolitik" perspective offered is fourfold.[39] First, by expanding Hersey and Blanchard's concept of "follower readiness" to include careerists' differential propensity and capacity to resist policy initiatives, the noncompliance delay effect affords appointees a diagnostic tool to anticipate the nature, intensity, and duration of bureaucratic resistance.[40] Second, the level of diagnosed bureaupolitical resistance or "readiness" in turn suggests the extent to which appointees can profit from constructively engaging careerists using the four styles of executive leadership identified by Hersey and Blanchard: telling, selling, participating, and delegating. Third, to be effective, these four styles need to be more fully elaborated to include all the leadership tools associated with the administrative presidency, as well as those identified by Heclo. And finally, to help advance a public service ethic within the federal bureaucracy, appointees must heed Hersey and Blanchard's charge for leaders to nurture rather than stunt growth in careerists' readiness levels.

Recall that Hersey and Blanchard's four follower-based leadership styles are derived deductively from the interaction of two key leadership behaviors: task and relationship. The former refers to the degree of managerial direction that leaders try to exercise over members in their work group as measured by how precisely and forcefully they structure and define their followers' tasks, bureaucratic routines, and worldviews. The latter refers to how mightily leaders strive to maintain personal relationships with followers by opening communication channels, providing "socioemotional" support, exhibiting facilitative behavior, and proffering "psychological strokes." Thus, telling strategies involve high-task, low-relationship behaviors; selling strategies exhibit high-task, high-relationship behaviors; participating strategies evince low-task, high-relationship behaviors; and delegating strategies invoke low-task, low-relationship behaviors (see Figure 10–3).

When selecting among these styles, Hersey and Blanchard urge leaders to link their choice of style to the readiness levels of their followers—i.e., how ready their subordinates are to take on a particular task. Thus, readiness is not a static personality trait (as bureauphobes and bureauphiles imply when discussing careerists), but an assessment of how ready a person is to perform a particular task at a particular time. Here, two factors are critical. The first, job maturity, reveals the extent to which followers have the ability and technical knowledge needed for work assignments. The second, psychological maturity, indicates whether followers exhibit sufficient self-confidence, self-respect, and willingness to assume personal responsibility for goal realization.

In essence, Hersey and Blanchard's primary prescriptions are threefold for determining the "high-probability [match and] combination of task and relationship behavior for success."[41] First, the higher the maturity level exhibited by followers with regard to a

Figure 10–3
Political Appointee–Careerist Relations: A Strategic Perspective

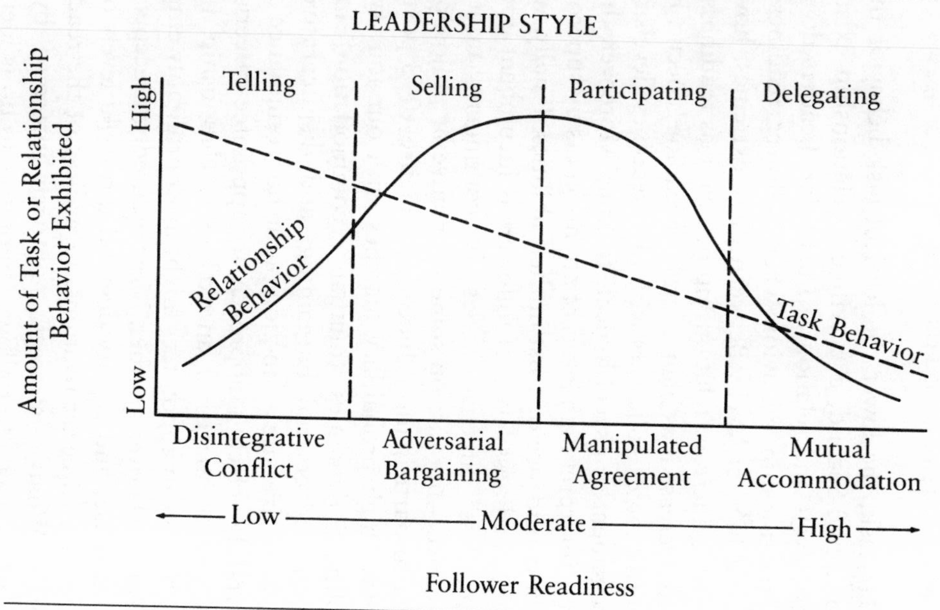

LEADERSHIP STYLE

| Telling | Selling | Participating | Delegating |

Task Behavior

Relationship Behavior

Amount of Task or Relationship Behavior Exhibited

High

Low

| Disintegrative Conflict | Adversarial Bargaining | Manipulated Agreement | Mutual Accommodation |

Low ——— Moderate ——— High

Follower Readiness

particular task, the lower the level of task behavior that leaders need to apply. Second, a curvilinear relationship exists between readiness levels and relationship behavior. Leaders do well to diminish relationship behavior when follower readiness is at its lowest and highest levels. Between these extremes, however, they should, first, increase relationship behavior as readiness increases, and then decrease it as higher levels of readiness occur. Hersey and Blanchard's logic? Followers with high readiness levels require less encouragement or psychological stroking. Moreover, they tend often to misinterpret high levels of attentiveness by superordinates as a lack of confidence or trust in their abilities. Finally, while developing the readiness levels of followers is incumbent upon leaders, adapting less directive styles is contingent upon follower performance—not just on some normative or philosophical commitment to participation. Indeed, (as Figure 10–3 portrays) these styles have high probability matches with our four types of bureaupolitical dynamics (mutual accommodation, manipulated agreement, adversarial bargaining, and disintegrative conflict), which themselves are a function of the noncompliance delay effect.

Certainly, Heclo's approach to appointee-careerist relations evokes similar images of an exchange relationship, but without elaborating when appointees might most profitably emphasize one leadership style over another. Most assuredly, precepts of decency, common sense, and comity demand threshold levels of civility in all appointee-careerist relations, regardless of the readiness levels exhibited. What a strategic approach informed by the noncompliance delay effect allows appointees to do is identify leadership styles, tactics, and targets most critical for crafting accomplishment in ways that also advance the values associated with a public service model of appointee-careerist relations.

Telling Strategies. Applying Hersey and Blanchard's logic, political appointees should find a highly directive, low-relationship leadership style (telling) most necessary, applicable, and effective in situations where they experience or strongly expect disintegrative conflict. Recall how disintegrative conflict produces unflagging and uncompromising resistance by careerists who perceive a political appointee's policy initiative as an illegitimate assault on agency, program, or careerist prerogatives. This perception leads ultimately—as it did during the revolt of civil rights attorneys at the Justice Department—to non-negotiable demands, hostility among the parties, and appeals to macropolitical sovereigns for an imposed resolution of the controversy. Thus, with the "readiness" of careerists at its nadir, cooperative strategies alone seem distinctly unlikely to create a "policy bias" sufficient to effect major policy reorientation. Rather, a strategy emphasizing a highly directive, top-down version of the administrative presidency seems most appropriate and profitable in the short run.

This is not to suggest that a bureauphobic approach animated by disdain and hostility for careerists will prove effective. Indeed, Hersey and Blanchard stress that being directive "does not mean being nasty," but being concerned with accomplishment of "leader-made" decisions through one-way communication of means and ends.[42] Moreover, the ill-will created within the bureaucracy by obtrusive telling strategies in one policy area— wielded capriciously, ideologically, or in paroxysms of bureauphobia—may jeopardize otherwise less contentious policy initiatives as well.

Most important, presidential appointees should not use a telling strategy indiscriminately with all careerists. Instead, they should target those program careerists whom Heclo labels opponents—individuals "who see vital interests harmed by [major] change and who are unalterably opposed to the efforts of political executives."[43] At the same time, appointees seeking both policy accomplishment and the creation of a public service ethos are well-advised to identify any staff bureaucrats, reformers, and institutionalists who sympathize with or can be induced (with positive or negative incentives) to adopt their policy goals. Thus, as one of Heclo's interviewees counseled, "A smart guy [a political appointee] should spend a while finding out who's productive, build on the ones who will help you do things, move them, use them to get other good people, and ride them as far as you can."[44] Here, intra-agency structural and procedural reforms become critical for reassigning responsibility, authority, and rule-making tasks to strategically located allies within the bureaucracy. In sum, under conditions of disintegrative conflict, bureauphobic strategies of intensive politicization, centralized decision making, and strict budget and management controls are probably unavoidable. Appointees, too, may have little choice but to employ "jigsaw puzzle" management against those careerists exhibiting bureaucratic intransigence, sabotage, and combativeness.

While frustrating to most appointees, strategies such as these are always and appropriately grist for extra-agency political intrigue by disgruntled careerists and their allies. This is especially true, however, under circumstances of disintegrative conflict, as careerists—or their allies—try to expand the scope of the conflict to a point of decisive advantage within the legislature, the courts, or other executive branch agencies. Thus, to hold their own in terms of policy and the values informing the public service model, appointees are virtually compelled to strategically and aggressively rally within advocacy coalitions allies who share their policy perspective. Coalition members, in turn, must become "fixers" poised to clean up bills, amendments, or appropriation riders hostile to their policy intentions. In sum, political appointees—contrary to the tactics of several prominent Reaganites—must eschew confrontational, standoffish, or "go-it-alone" relationships with congressional overseers. These only provoke more potential adversaries, unnecessarily risk estrangement of potential allies within Congress, and spawn contagious conflicts—precisely when appointees most need committed, savvy, and influential friends.

Selling Strategies. Recall how adversarial scenarios evince initially rigid and stalemated negotiating patterns that create long-term implementation delays. As distrust and skepticism about appointees' motives mount, program careerists, their interest group allies, and/or institutionalists welcome and appeal for intervention by other subsystem macropolitical actors. Yet, unlike disintegrative conflict, the disputants wish to avoid externally imposed, overall settlements. Instead, macropolitical intervention is sought only for discrete aspects of the dispute. Moreover, intervention is encouraged in ways designed largely to alter the benefit-cost decision calculations of appointees (e.g., judicial clarification of ambiguous statutory language, riders to appropriation bills preventing certain actions, and changes in funding formulae). In sum, careerists' readiness levels for political appointees' initiatives are distinctly higher than in disintegrative conflict situations.

With higher readiness levels probable among careerists, Hersey and Blanchard's approach suggests that political appointees are more likely to advance presidential policy and public service model goals by emphasizing a selling leadership strategy focused on Heclo's "reluctant" careerists. Reluctants are careerists who "may be opposed to change, but who are not immune to persuasion that there are some hitherto unrecognized advantages [to cooperation]—they will at least listen."[45] Put differently, political appointees might expand profitably the "zones of indifference" of reluctants by alerting them to these "hitherto unrecognized advantages" of cooperation. For example, in the TVA case mentioned earlier, the Authority altered significantly its cost-benefit calculus toward SO_2 compliance when it became clear that its power production future depended more on coal-fired power plants than on nuclear facilities.

What would a selling strategy entail for political appointees? With a different audience in mind, Hersey and Blanchard suggest gradually increasing relationship-oriented behavior with subordinates, while still maintaining a modicum of task-oriented behavior until a more substantial level of readiness develops. Thus, political appointees might strive to create a supportive and considerate implementation context, one characterized by explaining decisions, providing opportunities for clarification, and wielding positive and negative incentives with strategic savvy. Still, a selling strategy is limited most profitably to persuasion through either "intensified argument" or clarification of points of "mutual self-interest." As one of Heclo's interviewees pointed out, "You're [i.e., political appointees] looking for places where you can support him so he can support you, [but this] does not mean you bring the bureau chief into the secretary or undersecretary's office and lay out all the sensitive information that he can then use against you with [the interest groups] and Congress."[46]

What specific tools of the administrative presidency can political appointees emphasize under these circumstances? Again, Heclo is instructive when he suggests the utility of such communication devices as formal task forces, indirect pressures brought by third-party actors, and quid pro quo side payments. In addition, Hersey and Blanchard's narrower concept of readiness provides additional "currency" for side payments. That is, with different programmatic imperatives competing within organizations for scarce dollars and political advantage, appointees might coax compromise from Heclo's reluctants (and perhaps even critics) by adopting a "linkage" strategy of enhanced capacities. Specifically, appointees might premise the granting, withholding, or transferring of resources related to other program goals cherished by reluctants to good-faith bargaining over policy alternatives. In the process, careerists in other agencies who are part of a target program's implementation structure or governance network may try to exert third-party pressures toward compromise. They, too, stand to suffer or gain when appointees tie program resources in sister agencies to presidential policy initiatives.

Participating Strategies. Recall that in manipulated agreement scenarios the nature of communications between appointees and careerists is typically less precise, more anticipatory, and rife with respectfully competitive undertones. This tends to force appointees to mobilize external support unilaterally for their policy initiatives, but in this instance by manipulating political symbols (e.g., appeals to the "public interest"). These, of course, are used by appointees to seize the moral high ground, to dissuade careerists from mobilizing their allies or welcoming their support, and to save face for all involved. Still, since the policy initiatives are more of a nuisance than a source of principled opposition to careerists, their readiness to cooperate is decidedly higher than in adversarial bargaining situations.

With higher readiness levels among careerists, Hersey and Blanchard's logic suggests that appointees are more likely to advance policy and public service goals by adopting a participative leadership style. No longer do explaining decisions, providing opportunities for clarification, and persuasion through intensified argument seem sufficient. Instead, Hersey and Blanchard's approach calls for appointees to share ideas and to facilitate decision making. In their terms, participating should involve a "leader/follower-made or follower-made decision with encouragement from [the] leader."[47] Indeed, as Crowell did at the Forest Service, appointees might even consult program, staff, and reformer bureaucrats—as well as their interest group allies—when formulating policy objectives and initiatives. Concurrently, however, appointees must subtly communicate to careerists the consequences of obdurate disagreement—especially if escalated publicly—for their cherished programs, policies, or lifestyles. Again, however, "linkage," information exchange, joint decision documents, endorsement of related policies, capacity building, and promises of future cooperation might all be used deftly as strategic and face-saving bargaining resources.

Appointees pursuing this strategy also can expect to profit by paying special attention to the views of those careerists whom Heclo labels "critics." These are bureaucrats "who feel they have views to contribute and are willing to be supportive as long as what they have to say is seriously considered." Their concern is less with substance than with due process: "They do not feel that they [have] to win as long as they [can] gain access [to appointees] for their views." Fortunately, the complexity of many issues allows program, institutional, and staff bureaucrats who are critics the flexibility to rationalize a range of presidential initiatives. Indeed, as one of Heclo's interviewees mused, "The options aren't all that different regardless of which party is in power. . . . What many career people do care about is that their sorting out of alternatives comes into play . . . and that there is evidence they've [appointees] paid attention and at least had to wrestle with the issues worrying us."[48]

Delegating Strategies. Applying the logic of Hersey and Blanchard's contingency theory, political appointees confronting mutual accommodation scenarios should emphasize delegating strategies to accomplish their goals and to foster a public service ethic within the executive branch. Recall how careerists in this situation exhibit their highest levels of readiness to forego prolonged challenges and to settle disagreements dispassionately if an environment is constructed of mutual trust, joint problem solving, clear communication, and adequate training and resources. Most especially, it behooves political appointees to avoid ignoring or creating what Heclo terms "forgotten" careerists within the target agency. These are careerists whose failure to support political executives "stems [more] from their failure to hear what is wanted or to hear correctly . . . than from outright opposition to policy goals."[49] Thus, appointees do well to identify previously forgotten careerists and to foster clear, consistent, and collegial communication processes with them and all of Heclo's remaining bureaucratic types. What is more, with readiness levels at their apogee, no longer do sharing ideas and facilitating decision making seem a "high probability match" between situation and leadership style. Instead, high follower readiness decreases the risk to appointees of turning over to careerists responsibility for decisions and implementation—as long as accountability mechanisms accompany this delegation.

As Heclo suggests, appointees in this situation might stress informal reminders, written communication of expectations, performance reporting procedures, and personalized discussion networks. Having mutually established with careerists in word, action, and reporting system the general parameters of acceptable action, appointees then can delegate authority to them reasonably confident that "implementation monsters" will not occur.[50] Indeed, appointees might even delegate responsibility to careerists for choosing among policy alternatives, or at least grant them considerable autonomy over implementation details and mechanics, as did Secretary Weinberger in the case of multi-year funding at the Defense Department. Appointees enhance their probability of success by emphasizing unobtrusive monitoring of program performance (outputs and outcomes) rather than obtrusive control of implementation processes. In sum, appointees can anticipate that careerists will be sufficiently self-motivated or self-interested to pursue faithfully a presidential initiative that is effectively and persistently communicated, funded, and monitored for program performance rather than control.

TOWARD A PUBLIC SERVICE MODEL IN THE 1990s?

Certainly much remains to be done before a robust, contingency-based approach to appointee-careerist relations exists, especially one that fosters rather than undermines the normative ends promoted by Ingraham and Ban's public service model. The types of bureaupolitical behavior and related styles of leadership discussed in this chapter hardly are exhaustive and must be further elaborated, tested, and refined empirically. Still, the rudiments are offered of a framework for anticipating, understanding, and strategically addressing appointee-careerist relations. Moreover, these recommendations avoid simplistic "bureauphobic" or "bureauphilic" prescriptions and promote the ends of the public service model. They do so in two ways. First, they are more "conditionally cooperative" than most bureauphilic prescriptions. Second, they are more grounded in notions of shared responsibility for lawful government than most bureauphobic strategies.

Unabashedly, the strategic logic proffered in this chapter is premised on a particular normative end. Put simply, it is designed to promote public interest–oriented policy accomplishment through "creative" appointee-careerist engagement. Specifically, appointees must respect careerists' concerns relating to management development and program capacity; careerists must respect the appointees' concerns for partisan policy objectives, expeditious results, and responsiveness to legal presidential goals. Obviously, other normative premises could lead others to different prescriptions. Yet this argument presumes that Ingraham and Ban's "joint tempering and seasoning" is a worthy goal that is most likely to flourish (1) when appointees and careerists understand each others' motives; (2) when realism informs their strategic judgments; and (3) when sustained, persistent, and good-faith interaction prevails between the two sets of government officials.

This is not to suggest that better communication is a panacea for nurturing the values associated with the public service model. Indeed, should appointees fail when confronted by intransigent careerists to wield the tools (Theory X included) of the administrative presidency in favor of their legitimate policy ends, good-faith dialogue may cease altogether as the resolve of appointees becomes questioned. In such an event, bureauphiles who fail to craft a climate of implementation expectations among careerists arguably foil the ideals of the public service model as much as bureauphobes do. It *is* to suggest, however, that progress in appointee-careerist relations requires appointees to (1) appreciate that heterogeneity rather than homogeneity exists among careerists in their attitudes toward change; (2) recognize that in a constitutional system of factored problems, fragmented authority, and plural executives careerists must—and do—accommodate their behavior to the cues of a variety of legitimate sovereigns, not just the President; (3) realize that bureaucratic resistance varies across different tasks and policy initiatives; and (4) take a dynamic and developmental rather than a static and deterministic view of careerist "readiness." In the process, Lowi's "personal" presidents and their appointees gain important insights for anticipating, navigating, and constructively confronting responses to their policy initiatives in the contemporary administrative state.

SUMMING UP

As for this book's overall implications for the values cherished in a democracy, two are readily apparent. One is substantive and the other is research-related. First, should presidents, their political appointees, or scholars view the administrative presidency as a way of diminishing or entirely circumventing micro- or macropolitical influence over policy making, they will be sorely disappointed. Ergo, while the tools of the administrative presidency are distinctly managerial in nature, they are means nonetheless to decidedly political ends. These ends, in turn, engender ranges of political conflict depending partially on their mode and tempo. Arguably, then, the term "administrative presidency" is a misnomer to the extent that it connotes or is misinterpreted to be a distinctly technical, less visible, and less politically-charged managerial approach to policy reorientation. Thus, the Republic has little to fear that the administrative presidency will asymmetrically advantage presidents relative to other macropolitical system actors. The administrative presidency does offer an opportunity to create a policy bias in favor of presidential agendas. But it offers no guarantee or warning of presidential dominance or success. What is more, success depends largely on (1) the political savvy and acumen of presidents and their appointees; (2) their ability to link short-term tactics adroitly to strategic goals; and (3) the extent to which they (a) employ reversible logic implementation strategies, (b) eschew notions of "simplistic sovereignty," and (c) approach their mission as one of accomplishment rather than control.

The second, more research-oriented implication of this book is that much conceptual and empirical work remains before the full implications of the administrative presidency are understood for Heclo's "larger organizational life of government." The cases examined here provide "peripheral vision" too crabbed to satisfy his criteria for studying the administrative presidency longitudinally, across a broad range of policy types and domains, and in interaction with a variety of other policy initiatives. In addition, the types of policy initiatives, bureaucratic responses, and political dynamics outlined are hardly exhaustive, must be further elaborated, and require empirical testing.

Still, the book has examined the administrative presidency at the grassroots in systematic and unprecedented ways. As such, it offers the rudiments of conceptual and analytical frameworks capable of doing two things: informing future research on this important yet understudied topic, and affording competent process standards against which to measure future administrative strategies. Unlike von Weber's, *Der Freischutz*, the tools of the administrative presidency are not "magic bullets" guaranteed always to hit their mark. Neither are they necessarily bullets cast by "devilish" presidents bent on or capable of subverting our constitutional system. What they are, and will remain, are attractive tools for presidents striving to create a policy bias in favor of their agendas within our hyperpluralistic, Madisonian system. Consequently, their bureaupolitical dynamics and implications are distinctly worthy of our sustained, persistent, and systematic attention in the 1990s and beyond.

NOTES

PREFACE

1. Hugh Heclo, "An Executive's Success Can Have Costs," pp. 371–374 in Lester M. Salamon and Michael S. Lund, eds., *The Reagan Presidency and the Governing of America* (Washington DC: The Urban Institute Press, 1984).

CHAPTER 1: A PASSION TO PREVAIL

1. Bert A. Rockman, *The Leadership Question: The Presidency and the American System* (New York: Praeger, 1984), p. 71.

2. For example, Richard E. Neustadt, *Presidential Power: The Politics of Leadership from FDR to Carter* (New York: Wiley, 1980; Theodore J. Lowi, *The Personal President: Power Invested, Promise Unfulfilled* (Ithaca NY: Cornell University Press, 1985); James McGregor Burns, *The Power to Lead: The Crisis of the American Presidency* (New York: Simon & Schuster, 1984).

3. Hugh Heclo and Lester Salamon, eds., *The Illusion of Presidential Government* (Boulder CO: Westview Press, 1981); Paul C. Light, *The President's Agenda: Domestic Policy Choice from Kennedy to Carter* (Baltimore: Johns Hopkins University Press, 1982); Barbara Kellerman, *The Political Presidency: Practice of Leadership* (New York: Oxford University Press, 1984). The extended quotation is from C. Calvin MacKenzie, *The Politics of Presidential Appointments* (New York: Free Press, 1981), p. 248.

4. Lowi, *The Personal President.*

5. The term "administrative presidency" is attributed to Richard Nathan. See Richard P. Nathan, *The Plot That Failed* (New York: Wiley, 1975) and Richard P. Nathan, *The Administrative Presidency* (New York: Wiley, 1983). The characterization of the administrative presidency as a low-visibility, low-political risk strategy is attributed to, among many others, Arnold J. Meltsner. See Arnold J. Meltsner, ed., *Politics and the Oval Office* (San Francisco: Institute for Contemporary Studies, 1981).

6. Richard P. Nathan, "The Administrative Presidency," *The Public Interest,* vol. 44 (Summer 1976), pp. 40–54.

7. James D. Carroll, A. Lee Fritschler, and Bruce L.R. Smith, "Supply-Side Management in the Reagan Administration," *Public Administration Review,* vol. 45 (November/December 1985), pp. 805–814.

8. See, for example, Michael Sanera, "Implementing the Mandate," pp. 457–545 in Stuart M. Butler, Michael Sanera, and W. Bruce Weinrod, eds.,

Mandate for Leadership II: Continuing the Conservative Revolution (Washington DC: Heritage Foundation, 1984); Terry M. Moe, "The Politicized Presidency," pp. 235–271 in John E. Chubb and Paul E. Peterson, eds., *The New Direction in American Politics* (Washington DC: Brookings Institution, 1985); Lloyd N. Cutler, "The Case for Presidential Intervention in Regulatory Rulemaking by the Executive Branch," *Tulane Law Review,* vol. 56 (1982), pp. 830–848; and Ben W. Heineman, Jr. and Curtis Hessler, *Memorandum for the President: Managing the Domestic Agenda in the 1980s* (New York: Random House, 1980).

9. See, for example, Hugh Heclo, "OMB and the Presidency—The Problem of 'Neutral Competence'," *The Public Interest,* vol. 38 (Winter 1975), pp. 80–98; Chester A. Newland, "A Mid-Term Appraisal—The Reagan Presidency: Limited Government and Political Administration," *Public Administration Review,* vol. 43 (January/February 1983), pp. 1–21; Frederick C. Mosher, "Denigration of the Public Servant," pp. 405–409 in Lester M. Salamon and Michael S. Lund, eds., *The Reagan Presidency and the Governing of America* (Washington DC: Urban Institute Press, 1984); James P. Pfiffner, "Political Public Administration," *Public Administration Review,* vol. 45 (March/April 1985), pp. 352–356; James P. Pfiffner, "Political Appointees and Career Executives: The Democracy-Bureaucracy Nexus in the Third Century," *Public Administration Review,* vol. 47 (January/February 1987), pp. 57–65.

10. See, for example, George C. Eads and Michael Fix, *Relief or Reform? Reagan's Regulatory Dilemma* (Washington DC: Urban Institute Press, 1984). For a somewhat different perspective on Reagan's legacy, see Bert Rockman, "Conclusions: An Imprint But Not a Revolution," pp. 191–206 in B.B. Kymlicka and Jean V. Matthews, eds., *The Reagan Revolution* (Chicago: Dorsey, 1988).

11. The literature dealing either centrally or tangentially with this topic is too extensive to cite comprehensively. Leading entries include: Fred I. Greenstein, ed., *The Reagan Presidency: An Early Assessment* (Baltimore: Johns Hopkins University Press, 1983); Nathan, "The Administrative Presidency"; Eads and Fix, *Relief or Reform?*; Newland, "A Mid-Term Appraisal"; Richard W. Waterman, *Presidential Influence and the Administrative State* (Knoxville: University of Tennessee Press, 1989); James P. Pfiffner, *The Strategic Presidency: Hitting the Ground Running* (Chicago: Dorsey, 1988); John L. Palmer and Isabel V. Sawhill, eds., *The Reagan Record* (Cambridge MA: Ballinger, 1984); John D. Lees and Michael Turner, *Reagan's First Four Years: A New Beginning?* (Manchester: Manchester University Press, 1988); Richard P. Nathan, Fred C. Doolittle, and Associates, *The Consequences of Cuts: The Effects of the Reagan Domestic Program on State and Local Governments* (Princeton NJ: Princeton University Press, 1983).

There is also a growing body of literature that specifically addresses the use of the administrative presidency in the natural resources arena. This literature includes: Michael E. Kraft and Norman J. Vig, eds., *Environmental Politics in the 1980s: Reagan's New Agenda* (Washington DC: Congressional Quarterly Press, 1984); Paul R. Portney, ed., *Natural Resources and the Environment: The Reagan Approach* (Washington DC: Urban Institute Press, 1984); Tom Arrandale, *The Battle for Natural Resources* (Washington DC: Congressional Quarterly Press, 1983); Jeanne N. Clarke and Daniel McCool, *Staking Out the Terrain: Power Differentials Among Natural Resource Management Agencies* (Albany: State University of New York Press, 1985); Michael E. Kraft and Regina Axelrod, "Political Constraints on Development of Alternative Energy Sources: Lessons from the Reagan Administration," *Policy Studies Journal,* vol. 13 (December 1984), pp. 319–330; Donald C. Menzel, "Redirecting the Implementation of a Law: The Reagan Administration and Coal Surface Mining," *Public Administration Review,* vol. 43 (May/June 1983), pp. 411–420; David M. Hedge and Donald C. Menzel, "Loosening the Regulatory Ratchet: A Grassroots View of Environmental Deregulation," *Policy Studies Journal,* vol. 13 (March 1985), pp. 599–606; Howard E. McCurdy, "Public Ownership of Land and the 'Sagebrush Rebellion'," *Policy Studies Journal,* vol. 12 (March 1984), pp. 483–490; Paul R. Portney, "Natural Resources and the Environment: More Controversy than Change," pp. 141–175 in Palmer and Sawhill, *The Reagan Record.*

12. Notable exceptions to this generalization are McCurdy, "Public Ownership"; Menzel, "Redirecting the Implementation"; Nathan, Doolittle, and Associates, *The Consequences of Cuts*; and Waterman, *Presidential Influence.*

13. Bruce Buchanan, *The Citizen's Presidency* (Washington DC: Congressional Quarterly, 1987).

14. See, for example, Patricia Wald, "The Realpolitik of Judicial Review in a Deregulation Era," *Journal of Policy Analysis and Management,* vol. 5 (1986), pp. 535–546; John D. Leshy, "Natural Resource Policy," pp. 13–46 in Paul R. Portney, ed., *Natural Resources and the Environment;* Robert W. Crandall and Paul R. Portney, "Environmental Policy," pp. 47–81 in Portney, ed., *Natural Resources and the Environment*; Michael E. Kraft and Norman Vig, "Environmental Policy in the Reagan Presidency," *Political Science Quarterly,* vol. 99 (Fall 1984), pp. 415–439. One excellent effort that does seek to link specific leadership styles and strategies of Reagan appointees to specific outcomes of managerial objectives is Laurence E. Lynn, Jr., "The Reagan Administration and the Renitent Bureaucracy," pp. 339–370 in Salamon and Lund, *The Reagan Presidency.*

15. See, for example, Irene S. Rubin, *Shrinking the Federal Government: The Effect of Cutbacks on Five Federal Agencies* (New York: Longman, 1985); Edie N. Goldenberg, "The Permanent Government in an Era of Retrenchment and Redirection," pp. 381–404 in Salamon and Lund, *The Reagan Presidency*; Carolyn Ban and Patricia Ingraham, "Short-Timers: Political Appointee Mobility and Its Impact on Political-Career Relations in the Reagan Administration," *Administration & Society,* vol. 22 (May 1990), pp. 106–124;

16. See, for example, James L. Regens and Robert W. Rycroft, "Funding for Environmental Protection: Comparing Congressional and Executive Influences," *The Social Science Journal,* vol. 26, no. 2 (1989), pp. 289–301; Paul J. Culhane, "Sagebrush Rebels in Office: Jim Watt's Land and Water Politics," pp. 293–317 in Vig and Kraft, *Environmental Policy in the 1980s*; B. Dan Wood, "Principals, Bureaucrats, and Responsiveness," *American Political Science Review,* vol. 82 (1988), pp. 213–234; B. Dan Wood, "Principal-Agent Models of Political Control of Bureaucracy," *American Political Science Review,* vol. 83 (September 1989), pp. 965–988; Jonathan Bender, Serge Taylor, and Roland Van Gaalen, "Stacking the Deck: Bureaucratic Missions and Policy Design," *American Political Science Review,* vol. 81 (September 1987), pp. 873–896; Jonathan Bender and Terry Moe, "An Adaptive Model of Bureaucratic Politics," *American Political Science Review,* vol. 79 (September 1985), pp. 755–774; John T. Scholz and Feng Heng Wei, "Regulatory Enforcement in a Federalist System," *American Political Science Review,* vol. 80 (December 1986), pp. 1187–1207; Randall L. Calvert, Mathew D. McCubbins, and Barry R. Weingast, "A Theory of Political Control and Agency Discretion," *American Journal of Political Science,* vol. 33 (August 1989), pp.

581–611; Joseph Stewart, Jr., and Jane S. Cromartie, "Partisan Presidential Change and Regulatory Policy: The Case of the FTC and Deceptive Practices Enforcement, 1938–1974," *Presidential Studies Quarterly*, vol. 12 (Fall 1982), pp. 568–573.

17. See, for example, Frank J. Thompson and Michael J. Scicchitano, "State Enforcement of Federal Regulatory Policy: The Lessons of OSHA," *Policy Studies Journal*, vol. 13 (March 1985), pp. 591–598.

18. See, for example, Richard Rose, *Managing Presidential Objectives* (New York: Free Press, 1976); Richard L. Cole and David A. Caputo, "Presidential Control of the Senior Civil Service: Assessing the Strategies of the Nixon Years," *American Political Science Review*, vol. 73 (June 1979), pp. 399–413; Newland, "A Mid-Term Appraisal"; James L. Sundquist, "Jimmy Carter as Public Administrator: An Appraisal at Midterm," *Public Administration Review*, vol. 39 (January/February 1979), pp. 3–11; Colin Campbell, *Governments Under Stress* (Toronto: University of Toronto Press, 1983); Margaret Jane Wyszomirski, "The De-Institutionalization of Presidential Staff Agencies," *Public Administration Review*, vol. 42 (September/October 1982), pp. 448–458.

19. For an excellent summary of the logic of the New Resource Economics, see Andrew Dana and John Baden, "The New Resource Economics: Toward an Ideological Synthesis," *Policy Studies Journal*, vol. 14 (December 1985), pp. 233–243.

20. Clarke and McCool, *Staking Out the Terrain*.

21. See, for example, Sally K. Fairfax, "Beyond the Sagebrush Rebellion: The BLM as Neighbor and Manager in the Western States," pp. 79–91 in John G. Francis and Richard Ganzel, eds., *Western Public Lands: The Management of Natural Resources in a Time of Declining Federalism* (Totowa NJ: Rowman and Allanheld, 1984); John G. Francis, "Environmental Values, Intergovernmental Politics, and the Sagebrush Rebellion," pp. 29–46 in Francis and Ganzel, *Western Public Lands*; R. Burnell Held, "Federal-State Relations in Public Land Administration," *Policy Studies Journal*, vol. 14 (December 1985), pp. 296–304; Barney Dowdle, "Perspective on the Sagebrush Rebellion," *Policy Studies Journal*, vol. 12 (March 1984), pp. 473–482.

22. James R. Meindl, Sanford B. Ehrlich, and Janet M. Dukerich, "The Romance of Leadership," *Administrative Science Quarterly*, vol. 30 (1985), p. 78.

23. These categories are premised on observations offered by Meindl, Ehrlich, and Dukerich, "The Romance of Leadership."

24. Erwin C. Hargrove and Michael Nelson, *Presidents, Politics, and Policy* (Baltimore: Johns Hopkins University Press, 1984).

25. Representative of the "Savior" perspective on powerful presidents acting as a force for good are such classics as: James McGregor Burns, *The Power to Lead* (New York: Simon and Schuster, 1984); Richard Neustadt, *Presidential Power* (New York: Wiley, 1980); Arthur Schlesinger, Jr., *A Thousand Days* (Boston: Houghton Mifflin, 1965); and most political science textbooks published during the 1950s and 1960s: See Thomas Cronin, "Superman—Our Textbook President," *The Washington Monthly*, October 1970, pp. 47–54. Representative of the "Satan" perspective is Arthur Schlesinger, Jr.'s, *The Imperial Presidency* (Boston: Houghton Mifflin, 1973).

26. For an excellent summary of these perspectives, see Bert A. Rockman, *The Leadership Question: The Presidency and the American System* (New York: Praeger, 1984). Also see Erwin C. Hargrove, *The Power of the Modern Presidency*

(New York: Knopf, 1974); Paul C. Light, "The President's Agenda: Notes on the Timing of Domestic Choice," *Presidential Studies Quarterly*, vol. 11 (Winter 1981), pp. 67–82; James L. Sundquist, *The Decline and Resurgence of Congress* (Washington DC: Brookings Institution, 1981); David W. Brady, "Critical Elections, Congressional Parties, and Clusters of Policy Changes," *British Journal of Political Science*, vol. 8 (January 1978), pp. 79–99; Donald R. Kinder and D. Roderick Kiewiet, "Sociotropic Politics: The American Case," *British Journal of Political Science*, vol. 11 (January 1981), pp. 129–161; George C. Edwards III, *The Public Presidency* (New York: St. Martin's Press, 1983); Edward R. Tufte, *Political Control of the Economy* (Princeton NJ: Princeton University Press, 1978); Anthony Downs, "Up and Down with Ecology: The Issue-Attention Cycle," *The Public Interest*, vol. 28 (Summer 1972); Light, *The President's Agenda*.

27. Meindl, Ehrlich, and Dukerich, "The Romance of Leadership," p. 79.

28. See, for example, Godfrey Hodgson, *All Things to All Men: The False Promise of the Modern American Presidency* (New York: Simon and Schuster, 1980); Fred Greenstein, "Change and Continuity in the Modern Presidency," pp. 45–85 in Anthony King, ed., *The New American Political System* (Washington DC: American Enterprise Institute, 1978); Thomas Franck, ed., *The Tethered Presidency* (New York: New York University Press, 1981); Francis E. Rourke, *Bureaucracy, Politics, and Public Policy*, 3rd ed. (Boston: Little, Brown, 1984); Richard Pious, *The American Presidency* (New York: Basic Books, 1979).

29. Lowi, *The Personal President*.

30. The President's Committee on Administrative Management, *Report of the President's Committee* (Washington DC: U.S. Government Printing Office, 1937).

31. David Rosenbloom, "Public Administrative Theory and the Separation of Powers," *Public Administration Review*, vol. 43 (May/June 1983), pp. 219–227.

32. For excellent treatments of these developments, see Marion Clawson, *The Federal Lands Revisited* (Baltimore: Resources for the Future, 1983); Paul J. Culhane, *Public Lands Politics* (Baltimore: Johns Hopkins University Press, 1981); Richard O. Miller, "FLPMA: A Decade of Management Under the BLM Organic Act," *Policy Studies Journal*, vol. 14 (December 1985), pp. 265–273; Clarke and McCool, *Staking Out the Terrain*. For an extensive and informative treatment of the evolving legal framework of public land management, see George C. Coggins, Parthenia B. Evans, and Margaret Lindeberg-Johnson, "The Law of Public Rangeland Management I: The Extent and Distribution of Federal Power," *Environmental Law*, vol. 12 (Spring 1982), pp. 535–622; George C. Coggins and Margaret Lindeberg-Johnson, "The Law of Public Rangeland Management II: The Commons and the Taylor Act," *Environmental Law*, vol. 13 (Fall 1982), pp. 1–102; George C. Coggins, "The Law of Public Rangeland Management III: A Survey of Creeping Regulation at the Periphery, 1934–1982," *Environmental Law*, vol. 13 (Winter 1983), pp. 295–365; George C. Coggins, "The Law of Public Rangeland Management IV," *Environmental Law*, vol. 14 (Fall 1983), pp. 1–132; George C. Coggins, "The Law of Public Rangeland Management V: Prescriptions for Reform," *Environmental Law*, vol. 14 (Spring 1984), pp. 497–546.

33. In 1980, federally owned land as a percentage of total state acreage in each of the 11 Western states plus Alaska was as follows: Alaska, 89%; Arizona, 44%; California, 47%; Colorado, 36%; Idaho, 64%; Montana, 30%; Nevada,

86%; New Mexico, 33%; Oregon, 53%; Utah, 64%; Washington, 29%; and Wyoming, 49%. The source for these data is BLM, *Public Land Statistics* (Washington DC: U.S. Government Printing Office, 1980).

34. Classic studies reviewing the influence of traditional users in BLM policy making include: Phillip O. Foss, *Politics and Grass* (Seattle: University of Washington Press, 1960); Wesley Calef, *Private Grazing and Public Lands* (Chicago: University of Chicago Press, 1960); Samuel P. Hays, *Conservation and the Gospel of Efficiency* (Cambridge MA: Harvard University Press, 1959).

35. Paul J. Culhane and H. Paul Friesma, "Land Use Planning for the Public Lands," *Natural Resources Journal*, vol. 19 (January 1979), as cited in Richard Miller, "FLPMA: A Decade of Management Under the BLM Organic Act."

36. Woodrow Wilson, "The New Meaning of Government," reprinted in *Public Administration Review*, vol. 44 (May/June 1984), pp. 193–195. For a thoughtful and insightful discussion of the relationship between the Progressive conservationist ethic and the philosophy of Reagan's first Interior Secretary, James Watt, see R. McGreggor Cawley and William Chaloupka, "James Watt and the Environmentalists: A Clash of Ideologies," *Policy Studies Journal*, vol. 14 (December 1985), pp. 244–254.

37. Clawson, *The Federal Lands Revisited*, especially Ch. 2. Since Clawson does not always place specific dates on these eras, those noted in this discussion are my own interpretation of Clawson's text and tables.

38. The most significant of these activities included the Louisiana, Gadsden, and Alaska purchases; peace treaties with Mexico, in the Guadalupe-Hidalgo pact, and with various Indian tribes; and the agreement with Great Britain for the Pacific Northwest.

39. The most significant among these congressional initiatives were the Homestead Act, the Desert Land Act, the Mining Law of 1872, and the Timber and Stone Act.

40. In the original Homestead Act of 1862, a citizen could buy up to 160 acres of public domain at a nominal fee as long as he resided on and cultivated the land for five years. In 1909, this was raised to 320 acres, and then to 640 acres in the Stockraising Homestead Act of 1916. Most agronomists have concluded that the low productivity of BLM lands today ranges from 6.1 acres per animal-unit-month in Montana to 22 acres per animal-unit-month in Nevada.

41. Clarke and McCool, *Staking Out the Terrain*.

42. Fairfax, "Beyond the Sagebrush Rebellion."

43. Robert H. Nelson, "Economic Analysis in Public Rangeland Management," pp. 47–78 in John G. Francis and Richard Ganzel, eds., *Western Public Lands: The Management of Natural Resources in a Time of Declining Federalism* (Totowa NJ: Rowman and Allanheld, 1984); Robert H. Nelson, "A Long Term Strategy for the Public Lands," in *Resource Conflicts in the West* (Reno: Nevada Public Affairs Institute, University of Nevada, 1983).

44. Outstanding reviews of these developments include: Richard B. Stewart, "The Reformation of American Administrative Law," *Harvard Law Review*, vol. 88 (1975), pp. 1667–1813; R. Shep Melnick, *Regulation and the Courts: The Case of the Clean Air Act* (Washington DC: Brookings Institution, 1983); Abraham Chayes, "The Role of the Judge in Public Law Litigation," *Harvard Law Review*, vol. 89 (1976), pp. 1281–1316; Martin M. Shapiro, *Guarding the Guardians* (Athens: University of Georgia Press, 1988).

45. *National Environmental Policy Act*, Pub. L. 91–190. In *NRDC v. Mor-*

ton, 388 F. Supp. 840, 841 (1974), the BLM was ordered to perform 212 separate EISs. This number was later reduced to 144 in *Natural Resources Defense Council v. Andrus*, 448 F. Supp. 802 (1978).

46. Robert H. Nelson, "*National Resources Defense Council v. Morton*: The Role of Judicial Policy Making in Public Rangeland Management," *Policy Studies Review*, vol. 14 (December 1985), p. 259.

47. *Natural Resources Defense Council v. Hughes*, 437 F. Supp. 981 (D.C. Cir., 1977), and *Valdez et al. v. Applegate*, 616 F. 2d 570 (1980).

48. Leshy, "Natural Resource Policy."

49. Leshy, "Natural Resource Policy," p. 45; also see Butler, Sanera, and Weinrod, *Mandate for Leadership II*.

50. Hugh Heclo, "An Executive's Success Can Have Costs," pp. 371–374 in Salamon and Lund, *The Reagan Presidency*.

51. In the private management literature, two different techniques for assessing strategic processes have been developed: the "indirect" and the "direct" approaches to strategic planning evaluation. While the former examines specific internal performance measures to interpret the worth of the strategic process employed, the direct approach relates the features and characteristics of the system to external planning standards. Specifically, the internal consistency of a business' strategic choice elements—viz., its mission, goals, objectives, resource allocations, and feedback—is evaluated against external criteria.

CHAPTER 2: PROMETHEUS UNBOUND OR SISYPHUS REDUX?

1. Moe, "The Politicized Presidency," p. 271.
2. Carroll, Fritschler, and Smith, "Supply-Side Management," p. 806.
3. Pious, *The American Presidency*.
4. Pious, *The American Presidency*, p. 254.
5. Many excellent summaries of the issues, claims, and empirical findings of the reorganization literature exist. The classic statement, however, remains Harold Seidman and Robert Gilmour, *Politics, Position, and Power: From the Positive to the Regulatory State*, 4th ed. (New York: Oxford University Press, 1984). Also see James March and Johan Olsen, "Organizing Political Life: What Administrative Reorganization Tells Us About Government," *American Political Science Review*, vol. 77 (1983), pp. 282–296; Peri E. Arnold, *Making the Managerial Presidency: Comprehensive Reorganization Planning, 1905–1980* (Princeton NJ: Princeton University Press, 1986).
6. Seidman and Gilmour, *Politics, Position, and Power*, p. 15.
7. Robert T. Golembiewski, "Public Sector Organization: Why Theory and Practice Should Emphasize Purpose, and How to Do So?" pp. 433–474 in Ralph C. Chandler, *A Centennial History of the American Administrative State* (New York: The Free Press, 1987); Alfred D. Chandler, *Strategy and Structure* (Cambridge MA: MIT Press, 1962); Tom Peters, *Thriving on Chaos: Handbook for a Management Revolution* (New York: Knopf, 1987).
8. March and Olsen, "Organizing Political Life," p. 288.
9. March and Olsen, "Organizing Political Life," p. 290.
10. See, for example, Pfiffner, *The Strategic Presidency*; Mackenzie, *The Politics of Presidential Appointments*.

11. Morton Halperin, *Bureaucratic Politics and Foreign Policy* (Washington DC: Brookings Institution, 1974).

12. See, for example, James Pfiffner, "Political Appointees and Career Executives"; Patricia W. Ingraham, "Building Bridges or Burning Them? The President, the Appointees, and the Bureaucracy," *Public Administration Review*, vol. 47 (September/October 1987), pp. 425–435; Joel D. Aberbach and Bert A. Rockman, "Mandates or Mandarins? Control and Discretion in the Modern Administrative State," *Public Administration Review*, vol. 48 (March/April 1988), pp. 606–612; Hugh Heclo, "OMB and the Presidency"; Ban and Ingraham, "Short-Timers."

13. Heclo, "OMB and the Presidency," p. 84.

14. Pfiffner, "Political Appointees"; Ingraham, "Building Bridges."

15. See, for example, Heclo, "OMB and the Presidency"; Pfiffner, "Political Appointees"; Chester A. Newland, "Public Executives: Imperium, Sacerdotium, Collegium? Bicentennial Leadership Challenges," *Public Administration Review*, vol. 47 (January/February 1987), pp. 45–56; National Academy of Public Administration, *Leadership in Jeopardy: The Fraying of the Presidential Appointment System* (Washington DC: NAPA, November 1985); Elliot Richardson et al., *Politics and Performance: Strengthening the Executive Leadership System* (Washington DC: Volcker Commission, 1989).

16. Jack Knott and Gary Miller, *Reforming Bureaucracy: The Politics of Institutional Choice* (Englewood Cliffs NJ: Prentice-Hall, 1987). For an important and compelling counter argument, see Francis E. Rourke, "American Bureaucracy in a Changing Political Setting," *Journal of Public Administration Research and Theory*, vol. 1 (1991), pp. 111–129. And for an argument taking a more contingent perspective, see Robert F. Durant, "Whither Bureaucratic Influence?: A Cautionary Note," *Journal of Public Administration Research and Theory*, vol. 1 (October 1991), pp. 461–476.

17. Nathan, *The Administrative Presidency*; Moe, "The Politicized Presidency."

18. Sanera, "Implementing the Mandate."

19. Sanera, "Implementing the Mandate," p. 514.

20. See Goldenberg, "The Permanent Government."

21. Ban and Ingraham, "Short-Timers."

22. These data are compiled from Ingraham, "Building Bridges," and Clyde Linsley, "Politics and the Civil Service," *Government Executive* (November/December 1987), pp. 48–54.

23. Ingraham, "Building Bridges," p. 428.

24. Naomi Caiden, "The New Rules of the Federal Budget Game," *Public Administration Review*, vol. 44 (March/April 1984), p. 110.

25. See, for example, Lance T. LeLoup, "Agency Policy Actions: Determinants of Non-Incremental Change," Ch. 5 in Randall Ripley and Grace Franklin, eds., *Policy Making in the Federal Executive Branch* (Washington DC: Free Press, 1975); John Wanat, "The Bases of Budgetary Incrementalism," *American Political Science Review*, vol. 68 (September 1974), pp. 1221–1228; Mark Kamlet and David Mowery, "The Budgetary Base in Federal Resource Allocation," *American Journal of Political Science*, vol. 25 (November 1980), pp. 804–821.

26. Wyszomirski, "The De-Institutionalization of Presidential Staff Agencies."

27. Ralph Hummel, *The Bureaucratic Experience*, 3rd ed. (New York: St. Martin's Press, 1987), pp. 254–255.

28. Richard Rose, *Managing Presidential Objectives* (New York: Free Press, 1976).

29. Benny Hjern and David O. Porter, "Implementation Structures: A New Unit of Administrative Analysis," *Organization Studies*, vol. 2 (1981), pp. 211–227.

30. Paul R. Schulman, "The Politics of 'Ideational Policy'," *Journal of Politics*, vol. 38 (1988), pp. 1014–1023.

31. Seidman and Gilmour, *Politics, Position, and Power.*

32. Nathan, "The Administrative Presidency," p. 54.

33. Quoted in Seidman and Gilmour, *Politics, Position, and Power*, p. 35.

34. Eads and Fix, *Relief or Reform?*

35. See, for example, Rockman, "Conclusions."

36. Newland, "A Mid-Term Appraisal."

CHAPTER 3: PUBLIC LANDS, THE BLM, AND THE REAGAN REVOLUTION

1. Donald Regan, quoted by William Safire, "On Language," *The New York Times Magazine*, March 19, 1989, p. 3.

2. During the two terms of the Reagan presidency, three Interior Secretaries served: James Watt, William Clark, and Donald Hodel.

3. For a thoughtful and insightful discussion of the relationship between the Progressive conservation ethic and the philosophy of Interior Secretary James Watt, see Cawley and Chaloupka, "James Watt and the Environmentalists."

4. Quoted in Ronald Brownstein and Nina Easton, *Reagan's Ruling Class: Portraits of the President's Top 100 Officials* (Washington DC: Presidential Accountability Group, 1982), p. 115.

5. Interview, Frank DuBois, Deputy Assistant Secretary for Land and Water Resources, U.S. Department of Interior, Las Cruces, New Mexico, January 23, 1986.

6. For a sample of Watt's attitudes, see Hearings, U.S. House of Representatives Committee on Appropriations, Subcommittee on the Department of Interior and Related Agencies, *Department of Interior and Related Agencies Appropriations for 1982*, 97th Cong., 1st sess., part 9; and James G. Watt, Interior Secretary, Remarks Before the National Public Lands Council, Reno, NV, September 21, 1982.

7. Garrey Carruthers, Assistant Secretary for Land and Water Resources.

8. These statistics are culled from various sources, including: Clarke and McCool, *Staking Out the Terrain*, Ch. 4; Portney, "Natural Resources and the Environment"; Leshy, "Natural Resource Policy"; "Watt's Clashes with Congress Stall Programs," *Congressional Quarterly Weekly Reports*, July 11, 1981, pp. 1256–1258.

9. See Dana and Baden, "The New Resource Economics."

10. Dana and Baden, "The New Resource Economics."

11. Portney, "Natural Resource Policy."

12. Quoted in Ron Arnold, *At the Eye of the Storm: James Watt and the Environmentalists* (Chicago: Regnery Gateway Press, 1982).

13. Richard F. Elmore, "Backward Mapping: Implementation Research and Policy Decisions," p. 20 in Walter Williams et al., *Studying Implementation: Methodological and Administrative Issues* (Chatham NJ: Chatham House Publishers, 1982).

14. Quoted in Brownstein and Easton, *Reagan's Ruling Class*, pp. 134, 135.

15. Clarke and McCool, *Staking Out the Terrain.*

16. See *BLM/Forest Service Interchange: National Summary and Legislative Proposal* (Washington DC: U.S. Forest Service and Bureau of Land Management, February 1986).

17. States with sizeable quantities of mineral, oil, and gas resources, in BLM staffers' terminology.

CHAPTER 4: POLITICS, POSITION, AND POWER PRODUCTION

1. Richard Corrigan, *National Journal*, August 18, 1981, p. 1280 as quoted in William Hogan, "Energy Policy," pp. 83–109 in Paul R. Portney, ed., *Natural Resources.* Also see Joe Kalt and Peter Navarro, "Administration Backsliding on Energy Policy," *Wall Street Journal*, February 9, 1982, p. 24; Robert L. Bradley, "Energy Policies: A Few Bright Spots," pp. 305–319 in David Boaz, ed., *Assessing the Reagan Years* (Washington DC: Cato Institute, 1988).

2. Hogan, "Energy Policy," p. 83.

3. Interview with Pete Hannigan, Santa Fe, New Mexico, January 24, 1986.

4. Eugene Ward, "Energy Conservation Steps Could Cost Jobs, Up Taxes," *Albuquerque Journal*, September 20, 1977.

5. "Carter Analysis Gets Praise from Schmitt and Domenici," *Las Cruces Sun-News*, November 9, 1977.

6. "Domenici Asks Change in Coal Lease Policy," *Albuquerque Journal*, January 10, 1980; "New Mexico Delegates Disappointed in Carter," *Albuquerque Journal*, April 21, 1977.

7. "Oil Leasing Halt Called 'Ridiculous'," *Albuquerque Journal*, March 2, 1980.

8. Bureau of Land Management, *District Office/Resource Area Organization Study* (Washington DC: Deputy Director for Services, Division of Management Research, Bureau of Land Management, Deputy Director for Services, 1981), p. II–4. Henceforth cited as *DO/RA Study I.*

9. Geoff Middaugh, *Issue Paper: Increasing Management Flexibility with the Existing FMS and Budget System*, Internal BLM Discussion Document, May 15, 1986, p. 1. Hereafter cited as *Issue Paper.*

10. *DO/RA Study I*, p. III-13.

11. *DO/RA Study I*, pp. III-13 and III-14.

12. Bureau of Land Management, *Final State Office Organization Study* (Washington DC: Deputy Director for Services, Division of Management Research, Bureau of Land Management, October 2, 1981), p. III-4.

13. For a most thorough discussion of the rational choice perspective applied to public bureaucracy, see Jack Knott and Gary Miller, *Reforming Bureaucracy.* They argue that applying the administrative orthodoxy to organizations (viz., hierarchy, functional departmentalization, rules and regulations) produces an incentive structure in which rational individuals respond to perverse incentives. In the process, the sum total of rational individuals pursuing their own self-interest within this context produces negative collective outcomes. A kind of "tragedy of the commons" results (e.g., goal displacement, goal suboptimization, making decisions on the basis of biased information, and rational ignorance). This is discussed further in Chapter 9.

14. Bureau of Land Management, *BLM Role Clarification Study* (Washington DC: Department of the Interior, May 9, 1986). Hereafter, cited as *RC Study*.

15. *RC Study*.

16. *RC Study*, p. 17.

17. *RC Study*, p. 17.

18. *Issue Paper*, p. 3.

19. *RC Study*, p. 20.

20. Matthew McCubbins and Thomas Schwartz, "Congressional Oversight Overlooked: Police Patrols vs. Fire Alarms," *American Journal of Political Science*, vol. 29 (February 1984), pp. 165–179.

21. David Linowes, *Report of the Commission on Fiscal Accountability of the Nation's Energy Resources* (Washington DC: U.S. Government Printing Office, January 1982), "Summary," p. xv. Hereafter cited as *Linowes I.*.

22. *Linowes I*, p. 142.

23. *Linowes I*, pp. 143–145.

24. Steven Maynard-Moody, Donald D. Stull, and Jerry Mitchell, "Reorganization as Status Drama," *Public Administration Review*, vol. 46 (July/August 1986), pp. 301–302. Also see Edgar Schein, *Organizational Culture and Leadership* (San Francisco: Jossey-Bass, 1985).

25. This finding and perceptions related to the nature of the reorganization at BLM are premised on a series of semi-structured interviews conducted by the author with several former MMS personnel during June and July 1985. Many of these under the circumstances wished to remain anonymous. However, their comments were corroborated by interviews with John Lopez, Director, Personnel Branch, State Office BLM, Santa Fe, New Mexico; Michelle Chavez, personnel specialist at that location; and Pete Hannigan, former President, New Mexico Oil and Gas Association, Santa Fe, New Mexico. These interviews were conducted in July 1984, June 1985, January 1986, June 1986, and July 1986.

26. For a more precise list of complaints, see 49 *Fed. Reg.* 37356 et seq. (1984).

27. Interviews at BLM; see Note 25.

28. *RC Study*, p. 20.

29. Robert L. Bradley, Jr., "Energy Policies: A Few Bright Spots," p. 312 in Boaz, *Assessing the Reagan Years*. Moreover, as Portney points out, "When weighed against the administration's own goals, however, even the successes are few and far between" ("Natural Resources," p. 175). Using the same logic, Leshy indicts the totality of Reagan's natural resource policy: "Underneath its ambitious rhetoric, then, the Reagan administration's performance in natural resource policy has produced few dramatic departures or lasting changes. By preaching the need for a fundamentally different course, the Reagan administration has asked to be judged by that standard, and by that measure, it has failed" ("Natural Resource Policy," p. 46).

30. Lopez July 1984 interview.

31. David Linowes, *Report of the Commission on Fair Market Value Policy for Federal Coal Leasing* (Washington DC: U.S. Government Printing Office, February 1984). Hereafter cited as *Linowes II*.

32. *Linowes II*, pp. 351–352.

33. *Linowes II*, p. 360.

34. *RC Study*, p. 14.

CHAPTER 5: BACKDOOR PRIVATIZATION, "COW WELFARE," AND THE BLM

1. Interview with Robert "Bob" Jones, New Mexico Cattle Growers Association, Del City, Texas, May 25, 1983.

2. Jim Zumbo, "The Sagebrush Rebellion," *The Country Gentleman*, Summer 1981, p. 53.

3. "Cattleranchers Battle BLM for Control of Grazing Land," *Albuquerque Journal*, October 12, 1982; also "'Sagebrush Rebellion' Grows Against BLM Controls," *Albuquerque Journal*, June 4, 1979.

4. Jones interview.

5. "BLM, Ranchers Discuss Report," *Albuquerque Journal*, September 26, 1980; Interview with Gene Ross, New Mexico State University Agricultural Extension Service, Las Cruces, May 25, 1983; "Foes Clash at Hearing on Land Use," *Albuquerque Journal*, August 26, 1979. For an insightful critique of BLM's range inventory methods and environmental emphasis, see Robert H. Nelson, "Economic Analysis."

6. "Full-force-and-effect" orders meant that grazing reductions took effect immediately, even though administrative appeals to the BLM were not exhausted or completed.

7. *Valdez et al. v. Applegate*, 616 Fed. Rep. 570 (1978).

8. "Memorandum of Understanding Between the Governor of New Mexico and the New Mexico State Director, Bureau of Land Management, U.S. Department of the Interior," July 30, 1980 (also referred to as the *Zimmerman Report*). Also, letter from Larry L. Woodward, Acting Director, New Mexico State BLM, to Governor Bruce King, November 14, 1979.

9. "Utah BLM Manager Fights Sagebrush Rebellion," *Albuquerque Journal*, December 25, 1980.

10. "Instruction Memorandum No. 81–296, BLM Director to All Washington and Field Officials," September 22, 1981. Hereafter cited as "Instruction Memo."

11. For a review of such resistance in southeastern New Mexico from the perspectives of both ranchers and BLM staff, see "Cattle Ranchers Battle BLM for Control of Grazing Land," *Albuquerque Journal*, October 12, 1982.

12. See, for example, "Ranchers Oppose Land Upkeep Plan," *Albuquerque Journal*, December 8, 1981.

13. "Ranchers Oppose."

14. Rick Hanks, Rio Puerco Resource Area Manager, quoted in Minutes, Pan Am Pipeline Meeting, Cuba, New Mexico, March 11, 1983. Thor Stephanson, among others, gives the reason for their position: "Ranchers in the West are generally in favor of the policy to give them maintenance responsibility as this will give them vested (and priority) interest" over competing users. Quoted in Memorandum from Don Brewer, BLM, to Planning Files, "Meeting with New Mexico Game and Fish," November 29, 1983, p. 2).

15. "Sagebrush Rebellion May Have Lost Momentum," *Las Cruces Sun-News*, May 6, 1982; Neil Peirce, "Is Sagebrush Rebellion a Misstep—In the Right Direction," editorial, *Albuquerque Journal*, February 22, 1981.

16. Memorandum from Area Manager, Rio Puerco, to Albuquerque District

Manager, "Interim Rangeland Improvement Policy and the Rio Puerco Resource Area," February 29, 1982. Henceforth referred to as Rick Hanks Memo.

17. Rick Hanks Memo, p. 4.

18. Letter from Jerry G. Schickedanz, Rangeland Improvement Task Force Coordinator, Cooperative Extension Service, New Mexico State University, to Charles W. Luscher, BLM New Mexico State Director, November 16, 1982, p. 2. Hereafter referred to as Schickedanz Memo.

19. Memorandum from Bob Reed, Chief, Division of Operations, NM State BLM, to Rick Hanks, Rio Puerco Resource Area Manager, "Response to the Proposed Policies Regarding Maintenance of Range Improvements and the Redistribution of RB (8100) Funds," February 25, 1982, p. 1. Hereafter referred to as Reed Memo.

20. Reed Memo, p. 1.

21. DuBois interview.

22. Schickedanz Memo and attachment, "Ranch Improvement Maintenance and Depreciation Costs: Northwestern New Mexico, 1978 and 1982," Range Improvement Task Force, New Mexico State University, November 16, 1982.

23. Nancy Harbert, "NM Cattle Growers Support Proposed BLM Cuts," *Albuquerque Journal*, March 29, 1983.

24. Memorandum from District Manager, BLM, Albuquerque, New Mexico, to State Director, BLM, "Deputy Assistant Secretary's Request for Information on the Rio Puerco Pipeline Systems Maintenance Proposal," October 26, 1982, p. 3.

25. Referred to in Minutes, Chiuilla Pipeline, Cuba, New Mexico, March 7, 1983.

26. Minutes, Piedra Lumbre Pipeline Meeting, March 10, 1983; see also, for example, Memorandum from Robbie Smith, Range Conservationist, BLM, to District Manager, BLM, through Dave Koehler, Acting Resource Area Manager, "Pipeline Maintenance Meeting with Core Allottees," July 1, 1983; and most especially "Resolution and Survey," attached to Letter from Manuel F. Martinez, Secretary/Treasurer, Rio Puerco Livestock Association, to Herrick E. (Rick) Hanks, Manager, Rio Puerco Resource Area, July 30, 1983.

27. Minutes, Piedra Lumbre Pipeline Meeting, March 10, 1983; and Minutes, Chiuilla Pipeline Meeting, Cuba, NM, March 7, 1983.

28. Minutes, District Advisory Council Meeting, BLM, Albuquerque District Office, July 26, 1983, p. 2.

29. Schickedanz Memo and "Ranch Improvement Maintenance Study."

30. Unidentified BLM official quoted in *Albuquerque Journal*, March 3, 1983.

31. The following section, "The Water Rights Exemption Question," relies on an exchange of letters between April 19, 1982 and October 25, 1983 among: Steve E. Reynolds, New Mexico State Engineer; Charles W. Luscher, State Director, New Mexico State Office, BLM; and William P. Stephens, Secretary, New Mexico Department of Agriculture.

32. Paul Sabatier, "Top-Down and Bottom-Up Approaches to Implementation," *Journal of Public Policy*, vol. 6 (1987), pp. 21–48.

33. Minutes, Las Cruces District Grazing Advisory Board, January 14, 1982, p. 4. In these minutes, for example, Board members had to scuttle plans for four out of seven range improvement issue areas scheduled under the area's Man-

agement Framework Plan. The reason? There "were not enough funds to address all seven issues": rangeland management, wildlife management, off-road vehicle designations, wilderness, energy minerals, access, and special areas. Also see Minutes, Las Cruces District Grazing Advisory Board, Las Cruces, NM, April 8, 1982.

34. See, for example, Minutes, Las Cruces Board, April 8, 1982, p. 3.

35. U.S. House of Representatives, *Subcommittee on the Department of the Interior and Related Agencies Appropriations for 1982* (Washington DC: Government Printing Office, 1981), p. 469.

36. U.S. House of Representatives, *Subcommittee on the Department of the Interior and Related Agencies Appropriations for 1985* (Washington DC: Government Printing Office, 1984), p. 833.

37. U.S. House, *Subcommittee on Interior Appropriations 1985,* p. 833.

38. U.S. House, *Subcommittee on Interior Appropriations,* pp. 911–912, 914.

CHAPTER 6: TOWARD BECOMING "A GOOD URBAN NEIGHBOR"?

1. Statement of Robert F. Burford, Director, Bureau of Land Management, U.S. Senate Committee on Energy and Natural Resources, *Workshop on Public Land Acquisition and Alternatives,* 97th Cong., 1st sess. (Washington DC: U.S. Government Printing Office, 1981), pp. 48–49. Hereafter cited as *Workshop.*

2. 43 U.S.C. 869 (1954).

3. Summarized in *Workshop,* p. 721.

4. See *Workshop,* p. 714, for a list of exceptions to this process.

5. *Workshop,* pp. 332–333.

6. *Workshop,* p. 215.

7. Culhane, "Sagebrush Rebels in Office," p. 309.

8. *Workshop,* p. 42.

9. *Workshop,* pp. 21, 663.

10. *Workshop,* p. 27.

11. *Workshop,* p. 29.

12. *Workshop,* p. 410.

13. *Workshop,* p. 33.

14. *Workshop,* p. 219.

15. See, for example, Joseph A. Davis, "Congress Decidedly Cool to Reagan Land-Sale Plan," *Congressional Quarterly Weekly Report,* July 17, 1982, pp. 1687–1690.

16. *Workshop,* p. 9.

17. *Workshop,* p. 844.

18. *Workshop,* p. 863.

19. *Workshop,* p. 413.

20. Information concerning Las Cruces' efforts and arguments was culled from the following sources: Letter from Dean Bibles, Assistant Director, BLM, to Congressman Harold Runnels, August 5, 1980; Letter from Ed Garland, Property Manager, City of Las Cruces, to U.S. Senator Harrison Schmitt, October 2, 1980; and Letter from Daniel C. B. Rathbun, Las Cruces District Manager, BLM, to Ed Garland, Property Manager, City of Las Cruces, December 15, 1980.

21. Quoted in letter from Larry L. Morgan, Administrator, Second District, Office of Congressman Harold Runnels, to Richard P. Schroats, Chairman, Airport Advisory Board, City of Las Cruces, August 14, 1980.

22. Letter from Gene Elliott, President, Las Cruces Chamber of Commerce, to U.S. Senator Harrison Schmitt, April 20, 1981; Letter from Joe Camunez, Mayor, City of Las Cruces, to U.S. Senator Harrison Schmitt, June 4, 1981; Letter from U.S. Senator Harrison Schmitt to Donald P. Hodel, Undersecretary, Department of the Interior, May 22, 1981.

23. Quoted in letter from Bill J. Howard, Chief, Airports District Office, Federal Aviation Administration, Department of Transportation, to Ed Garland, Airport Manager, City of Las Cruces, June 12, 1981.

24. Howard to Garland letter, p. 2.

25. Schmitt to Hodel letter.

26. Letter from Donald P. Hodel, Undersecretary, Department of the Interior, to U.S. Senator Harrison Schmitt, May 1, 1981.

27. For background on the Elena Gallegos–Albuquerque Boys Academy Exchange, see "Failure to OK Appraisal Snags Land Acquisition," *Albuquerque Journal*, March 20, 1980; Glen Warchol, "City in Quandary over BLM's Deal," *Las Cruces Sun-News*, June 19, 1981; Marvin Tessneer, "Schmitt Assures City," *Las Cruces Sun-News*, June 21, 1981. It should also be noted that Lujan was not only suffering from attacks by environmentalists at this time. As Wayne Ciddio of the Albuquerque Chamber of Commerce points out, the congressman was also widely perceived as a "casework," rather than an "issue-oriented," representative. Thus, when Senator Domenici didn't get immediately interested in the exchange, Lujan "jumped in" to demonstrate his "new issue-orientation." Interview with Wayne Ciddio, Albuquerque Chamber of Commerce and former Albuquerque District Office Manager, U.S. Senator Harrison Schmitt, Albuquerque, New Mexico, June 17, 1986.

28. Quoted in "Lujan, Schmitt Tell Rusk to Work Out Land-Deal Problem," *Albuquerque Journal*, March 7, 1981.

29. "Lujan, Schmitt Tell Rusk." Also see Memorandum from Tom Baca, Las Cruces District Office Manager, to U.S. Senator Harrison Schmitt and his staff, "Meeting of July 7 on the Las Cruces Airport Industrial Park Issue," July 9, 1981 (Hereafter, Baca Memo); and "Industrial Park Prospects Bleak," *Las Cruces Sun-News*, July 7, 1981.

30. Ciddio interview.

31. "City in Quandary over BLM's Deal." Also see Memorandum from Ed Garland, Property Manager, City of Las Cruces, to J.W. Harrison, City Manager, City of Las Cruces, "Las Cruces Crawford Industrial Park Proposed Site," June 16, 1981.

32. Quoted in Warchol, "City in Quandary."

33. Letter from M.J. Hassell, Regional Forester, U.S. Forest Service, to Ed Garland, Property Manager, City of Las Cruces, June 16, 1981.

34. This account relies heavily on Baca Memo and Memorandum from J.W. Harrison, City Manager, Las Cruces, NM, to Las Cruces City Commission, "A Meeting Regarding Lands for the Proposed Industrial Park," August 17, 1981; Harrison Memo.

35. Baca Memo, p. 3.

36. Glen Warchol, "City Seeks to Save Land," *Las Cruces Sun-News*, July 6, 1981. City Property Manager Garland was equally upbeat. See, for exam-

ple, Glen Warchol, "Industrial Park Hopes Up," *Las Cruces Sun-News*, July 8, 1981.

37. Quoted in Nancy Harbert, "Cruces Official Unveils East Mesa Plans," *Las Cruces Sun-News*, November 14, 1981.

38. Interview with Dan Rathbun, Las Cruces District Office Manager, BLM, Las Cruces, NM, August 5, 1982; "City Seeks Withdrawal of Park Site," *Las Cruces Sun-News*, February 23, 1982; Interview with Tom Baca, Las Cruces District Office Manager, U.S. Senator Harrison Schmitt, Las Cruces, NM, July 1985.

39. "'Another Tool' Introduced for Land Grant Tract Buy," *Las Cruces Sun-News*, January 28, 1982.

40. "Land Swap Deal Reached, Lujan Says," *Albuquerque Journal*, December 5, 1981.

41. "Land Swap."

42. Rick Nathanson, "City Group Says Tax Boost Could Finance Land Deal," *Albuquerque Journal*, February 8, 1982.

43. Letter from Richard G. Elkins, President, Albuquerque Academy Board of Trustees, to Joe Camunez, Mayor, City of Las Cruces, February 12, 1982.

44. Quoted in Nancy Harbert, "U.S. Out of Cruces Land Swap," *Albuquerque Journal*, January 29, 1982.

45. Letter from Las Cruces City Commission to M.J. Hassell, Regional Forester, U.S. Forest Service, February 18, 1982.

46. Quoted in Gregory J. Vigil, "City Seeks Withdrawal of Park Site," *Las Cruces Sun-News*, February 23, 1982.

47. Quoted in Marcus Walton, "Land Swap to Proceed as Planned," *Las Cruces Sun-News*, March 2, 1982.

48. Telephone interview with Robert Armstrong, U.S. Forest Service, Southwest Region, Albuquerque, NM, July 1, 1986.

49. Interview with Eric G. Johanson III, U.S. Forest Service, Southwest Region, Albuquerque, NM, June 19, 1986.

50. Armstrong interview.

51. Johanson interview; Armstrong interview. Also see "Elena Gallegos Grant Exchange, General Cost Analysis," U.S. Forest Service.

52. Armstrong interview.

53. Johanson interview.

54. Johanson interview.

55. Armstrong interview, Johanson interview, and anonymous interviewees at the Forest Service. Also see Rathbun interview; Joint interview with Dan Rathbun, BLM, Las Cruces District Office Manager, Las Cruces, NM, and Robert Calkins, BLM, Las Cruces Assistant District Office Manager, Las Cruces, NM, August 5, 1982; Ciddio interview; interview with Bill Harkenrider, Las Cruces Area Resource Manager, BLM, Las Cruces, NM, January 22, 1986.

56. Johanson interview; Harkenrider interview; Armstrong interview.

57. This discussion of Wittern's private-sector initiative is based on the following: interview with Klaus Wittern, Las Cruces, New Mexico, June 25, 1986; "Alternative on Industrial Park Offered," *Las Cruces Sun-News*, October 20, 1981; "Wittern's Choice," *El Paso Times*, August 23, 1981; "Industrial Park Developer Wants Federal Activity," *El Paso Times*, October 16, 1981; "Klaus Wittern Is Still in Business," *Las Cruces Sun-News*, February 21, 1982.

58. "Industrial Park Developer."

59. "Wittern's Choice."

60. "Industrial Park Developer."

61. "Industrial Park Developer."

62. "Alternative on Industrial Park."

63. "City May Give Wittern More Time," *Las Cruces Sun-News*, October 27, 1981.

64. See "Land Purchase Agreement," signed by David M. Steinborn, Mayor, City of Las Cruces, and Frank A. Kleinhenz, Chief Administrative Officer, City of Albuquerque, December 7, 1982.

65. Johanson interview.

66. "Reagan Administration Backs Swap Involving Elena Gallegos Grant," *Albuquerque Journal*, May 28, 1983.

CHAPTER 7: THOU SHALT NOT COVET THY NEIGHBOR'S WATER

1. Catherine Lovell, "Where We Are in Intergovernmental Relations and Some of the Implications," *Southern Review of Public Administration*, vol. 3 (June 1979), p. 6.

2. The data in this section on the history and subsidized costs of water projects in the West relies on Ira G. Clark, *Water in New Mexico: A History of Its Management and Use* (Albuquerque: University of New Mexico Press, 1987); Arrandale, *Battle for Natural Resources*, esp. Ch. 9; Clarke and McCool, *Staking Out the Terrain*, esp. Chs. 2 and 4; Portney, *Natural Resources and the Environment*; Culhane, "Sagebrush Rebels in Office"; F. Lee Brown and Helen Ingram, *Water and Poverty in the Southwest* (Tucson: University of Arizona Press, 1987). For a comprehensive and very informative series of essays on the West's water future, see Zachary A. Smith, ed., *Water and the Future of the Southwest* (Albuquerque: University of New Mexico Press, 1990); Helen Ingram, "Water Rights in the Western States," *Academy of Political Science Proceedings*, vol. 34, no. 3 (1982), pp. 134–143.

3. Arrandale, *Battle for Natural Resources*.

4. For an excellent review of this situation, see Douglas L. Grant, "Reasonable Groundwater Pumping Levels Under the Appropriation Doctrine: The Law and Underlying Economic Goals," *Natural Resources Journal*, vol. 21 (January 1981), pp. 1–36. Figures on state dependence on groundwater are culled from this article, note 8.

5. See, for example, "Secretary Avoids Backing NM in Water Suit," *El Paso Sun-Times*, November 3, 1981; Leah Leach, "State Stockmen Given Warning on Water Suit," *Albuquerque Journal*, July 30, 1981. To appreciate the passion involved on both sides in the dispute, see "New Mexico Water Is Not Negotiable," editorial, *Las Cruces Sun-News*, December 13, 1981. In addition, an economic boycott of El Paso businesses was initiated in southern New Mexico, a boycott led by Stahmann Farms, the largest pecan producer in the United States. In the most noteworthy manifestation of the boycott, William Stahmann withdrew the company's multi-million dollar assets from El Paso banks. Interestingly, Stahmann would later become a leading advocate of negotiation with El Paso. See "Stahmann Debunks Myths of El Paso Water Suit," *Las Cruces Sun-News*, June 26, 1984.

6. Don Frederick, "Briefs: Water Suit Faulty," *El Paso Times*, April 9, 1982; Marvin Tessneer, "Water Arguments Challenged," *Las Cruces Sun-News*, March 3, 1982.

7. For excellent reviews of the nature and consequences of New Mexico groundwater law, see "New Mexico Water Law: An Overview and Discussion of Current Issues," *Natural Resources Journal*, vol. 22 (October 1982), pp. 1045-1062. For a corresponding view on Texas' groundwater regulatory regime, see Corwin W. Johnson, "Texas Groundwater Law: A Survey and Some Proposals," *Natural Resources Journal*, vol. 22 (October 1982), pp. 1017–1029.

8. This discussion relies heavily on: John Hedderson, "The Population of Texas Counties Along the Mexico Border," *Natural Resources Journal*, vol. 22 (October 1982), pp. 765–781; Neal E. Armstrong, "Anticipating Transboundary Needs and Issues in the Mexico–United States Border Region in the Rio Grande Basin," *Natural Resources Journal*, vol. 22 (October 1982), pp. 877–906; Ken Ortolon, "Texas, New Mexico Battle over Control of Groundwater," *El Paso Herald Post*, December 16, 1983; and Albert E. Utton, "An Assessment of the Management of U.S.–Mexican Water Resources," *Natural Resources Journal*, vol. 22 (October 1982), esp. pp. 1095-1096.

9. *The City of El Paso v. S.E. Reynolds*, Memorandum Opinion, U.S. District Court for the District of New Mexico, January 17, 1983. Hereafter referred to as *Memorandum Opinion*.

10. Marvin Tessneer, "Plan Would Deplete Water, Expert Says," *Las Cruces Sun-News*, January 14, 1982.

11. See, for example, Leshy, "Natural Resource Policy." Also see Culhane, "Sagebrush Rebels in Office."

12. *Special Analyses: Budget of the United States Government, FY 1985* (Washington DC: U.S. Government Printing Office, 1984). While Congress overrode the president's veto of the state grant program by reauthorizing $36 million annually for water research through 1989, significant concessions were made to the Administration. Not only was the House's original call for a $60 million reauthorization nearly cut in half, but state matching requirements were enacted that would reduce the federal share to one dollar for every two nonfederal dollars by 1988.

13. This, despite repeated assurances that the Administration's aim was to enhance state regulatory control. See, for example, Mary Wormley, "Carruthers Says Nation Must Intensify Water Management," *Las Cruces Sun-News*, May 8, 1981. Just how severe these funding cuts were for New Mexico is summarized in Paul Weick, "New Mexico Projects May Be Cut," *Albuquerque Journal*, March 11, 1981; and Testimony of Thomas G. Bahr, Director, Office of Water Policy, Department of the Interior, U.S. Senate, Committee on Environment and Public Works, Subcommittee on Water Resources, *The Impact of the Supreme Court Decision in Sporhase Versus Nebraska*, 97th Cong., 2nd Sess., (Washington DC: Congressional Printing Office, September 15, 1982), pp. 12–20.

14. Background on the context and positions taken by the litigants on this issue relies heavily on the following sources: *S.E. Reynolds, et al. v. The City of El Paso, et al.*, 10th Circuit Court of Appeals, April 21, 1983; Jesse B. Gilmour, "The Rio Grande Compact," pp. 53–60 in New Mexico Water Resources Research Institute, *Water Law in the West* (Las Cruces, NM: New Mexico State University, 1988); Clark, *Water in New Mexico*; Don Frederick, "NM, El Paso Outline Views on Water Suit," *El Paso Times*, December 30, 1981.

15. Jolene Crane, "*Sporhase v. Nebraska, ex rel. Douglas*: A Call for Groundwater Legislation," *Denver Law Journal*, vol. 60 (1983), p. 643.

16. For fine discussions of the evolution of this doctrine, see Philip M. Barnett, "Mixing Water and the Commerce Clause: The Problems of Practice, Precedent, and Policy in *Sporhase v. Nebraska*," *Natural Resources Journal*, vol. 24 (January 1984), pp. 161–194; Thomas K. Anson and P.M. Schenkkan, "Federalism, the Dormant Commerce Clause, and State-Owned Resources," *Texas Law Review*, vol. 59 (1980), pp. 71–99.

17. Quoted in Don Frederick, "EP Official: NM Water Is Not Vital," *El Paso Times*, December 30, 1981.

18. Don Frederick, "NM, El Paso Outline."

19. *Sporhase v. Nebraska, ex rel. Douglas*, 102 S. Ct. at 3456 (1982).

20. Marvin Tessneer, "Water Ruling is Conditional, " *Las Cruces Sun-News*, July 12, 1982.

21. *Sporhase v. Nebraska*.

22. The information relating to the Reagan Administration's position on the coal slurry pipeline relies primarily on two sources: (1) "Statement of Carol E. Dinkins, Assistant Attorney General, Land and Natural Resources Division," U.S. House of Representatives, Committee on Public Works and Transportation, Subcommittee on Surface Transportation, *Regarding H.R. 1010 and Related Coal Slurry Pipeline Legislation*, 97th Congress, 2nd Sess. (Washington DC: Government Printing Office, September 15, 1982), hereafter cited as *Dinkins I*; and (2) "Statement of Carol Dinkins," U.S. Senate Committee on Energy and Natural Resources, *Coal Distribution and Utilization Act of 1983*, 98th Congress, 1st Sess. (Washington DC: Government Printing Office, March 14, 1983), hereafter cited as *Dinkins II*. Also useful was U.S. House of Representatives, Committee on Public Works and Transportation, Subcommittee on Surface Transportation, *Hearings on The Coal Pipeline Act of 1983*, 98th Congress, 1st Sess. (Washington DC: Government Printing Office, April 13 and 19, 1983).

23. For details and an analysis of the Cheney Amendment, see "Testimony of Paul L. Bloom, Attorney at Law," U.S. House of Representatives, Committee on Public Works and Transportation, Subcommittee on Surface Transportation, April 19, 1983, pp. 487–494 in *Hearings on The Coal Pipeline Act of 1983*.

24. *Dinkins I*, p. 42.

25. Thomas G. Bahr, "Legal, Hydrological, and Environmental Issues Surrounding the El Paso Water Suit," pp. 45–46 in *Water Law in the West*. Along with calling for congressional action spelling out states' primacy in governing their own allocation of water rights, Bahr called upon New Mexico to start looking at importing water from other states, both in the Southwest and from the Great Lakes and Columbia River.

26. Brownstein and Easton, *Reagan's Ruling Class*, pp. 404–408. At this point, it is important to note the disunity between the Justice Department speaking "for the Administration," and the Interior Department, with Bahr representing "the Administration's position." Dinkins opposed all comprehensive efforts to deal with the dormant commerce clause issue. In contrast, Bahr stated that the Administration opposed any effort by Congress to legislate a reduced role for the states. However, he claimed that legislative action designed to strengthen state control would not be opposed. This mixed message, coupled with the Administration's ultimate failure to support this type of legislation, was somewhat frustrating.

(interview with Thomas Bahr in Las Cruces, NM, January 23, 1986). Also, see "Testimony of Thomas G. Bahr," *The Impact of the Supreme Court Decision in Sporhase vs. Nebraska*, p. 15.

27. "New Mexico Water is Not Negotiable."

28. For an informative analysis of the federal implied reserved water rights issue (also known as the "Doctrine of Nonreserved Federal Water Rights"), see Coggins et al., "The Law of Public Rangeland Management I," pp. 578–588. Also see *United States v. New Mexico*, 438 U.S. 696 (1978).

29. This section is based on *Dinkins I* and *II*.

30. See, for example, "Anaya Vows to Appeal Ruling on Water Law," *Albuquerque Journal*, January 22, 1983; "State Senate Boosts Bill to Limit Water Export," *Albuquerque Journal*, February 18, 1983. It is also important to note that six additional Western states with water export laws similar to New Mexico's intervened on the state's behalf.

31. "New Mexico Fights El Paso Challenge to New Water Law," *Albuquerque Journal*, May 15, 1983.

32. Idaho, Montana, and Wyoming had already chosen state ownership as a regulatory framework. Also see New Mexico Water Resources Research Institute and University of New Mexico Law School, *State Appropriation of Unappropriated Groundwater: A Strategy for Insuring New Mexico a Water Future* (Las Cruces: New Mexico State University, 1986).

33. "Judge: NM Can Limit Water Export," *El Paso Times*, August 4, 1984.

34. See, for example, Nancy E. Hetrick, "Recent Developments in the El Paso/New Mexico Interstate Groundwater Controversy—The Constitutionality of New Mexico's New Municipality Water Planning Statute," *Natural Resources Journal*, vol. 29 (Winter 1989), pp. 223–249.

35. "New Mexico Hunts Ways to Plug Drain," *El Paso Times*, January 20, 1983.

36. "Schmitt Prepares Bill to Save Water," *Las Cruces Sun-News*, December 7, 1981.

37. Quoted in Leach, "State Stockman Given Warning."

38. "Lujan Calls Governors' Reaction to Water Plan Encouraging," *Albuquerque Journal*, May 31, 1982.

39. Stephen F. Williams, "The Requirement of Beneficial Use as a Cause of Waste in Water Resource Development," *Natural Resources Journal*, vol. 23 (January 1983), p. 7.

40. *State Appropriation*, p. 2; Report of the New Mexico Governor's Water Law Study Committee, "The Impact of Recent Court Decisions Concerning Water and Interstate Commerce on Water Resources in the State of New Mexico," *Natural Resources Journal*, vol. 24 (July 1984), pp. 689–744.

41. *State Appropriation*, pp. 9, 10.

42. *State Appropriation*, p. 87.

43. *State Appropriation*. Groundwater appropriation by states is a quite controversial approach. For a critique, see Rika Murray, "Allocation of Groundwater After *Sporhase v. Nebraska*: A Proposal for Combined Federal-State Regulation," *Albany Law Review*, vol. 48 (1984), pp. 494–520; Ann Berkely Rodgers, "The Limits of State Activity in the Interstate Water Market," *Land and Water Law Review*, vol. 21 (1986), pp. 357–380.

44. Robert Burnson, "Stahmann Is Hoping for Water Settlement," *Las Cruces Sun-News*, July 12, 1986.

45. "Irrigation District Wants AG Off Case," *Las Cruces Sun-News*, July 10, 1986.

46. This discussion relies heavily on John B. Regnell, "United States Department of the Interior Endeavors to Accommodate to the New Western Water Policy Agenda," *SNREA News*, vol. 2 (Summer 1987), pp. 1–3.

47. Quoted in Regnell, "U.S. Dept. of Interior Endeavors," pp. 2, 3.

CHAPTER 8: WILDERNESS, KING COAL, AND THE SAN JUAN BASIN

1. Leshy, "Natural Resource Policy," p. 41.

2. *Secretarial Issue Document, 1979: Federal Coal Management Program* (Washington DC: U.S. Government Printing Office, 1979), p. 1, henceforth cited as *1979 Issue Document*.

3. *1979 Issue Document*, p. 2. This history of events relies heavily on the *1979 Issue Document*. Also informative was the *Secretarial Issue Document, 1986: Federal Coal Management Program* (Washington DC: Government Printing Office, 1986).

4. *1979 Issue Document*, p. 4.

5. Prior to enactment of the Federal Coal Leasing Amendments Act (FCLAA) of 1976, a permittee could submit a preference right lease application (PRLA) as a result of activity undertaken under a prospecting permit issued pursuant to Section 2(b) of the Mineral Lands Leasing Act of 1920. If the Interior Secretary ascertained that coal existed in commercial quantities on the permitted lands in question, s/he could issue a noncompetitive preference right lease. Thus, the permittee would become owner without having to compete with others in a competitive bidding process. FCLAA, however, abolished preference right leasing except for PRLAs that resulted from prospecting permits issued on or before August 4, 1976. See *Federal Coal Management Report: FY 1984* (Washington DC: Department of the Interior, 1984), esp. p. 27. As pointed out in the *1979 Issue Document*, coal supplies on PRLAs were significant: As of that year, there were 172 PRLAs, holding an estimated 9.9 billion tons of recoverable reserves. See *1979 Issue Document*, p. 128.

6. Arrandale, *Battle for Natural Resources*, p. 93.

7. *NRDC v. Burford*, D.D.C, Civil No. 82–2763.

8. Background on the sociopolitical, economic, and ecological characteristics of the SJB is culled from *Draft San Juan Basin Cumulative Overview* (Washington DC: Bureau of Land Management, November 1982); *Final San Juan River Regional Coal Environmental Impact Statement* (Washington DC: Bureau of Land Management, 1984); and *Draft EIS: Public Service Company of New Mexico's Proposed New Mexico Generating Station and Possible New Town* (Washington DC: Bureau of Land Management, November 1982).

9. 46 *Fed. Reg.* 53528 (October 29, 1981).

10. "Bisti Dropped as Potential Wild Area," *Albuquerque Journal*, December 28, 1982; Nolan Hester, "Wilderness Sites May Be Cut," *Albuquerque Journal*, October 26, 1982. As summarized by BLM spokesman John Gumert, Watt used the administrative presidency to eliminate the proposed wilderness areas by more narrowly interpreting the Bureau's 1976 reorganization legislation. "Under the Federal Land Policy and Management Act, . . . the Bureau may create a wil-

derness from an area with fewer than 5,000 acres only if it has some outstanding or unique feature" ("Wilderness Sites").

11. "Split estates" are those properties where the BLM controls surface but not subsurface mineral rights.

12. "Minutes of the December 13, 1983, Regional Coal Team Meeting," BLM, Santa Fe, NM, January 25, 1984, p. 1-1.

13. This discussion relies heavily on *Linowes II*. Also see General Accounting Office, *Analysis of the Powder River Basin Federal Coal Lease Sale: Economic Valuation Improvements and Legislative Changes Needed* (Washington DC: U.S. Government Printing Office, May 1983). The GAO estimated that Carruther's approach cost the government $100 million in lost lease revenue.

14. See "U.S. to Prepare New Study on Impact of Coal Leasing," *Albuquerque Journal*, August 31, 1984.

15. For the most complete summary of public reaction to much of the Interior Department's actions during this time, see Bureau of Land Management, *Final San Juan Basin Cumulative Overview and Comment Letters* (Santa Fe NM: Bureau of Land Management, September 1983), hereafter cited as *Cumulative Comments*. The following discussion relies heavily on this document, as well as the minutes of the following public hearings: *Comment Summary: San Juan River Regional Coal DEIS* (Washington DC: Bureau of Land Management, April 1983); and Bureau of Land Management, *Proceedings in the Matter of the Federal Coal Management Program Draft EIS Supplement* (Albuquerque NM: Blasing & Townsend, Inc., March 20, 1985).

16. *Cumulative Comments*, p. CL-31.

17. *Cumulative Comments*, p. CL-31.

18. Letter and Comments from Daniel Kirshner, Economic Analyst, Environmental Defense Fund, to State Director, New Mexico State Office, BLM, April 7, 1983, pp. II-5–II-15.

19. Talli Nauman, "U.S. Cancels Session on San Juan Coal," *Albuquerque Journal*, March 6, 1984. Glowka made similar points in a wide-ranging interview with the author in Albuquerque, NM, June 20, 1986.

20. Bureau of Land Management, "Minutes of December 13, 1983."

21. Letter from Patrick H. Beckett, Chairman, NM Cultural Properties Review Committee, to Curtis F. Schaafsma, NM State Archaeologist, December 1, 1982.

22. Letter from Beckett to Schaafsma.

23. *NRDC v. Morton*, and *NRDC v. Berglund*, 458 F. Supp. 925 [D.D.C.] (1978).

24. Rex Weyler, *Blood of the Land* (New York: Vintage Books, 1984), p. 102. For an insightful and comprehensive review of the plight of American Indians historically in water rights conflicts, see Daniel McCool, *Command of the Waters: Iron Triangles, Federal Water Development, and Indian Water Rights* (Berkeley and Los Angeles: University of California Press, 1988).

25. This discussion relies on several sources, including: Navajo and Hopi Indian Relocation Commission, *Interim Progress Report* (Flagstaff AZ: U.S. Government, December 7, 1978), esp. Ch. 1; Navajo and Hopi Indian Relocation Commission, *Report and Plan* (Flagstaff AZ: U.S. Government, April 1981), esp. "Executive Summary and Recommendations."

26. Public Law 93–531.

27. *Healing v. Jones*, 210 F. Supp. 125 (1963).

28. Nancy Harbert, "Navajos Want to Stay on Coal Land," *Albuquerque Journal*, November 9, 1983.

29. See, for example, Peter Katel, "Interior Dept. Accused of Indian Policy Shifts," *Albuquerque Journal*, March 12, 1982; Paul R. Wieck, "Reagan Budget Would Slash BIA Funds," *Albuquerque Journal*, February 3, 1982.

30. "Reagan Administration Told It Must Act on Indian Claims," *Albuquerque Journal*, December 23, 1982.

31. Katel, "Interior Dept. Accused."

32. Talli Nauman, "2 Million Acres Claimed in Suit Filed by Navajos," *Albuquerque Journal*, October 7, 1982.

33. "Watt Heads Off Indian Tribe-PNM Dispute Possibility," *Albuquerque Journal*, March 6, 1982.

34. Talli Nauman, "Navajos Sue for Coal-Rich Ranchland," *Albuquerque Journal*, November 23, 1983.

35. John Kingdon, *Agendas, Alternatives, and Public Policy* (Boston MA: Little, Brown, 1984).

36. See, for example, Peter Katel, "New Navajo Chairman Promises to Share Power," *Albuquerque Journal*, December 19, 1982.

37. Glowka interview.

38. See Paul R. Wieck, "Bisti Wilderness Plan Gets Mixed Reception," *Albuquerque Journal*, May 18, 1983; Paul R. Wieck, "Richardson Backs Lujan's San Juan Wilderness Compromise," *Albuquerque Journal*, April 24, 1984.

39. Wieck, "Bisti Wilderness Plan."

40. Paul R. Wieck, "Lujan Agrees to Support Larger Bisti Wilderness," *Albuquerque Journal*, October 22, 1983.

41. Paul R. Wieck, "Navajos Claim Right to Steer Strip Mining," *Albuquerque Journal*, March 20, 1984.

42. See Paul R. Wieck, "Richardson Defends Navajo Land Proposal," *Albuquerque Journal*, January 27, 1984; "Lujan Against Plan Doubling Acreage for Navajo Relocation," *Albuquerque Journal*, January 24, 1984.

43. Paul R. Wieck, "San Juan Plan Displeases Domenici," *Albuquerque Journal*, January 26, 1984.

44. "Lujan Against Plan."

45. Paul R. Wieck, "Richardson Backs Off Extended Limit for Navajo Land Search," *Albuquerque Journal*, March 2, 1984.

46. "Differences Hold Up Passage of San Juan Wilderness Bill," *Albuquerque Journal*, October 4, 1984.

47. "Reagan Signs Four Corners Wilderness Bill," *Albuquerque Journal*, October 31, 1984.

CHAPTER 9: MISSING LINKS, LINKS GONE MISSING, AND NATURAL RESOURCE MANAGEMENT

1. Erwin C. Hargrove, *The Missing Link* (Washington DC: Urban Institute, 1975).

2. For excellent summaries and critiques of the present state of these efforts, see Malcolm Goggin, Ann O'M. Bowman, James Lester, and Laurence J. O'Toole, Jr., *Implementation Theory and Practice* (Boston: Scott Foresman/Little, Brown,

1990); Steven H. Linder and B. Guy Peters, "A Design Perspective on Policy Implementation: The Failures of Misplaced Prescription," *Policy Studies Review*, vol. 6 (February 1987), pp. 459–475; Malcolm L. Goggin, "The 'Too Few Cases/Too Many Variables' Problem in Implementation Research," *The Western Political Quarterly*, vol. 59 (June 1986), pp. 328–347.

3. Benny Hjern, "Implementation Research—The Link Gone Missing," *Journal of Public Policy*, vol. 2 (August 1982), pp. 301–308.

4. See, for example, Wood, "Principal-Agent Models"; Robert Rector and Michael Sanera, eds., *Steering the Elephant: How Washington Works* (New York: University Books, 1987); Waterman, *Presidential Influence;* Francis E. Rourke, "Executive Responsiveness to Presidential Policies: The Reagan Presidency," *Congress and the Presidency,* vol. 17 (Spring 1990), pp. 1–11; Susan Gluck Mezey, *No Longer Disabled: The Federal Courts and the Politics of Social Security Disability* (Westport CT: Greenwood Press, 1988); Abigail M. Thernstrom, *Whose Votes Count? Affirmative Action and Minority Voting Rights* (Cambridge MA: Harvard University Press, 1987).

5. For example, see Arnold J. Meltsner, ed., *Politics and the Oval Office*, esp. Ch. 1.

6. See, for example, Rector and Sanera, *Steering the Elephant*.

7. Seymour Scher, "Conditions for Legislative Control," *Journal of Politics*, vol. 28 (1963), pp. 526–551; John Bibby, "Congress' Neglected Function," pp. 477–488 in Melvin R. Laird, ed., *The Republican Papers* (New York: Anchor Books, 1968); Morris S. Ogul, *Congress Oversees the Bureaucracy: Studies in Legislative Supervision* (Pittsburgh: University of Pittsburgh Press, 1976).

8. See, for example, Kenneth J. Meier, *Politics and the Bureaucracy*, 2nd ed. (Monterey CA: Brooks/Cole, 1987), and most of the "bottom up" research in the policy implementation literature (see Note 2, above).

9. See, for example, McCubbins and Schwartz, "Police Patrols and Fire Alarms"; Joel D. Aberbach, *Keeping a Watchful Eye: The Politics of Congressional Oversight* (Washington DC: Brookings Institution, 1990); Randall L. Calvert, Mark J. Moran, and Barry R. Weingast, "Congressional Influence over Policy Making: The Case of the FTC," pp. 493–522 in Matthew D. McCubbins and Terry Sullivan, eds., *Theories on Congress: The New Institutionalism* (Cambridge: Cambridge University Press, 1986); R. Douglas Arnold, *Congress and the Bureaucracy: A Theory of Influence* (New Haven CT: Yale University Press, 1979); Terry Moe, "The Politics of Bureaucratic Structure," pp. 267–329 in John E. Chubb and Paul E. Peterson, *Can the Government Govern?* (Washington DC: Brookings Institution, 1989); B. Dan Wood, Response to Brian J. Cook in "Principal-Agent Models of Political Control of the Bureaucracy," *American Political Science Review*, vol. 83 (September 1989), pp. 965–978.

10. As Paul Schulman suggests, a policy is a "hypothesis" or an "idea set." It is comprised of three components: central concepts, axioms, and deductive propositions ("If . . . then" statements). For instance, in deciding to deploy the MX missile, the core concept of "deterrence" is coupled with the axiomatic premise that "nations act rationally" to produce the deductive proposition that "mutually assured destruction will deter aggression." Thus, a policy or idea set "offers a causal explanation for a given social condition or problem state, a forecast regarding future states, and a prescriptive inference for policy intervention on behalf of a desired outcome" (p. 265). What is more, changes can occur in any of the three components of the idea set at any time, thus qualitatively changing or bringing

about a new policy alternative. See Paul R. Schulman, "The Politics of 'Ideational Policy'," *Journal of Politics*, vol. 38 (1988), pp. 263–291. More on this concept and its dynamics appears in Chapter 10.

11. The term "policy softening" is derived from John Kingdon's work on agenda processes. See Kingdon, *Agendas, Alternatives, and Public Policy*.

12. The logic underlying the assumption here is akin to Lowi's notion of policy types. As posited by him, the perceptions of individuals about what is at stake for them will vary by policy type (distributive, regulatory, and redistributive). In turn, these perceptions will shape or condition the nature of the politics that these types occasion. Similarly, the logic in this chapter is that variations on policy validity and policy softening (or tempo) conditioned or helped foster the types of bureaupolitical dynamics witnessed in the different cases. See Theodore Lowi, "American Business, Public Policy, Case Studies, and Political Theory," *World Politics*, vol. 16 (1964), pp. 675–715; Randall B. Ripley and Grace A. Franklin, *Policy Implementation and Bureaucracy*, 2nd ed. (Chicago: The Dorsey Press, 1986).

13. See Note 10 above.

14. Kingdon, *Agendas, Alternatives, and Public Policy*, pp. 134–135.

15. Laurence J. O'Toole, Jr., and Robert S. Montjoy, "Interorganizational Policy Implementation: A Theoretical Perspective," *Public Administration Review*, vol. 44 (November/December 1984), pp. 491–503.

16. Eugene Bardach, *The Implementation Game* (Cambridge MA: MIT Press, 1977).

17. Peggy Noonan, *What I Saw at the Revolution: A Political Life in the Reagan Era* (New York: Random House, 1990).

18. These concepts are defined and elaborated in Karen M. Hult and Charles Walcott, *Governing Public Organizations: Politics, Structures, and Institutional Design* (Pacific Grove CA: Brooks/Cole, 1990).

19. Hult and Walcott, *Governing Public Organizations*, p. 5.

20. Hult and Walcott, *Governing Public Organizations*, p. 9.

21. Benny Hjern and David O. Porter, "Implementation Structures: A New Unit of Administrative Analysis," *Organization Studies*, vol. 2, no. 3 (1981), p. 211.

22. Rockman, "Conclusions: An Imprint."

23. Martin Landau and Russell Stout, "To Manage Is Not to Control: The Folly of Type II Errors," *Public Administration Review*, vol. 39 (March/April 1979), pp. 148–156.

24. Richard F. Elmore, "Forward and Backward Mapping: Reversible Logic in the Analysis of Public Policy," pp. 33–70 in Kenneth Hanf and Theodore A.J. Toonen, eds., *Policy Implementation in Federal and Unitary Systems: Questions of Analysis and Design* (Dordrecht: Martinus Nijhoff, 1985).

25. Elmore, "Forward and Backward Mapping," p. 67.

26. Elmore, "Forward and Backward Mapping," p. 34.

27. Elmore, "Forward and Backward Mapping," p. 36.

28. Noonan, *What I Saw at the Revolution*, p. 233.

29. Golembiewski, "Public-Sector Organizations," p. 437.

30. Knott and Miller, *Reforming Bureaucracy*.

31. Moe, "Politics of Bureaucratic Structure."

32. Golembiewski, "Public-Sector Organizations," p. 437.

33. Donald P. Warwick, *A Theory of Public Bureaucracy* (Cambridge MA: Harvard University Press, 1975).

34. Anthony Downs, *Inside Bureaucracy* (Boston MA: Little, Brown, 1967).

35. Constance Horner, "Beyond Mr. Gradgrind: The Case for Deregulating the Public Sector," *Policy Review*, vol. 44 (Spring 1988), p. 34.

36. See Horner, "Beyond Mr. Gradgrind"; Tom Price, "Pentagon Wants Leeway to Manage," *Atlanta Journal Constitution*, April 6, 1990.

37. Horner, "Beyond Mr. Gradgrind," p. 36.

38. Middaugh, *Issue Paper*, pp. 2–3.

39. Dana and Baden, "The New Resource Economics."

40. Dana and Baden, "The New Resource Economics," p. 242.

41. See, for example, James R. Udall, "Just Add Water Marketing," *Sierra*, vol. 72 (March/April 1987), pp. 37–42.

42. Brown and Ingram, *Water and Poverty*.

43. William G. Ouchi, "Markets, Bureaucracies, and Clans," *Administrative Science Quarterly*, vol. 25 (March 1980), p. 132.

44. See Timothy Egan, "Forest Service Abusing Role, Dissidents Say," *New York Times*, March 4, 1990, pp. 1, 21.

45. Herbert Kaufman, *The Forest Ranger* (Baltimore: Johns Hopkins University Press, 1960).

46. Golembiewski, "Public-Sector Organization," p. 450.

47. Golembiewski, "Public-Sector Organization," pp. 452–453.

48. Peters, *Thriving on Chaos*, p. 380.

49. Golembiewski, "Public-Sector Organization." In collateral or parallel structures, the "formal organizational structure is retained, and a temporary or episodically activated structure is constituted for specific purposes or a defined period" (p. 457). In contrast, project management "retains the functional model, but adds major structural counterbalance to it in the role of the project manager or director" (p. 31). The mature matrix is "an amalgam of various prominent features of the functional model," as well as of project management and parallel structures (p. 35).

50. Golembiewski, "Public-Sector Organization," p. 461.

51. Here, the Reagan Administration would have had to deal with two types of middle-level constraints: (1) those resulting from statutes and (2) those imposed by and under the exclusive authority of other agencies. Thus, while appointees could have permanently or on an ad hoc basis waived the latter, the former would have required congressional waivers, a distinctly more difficult task requiring "softening" of legislative sovereigns over prolonged periods. The Administration, at least, would have had to begin that formidable task. Finally, recognizing that policy accomplishment depends most often today on interorganizational cooperation within implementation structures (or "governance networks"), the Administration could have begun the long and arduous task of educating key members of Congress about the wisdom of a legislative oversight process that conditions congressional largesse at least partially upon interagency cooperation rather than conflict.

52. See, for example, Nancy Whelan, "Suspending the Rules and Improving Business," *Government Executive*, April 1987, esp. pp. 18–19.

53. Whelan, "Suspending the Rules," p. 19.

54. Middaugh, *Issue Document*, pp. 2–3.

55. Golembiewski, "Public-Sector Organization," p. 464.

CHAPTER 10: "FIRE ALARMS," "GARBAGE CANS," AND THE ADMINISTRATIVE PRESIDENCY

1. Kingdon uses the term "pre-decision policy processes" to subsume two analytically distinct components of agenda processes, which he identifies as agenda setting (selecting from among all possible problems or subjects those that are worthy of priority attention by decision makers) and alternative specification (selecting the set of conceivable alternative ways available for addressing each problem). For him, Cohen, March, and Olsen's "garbage can model" of decision-making adequately captures the dynamics of agenda setting, while Lindblom's incrementalism captures those of alternative specification. See Kingdon, *Agendas, Alternatives, and Public Policy* (Boston: Little, Brown, 1984). Also, for a perspective that maintains that alternative specification is better conceptualized as both incremental and nonincremental, see Robert F. Durant and Paul F. Diehl, "Agendas, Alternatives, and Public Policy: Lessons from the U.S. Foreign Policy Arena," *Journal of Public Policy*, vol. 9 (April/June 1989), pp. 179–205.

2. See, for example, E.E. Schattschneider, *The Semisovereign People* (New York: Holt, Rinehart and Winston, 1960); Roger W. Cobb and Charles D. Elder, *Participation in American Politics: The Dynamics of Agenda Building* (Baltimore: Johns Hopkins University Press, 1972); Downs, "Up and Down with Ecology"; Paul C. Light, *The President's Agenda: Domestic Policy Choice from Kennedy to Carter* (Baltimore: Johns Hopkins University Press, 1982); David Dery, *Problem Definition in Policy Analysis* (Lawrence: University Press of Kansas, 1984); Nelson W. Polsby, *Political Innovation in America: The Politics of Policy Initiation* (New Haven CT: Yale University Press, 1984).

3. See, for example, Karl W. Deutsch, *The Nerves of Government* (New York: Free Press, 1963); Robert Axelrod, *The Evolution of Cooperation* (New York: Basic Books, 1984).

4. Schulman, "The Politics of 'Ideational Policy'," p. 265.

5. The terms borrowed from evolutionary theory are akin to, but not isomorphic with, concepts developed by Lindblom. See Charles Lindblom, "The Science of 'Muddling Through'," *Public Administration Review*, vol. 19 (1959), pp. 79–88. As terms used by natural scientists to portray modes of evolutionary transformation, they are better suited than Lindblom's binary concepts to connote the disparate types, pace, and nuances of evolution undergirding various presidential policy initiatives. In particular, they better capture both incremental and nonincremental policy alternatives. For the biological origins of these terms, see Niles Eldridge and Stephen Jay Gould, "Punctuated Equilibria: An Alternative to Phyletic Gradualism," pp. 82–115 in T.J.M. Schopf, *Models in Paleobiology* (San Francisco CA: Freeman, Cooper, 1972).

6. Terms requiring definition at this point include "policy community," "policy sectors," "issue networks," "advocacy coalitions," and "dominant coalitions." According to Kingdon (*Agendas, Alternatives, and Public Policies*, p. 92), there exists a "policy community of specialists—bureaucrats, people in the planning and evaluation and in the budget offices, [Capitol] Hill staffers, academics, interest groups, researchers—which concentrates on generating policy proposals" in their substantive areas of expertise. As defined by Welborn and Brown, a policy sector is differentiated between core and peripheral actors. The former's participa-

tion in policy formulation is persistent, stable over time, and formidable in influence. The latter's is episodic, fleeting, and more problematic. See David M.· Welborn and Anthony E. Brown, *Regulatory Policy and Processes* (Knoxville: Bureau of Public Administration, University of Tennessee, 1980). Similarly, Heclo defines "issue networks" relative to "iron triangles" as largely shifting, fluid, and anonymous. That is, issue networks are extremely diverse, with numerous actors—holding intellectual or emotional rather than material stakes in policy outcomes—moving in and out of these transitory networks. See Hugh Heclo, "Issue Networks and the Executive Establishment," pp. 87–124 in Anthony King, ed., *The New American Political System* (Washington DC: American Enterprise Institute, 1978). Further elaborating on this notion, Sabatier and Pelkey define advocacy coalitions as "composed of elite actors from a variety of sources—interest groups, agency officials, legislators, executive overseers, intellectuals—who share a general set of normative and causal beliefs concerning the policy area"; this coalition uses "a variety of legal and political instruments to achieve their policy objectives over time" (p. 237). See Paul Sabatier and Neal Pelkey, "Incorporating Multiple Actors and Guidance Instruments into Models of Regulatory Policymaking: An Advocacy Coalition Framework," *Administration & Society*, vol. 19 (1987), pp. 236–263. Finally, the term "dominant coalition" refers to that coalition *within* an agency that determines what its capabilities and its ends should be. Of course, the ability of these actors to do so often depends partially on their linkage with key external actors (e.g., legislative sovereigns, clientele groups, etc.).

7. Christopher Hood, *The Tools of Government* (Chatham NJ: Chatham House Publishers, 1986).

8. See Sabatier, "Top-Down and Bottom-Up Approaches," pp. 21–48.

9. The term "counterbureaucracy" refers to the attempts of recent presidents to circumvent the permanent federal bureaucracy by assigning the latter's policy-proposing functions to units within the White House staff that are presumably more loyal to the President (see Nathan, *The Administrative Presidency*). Also see Francis E. Rourke and Paul R. Schulman, "Adhocracy in Policy Development," *The Social Science Journal*, vol. 26 (1989), pp. 131–142.

10. Sabatier, "Top-Down and Bottom-Up Approaches," p. 45.

11. See, for example, Rector and Sanera, *Steering the Elephant*; Waterman, *Presidential Influence*; B. Dan Wood, "Principals, Bureaucrats, and Responsiveness"; B. Dan Wood, Response to Brian Cook.

12. The patterns of bureaucratic politics identified are heavily dependent upon the collective works of Louis C. Gawthrop, James G. March and Herbert A. Simon, A. Lee Fritschler and Morley Segal, Robert A. Dahl and Charles E. Lindblom, and Robert S. Montjoy and Laurence J. O'Toole, Jr. Two points are important to note. First, the resistance of careerists—principled or otherwise—to lawful policy initiatives can take many forms and be either overt or covert and direct or indirect. Thus, as Guy Peters suggests in a cross-national perspective, "Bureaucrats defeat politicians by obfuscation, delay, use of rules, regulations, and procedures"; B. Guy Peters, *The Politics of Bureaucracy*, 3rd ed. (New York: Longman, 1989), p. 194. Second, the categories used in this typology refer to behaviors, characteristics, and dynamics exhibited by the full range of micro- and macropolitical actors involved in each scenario.

13. Austin Sarat and Joel B. Grossman, "Courts and Conflict Resolution:

Problems in Mobilization of Adjudication," *American Political Science Review*, vol. 69 (1975), p. 1211.

14. Robert F. Durant, Larry W. Thomas, Roger G. Brown, and E. Fletcher McClellan, "From Complacence to Compliance: Toward a Theory of Intragovernmental Regulation," *Administration & Society*, vol. 17 (February 1986), pp. 433–459.

15. The concept of institutional or program mission refers to an organization or program's dominant official philosophy or administrative ideology and is directly associated with its maintenance and survival needs. It is analogous to what Laurence E. Lynn, Jr., (*Managing Public Policy* [Boston: Little, Brown, 1987] p. 245) terms the "core activity" of an organization ("that activity that defines the organization's raison d'etre in the minds of its employees and constituents"). Among others who have made use of the term are James Q. Wilson, *Bureaucracy* (New York: Basic Books, 1989); Jonathan Bendor, *Parallel Systems: Redundancy in Government* (Berkeley and Los Angeles: University of California Press, 1985); Jerry Mashaw, *Bureaucratic Justice* (New Haven CT: Yale University Press, 1983); and Martha Derthick, *Policymaking for Social Security* (Washington DC: Brookings Institution, 1979).

16. Lynn, *Managing Public Policy*, pp. 153–155.

17. U.S. Advisory Commission on Intergovernmental Relations, *Regulatory Federalism: Policy, Process, Impact, and Reform* (Washington DC: ACIR, 1984).

18. James Q. Wilson and Patricia Rachal, "Can Government Regulate Itself?" *The Public Interest*, vol. 46 (March 1977), pp. 3–14. As defined by Wilson (*Bureaucracy*, p. 129), contextual goals are "descriptions of desired states of affairs other than the one the agency was brought into being to create. . . . These define the context within which the primary goals can be sought."

19. Lynn, *Managing Public Policy*, pp. 251–256.

20. Robert F. Durant, *When Government Regulates Itself: EPA, TVA, and Pollution Control in the 1970s* (Knoxville: The University of Tennessee Press, 1985).

21. Rowland Evans, Jr., and Robert D. Novak, *Nixon in the White House: The Frustration of Power* (New York: Random House, 1971), esp. Ch. 6.

22. Rector and Sanera, *Steering the Elephant*, p. 427.

23. Aaron Wildavsky, "Forward: The Human Side of Government," pp. xiii–xviii in Rector and Sanera, *Steering the Elephant*.

24. Patricia W. Ingraham and Carolyn Ban, "Politics and Merit: Can They Meet in a Public Service Model?" *Review of Public Personnel Administration*, vol. 8 (Spring 1988), p. 13.

25. Waterman, *Presidential Influence*.

26. Woodrow Wilson, "The Study of Administration," p. 29 in Dean L. Yarwood, ed., *Public Administration: Politics and People* (New York: Longman, 1987).

27. John Rohr, *To Run a Constitution* (Lawrence: University Press of Kansas, 1986).

28. See, for example, The National Commission on the Public Service, *Leadership for America: Rebuilding the Public Service* (Washington DC: National Commission on the Public Service, 1989).

29. Hugh Heclo, "In Search of a Role: America's Higher Civil Service," pp.

8–34 in Ezra Suleiman, ed., *Bureaucrats and Policy Making* (New York: Holmes & Meier Publishers, 1984).

30. The general tone of this perspective is reflected in James Pfiffner's writing: "The argument here is that most career executives will willingly support a new administration and not resist its legitimate policy initiatives"; "Career bureaucrats will cooperate with a new administration for two reasons: their role perception and their own self-interest." See Pfiffner, *The Strategic Presidency*, pp. 104, 102.

31. Laurence E. Lynn, "The Manager's Role in Public Management," *The Bureaucrat*, vol. 13 (Winter 1984–85), p. 20.

32. Lynn, "The Manager's Role," p. 20.

33. Moe, "The Politics of Bureaucratic Structure," p. 267.

34. See, for example, Butler, Sanera, and Weinrod, *Mandate for Leadership II.* See especially Sanera, "Implementing the Mandate," pp. 457–545. Similar perspectives are presented in Rector and Sanera, eds., *Steering the Elephant.* Sanera and others take pains to deny an uncomplimentary view of the career bureaucracy by referring to the need for cooperation, balance, and avoiding paranoia and confrontation with careerists. Still, their tone belies this when it comes to policy formulation in the executive branch. Sanera, for example, writes "the political executive must decide how he can gain more control over the policy-making process" (p. 479). To these ends, he continues, "Career staff will supply information, but they should never become involved in the formulation of agenda-related policy objectives." And in warning against building a fortress mentality (a mentality that is discouraged for "administrative" matters, but not for policy formulation or agenda setting), Sanera writes, "Even though the political executive will soon be face-to-face with a number of first class 'mess-makers,' he should keep his hostility in check" (p. 516).

35. Sanera, "Implementing the Mandate," p. 513.

36. See, for example, Rourke, *Bureaucracy, Politics, and Public Policy,* and Meier, *Politics and Bureaucracy.*

37. Hugh Heclo, *A Government of Strangers: Executive Politics in Washington* (Washington DC: Brookings Institution, 1977).

38. Heclo, *Government of Strangers,* p. 193. According to Heclo (pp. 149–150), "program" bureaucrats (or advocates) are those careerists with operating responsibility who primarily try to defend or advance established program activities as best they can. "Staff" bureaucrats (e.g., budgeteers, personnel managers, management specialists) are concerned primarily with internal administrative processes that cut across programs in an agency. They thus have fewer commitments to existing programs, subject matter, or clients, and are less threatened by changes in political leadership. "Reformers" are much less enamored by the ways programs have been run in the past, are typically associated with policy analysis units, and may have had proposals for reform rejected in the past (i.e., they "identify themselves as 'partisans for more rational decisionmaking'." Finally, "institutionalists" are concerned with getting things implemented effectively and with "maintaining an independent view up to the point of a political decision." This bureaucratic type is not resistant to change, but becomes so when appointee initiatives fall outside the bounds of legitimacy, particularly when they are patently illegal.

39. Some might question the ability of appointees to analyze the environment or situation they are entering or involved in and then to alter their leader-

ship style accordingly. While a formidable task, appointees have been aided in their diagnostic abilities in recent years by assessments done by presidential transition teams and independent think tanks. Moreover, according to Heclo, the "in-and-outer" system has brought to Washington "public careerists" with policy, organizational, and political knowledge garnered from participation in issue networks and previous service in federal agencies. As for leadership styles, the literature is mixed in its assessment of the capability of managers to alter their styles to fit particular contingencies. Part of the purpose of this chapter, however, is to demonstrate how and why applying different managerial styles is important when pursuing policy reorientation in disparate situations.

40. Paul Hersey and Kenneth H. Blanchard, *Management of Organizational Behavior: Utilizing Human Resources*, 5th ed. (Englewood Cliffs NJ: Prentice-Hall, 1988).

41. Hersey and Blanchard, *Management of Organizational Behavior,* p. 177.

42. Hersey and Blanchard, *Management of Organizational Behavior,* p. 172.

43. Heclo, *Government of Strangers,* p. 204.

44. Heclo, *Government of Strangers,* p. 215.

45. Heclo, *Government of Strangers,* pp. 204–205.

46. Heclo, *Government of Strangers,* p. 210, fn. 6.

47. Hersey and Blanchard, *Management of Organizational Behavior,* p. 182.

48. Heclo, *Government of Strangers,* pp. 205, 208.

49. Heclo, *Government of Strangers,* p. 205.

50. Giandomenico Majone and Aaron Wildavsky, " Implementation as Evolution," in Jeffrey Pressman and Aaron Wildavsky, eds., *Implementation,* 3rd ed. (Berkeley and Los Angeles: University of California Press, 1984), p. 173.

REFERENCES

BOOKS

Aberbach, Joel D. *Keeping a Watchful Eye: The Politics of Congressional Oversight.* Washington, DC: The Brookings Institution, 1990.

Arnold, Peri E. *Making the Managerial Presidency: Comprehensive Reorganization Planning, 1905–1980.* Princeton, NJ: Princeton University Press, 1986.

Arnold, R. Douglas. *Congress and the Bureaucracy: A Theory of Influence.* New Haven, CT: Yale University Press, 1979.

Arnold, Ron. *At the Eye of the Storm: James Watt and the Environmentalists.* Chicago: Regnery Gateway Press, 1982.

Arrandale, Tom. *The Battle for Natural Resources.* Washington, DC: Congressional Quarterly Press, 1983.

Axelrod, Robert. *The Evolution of Cooperation.* New York: Basic Books, 1984.

Bardach, Eugene. *The Implementation Game.* Cambridge, MA: The MIT Press, 1977.

Bendor, Jonathan. *Parallel Systems: Redundancy in Government.* Berkeley and Los Angeles: University of California Press, 1985.

Boaz, David, ed. *Assessing the Reagan Years.* Washington, DC: Cato Institute, 1988.

Brown, F. Lee, and Helen Ingram. *Water and Poverty in the Southwest.* Tucson: University of Arizona Press, 1987.

Brownstein, Ronald, and Nina Easton. *Reagan's Ruling Class: Portraits of the President's Top 100 Officials.* Washington, DC: Presidential Accountability Group, 1982.

Buchanan, Bruce. *The Citizen's Presidency.* Washington, DC: Congressional Quarterly, 1987.

Burns, James McGregor. *The Power to Lead: The Crisis of the American Presidency.* New York: Simon & Schuster, 1984.

Butler, Stuart M., Michael Sanera, and W. Bruce Weinrod, eds. *Mandate for Leadership II: Continuing the Fight.* Washington, DC: Heritage Foundation, 1984.

Calef, Wesley. *Private Grazing and Public Lands*. Chicago: University of Chicago Press, 1960.

Campbell, Colin. *Governments Under Stress*. Toronto: University of Toronto Press, 1983.

Chandler, Alfred D. *Strategy and Structure*. Cambridge, MA: MIT Press, 1962.

Chandler, Ralph C. *A Centennial History of the American Administrative State*. New York: Free Press, 1987.

Chubb, John E., and Paul E. Peterson, eds. *Can the Government Govern?* Washington, DC: Brookings Institution, 1989.

Chubb, John E., and Paul E. Peterson, eds. *The New Direction in American Politics*. Washington, DC: Brookings Institution, 1985.

Clark, Ira G. *Water in New Mexico: A History of Its Management and Use*. Albuquerque: University of New Mexico Press, 1989.

Clarke, Jeanne N., and Daniel McCool. *Staking Out the Terrain: Power Differentials Among Natural Resource Management Agencies*. Albany: State University of New York Press, 1985.

Clawson, Marian. *The Federal Lands Revisited*. Baltimore: Resources for the Future, 1983.

Cobb, Roger W., and Charles D. Elder. *Participation in American Politics: The Dynamics of Agenda Building*. Baltimore: Johns Hopkins University Press, 1972.

Culhane, Paul J. *Public Lands Politics*. Baltimore: Johns Hopkins University Press, 1981.

Dahl, Robert A., and Charles E. Lindblom. *Politics, Economics, and Welfare*. New York: Harper & Row, 1953.

Davis, Vincent, ed. *The Post-Imperial Presidency*. New Brunswick, NJ: Transaction, 1980.

Derthick, Martha. *Policymaking for Social Security*. Washington, DC: Brookings Institution, 1979.

Dery, David. *Problem Definition in Policy Analysis*. Lawrence: University Press of Kansas, 1984.

Deutsch, Karl W. *The Nerves of Government*. New York: Free Press, 1963.

Downs, Anthony. *Inside Bureaucracy*. Boston, MA: Little, Brown, 1967.

Durant, Robert F. *When Government Regulates Itself: EPA, TVA, and Pollution Control in the 1970s*. Knoxville: University of Tennessee Press, 1985.

Eads, George C., and Michael Fix. *Relief or Reform? Reagan's Regulatory Dilemma*. Washington, DC: Urban Institute Press, 1984.

Edwards, George C., III. *The Public Presidency*. New York: St. Martin's Press, 1983.

Evans, Rowland, Jr., and Robert D. Novak. *Nixon in the White House: The Frustration of Power*. New York: Random House, 1971.

Foss, Phillip O. *Politics and Grass*. Seattle: University of Washington Press, 1960.

Francis, John G., and Richard Ganzel, eds. *Western Public Lands: The Management of Natural Resources in a Time of Declining Federalism*. Totowa, NJ: Roman and Allanheld, 1984.

Franck, Thomas, ed. *The Tethered Presidency*. New York: New York University Press, 1981.

Gawthrop, Louis C. *Bureaucratic Behavior in the Executive Branch*. New York: Free Press, 1969.

Goggin, Malcolm, Ann O'M. Bowman, James Lester, and Laurence J. O'Toole, Jr. *Implementation Theory and Practice*. Boston: Scott Foresman/Little, Brown, 1990.

Golembiewski, Robert T. *Men, Management, and Morality: Toward a New Organizational Ethic*. New York: McGraw-Hill, 1965.

Golembiewski, Robert T., and Michael Cohen, eds. *People in Public Service*. Itasca, IL: F. E. Peacock, 1970.

Greenstein, Fred I., ed. *The Reagan Presidency: An Early Assessment*. Baltimore: Johns Hopkins University Press, 1983.

Halperin, Morton. *Bureaucratic Politics and Foreign Policy*. Washington, DC: Brookings Institution, 1974.

Hanf, Kenneth, and Theo. A.J. Toonen, eds. *Policy Implementation in Federal and Unitary Systems: Questions of Analysis and Design*. Dordrecht: Martinus Nijhoff, 1985.

Hargrove, Erwin C. *The Missing Link*. Washington, DC: Urban Institute, 1975.

Hargrove, Erwin C. *The Power of the Modern Presidency*. New York: Knopf, 1974.

Hargrove, Erwin C., and Michael Nelson. *Presidents, Politics, and Policy*. Baltimore: Johns Hopkins University Press, 1984.

Hays, Samuel P. *Conservation and the Gospel of Efficiency*. Cambridge, MA: Harvard University Press, 1959.

Heclo, Hugh. *A Government of Strangers: Executive Politics in Washington*. Washington, DC: Brookings Institution, 1977.

Heclo, Hugh, and Lester Salamon, eds. *The Illusion of Presidential Government*. Boulder, CO: Westview Press, 1981.

Heineman, Ben W., Jr., and Curtis Hessler. *Memorandum for the President: Managing the Domestic Agenda in the 1980s*. New York: Random House, 1980.

Hersey, Paul, and Kenneth H. Blanchard. *Management of Organizational Behavior: Utilizing Human Resources*, 5th ed. Englewood Cliffs, NJ: Prentice-Hall, 1988.

Hodgson, Godfrey. *All Things to All Men: The False Promise of the Modern American Presidency*. New York: Simon and Schuster, 1980.

Hood, Christopher. *The Tools of Government*. Chatham, NJ: Chatham House Publishers, 1986.

Hult, Karen M., and Charles Walcott. *Governing Public Organizations: Politics, Structures, and Institutional Design*. Pacific Grove, CA: Brooks/Cole, 1990.

Hummel, Ralph. *The Bureaucratic Experience*, 3rd ed. New York: St. Martin's Press, 1987.

Kaufman, Herbert. *The Forest Ranger*. Baltimore: Johns Hopkins University Press, 1960.

Kellerman, Barbara. *The Political Presidency: Practice of Leadership*. New York: Oxford University Press, 1984.

King, Anthony King, ed. *The New American Political System*. Washington, DC: American Enterprise Institute, 1978.

Kingdon, John. *Agendas, Alternatives, and Public Policy*. Boston, MA: Little, Brown, 1984.

Knott, Jack, and Gary Miller. *Reforming Bureaucracy: The Politics of Institutional Choice*. Englewood Cliffs, NJ: Prentice-Hall, 1987.

Kraft, Michael, E., and Normal J. Vig, eds. *Environmental Politics in the 1980s: Reagan's New Agenda*. Washington, DC: Congressional Quarterly Press, 1984.

Kymlicka, B.B., and Jean V. Matthews, eds. *The Reagan Revolution*. Chicago: Dorsey, 1988.

Laird, Melvin R., ed. *The Republican Papers*. New York: Anchor Books, 1968.

Lees, John D., and Michael Turner. *Reagan's First Four Years: A New Beginning?* Manchester: Manchester University Press, 1988.

Light, Paul C. *The President's Agenda: Domestic Policy Choice from Kennedy to Carter*. Baltimore: Johns Hopkins University Press, 1982.

Lynn, Laurence E., Jr. *Managing Public Policy*. Boston: Little/Brown, 1987.

Lowi, Theodore J. *The Personal President: Power Invested, Promise Unfulfilled*. Ithaca, NY: Cornell University Press, 1985.

Mackenzie, Calvin C. *The Politics of Presidential Appointments*. New York: Free Press, 1981.

March, James G., and Herbert A. Simon. *Organizations*. New York: John Wiley, 1958.

Mashaw, Jerry. *Bureaucratic Justice*. New Haven, CT: Yale University Press, 1983.

McCool, Daniel. *Command of the Waters: Iron Triangles, Federal Water Development, and Indian Water Rights*. Berkeley and Los Angeles: University of California Press, 1988.

McCubbins, Matthew D., and Terry Sullivan, eds. *Theories on Congress: The New Institutionalism*. Cambridge: Cambridge University Press, 1986.

Meier, Kenneth J. *Politics and the Bureaucracy*, 2nd ed. Monterey, CA: Brooks/Cole, 1987.

Melnick, R. Shep. *Regulation and the Courts: The Case of the Clean Air Act*. Washington, DC: Brookings Institution, 1983.

Meltsner, Arnold J., ed. *Politics and the Oval Office: Towards Presidential Governance*. San Francisco, CA: Institute for Contemporary Studies, 1981.

Mezey, Susan Gluck. *No Longer Disabled: The Federal Courts and the Politics of Social Security Disability*. Westport, CT: Greenwood Press, 1987.

Nathan, Richard P. *The Administrative Presidency*. New York: Wiley, 1983.

Nathan, Richard P. *The Plot That Failed*. New York: Wiley, 1975.

National Academy of Public Administration. *Leadership in Jeopardy: The Fraying of the Presidential Appointment System*. Washington, DC: National Academy of Public Administration, November 1985.

The National Commission on the Public Service. *Leadership for America: Rebuilding the Public Service*. Washington, DC: The National Commission on the Public Service, 1989.

Neustadt, Richard E. *Presidential Power: The Politics of Leadership from FDR to Carter*. New York: Wiley, 1980.

New Mexico Water Resources Research Institute. *Water Law in the West*. Las Cruces: New Mexico State University, 1984.

New Mexico Water Resources Research Institute and the University of New Mexico Law School. *State Appropriation of Unappropriated Groundwater: A Strategy for Insuring New Mexico a Water Future*. Las Cruces: New Mexico State University, 1986.

Noonan, Peggy. *What I Saw at the Revolution: A Political Life in the Reagan Era*. New York: Random House, 1990.

Ogul, Morris S. *Congress Oversees the Bureaucracy: Studies in Legislative Supervision*. Pittsburgh: University of Pittsburgh Press, 1976.

Palmer, John L., and Isabel V. Sawhill, eds. *The Reagan Record*. Cambridge, MA: Ballinger, 1984.

Palumbo, Dennis J., and Donald J. Calista, eds. *Implementation and the Policy Process*. New York: Greenwood Press, 1990.

Peters, B. Guy. *The Politics of Bureaucracy*, 3rd ed. New York: Longman, 1989.

Peters, Tom. *Thriving on Chaos: Handbook for a Management Revolution*. New York: Knopf, 1987.

Pfiffner, James P. *The Strategic Presidency: Hitting the Ground Running.* Chicago: Dorsey, 1988.

Pious, Richard. *The American Presidency.* New York: Basic Books, 1979.

Polsby, Nelson W. *Political Innovation in America: The Politics of Policy Initiation.* New Haven, CT: Yale University Press, 1984.

Portney, Paul R., ed. *Natural Resources and the Environment: The Reagan Approach.* Washington, DC: Urban Institute Press, 1984.

Pressman, Jeffrey, and Aaron Wildavsky, eds. *Implementation,* 3rd ed. Berkeley and Los Angeles: University of California Press, 1984.

Rector, Robert, and Michael Sanera, eds. *Steering the Elephant: How Washington Works.* New York: Universe Books, 1987.

Richardson, Elliot. *Politics and Performance: Strengthening the Executive Leadership System.* Washington, DC: Volcker Commission, 1989.

Ripley, Randall B., and Grace A. Franklin. *Policy Implementation and the Bureaucracy.* Chicago: Dorsey, 1986.

Ripley, Randall B., and Grace A. Franklin. *Policy Making in the Federal Executive Branch.* Washington, DC: Free Press, 1975.

Rockman, Bert A. *The Leadership Question: The Presidency and the American System.* New York: Praeger, 1984.

Rohr, John. *To Run a Constitution.* Lawrence: University Press of Kansas, 1986.

Rose, Richard. *Managing Presidential Objectives.* New York: Free Press, 1976.

Rourke, Francis E. *Bureaucracy, Politics, and Public Policy,* 3rd ed. Boston: Little, Brown, 1984.

Rubin, Irene S. *Shrinking the Federal Government: The Effect of Cutbacks on Five Federal Agencies.* New York: Longman, 1985.

Salamon, Lester M., and Michael S. Lund, eds. *The Reagan Presidency and the Governing of America.* Washington, DC: Urban Institute Press, 1984.

Schattschneider, E. E. *The Semisovereign People.* New York: Holt, Rinehart and Winston, 1960.

Schein, Edgar. *Organizational Culture and Leadership.* San Francisco: Jossey-Bass, 1985.

Schlesinger, Arthur, Jr. *The Imperial Presidency.* Boston: Houghton Mifflin, 1973.

Schlesinger, Arthur, Jr. *A Thousand Days.* Boston: Houghton Mifflin, 1965.

Schopf, T.J.M. *Models in Paleobiology.* San Francisco, CA: Freeman, Cooper, 1972.

Seidman, Harold, and Robert Gilmour. *Politics, Position, and Power:*

From the Positive to the Regulatory State, 4th ed. New York: Oxford University Press, 1984.

Shapiro, Martin M. *Guarding the Guardians.* Athens: The University of Georgia Press, 1988.

Smith, Zachary, A., ed. *Water and the Future of the Southwest.* Albuquerque: University of New Mexico Press, 1990.

Suleiman, Ezra, ed. *Bureaucrats and Policy Making.* New York: Holmes & Meier, 1984.

Sundquist, James L. *The Decline and Resurgence of Congress.* Washington, DC: Brookings Institution, 1981.

Thernstrom, Abigail M. *Whose Votes Count? Affirmative Action and Minority Voting Rights.* Cambridge, MA: Harvard University Press, 1987.

Tufte, Edward R. *Political Control of the Economy.* Princeton, NJ: Princeton University Press, 1978.

Vig, Norman, and Michael Kraft. *Environmental Policy in the 1980s: Reagan's New Agenda.* Washington, DC: Congressional Quarterly Press, 1984.

Warwick, Donald P. *A Theory of Public Bureaucracy.* Cambridge, MA: Harvard University Press, 1975.

Waterman, Richard W. *Presidential Influence and the Administrative State.* Knoxville: University of Tennessee Press, 1989.

Welborn, David M., and Anthony E. Brown. *Regulatory Policy and Processes.* Knoxville: Bureau of Public Administration, University of Tennessee, 1980.

Weyler, Rex. *Blood of the Land.* New York: Vintage Books, 1984.

Williams, Walter, ed. *Studying Implementation: Methodological and Administrative Issues.* Chatham, NJ: Chatham House Publishers, 1982.

Wilson, James Q. *Bureaucracy.* New York: Basic Books, 1989.

Yarwood, Dean L., ed. *Public Administration: Politics and People.* New York: Longman, 1987.

BOOK AND JOURNAL ARTICLES

Aberbach, Joel D., and Bert A. Rockman. "Mandates or Mandarins? Control and Discretion in the Modern Administrative State." *Public Administration Review,* vol. 48 (March/April 1988), pp. 606–612.

Anson, Thomas K., and P. M. Schenkkan. "Federalism, the Dormant Commerce Clause, and State-Owned Resources." *Texas Law Review,* vol. 59 (1980), pp. 71–99.

Armstrong, Neal E. "Anticipating Transboundary Needs and Issues in the Mexico–United States Border Region in the Rio Grande Basin." *Natural Resources Journal,* vol. 22 (October 1982), pp. 877–906.

Bahr, Thomas G. "Legal, Hydrological, and Environmental Issues Surrounding the El Paso Water Suit," pp. 45–46 in New Mexico Water Resources Research Institute. *Water Law in the West* (Las Cruces: New Mexico State University, 1984).

Ban, Carolyn, and Patricia Ingraham. "Short-Timers: Political Appointee Mobility and Its Impact on Political-Career Relations in the Reagan Administration." *Administration & Society,* vol. 22 (May 1990), pp. 106–124.

Barnett, Philip M. "Mixing Water and the Commerce Clause: The Problems of Practice, Precedent, and Policy in *Sporhase v. Nebraska.*" *Natural Resources Journal,* vol. 24 (January 1984), pp. 161–194.

Bendor, Jonathan, Serge Taylor, and Roland Van Gaalen. "Stacking the Deck: Bureaucratic Missions and Policy Design." *American Political Science Review,* vol. 81 (September 1987), pp. 873–896.

Bendor, Jonathan and Terry Moe. "An Adaptive Model of Bureaucratic Politics." *American Political Science Review,* vol. 79 (September 1985), pp. 755–774.

Bibby, John. "Congress' Neglected Function," pp. 477–488 in Melvin R. Laird, ed. *The Republican Papers* (New York: Anchor Books, 1968).

Bradley, Robert L. "Energy Policies: A Few Bright Spots," pp. 305–319 in David Boaz, ed. *Assessing the Reagan Years* (Washington, DC: Cato Institute, 1988).

Brady, David W. "Critical Elections, Congressional Parties, and Clusters of Policy Changes." *British Journal of Political Science,* vol. 8 (January 1978), pp. 79–99.

Caiden, Naomi. "The New Rules of the Federal Budget Game." *Public Administration Review,* vol. 44 (March/April 1984), pp. 109–117.

Calvert, Randall L., Mark J. Moran, and Barry R. Weingast. "Congressional Influence over Policy Making: The Case of the FTC," pp. 493–522 in Matthew D. McCubbins and Terry Sullivan, eds. *Theories on Congress: The New Institutionalism* (Cambridge: Cambridge University Press, 1986).

Calvert, Randall L., Matthew D. McCubbins, and Barry R. Weingast. "A Theory of Political Control and Agency Discretion." *American Political Science Review,* vol. 33 (August 1989), pp. 588–611.

Carroll, James D., A. Lee Fritschler, and Bruce L. R. Smith. "Supply-Side Management in the Reagan Administration." *Public Administration Review,* vol. 45 (November/December 1985), pp. 805–814.

Cawley, R. McGreggor, and William Chaloupka. "James Watt and the Environmentalists: A Clash of Ideologies." *Policy Studies Journal,* vol. 14 (December 1985), pp. 244–254.

Chayes, Abraham. "The Role of the Judge in Public Law Litigation." *Harvard Law Review,* vol. 89 (1976), pp. 1281–1316.

Coggins, George C. "The Law of Public Rangeland Management III: A Survey of Creeping Regulation at the Periphery, 1934–1982." *Environmental Law,* vol. 13 (Winter 1983), pp. 295–365.

Coggins, George C. "The Law of Public Rangeland Management IV." *Environmental Law,* vol. 14 (Fall 1983), pp. 1–132.

Coggins, George C. "The Law of Public Rangeland Management V: Prescriptions for Reform." *Environmental Law,* vol. 14 (Spring 1984), pp. 497–546.

Coggins, George C., and Margaret Lindeberg-Johnson. "The Law of Public Rangeland Management II: The Commons and the Taylor Act." *Environmental Law,* vol. 13 (Fall 1982), pp. 1–102.

Coggins, George C., Parthenia B. Evans, and Margaret Lindeberg-Johnson. "The Law of Public Rangeland Management I: The Extent and Distribution of Federal Power." *Environmental Law,* vol. 12 (Spring 1982), pp. 535–622.

Cohen, Michael D., James G. March, and Johan P. Olsen. "A Garbage Can Model of Organizational Choice." *Administrative Science Quarterly,* vol. 17 (1972), pp. 1–25.

Cole, Richard L., and David A. Caputo. "Presidential Control of the Senior Civil Service: Assessing the Strategies of the Nixon Years." *American Political Science Review,* vol. 73 (June 1979), pp. 399–413.

Crandall, Robert W., and Paul R. Portney. "Environmental Policy," pp. 47–81 in Paul R. Portney, ed. *Natural Resources and the Environment: The Reagan Approach* (Washington, DC: Urban Institute Press, 1984).

Crane, Jolene. "*Sporhase v. Nebraska, ex rel. Douglas:* A Call for Groundwater Legislation." *Denver Law Journal,* vol. 60 (1983), pp. 631–643.

Culhane, Paul J. "Sagebrush Rebels in Office: Jim Watt's Land and Water Politics," pp. 293–317 in Norman Vig and Michael Kraft, *Environmental Policy in the 1980s: Reagan's New Agenda* (Washington, DC: Congressional Quarterly Press, 1984).

Culhane, Paul J., and H. Paul Friesma. "Land Use Planning for the Public Lands." *Natural Resources Journal,* vol. 19 (January 1979), as cited in Richard Miller. "FLPMA: A Decade of Management Under the BLM Organic Act." *Policy Studies Journal,* vol. 14 (December 1985), pp. 265–273.

Cutler, Lloyd N. "The Case for Presidential Intervention in Regulatory Rulemaking by the Executive Branch." *Tulane Law Review*, vol. 56 (1982), pp. 830–848.

Dana, Andrew, and John Baden. "The New Resource Economics: Toward an Ideological Synthesis." *Policy Studies Journal*, vol. 14 (December 1985), pp. 233–243.

Davis, Joseph A. "Congress Decidedly Cool to Reagan Land-Sale Plan." *Congressional Quarterly Weekly Report*, July 17, 1982, pp. 1687–1690.

Dodd, Lawrence C. "Congress, the President, and the Cycles of Power," in Vincent Davis, ed. *The Post-Imperial Presidency* (New Brunswick, NJ: Transaction, 1980).

Dowdle, Barney. "Perspective on the Sagebrush Rebellion." *Policy Studies Journal*, vol. 12 (March 1984), pp. 473–482.

Downs, Anthony. "Up and Down with Ecology—the Issue-Attention Cycle." *The Public Interest*, vol. 28 (Summer 1972), pp. 38–50.

Durant, Robert F. "Whither Bureaucratic Influence?: A Cautionary Note." *Journal of Public Administration Research and Theory*, vol. 1 (October 1991), pp. 461–476.

Durant, Robert F., and Paul F. Diehl. "Agendas, Alternatives, and Public Policy: Lessons from the U.S. Foreign Policy Arena." *Journal of Public Policy*, vol. 9, no. 2 (April/June 1989), pp. 179–205.

Durant, Robert F., Larry W. Thomas, Roger G. Brown, and E. Fletcher McClellan. "From Complacence to Compliance: Toward a Theory of Intragovernmental Regulation." *Administration & Society*, vol. 17 (February 1986), pp. 433–459.

Eldridge, Niles, and Stephen Jay Gould. "Punctuated Equilibria: An Alternative to Phyletic Gradualism," pp. 82–115 in T.J.M. Schopf, *Models in Paleobiology* (San Francisco, CA: Freeman, Cooper, 1972).

Elmore, Richard F. "Backward Mapping: Implementation Research and Policy Decisions," pp. 18–35 in Walter Williams, ed., *Studying Implementation: Methodological and Administrative Issues* (Chatham, NJ: Chatham House Publishers, 1982).

Elmore, Richard F. "Forward and Backward Mapping: Reversible Logic in the Analysis of Public Policy," pp. 33–70 in Kenneth Hanf and Theo. A. J. Toonen, eds. *Policy Implementation in Federal and Unitary Systems: Questions of Analysis and Design* (Dordrecht: Martinus Nijhoff, 1985).

Fairfax, Sally K. "Beyond the Sagebrush Rebellion: The BLM as Neighbor and Manager in the Western States," pp. 79–91 in John G. Francis and Richard Ganzel, eds. *Western Public Lands: The Management of*

Natural Resources in a Time of Declining Federalism (NJ: Rowman and Allanheld, 1984).

Francis, John G. "Environmental Values, Intergovernmental Politics, and the Sagebrush Rebellion," pp. 29–46 in John G. Francis and Richard Ganzel, eds. *Western Public Lands: The Management of Natural Resources in a Time of Declining Federalism* (NJ: Rowman and Allanheld, 1984).

Fritschler, A. Lee and M. Segal. "Intergovernmental Relations and Contemporary Political Science: Developing an Integrated Typology." *Publius*, vol. 1 (Winter 1972), pp. 95–122.

Gilmour, Jesse B. "The Rio Grande Compact," pp. 53–60 in New Mexico Water Resources Research Institute, *Water Law in the West* (Las Cruces: New Mexico State University, 1984).

Goggin, Malcolm L. "The 'Too Few Cases/Too Many Variables' Problem in Implementation Research." *The Western Political Quarterly*, vol. 59 (June 1986), pp. 328–347.

Goldenberg, Edie N. "The Permanent Government in an Era of Retrenchment and Redirection," pp. 381–404 in Lester M. Salamon and Michael S. Lund, eds. *The Reagan Presidency and the Governing of America* (Washington, DC: Urban Institute Press, 1984).

Golembiewski, Robert T. "Organizational Patterns of the Future: What They Mean to Personnel Administration," pp. 198–216 in Robert T. Golembiewski and Michael Cohen, eds. *People in Public Service* (Itasca, IL: F. E. Peacock, 1970).

Golembiewski, Robert T. "Public-Sector Organization: Why Theory and Practice Should Emphasize Purpose, and How to Do So?" pp. 433–474 in Ralph C. Chandler, ed. *A Centennial History of the American Administrative State* (New York: Free Press, 1987).

Grant, Douglas L. "Reasonable Groundwater Pumping Levels Under the Appropriation Doctrine: The Law and Underlying Economic Goals." *Natural Resources Journal*, vol. 21 (January 1982), pp. 1–36.

Greenstein, Fred. "Change and Continuity in the Modern Presidency," pp. 45–85 in Anthony King, ed. *The New American Political System* (Washington, DC: American Enterprise Institute, 1978).

Heclo, Hugh. "An Executive's Success Can Have Costs," pp. 371–374 in Lester M. Salamon and Michael S. Lund, eds. *The Reagan Presidency and the Governing of America.* (Washington, DC: Urban Institute Press, 1984).

Heclo, Hugh. "In Search of a Role: America's Higher Civil Service," pp. 8–34 in Ezra Suleiman, ed. *Bureaucrats and Policy Making* (New York: Holmes & Meier, 1984).

Heclo, Hugh. "Issue Networks and the Executive Establishment," pp. 87–124 in Anthony King, ed. *The New American Political System* (Washington, DC: American Enterprise Institute, 1978).

Heclo, Hugh. "OMB and the Presidency—The Problem of 'Neutral Competence'." *The Public Interest,* vol. 38 (Winter 1975), pp. 80–98.

Hedderson, John. "The Population of Texas Counties Along the Mexico Border." *Natural Resources Journal,* vol. 22 (October 1982), pp. 765–781.

Hedge, David M., and Donald C. Menzel. "Loosening the Regulatory Ratchet: A Grassroots View of Environmental Deregulation." *Policy Studies Journal,* vol. 13 (March 1985), pp. 599–606.

Held, R. Burnell. "Federal-State Relations in Public Land Administration." *Policy Studies Journal,* vol. 14 (December 1985), pp. 296–304.

Hetrick, Nancy E. "Recent Developments in the El Paso/New Mexico Interstate Groundwater Controversy—The Constitutionality of New Mexico's New Municipality Water Planning Statute." *Natural Resources Journal,* vol. 29 (Winter 1989), pp. 223–249.

Hjern, Benny. "Implementation Research—The Link Gone Missing." *Journal of Public Policy,* vol. 2 (August 1982), pp. 301–308.

Hjern, Benny, and David O. Porter. "Implementation Structures: A New Unit of Administrative Analysis." *Organization Studies,* vol. 2, no. 3 (1981), pp. 211–227.

Hogan, William. "Energy Policy," pp. 83–109 in Paul R. Portney, ed. *Natural Resources and the Environment* (Washington, DC: Urban Institute Press, 1984).

Horner, Constance. "Beyond Mr. Gradgrind: The Case for Deregulating the Public Sector." *Policy Review,* vol. 44 (Spring 1988), pp. 34–38.

Ingraham, Patricia W. "Building Bridges or Burning Them? The President, the Appointees, and the Bureaucracy." *Public Administration Review,* vol. 47 (September/October 1987), pp. 425–435.

Ingraham, Patricia W., and Carolyn Ban. "Politics and Merit: Can They Meet in a Public Service Model?" *Review of Public Personnel Administration,* vol. 8 (Spring 1988), pp. 7–19.

Ingram, Helen. "Water Rights in the Western States." *Academy of Political Science Proceedings,* vol. 34, no. 3 (1982) pp. 134–143.

Johnson, Corwin W. "Texas Groundwater Law: A Survey and Some Proposals." *Natural Resources Journal,* vol. 22 (October 1982), pp. 1017–1029.

Kamlet, Mark, and David Mowery. "The Budgetary Base in Federal Resource Allocation." *American Journal of Political Science,* vol. 25 (November 1980), pp. 461–472.

Kinder, Donald R., and D. Roderick Kiewiet. "Sociotropic Politics: The

American Case." *British Journal of Political Science,* vol. 11 (January 1981), pp. 129–161.

Kraft, Michael E., and Norman Vig. "Environmental Policy in the Reagan Presidency." *Political Science Quarterly,* vol. 99 (Fall 1984), pp. 415–439.

Kraft, Michael E., and Regina Axelrod. "Political Constraints on Development of Alternative Energy Sources: Lessons from the Reagan Administration." *Policy Studies Journal,* vol. 13 (December 1984), pp. 319–330.

Landau, Martin, and Russell Stout. "To Manage Is Not to Control: The Folly of Type II Errors." *Public Administration Review,* vol. 39 (March/April 1979), pp. 148–156.

LeLoup, Lance T. "Agency Policy Actions: Determinants of Non-Incremental Change," in Randall Ripley and Grace Franklin, eds. *Policy Making in the Federal Executive Branch* (Washington, DC: Free Press, 1975).

Leshy, John D. "Natural Resource Policy," pp. 13–46 in Paul R. Portney, ed. *Natural Resources and the Environment: The Reagan Approach* (Washington, DC: Urban Institute Press, 1984).

Light, Paul C. "The President's Agenda: Notes on the Timing of Domestic Choice." *Presidential Studies Quarterly,* vol. 11 (Winter 1981), pp. 67–82.

Lindblom, Charles E. "The Science of 'Muddling Through'." *Public Administration Review,* vol. 19 (1959), pp. 79–88.

Linder, Steven H., and B. Guy Peters. "A Design Perspective on Policy Implementation: The Failures of Misplaced Prescription." *Policy Studies Review,* vol. 6 (February 1987), pp. 459–475.

Linsley, Clyde. "Politics and the Civil Service." *Government Executive,* November/December 1987, pp. 48–54.

Lovell, Catherine. "Where We Are in Intergovernmental Relations and Some of the Implications." *Southern Review of Public Administration,* vol. 3 (June 1979), pp. 6–20.

Lowi, Theodore. "American Business, Public Policy, Case Studies, and Political Theory." *World Politics,* vol. 16 (1964), pp. 675–715.

Lynn, Laurence E., Jr. "The Manager's Role in Public Management." *The Bureaucrat,* vol. 13 (Winter 1984–85), pp. 20–25.

Lynn, Laurence E., Jr. "The Reagan Administration and the Renitent Bureaucracy," pp. 339–370 in Lester M. Salamon and Michael S. Lund, eds. *The Reagan Presidency and the Governing of America* (Washington, DC: Urban Institute Press, 1984).

Majone, Giandomenico, and Aaron Wildavsky. "Implementation as Evolution," pp. 163–180 in Jeffrey Pressman and Aaron Wildavsky, eds.

Implementation, 3rd ed. (Berkeley and Los Angeles: University of California Press, 1984).

March, James, and Johan P. Olsen. "Organizing Political Life: What Administrative Reorganization Tells Us About Government." *American Political Science Review,* vol. 77 (1983), pp. 282–296.

Maynard-Moody, Steven, Donald D. Stull, and Jerry Mitchell. "Reorganization as Status Drama: Building, Maintaining, and Displacing Dominant Subcultures." *Public Administration Review,* vol. 46 (July/August 1986), pp. 301–302.

McCubbins, Matthew, and Thomas Schwartz. "Congressional Oversight Overlooked: Police Patrols vs. Fire Alarms." *American Journal of Political Science,* vol. 29 (February 1984), pp. 165–179.

McCurdy, Howard E. "Public Ownership of Land and the 'Sagebrush Rebellion'." *Policy Studies Journal,* vol. 12 (March 1984), pp. 483–490.

Meindl, James R., Sanford B. Ehrlich, and Janet M. Dukerich. "The Romance of Leadership." *Administrative Science Quarterly,* vol. 30 (1985), pp. 78–102.

Menzel, Donald C. "Redirecting the Implementation of a Law: The Reagan Administration and Coal Surface Mining." *Public Administration Review,* vol. 43 (May/June 1983), pp. 411–420.

Miller, Richard O. "FLPMA: A Decade of Management Under the BLM Organic Act." *Policy Studies Journal,* vol. 14 (December 1985), pp. 265–273.

Moe, Terry M. "The Politicized Presidency," pp. 235–272 in John E. Chubb and Paul K. Peterson, eds. *The New Direction in American Politics* (Washington, D.C.: The Brookings Institution, 1985).

Moe, Terry M. "The Politics of Bureaucratic Structure," pp. 267–329 in John E. Chubb and Paul E. Peterson, eds. *Can the Government Govern?* (Washington, DC: Brookings Institution, 1989).

Mosher, Frederick C. "Denigration of the Public Servant," pp. 405–409 in Lester M. Salamon and Michael S. Lund, eds. *The Reagan Presidency and the Governing of America* (Washington, DC: Urban Institute Press, 1984).

Murray, Rika. "Allocation of Groundwater After *Sporhase v. Nebraska:* A Proposal for Combined Federal-State Regulation." *Albany Law Review,* vol. 48 (1984), pp. 494–520.

Nathan, Richard P. "The Administrative Presidency." *The Public Interest,* vol. 44 (Summer 1976), pp. 40–50.

Nelson, Robert H. "A Long Term Strategy for the Public Lands," in *Resource Conflicts in the West* (Reno: Nevada Public Affairs Institute, University of Nevada, 1983).

Nelson, Robert H. "Economic Analysis in Public Rangeland Management," pp. 47–78 in John G. Francis and Richard Ganzel, eds. *Western Public Lands: The Management of Natural Resources in a Time of Declining Federalism* (Totowa, NJ: Rowman and Allanheld, 1984).

Nelson, Robert H. "*NRDC v. Morton:* The Role of Judicial Policy Making in Public Rangeland Management." *Policy Studies Journal,* vol. 14 (December 1985), pp. 255–264.

Newland, Chester A. "A Mid-Term Appraisal—The Reagan Presidency: Limited Government and Political Administration." *Public Administration Review,* vol. 43 (January/February 1983), pp. 1–21.

Newland, Chester A. "Public Executives: Imperium, Sacerdotium, Collegium? Bicentennial Leadership Challenges." *Public Administration Review,* vol. 47 (January/February 1987), 45–56.

New Mexico Governor's Water Law Study Committee. "The Impact of Recent Court Decisions Concerning Water and Interstate Commerce on Water Resources in the State of New Mexico." *Natural Resources Journal,* vol. 24 (July 1984), pp. 689–744.

"New Mexico Water Law: An Overview and Discussion of Current Issues." *Natural Resources Journal,* vol. 22 (October 1982), pp. 1045–1062.

New Mexico Water Resources Research Institute. *Water Law in the West: Proceedings of the 29th Annual New Mexico Water Conference* (Las Cruces: New Mexico State University, 1984).

O'Toole, Laurence J., Jr., and Robert S. Montjoy. "Interorganizational Policy Implementation: A Theoretical Perspective." *Public Administration Review,* vol. 44 (November/December 1984), pp. 491–503.

Ouchi, William G. "Markets, Bureaucracies, and Clans." *Administrative Science Quarterly,* vol. 25 (March 1980), pp. 129–140.

Pfiffner, James P. "Political Appointees and Career Executives: The Democracy-Bureaucracy Nexus in the Third Century." *Public Administration Review,* vol. 47 (January/February 1987), pp. 57–65.

Pfiffner, James P. "Political Public Administration." *Public Administration Review,* vol. 45 (March/April 1985), pp. 352–356.

Portney, Paul R. "Natural Resources and the Environment: More Controversy Than Change," pp. 141–175 in John L. Palmer and Isabel V. Sawhill, eds. *The Reagan Record: An Assessment of America's Changing Domestic Priorities* (Cambridge, MA: Ballinger, 1984).

Rainey, Glenn W. "Implementation and Managerial Creativity," pp. 89–105 in Dennis J. Palumbo and Donald J. Calista, eds. *Implementation and the Policy Process* (New York: Greenwood Press, 1990).

Regens, James L., and Robert W. Rycroft. "Funding for Environmental Protection: Comparing Congressional and Executive Influences." *The Social Science Journal,* vol. 26, no. 2 (1989), pp. 289–301.

Rockman, Bert. "Conclusions: An Imprint But Not a Revolution," pp. 191–206 in B.B. Kymlicka and Jean V. Matthews, eds. *The Reagan Revolution* (Chicago: Dorsey, 1988).

Rodgers, Ann Berkely. "The Limits of State Activity in the Interstate Water Market." *Land and Water Law Review,* vol. 21 (1986), pp. 357–380.

Rosenbloom, David. "Public Administrative Theory and the Separation of Powers." *Public Administration Review,* vol. 43 (May/June 1983), pp. 219–227.

Rourke, Francis E. "American Bureaucracy in a Changing Political Setting." *Journal of Public Administration Research and Theory,* vol. 1, no. 2 (1991), pp. 111–129.

Rourke, Francis E. "Executive Responsiveness to Presidential Policies: The Reagan Presidency." *Congress and the Presidency,* vol. 17 (Spring 1990), pp. 1–11.

Rourke, Francis E., and Paul R. Schulman. "Adhocracy in Policy Development." *The Social Science Journal,* vol. 26 (1989), pp. 131–142.

Sabatier, Paul. "Top-Down and Bottom-Up Approaches to Implementation Research." *Journal of Public Policy,* vol. 6 (1987), pp. 21–48.

Sabatier, Paul, and Neal Pelkey. "Incorporating Multiple Actors and Guidance Instruments into Models of Regulatory Policymaking: An Advocacy Coalition Framework." *Administration & Society,* vol. 19 (1987), pp. 236–263.

Sanera, Michael. "Implementing the Mandate," pp. 457–545 in Stuart M. Butler, Michael Sanera, and W. Bruce Weinrod, eds. *Mandate for Leadership II: Continuing the Fight* (Washington, DC: Heritage Foundation, 1984).

Sarat, Austin, and Joel B. Grossman. "Courts and Conflict Resolution: Problems in Mobilization of Adjudication." *American Political Science Review,* vol. 69 (1975), pp. 1200–1217.

Scher, Seymour. "Conditions for Legislative Control." *Journal of Politics,* vol. 28 (1963), pp. 526–551.

Scholz, John T. and Feng Heng Wei. "Regulatory Enforcement in a Federal System." *American Political Science Review,* vol. 80 (December 1986), pp. 1249–1270.

Schulman, Paul R. "The Politics of 'Ideational Policy'." *Journal of Politics,* vol. 38 (1988), pp. 1014–1023.

Stewart, Joseph, Jr., and Jane S. Cromartie. "Partisan Presidential Change and Regulatory Policy: The Case of the FTC and Deceptive Practices Enforcement." *Presidential Studies Quarterly,* vol. 12 (Fall 1982), pp. 568–573.

Stewart, Richard B. "The Reformation of American Administrative Law." *Harvard Law Review,* vol. 88 (1975), pp. 1667–1813.

Sundquist, James L. "Jimmy Carter as Public Administrator: An Appraisal at Midterm." *Public Administration Review,* vol. 39 (January/February 1979), pp. 3–11.

Thompson, Frank J., and Michael J. Scicchitano. "State Enforcement of Federal Regulatory Policy: The Lessons of OSHA." *Policy Studies Journal,* vol. 13 (March 1985), pp. 591–598.

Utton, Albert E. "An Assessment of the Management of U.S.–Mexican Water Resources." *Natural Resources Journal,* vol. 22 (October 1982), esp. pp. 1095–1096.

Wald, Patricia. "The Realpolitik of Judicial Review in a Deregulation Era." *Journal of Policy Analysis and Management,* vol. 5 (1986), pp. 535–546.

Wanat, John. "The Bases of Budgetary Incrementalism." *American Political Science Review,* vol. 68 (September 1974), pp. 1221–1228.

Watt, James G., Interior Secretary, Remarks Before the National Public Lands Council, Reno, NV, September 21, 1982.

"Watt's Clashes with Congress Stall Programs." *Congressional Quarterly Weekly Reports,* July 11, 1981, pp. 1256–1258.

Wildavsky, Aaron. "Forward: The Human Side of Government," pp. xiii–xviii in Robert Rector and Michael Sanera, eds. *Steering the Elephant: How Washington Works* (New York: Universe Books, 1987).

Williams, Stephen F. "The Requirement of Beneficial Use as a Cause of Waste in Water Resource Development." *Natural Resources Journal,* vol. 23 (January 1983), pp. 7–23.

Wilson, James Q., and Patricia Rachal. "Can Government Regulate Itself?" *The Public Interest,* vol. 46 (March 1977), pp. 3–14.

Wilson, Woodrow. "The New Meaning of Government," reprinted in *Public Administration Review,* vol. 44 (May/June 1984), pp. 193–195.

Wilson, Woodrow. "The Study of Administration," pp. 20–30 in Dean L. Yarwood, ed. *Public Administration: Politics and People* (New York: Longman, 1987).

Wood, B. Dan. "Principal-Agent Models of Political Control of Bureaucracy." *American Political Science Review,* vol. 83 (September 1989), pp. 965–988.

Wood, B. Dan. Response to Brian J. Cook in "Principals, Bureaucrats, and Responsiveness in Clean Air Enforcements." *American Political Science Review,* vol. 82 (1988), pp. 213–234.

Wyszomirski, Margaret Jane. "The De-Institutionalization of Presidential Staff Agencies." *Public Administration Review,* vol. 42 (September/October 1982), pp. 448–458.

NEWSPAPER/MAGAZINE ARTICLES

"Alternative on Industrial Park Offered." *Las Cruces Sun-News*, October 20, 1981.

"Anaya Vows to Appeal Ruling on Water Law." *Albuquerque Journal*, January 22, 1983.

"'Another Tool' Introduced for Land Grant Tract Buy." *Las Cruces Sun-News*, January 28, 1982.

"Bisti Dropped as Potential Wilderness Area." *Albuquerque Journal*, December 28, 1982.

"BLM, Ranchers Discuss Report." *Albuquerque Journal*, September 26, 1980.

Burnson, Robert. "Stahmann Is Hoping for Water Settlement." *Las Cruces Sun-News*, July 12, 1986.

"Carter Analysis Gets Praise from Schmitt and Domenici." *Las Cruces Sun-News*, November 9, 1977.

"Cattle Ranchers Battle BLM for Control of Grazing Land." *Albuquerque Journal*, October 12, 1982.

"City May Give Wittern More Time." *Las Cruces Sun-News*, October 27, 1981.

"City in Quandary Over BLM's Deal." *Las Cruces Sun-News*, June 19, 1981.

"City Seeks Withdrawal of Park Site." *Las Cruces Sun-News*, February 23, 1982.

Cronin, Thomas. "Superman—Our Textbook President." *The Washington Monthly*, October 1970, pp. 47–54.

"Differences Hold Up Passage of San Juan Wilderness Bill." *Albuquerque Journal*, October 4, 1984.

"Domenici Asks Change in Coal Lease Policy." *Albuquerque Journal*, January 10, 1980.

Egan, Timothy. "Forest Service Abusing Role, Dissidents Say." *New York Times*, March 4, 1990.

"Failure to OK Appraisal Snags Land Acquisition." *Albuquerque Journal*, March 20, 1980.

"Foes Clash at Hearing on Land Use." *Albuquerque Journal*, August 26, 1979.

Frederick, Don. "Briefs: Water Suit Faulty." *El Paso Times*, April 9, 1982.

Frederick, Don. "EP Official: NM Water Is Not Vital." *El Paso Times*, December 30, 1981.

Frederick, Don. "NM, El Paso Outline Views on Water Suit." *El Paso Times*, December 30, 1981.

Harbert, Nancy. "Cruces Official Unveils East Mesa Plans." *Albuquerque Journal*, November 14, 1981.

Harbert, Nancy. "Navajos Want to Stay on Coal Land." *Albuquerque Journal,* November 9, 1983.

Harbert, Nancy. "NM Cattle Growers Support Proposed BLM Cuts." *Albuquerque Journal,* March 29, 1983.

Harbert, Nancy. "U.S. Out of Cruces Land Swap." *Albuquerque Journal,* January 29, 1982.

Hester, Nolan. "Wilderness Sites May Be Cut." *Albuquerque Journal,* October 26, 1982.

"Industrial Park Developer Wants Federal Activity." *El Paso Times,* October 16, 1981.

"Industrial Park Prospects Bleak." *Las Cruces Sun-News,* July 7, 1981.

"Irrigation District Wants AG Off Case." *Las Cruces Sun-News,* July 10, 1986.

"Judge: NM Can Limit Water Export." *El Paso Times,* August 4, 1984.

Kalt, Joe, and Peter Navarro. "Administration Backsliding on Energy Policy." *Wall Street Journal,* February 9, 1982.

Katel, Peter. "Interior Dept. Accused of Indian Policy Shifts." *Albuquerque Journal,* March 12, 1982.

Katel, Peter. "New Navajo Chairman Promises to Share Power." *Albuquerque Journal,* December 19, 1982.

"Klaus Wittern Is Still in Business." *Las Cruces Sun-News,* February 21, 1982.

"Land Swap Deal Reached, Lujan Says." *Albuquerque Journal,* December 5, 1981.

Leach, Leah. "State Stockmen Given Warning on Water Suit." *Albuquerque Journal,* July 30, 1981.

"Lujan Against Plan Doubling Acreage for Navajo Relocation." *Albuquerque Journal,* January 24, 1984.

"Lujan Calls Governors' Reaction to Water Plan Encouraging." *Albuquerque Journal,* May 31, 1982.

"Lujan, Schmitt Tell Rusk to Work Out Land-Deal Problem." *Albuquerque Journal,* March 7, 1981.

Nathanson, Rick. "City Group Says Tax Boost Could Finance Land Deal." *Albuquerque Journal,* February 8, 1982.

Nauman, Talli. "Navajos Sue for Coal-Rich Ranchland." *Albuquerque Journal,* November 23, 1983.

Nauman, Talli. "2 Million Acres Claimed in Suit Filed by Navajos." *Albuquerque Journal,* October 7, 1982.

Nauman, Talli. "U.S. Cancels Session on San Juan Coal." *Albuquerque Journal,* March 6, 1984.

"New Mexico Delegates Disappointed in Carter." *Albuquerque Journal,* April 21, 1977.

"New Mexico Fights El Paso Challenge to New Water Law." *Albuquerque Journal*, May 15, 1983.

"New Mexico Hunts Ways to Plug Drain." *El Paso Times*, January 20, 1983.

"New Mexico Water is Not Negotiable," editorial. *Las Cruces Sun-News*, December 13, 1981.

"Oil Leasing Halt Called 'Ridiculous'." *Albuquerque Journal*, March 2, 1980.

Ortolon, Ken. "Texas, New Mexico Battle over Control of Groundwater." *El Paso Herald Post*, December 16, 1983.

Peirce, Neal. "Is Sagebrush Rebellion a Misstep—In the Right Direction." *Albuquerque Journal*, February 22, 1981.

Price, Tom. "Pentagon Wants Leeway to Manage." *Atlanta Journal-Constitution*, April 6, 1990.

"Ranchers Oppose Land Upkeep Plan." *Las Cruces Sun-News*, December 8, 1981.

"Reagan Administration Backs Swap Involving Elena Gallegos Grant." *Albuquerque Journal*, May 28, 1983.

"Reagan Administration Told It Must Act on Indian Claims." *Albuquerque Journal*, December 23, 1982.

"Reagan Signs Four Corners Wilderness Bill." *Albuquerque Journal*, October 31, 1984.

Regnell, John B. "United States Department of the Interior Endeavors to Accommodate to the New Western Water Policy Agenda." *SNREA News*, vol. 2, Summer 1987.

Safire, William. "On Language." *New York Times Magazine*, March 19, 1989, p. 3.

"'Sagebrush Rebellion' Grows Against BLM Controls." *Albuquerque Journal*, June 4, 1979.

"Sagebrush Rebellion May Have Lost Momentum." *Las Cruces Sun-News*, May 6, 1982.

"Schmitt Prepares Bill to Save Water." *Las Cruces Sun-News*, December 7, 1981.

"Secretary Avoids Backing NM in Water Suit." *El Paso Sun-Times*, November 3, 1981.

"Stahmann Debunks Myths of El Paso Water Suit." *Las Cruces Sun-News*, June 26, 1984.

"State Senate Boosts Bill to Limit Water Export." *Albuquerque Journal*, February 18, 1983.

Tessneer, Marvin. "Plan Would Deplete Water, Expert Says." *Las Cruces Sun-News*, January 14, 1982.

Tessneer, Marvin. "Schmitt Assures City." *Las Cruces Sun-News,* June 21, 1981.

Tessneer, Marvin. "Water Arguments Challenged." *Las Cruces Sun-News,* March 3, 1982.

Tessneer, Marvin. "Water Ruling Is Conditional." *Las Cruces Sun-News,* July 12, 1982.

"U.S. to Prepare New Study on Impact of Coal Leasing." *Albuquerque Journal,* August 31, 1984.

"Utah BLM Manager Fights Sagebrush Rebellion." *Albuquerque Journal,* December 25, 1979.

Vigil, Gregory J. "City Seeks Withdrawal of Park Site." *Las Cruces Sun-News,* February 23, 1982.

Walton, Marcus. "Land Swap to Proceed as Planned." *Las Cruces Sun-News,* March 2, 1982.

Warchol, Glen. "City in Quandary Over BLM's Deal." *Las Cruces Sun-News,* June 19, 1981.

Warchol, Glen. "City Seeks to Save Land." *Las Cruces Sun-News,* July 6, 1981.

Warchol, Glen. "Industrial Park Hopes Up." *Las Cruces Sun-News,* July 8, 1981.

Ward, Eugene. "Energy Conservation Steps Could Cost Jobs, Up Taxes." *Albuquerque Journal,* September 20, 1977.

"Watt Heads Off Indian Tribe–PNM Dispute Possibility." *Albuquerque Journal,* March 6, 1982.

Whelan, Nancy. "Suspending the Rules and Improving Business." *Government Executive,* April 1987, pp. 18–19.

Wieck, Paul R. "Bisti Wilderness Plan Gets Mixed Reception." *Albuquerque Journal,* May 18, 1983.

Wieck, Paul R. "Lujan Agrees to Support Larger Bisti Wilderness." *Albuquerque Journal,* October 22, 1983.

Wieck, Paul R. "Navajos Claim Right to Steer Strip Mining." *Albuquerque Journal,* March 20, 1984.

Wieck, Paul R. "New Mexico Projects May Be Cut." *Albuquerque Journal,* March 11, 1981.

Wieck, Paul R. "Reagan Budget Would Slash BIA Funds." *Albuquerque Journal,* February 3, 1982.

Wieck, Paul R. "Richardson Backs Lujan's San Juan Wilderness Compromise." *Albuquerque Journal,* April 24, 1984.

Wieck, Paul R. "Richardson Backs Off Extended Limit for Navajo Land Search." *Albuquerque Journal,* March 2, 1984.

Wieck, Paul R. "Richardson Defends Navajo Land Proposal." *Albuquerque Journal,* January 27, 1984.

Wieck, Paul R. "San Juan Plan Displeases Domenici." *Albuquerque Journal,* January 26, 1984.
"Wittern's Choice." *El Paso Times,* August 23, 1981.
Wormley, Mary. "Carruthers Says Nation Must Intensify Water Management." *Las Cruces Sun-News,* May 8, 1981.
Zumbo, Jim. "The Sagebrush Rebellion." *The Country Gentleman,* Summer 1981, pp. 52–54, 61–63.

GOVERNMENT DOCUMENTS

BLM, *BLM Role Clarification Study.* Washington, DC: U.S. Department of the Interior, May 9, 1986.
BLM, *District Office/Resource Area Organization Study.* Washington, DC: Deputy Director for Services, Division of Management Research, Bureau of Land Management, 1981.
BLM, *Final San Juan Basin Cumulative Overview and Comment Letters.* Santa Fe, NM: Bureau of Land Management, September 1983.
BLM, *Final State Office Organization Study.* Washington, DC: Deputy Director for Services, Division of Management Research, Bureau of Land Management, October 2, 1981.
BLM, *Proceedings in the Matter of the Federal Coal Management Program Draft EIS Supplement.* Albuquerque, NM: Blasing & Townsend, Inc., March 20, 1985.
BLM/Forest Service Interchange: National Summary and Legislative Proposal. Washington, DC: U.S. Forest Service and Bureau of Land Management, February 1986.
Bureau of Land Management, *Public Land Statistics.* Washington, DC: U.S. Government Printing Office, FY 1976 through 1986, 1988 editions.
Comment Summary: San Juan River Regional Coal DEIS. Washington, DC: Bureau of Land Management, April 1983.
Draft Environmental Impact Statement: Public Service Company of New Mexico's Proposed New Mexico Generating Station and Possible New Town. Washington, DC: Bureau of Land Management, November 1982.
Draft San Juan Basin Cumulative Overview. Washington, DC: Bureau of Land Management, November 1982.
"Elena Gallegos Grant Exchange, General Cost Analysis," U.S. Forest Service. Data provided by Robert Armstrong, Southwest Region, U.S. Forest Service, Albuquerque, NM, October 1986.
Federal Coal Management Report: FY 1984. Washington, DC: U.S. Department of the Interior, 1984.

Final San Juan River Regional Coal Environmental Impact Statement. Washington, DC: Bureau of Land Management, 1984.

GAO, *Analysis of the Powder River Basin Federal Coal Lease Sale: Economic Valuation Improvements and Legislative Changes Needed.* Washington, DC: U.S. Government Printing Office, May 1983.

Hearings, U.S. House of Representatives, Committee on Appropriations, Subcommittee on the Department of Interior and Related Agencies, *Department of Interior and Related Agencies Appropriations for 1982,* 97th Cong., 1st sess., part 9.

"Instruction Memorandum No. 81–296, BLM Director to All Washington and Field Officials." Washington, DC, September 22, 1981.

"Land Purchase Agreement," signed by David M. Steinborn, Mayor, City of Las Cruces, and Frank A. Kleinhenz, Chief Administrative Officer, City of Albuquerque, December 7, 1982.

Linowes, David, *Report of the Commission on Fair Market Value Policy for Federal Coal Leasing.* Washington, DC: U.S. Government Printing Office, February 1984.

Linowes, David. *Report of the Commission on Fiscal Accountability of the Nation's Energy Resources.* Washington, DC: U.S. Government Printing Office, January 1982.

"Memorandum of Understanding Between the Governor of New Mexico and the New Mexico State Director, Bureau of Land Management, U.S. Department of the Interior," July 30, 1980.

Middaugh, Geoff, *Issue Paper: Increasing Management Flexibility with the Existing FMS and Budget System,* Santa Fe, NM, May 15, 1986.

Minutes, Chiuilla Pipeline Meeting, Cuba, NM, March 7, 1983.

Minutes of the December 13, 1983, Regional Coal Team Meeting, BLM, Santa Fe, NM, January 25, 1984.

Minutes, District Advisory Council Meeting, BLM District Office, Albuquerque, NM, July 26, 1983.

Minutes, Las Cruces District Grazing Advisory Board, Las Cruces, NM, January 14, 1982.

Minutes, Las Cruces District Grazing Advisory Board, Las Cruces, NM, April 8, 1982.

Minutes, Pan Am Pipeline Meeting, Cuba, NM, March 11, 1983.

Minutes, Piedra Lumbre Pipeline Meeting, March 10, 1983.

Navajo and Hopi Indian Relocation Commission, *Interim Progress Report.* Flagstaff, AZ: U.S. Government Printing Office, December 7, 1978.

Navajo and Hopi Indian Relocation Commission, *Report and Plan.* Flagstaff, AZ: U.S. Government Printing Office, April 1981.

The President's Committee on Administrative Management, *Report of the President's Committee on Administrative Management.* Washington, DC: U.S. Government Printing Office, 1937.

Range Improvement Task Force, "Ranch Improvement Maintenance and Depreciation Costs: Northwestern New Mexico, 1978 and 1982," Las Cruces: New Mexico State University, November 16, 1982.

Secretarial Issue Document, 1979: Federal Coal Management Program. Washington, DC: U.S. Government Printing Office, 1979.

Secretarial Issue Document, 1986: Federal Coal Management Program. Washington, DC: U.S. Government Printing Office, 1986.

Special Analyses: Budget of the United States Government, FY 1985. Washington, DC: U.S. Government Printing Office, 1984.

"Statement of Robert F. Burford, Director, Bureau of Land Management," U.S. House of Representatives, Committee on Public Works and Transportation, Subcommittee on Surface Transportation, *Regarding H.R. 1010 and Related Coal Slurry Pipeline Legislation,* 97th Congress, 2nd Sess., September 15, 1982.

"Statement of Robert F. Burford, Director, Bureau of Land Management," U.S. Senate Committee on Energy and Natural Resources, *Workshop on Public Land Acquisition and Alternatives,* 97th Cong., 1st Sess., Washington, DC: U.S. Government Printing Office, 1981, pp. 48–49.

"Statement of Carol E. Dinkins, Assistant Attorney General, Land and Natural Resources Division," U.S. House of Representatives, Committee on Public Works and Transportation, Subcommittee on Surface Transportation, *Regarding H.R. 1010 and Related Coal Slurry Pipeline Legislation,* 97th Congress, 2nd Sess., September 15, 1982.

"Statement of Carol Dinkins," U.S. Senate Committee on Energy and Natural Resources, *Coal Distribution and Utilization Act of 1983,* 98th Congress, 1st Sess., March 14, 1983.

"Testimony of Thomas G. Bahr, Director, Office of Water Policy, U.S. Department of the Interior," U.S. Senate Committee on Environment and Public Works, Subcommittee on Water Resources, *The Impact of the Supreme Court Decision in Sporhase Versus Nebraska,* 97th Cong., 2nd Sess., September 15, 1982, pp. 12–20.

"Testimony of Paul L. Bloom, Attorney at Law," U.S. House of Representatives, Committee on Public Works and Transportation, Subcommittee on Surface Transportation, April 19, 1983, pp. 487–494 in U.S. House of Representatives, Committee on Public Works and Transportation, Subcommittee on Surface Transportation, *Hearings on the Coal Pipeline Act of 1983,* 98th Congress, 1st Sess., April 13 and 19, 1983.

U.S. Advisory Commission on Intergovernmental Relations, *Regulatory Federalism: Policy, Process, Impact, and Reform.* Washington, DC: ACIR, 1984.

U.S. House of Representatives, Committee on Public Works and Transportation, Subcommittee on Surface Transportation, *The Coal Pipeline Act of 1983,* 98th Congress, 1st Sess., April 13 and 19, 1983.

U.S. House of Representatives, *Subcommittee on the Department of the Interior and Related Agencies Appropriations for 1982.* Washington, DC: U.S. Government Printing Office, 1981.

U.S. House of Representatives, *Subcommittee on the Department of the Interior and Related Agencies Appropriations for 1985.* Washington, DC: U.S. Government Printing Office, 1984.

U.S. Senate Committee on Energy and Natural Resources, *Workshop on Public Land Acquisition and Alternatives,* 97th Cong., 1st Sess., Washington, DC: U.S. Government Printing Office, 1981.

COURT CASES

The City of El Paso v. S. E. Reynolds, Memorandum Opinion, U.S. District Court for the District of New Mexico, January 17, 1983.

Healing v. Jones, 210 F. Supp. 125 (1963).

Natural Resources Defense Council v. Berglund, 458 F. Supp. 925 [D.D.C.] (1978).

Natural Resources Defense Council v. Burford, D.D.C. Civil No. 82-2763.

Natural Resources Defense Council v. Hughes, 437 F. Supp. 981 [D.C.C.] (1977).

Natural Resources Defense Council v. Morton, 388 F. Supp. 840, 841 (1974).

Natural Resources Defense Council v. Andrus, 448 F. Supp. 802 (1978).

S. E. Reynolds, et al. v. The City of El Paso, et al., 10th Circuit Court of Appeals, April 21, 1983.

Sporhase v. Nebraska, ex rel. Douglas, 102 S. Ct. at 3456 (1982).

United States v. New Mexico, 438 U.S. 696 (1978).

Valdez et al. v. Applegate, 616 Fed. Rep. 570 (1978).

Valdez et al. v. Applegate, 616 F. 2d. 570 (1980).

CORRESPONDENCE

Letter from Patrick H. Beckett, Chairman, New Mexico Cultural Properties Review Committee, to Curtis F. Schaafsma, New Mexico State Archaeologist, December 1, 1982.

Letter from Dean Bibles, Assistant Director, BLM, to Congressman Harold Runnels, August 5, 1980.

Letter from Joe Camunez, Mayor, City of Las Cruces, to U.S. Senator Harrison Schmitt, June 4, 1981.

Letter from Las Cruces City Commission to M.J. Hassell, Regional Forester, U.S. Forest Service, February 18, 1982.

Letter from Richard G. Elkins, President, Albuquerque Academy Board of Trustees, to Joe Camunez, Mayor, City of Las Cruces, February 12, 1982.

Letter from Gene Elliott, President, Las Cruces Chamber of Commerce, to U.S. Senator Harrison Schmitt, April 20, 1981.

Letter from Ed Garland, Property Manager, City of Las Cruces, to U.S. Senator Harrison Schmitt, October 2, 1980.

Letter from M.J. Hassell, Regional Forester, U.S. Forest Service, to Ed Garland, Property Manager, City of Las Cruces, June 16, 1981.

Letter from Donald P. Hodel, Undersecretary, Department of the Interior, to U.S. Senator Harrison Schmitt, May 1, 1981.

Letter from Bill J. Howard, Chief, Airports District Office, Federal Aviation Administration, to Ed Garland, Airport Manager, City of Las Cruces, June 12, 1981.

Letter and Comments from Daniel Kirshner, Economic Analyst, Environmental Defense Fund, to State Director, New Mexico State Office, BLM, April 7, 1983.

Letter to Files, Charles W. Luscher, State Director, New Mexico State Office, BLM, October 25, 1983.

Letter from Larry L. Morgan, Administrator, Second District, Office of Congressman Harold Runnels, to Richard P. Schroats, Chairman, Airport Advisory Board, City of Las Cruces, August 14, 1980.

Letter from Daniel C. B. Rathbun, Las Cruces District Manager, BLM, to Ed Garland, Property Manager, City of Las Cruces, December 15, 1980.

Letter from Steve E. Reynolds, New Mexico State Engineer, to Charles W. Luscher, State Director, New Mexico State Office, BLM, April 19, 1982.

Letter from Steve E. Reynolds, New Mexico State Engineer, to Charles W. Luscher, State Director, New Mexico State Office, BLM, September 21, 1983.

Letter from Steve E. Reynolds, New Mexico State Engineer, to William P. Stephens, New Mexico Secretary of Agriculture, July 5, 1983.

Letter from Jerry G. Schickedanz, Rangeland Improvement Task Force Coordinator, Cooperative Extension Service, New Mexico State University, to William Lusher, Director, New Mexico State Office, BLM, November 16, 1982.

Letter from U.S. Senator Harrison Schmitt, to Donald P. Hodel, Undersecretary, U.S. Department of the Interior, May 22, 1981.

Letter from William P. Stephens, New Mexico Secretary of Agriculture, to Charles W. Luscher, State Director, New Mexico State Office, BLM, August 10, 1983.

Letter from William P. Stephens, Secretary, New Mexico Department of Agriculture, to Steve E. Reynolds, New Mexico State Engineer, June 24, 1983.

Letter from Larry L. Woodward, Acting State BLM Director, to Governor Bruce King, November 14, 1979.

"Resolution and Survey," attached to Letter from Manuel F. Martinez, Secretary/Treasurer, Rio Puerco Livestock Association, to Herrick E. (Rick) Hanks, Manager, Rio Puerco Resource Area, BLM, July 30, 1983.

MEMORANDA

Memorandum from Area Manager, Rio Puerco, to Albuquerque District Manager, "Interim Rangeland Improvement Policy and the Rio Puerco Resource Area," February 29, 1982.

Memorandum from Tom Baca, Las Cruces District Office Manager, to U.S. Senator Harrison Schmitt and his staff, "Meeting of July 7 on the Las Cruces Airport Industrial Park Issue," July 9, 1981.

Memorandum from District Manager, Albuquerque, New Mexico, to State Director, "Deputy Assistant Secretary's Request for Information on the Rio Puerco Pipeline Systems Maintenance Proposal," October 26, 1982.

Memorandum from Don Brewer, BLM, to Planning Files, "Meeting with New Mexico Game and Fish," November 29, 1983.

Memorandum from Ed Garland, Property Manager, City of Las Cruces, to J.W. Harrison, City Manager, City of Las Cruces, "Las Cruces Crawford Industrial Park Proposed Site," June 16, 1981.

Memorandum from J.W. Harrison, City Manager, Las Cruces, NM, to Las Cruces City Commission, "A Meeting Regarding Lands for the Proposed Industrial Park," August 17, 1981.

Memorandum from Bob Reed, Chief, Division of Operations, to Rick Hanks, Rio Puerco Resource Area Manager, "Response to the Proposed Policies Regarding Maintenance of Range Improvements and the Redistribution of RB (8100) Funds," February 25, 1982.

Memorandum from Robbie Smith, BLM Range Conservationist, to District Manager, Through Dave Koehler, Acting Area Manager, "Pipeline Maintenance Meeting with Core Allottees," July 1, 1983.

INTERVIEWS

Armstrong, Robert. U.S. Forest Service, Albuquerque, New Mexico. Telephone Interview, July 1, 1986.

Baca, Thomas. Former Las Cruces District Office Manager for U.S. Senator Harrison Schmitt and Director of Real Property and Development, City of Las Cruces. Interviews in Las Cruces, New Mexico, July 5 and 30, 1985.

Bahr, Tom. New Mexico Water Resources Research Institute, New Mexico State University. Interview in Las Cruces, New Mexico, January 23, 1986.

Berry, Dan. Cattle Rancher and New Mexico State Legislator. Interview conducted by Wes Brownfield, June 10, 1982.

Boudenchuck, Mike. New Mexico Department of Agriculture, New Mexico State University. Interview in Las Cruces, New Mexico, March 17 and April 13, 1982.

Calkins, Robert. Associate Director, BLM Las Cruces District Office. Interview in Las Cruces, New Mexico, August 5, 1982.

Carruthers, Garrey. Former Assistant Secretary for Land and Water Resources, Department of the Interior. Interview in Las Cruces, New Mexico, July 30, 1985.

Chavez, Michelle. Branch of Personnel Management, BLM State Office. Interview in Santa Fe, New Mexico, June 18, 1986.

Chavez, Robert. Branch of Personnel Management, BLM, New Mexico State Office. Interview in Sante Fe, New Mexico, June 18, 1986.

Ciddio, Wayne, Albuquerque Chamber of Commerce. Interview in Albuquerque, New Mexico, June 17, 1986.

Clark, Ira. Emeritus Professor, New Mexico State University. Interview conducted by Michelle Deany in Las Cruces, New Mexico, March 12, 1982.

DuBois, Frank. New Mexico Department of Agriculture. Interview in Las Cruces, New Mexico, January 23, 1986.

Edwards, Punky. Public Affairs Specialist, BLM, Las Cruces District Office. Interview in Las Cruces, New Mexico, March 17, 1982.

Espinosa, Tom. Branch of Personnel, BLM, New Mexico State Office. Interview in Santa Fe, New Mexico, June 12, 1987.

Esquardo, Gil. Public Affairs Staff, BLM, New Mexico State Office. Interview in Santa Fe, New Mexico, June 21, 1982.

Glowka, Dave. Sierra Club. Interview in Albuquerque, New Mexico, June 20, 1986.

Hanks, Herrick (Rick). Area Manager, BLM, Rio Puerco Resource Area. Interview in Albuquerque, New Mexico, January 23, 1986.

Hannigan, Pete. President, New Mexico Oil and Gas Association. Interview in Santa Fe, New Mexico, January 24, 1986.

Harkenrider, Jr., William J. Las Cruces/Lordsburg Area Manager, BLM. Interview in Las Cruces, New Mexico, January 22, 1986.

Johanson, Eric G., III. Group Leader, Acquisitions and Exchange, Lands and Minerals, U.S. Forest Service, Southwest Region. Interview in Albuquerque, New Mexico, June 19, 1986.

Jones, Bob. Former Director, New Mexico Cattle Growers Association. Interview in Del City, Texas, May 25, 1983.

Jones, Dave. Division of Lands and Renewable Resources, BLM, New Mexico State Office. Interview in Albuquerque, New Mexico, June 24, 1986.

Joseph, Jon. Lands and Recreation Division, BLM, New Mexico State Office. Interviews in Sante Fe, New Mexico, January 24 and June 18, 1986.

Keesling, Lee. Public Affairs Staff, BLM, New Mexico State Office. Interview in Santa Fe, New Mexico, June 10, 1986.

Kenny, John. Planning and Environmental Coordination Division, BLM, New Mexico State Office. Interview in Santa Fe, New Mexico, January 24, 1986.

Larragoite, Marie. Solid Minerals Branch, BLM, New Mexico State Office. Interview in Sante Fe, New Mexico, January 24, 1986.

Lee, Charlie. Cattle Rancher and New Mexico State Senator. Interview in Del City, Texas, May 25, 1983.

Lopez, John. Director, Branch of Personnel, BLM, New Mexico State Office. Interviews in Sante Fe, New Mexico, July 17 and 18, 1984; June 6, 1985; and July 14 and 15, 1986.

McCaffery, Fred. Newspaper Reporter and Political Analyst, New Mexico. Interview in Sante Fe, New Mexico, June 21, 1982.

Middaugh, Geoff. Budget and Evaluation Program, BLM, New Mexico State Office. Interview in Sante Fe, New Mexico, June 18 and 19, 1986.

Mills, Ernie. New Mexico Newspaper and TV Political Analyst. Interview in Santa Fe, New Mexico, June 21, 1982.

Morris, James P. "Corky." Chairman, Bernalillo County Commission and former Republican Party Chairman, New Mexico. Interview in Albuquerque, New Mexico, June 22, 1982.

Pack, Al. Native American Program Coordinator, BLM, New Mexico State Office. Interview in Sante Fe, New Mexico, January 24, 1986.

Rathbun, Dan. District Manager, BLM, Las Cruces District Office. Interview in Las Cruces, New Mexico, August 5, 1982.

Reed, Robert. Division of Operations, BLM, Albuquerque District. Interview in Albuquerque, New Mexico, June 20, 1986.

Ross, Gene. New Mexico State University Agricultural Extension Service. Interviews in Las Cruces, New Mexico, March 14 and May 25, 1983.

Sanchez, Robert. Branch of Personnel, BLM, New Mexico State Office. Interview in Santa Fe, New Mexico, June 9 and 23, 1987.

Schultz, Robert. Biological Resources Branch, BLM, New Mexico State Office. Interview in Santa Fe, New Mexico, June 17, 1985 and January 20, 1986.

Stephens, William. New Mexico Secretary of Agriculture. Interview in Las Cruces, New Mexico, February 11, 1983.

Umshler, Dennis. Geologist, Branch of Solids, BLM, Albuquerque District Office. Interview in Albuquerque, New Mexico, June 18, 1986.

White, Ronald J. Director, Agricultural Programs and Resources, New Mexico Department of Agriculture. Materials provided in Las Cruces, New Mexico, June 25, 1986.

Wisely, Sally. Public Affairs Staff, BLM, New Mexico State Office. Interviews in Santa Fe, New Mexico, June 13, 1984 and July 22, 1986.

Wittern, Klaus. Developer. Interview in Las Cruces, New Mexico, June 25, 1986.

INDEX

Aberbach, Joel, 235, 251
Acid rain, 284
Acquired Lands Mineral Leasing Act, 15
Administrative orthodoxy, 33, 76, 87, 101, 258, 259, 262, 266, 272, 273
Administrative presidency
  authority tools of, 34–41
  communication tools, 45–50
  logic, 3, 4
  organizing tools of, 30–34
  research gaps, 5, 6, 321
  surrounding controversies, 4, 5, 233, 320
  treasury tools, 41–45
Advocacy coalitions, 314
Affirmative action, 296
Agenda item types
  convergent, 277, 285–287, 293
  emergent, 277, 283–285, 293, 299
  gradualist, 277, 287–288, 293, 296
  quantum, 247, 281–283, 293, 300, 301
Agenda processes (predecision), 276, 282
Agriculture Department (Department of Agriculture), 20
Ah-shi-sle-pah Wilderness Study Area, 205–208, 219, 221, 222, 223, 225
Aid to Families with Dependent Children (AFDC), 49
Alaska, 53
Albuquerque
  Boys Academy, 129, 141, 142, 144, 145, 146, 147, 149, 156, 242
  City Council, 141, 147, 157
Albuquerque district grazing advisory board, 119
American West, 12
Anaya, Toney, 187, 211, 212, 225, 236, 248
Andrus, Cecil, 84, 197, 202, 203, 204, 206, 210, 226, 227
Angrisani, Albert, 37
Annual Work Plans (AWP), 85, 86
Anthropocentrism, 293
Antiquities Act, 14
Applegate, Paul, 117
Appointee-careerist relations, 302–320
Archaeology and Historic Preservation Act, 17
Archuleta, Dickie, 119
Arizona, 8, 116, 166, 221
Armstrong, Robert, 152, 153, 154
Army Corps of Engineers, 265
Arrandale, Thomas, 165
Arthur, Chester, 216
Asset Management Program, 135, 143, 159, 243, 265
Auchter, Thorne, 37
Austrian economics, 54

Baca, Jim, 211
Baca, Tom, 146
Baden, John, 263, 264
Bahr, Tom, 177
Ban, Carolyn, 39, 303, 318, 319
Bardach, Eugene, 243

Bardacke, Paul, 175, 186, 211
Belief systems, 281, 283, 285
Berry, Dan, 104
Bibby, John, 234
Bidegain, Phillip, 110
Binghaman, Jeff, 105, 221, 223
Biocentric, 293
Biological model of public
    organizations, 249
Bisti Badlands, 205, 206, 207, 208,
    219, 221, 222, 225, 236, 243
Blanchard, Kenneth, 304, 309–313,
    315, 316, 317
BLM-Forest Service land exchange,
    60, 287
BLM-Forest Service tensions in New
    Mexico, 154
BLM-MMS reorganization, 94, 96,
    97, 98, 127, 153, 237, 258
BLM state directors, 61
Blue Ribbon Commission on Defense
    Management, 261
"Bottom-up" budgeting, 43
Brady Commission, 282
Bratton, Howard, 179, 181, 182
Brown, F. Lee, 265
Brown, Harold, 41
Brownlowian prescriptions for
    presidential power, 10
Buchanan, Bruce, 5
Budget and Impoundment Control
    Act of 1974, 41
Budget reconciliation process, 43
Burciaga, Juan, 220
Bureau Management Team (BMT),
    85, 86, 87, 89, 91, 101, 268
Bureau of Indian Affairs (BIA), 216,
    218, 226
Bureau of Land Management (BLM)
    allegations of data manipulation
        against, 212–213
    clientelism, 12–18, 22, 124, 127
    congressional moratoria against,
        213, 226, 236 (off-shore
        drilling), 248, 292

congressional scrutiny of, 12,
    286–287
culture, 20, 53, 88, 258, 266
district office roles (DO), 61
district office staffing
    patterns/needs, 65, 98, 101
Energy and Minerals Division, 59
impact of reorganizations, 99
in New Mexico, 7, 67
long-range planning within, 23
Memorandum of Understanding
    with New Mexico, 106, 292
minimalist management ethic, 20,
    21, 125
mission, 20
multiple-use advisory boards, 23
natural resource production trends
    in New Mexico, 76
need for role clarification, 61,
    84–89, 99
"new" BLM, 22–23
participative management, 87
personnel actions, 61
personnel retraining needs, 97
planning, 60
Planning and Environmental
    Coordination Division, 85, 86
predecessor agencies, 7
range improvement backlog,
    125–126
relationship to mining industry, 12,
    94–100
relationship to ranching industry,
    12, 101
relationship to timber industry, 12
renewable resources, 60
resource area roles (RA), 61
resource area staffing
    patterns/needs, 65, 98
Resource Management Division,
    85, 86
skill mix, 59–60
staffing patterns in New Mexico,
    67–73, 124
state office roles (SO), 61

state office staffing patterns, 65
Washington Office, 90, 109, 117, 240, 263, 271
wilderness management, 60, 90
Bureau of Reclamation (BuRec), 164, 188
"Bureaucracy problem" (the), 46, 259
"Bureaucrat bashing," 304
Bureaucratic culture, 10, 46
Bureaucratic rules and routines, 10
Bureaucratic types (Heclo)
  critics, 309, 316, 317
  forgottens, 309, 317
  institutionalists, 309, 317
  opponents, 309, 313
  program, 309, 316, 317
  reformers, 309, 316
  reluctants, 309, 315
  staff, 309, 316, 317
Bureaupathologies, 259
Bureauphiles, 302, 306–307, 310, 319
Bureauphobes, 302, 307–308, 310, 313, 319
Bureaupolitics
  adversarial, 244, 288, 289, 292, 293, 294, 298–300, 312, 314, 316
  disintegrative, 247, 288, 292, 293, 294, 300–302, 312, 313, 314
  manipulated agreement, 244, 288, 289, 293, 294, 296–298, 312, 316
  mutual accommodation, 240, 288, 289, 293, 294–296, 312, 317
Burford, Robert, 37, 59, 96, 97, 107, 110, 111, 113, 117, 123, 204, 213, 233, 240, 241, 287
Bush Administration, 187, 226, 247, 298
Bush, George, 287

Cabinet Councils, 49, 57, 171
Cabinet oversecretaries, 31

Calista, Donald, 269
Camp David Summit, 286
Camunez, Joseph, 144, 149, 150, 157
Carroll, James, 29
Carruthers, Garrey, 55, 95, 107, 165, 168, 172, 173, 178, 182, 183, 188, 209–210, 211, 222–223, 225
Carter Administration
  coal-leasing application backlog/mismanagement, 67
  deregulatory efforts at Interstate Commerce Commission, 305
  energy policy, 30, 84, 97, 195, 196, 197, 246
  federal water project assistance, 164
  focus on economic rationality, 39
  health policy, 41
  "hit list" of water projects, 67, 164
  natural resource policy, 6, 23, 24, 54, 60
  policy on federal nonreserved water rights, 178–179
  political appointee staffing patterns, 40
  position on Paragon Ranch, 220
  position on transfer of BLM lands to Las Cruces, 139
  rangeland policy, 103, 116, 118, 240, 244
  transition team, 31
  urban policy, 41
  use of rangeland betterment funds (8100 funds), 109, 190
Carter, Jimmy, 31, 35, 47, 49, 83, 197, 234, 299
Central Intelligence Agency (CIA), 84
Checkerboard land ownership patterns, 19–20, 67, 130
Cheney, Richard, 261
Child nutrition funding, 49
Childrens' legal rights, 301–302
China, 283, 287

Cibola National Forest, 129, 140, 141
City of El Paso v S.E. Reynolds, 179–181
Civil Service Reform Act of 1978, 37, 40
Civilian Conservation Corps, 112
Clans, 265–266
Clark, William, 51, 93, 94, 95, 99, 118, 204, 210, 213, 214
Clarke, Jeanne, 7, 20
Clean Air Act Amendments of 1977, 197
Clements, William, 178
Coal Management Plan (CMP), 197, 198, 204, 210, 226
Cohen, Michael, 276, 279
Collateral structures, 267
Colorado, 8, 59, 61, 166, 172
Color-of-Titles Acts, 15
Commission on Federal Water Policy, 171
Committee on the Present Danger, 37
Compensatory education funding, 49
Competent process standards, 5, 237, 275
Conditional cooperation, 304, 309, 319
Congressional bureaucracy, 307
Connally, John, 55, 178
Conservation Foundation, 133, 136
Consultation-Confrontation eras of land management, 22–23
"Consultation, cooperation, and coordination," 106, 110
Contextual goals, 296
Cooperative agreements, 110, 119, 120
Coors, Adolph, 59
Core beliefs, 123
Corrigan, Richard, 82
Council of Environmental Quality (CEQ), 59, 215
Counterbureaucratic strategy, 35, 282
Counterstaffing strategy, 39
Covert operations, 286

"Cow welfare," 56, 108, 111, 127, 289
Crane, Jolene, 174
Crausby, Raleigh, 143
"Creeping centralization," 86
Crowder Investment Company, 157
Crowell, John, 37, 134, 297–298, 316
"Crowfoot vigilantes," 104
Cuban Missile Crisis, 282
Culhane, Paul, 13
Custodial management, 20, 21

Dana, Andrew, 263, 264
D.C. Circuit Court of Appeals (U.S.), 219
Decade of the environment, 8
Decision settings, 252
DeConcini, Dennis, 217
De-na-zin Wilderness Study Area, 205, 206, 207, 208, 221, 222, 223, 225
Department of Agriculture, 38, 46, 134
Department of Commerce, 38, 46
Department of Defense, 32, 37, 41, 203, 294, 296, 318
Department of Education, 31, 40
Department of Energy, 30, 31, 34, 37
Department of Energy Reorganization Act of 1977, 197
Department of Health and Human Services, 38
Department of Health, Education, and Welfare, 35
Department of Justice, 34, 40, 183, 191, 300, 313
Department of State, 46
Department of the Treasury, 37, 46
Der Freischutz, 321
Devine, Donald, 38
Dinkins, Carol, 176–180
Direct-line democracy, 260
Dismantling of America, 4
District grazing advisory boards, 106, 124

Doctrine of prior appropriation and beneficial use, 168, 184, 189

Domenici, Pete, 55–56, 83, 84, 105, 107, 144, 147, 153, 159, 160, 183, 208, 217, 222–225, 243, 244, 246, 248, 292

Domestic Policy Council, 30

Dominant coalitions, 238, 294, 296

Dona Ana County, 138, 150, 170 (water supplies)

Dormant Commerce Clause, 167, 169, 174–179, 181, 185, 245

Downs, Anthony, 260–261

DuBois, Frank, 95, 107, 114, 116, 117, 240, 241, 254, 289

Due diligence standards, 194

Duerkson, Christopher, 137

Dust Bowl disaster, 21

Eads, George, 48

Economic protectionism, 175, 185

Economic Stabilization Act, 41

Edwards, Edwin, 37

Eisenhower, Dwight D., 31, 34, 47, 282

Elena Gallegos land grant, 140, 141, 227, 234, 235, 244, 252, 286

Elena Gallegos Trust Fund Committee, 148, 157

Elephant Butte Dam, 172, 182, 187

Elkins, Richard, 149

Elmore, Richard, 58, 251, 253, 254, 256

El Paso v. Reynolds, 163, 167, 184, 186, 292

Emergency Natural Gas Act of 1977, 83

Employment and Training Administration, 34, 37

End Results Budgeting (ERB), 270

Energy Minerals Allocation Recommendation System (EMARS I & II), 196, 233, 285

Environmental Defense Fund (EDF), 212–213

Environmental Impact Statements (EIS), 60

Environmental Protection Agency (EPA), 31, 45, 133, 299–300, 305

Environmental protection "unsuitability" criteria, 202, 204

Eppers, Bud, 104

Equal Employment Opportunity Commission (EEOC), 45

Equal value (land exchanges), 136–137

Exchange Theory, 308

Executive leadership
    Hersey and Blanchard's four follower-based styles:
    delegating, 310, 317–318
    participating, 309, 316–317
    selling, 309, 314–316
    telling, 309, 312–314
    Hersey and Blanchard's leader-follower behavioral components:
    follower-readiness, 309, 310, 312–318
    job maturity, 310
    psychological maturity, 310
    relationship behavior, 310, 312, 315
    task behavior, 310, 311, 315
    typology of, 9, 10

Executive Office of the President (EOP), 6, 30, 42, 307

Executive Order 12291, 49

Experimental Stewardship Program, 127

Fair market value (land exchanges), 131, 136, 138

Fairfax, Sally, 22

Farmington, New Mexico, 224

Federal Aviation Administration (FAA), 138, 140, 144

Federal Coal Leasing Amendments
    Act (FCLAA), 17, 197, 202,
    204, 213
Federal Communications Commission
    (FCC), 34
Federal homestead land disposal
    programs, 19
Federal Land Policy and Management
    Act (FLPMA), 13, 17–18, 22,
    53, 61, 65, 84, 103, 130, 131,
    135, 136, 138, 139, 193, 202,
    204
Federal Oil and Gas Royalty
    Management Act of 1982
    (FOGrMA), 96, 236
Federal Trade Commission (FTC), 37
Federal water assistance, 164
"Fire alarm" oversight, 91, 101, 147,
    155, 226, 238, 286, 287, 289,
    305
"Fiscalization" of the legislative
    process, 42
Fish and Wildlife Service, 53, 133,
    188
Fix, Michael, 48
Flow-of-work structures, 268, 269
Food for Peace program, 30
Ford Administration, 39, 49, 195, 196
Ford, B. Ford, 37, 297–298
Ford, Gerald, 31, 55
Foreign Service, 265
Forest Service, 20, 37, 133, 134, 140,
    142, 144, 145, 146, 148, 149,
    150, 151, 153, 156, 157, 162,
    203, 242, 243, 264, 265, 266,
    269–271, 289, 297, 298, 316
FORPLAN, 264
Fossil Forest, 223
Fowler, Mark, 37, 39
Frail Lands Program, 112
Franklin, Larry, 104
Friesma, Paul, 13
Fritschler, A. Lee, 29
Full force and effect orders, 106, 113,
    121

Functional departmentation, 259, 268
Fyfe, Paul, 218

Gallatin National Forest, 270
Galley, Fred, 145
Garbage can model of decision
    making, 276, 279
    access structures, 279–283, 285,
        287
    decision structures, 279–285, 287
    energy distributions, 279–283,
        285, 286
    energy loads, 279–283
    entry times, 279–287
Garland, Ed, 144
General Accounting Office, 83, 91,
    98, 135, 302
General Land Office, 7, 19
General Mining Law, 14
General Services Administration
    (GSA), 139, 140
Gilmour, Robert, 32, 47
Glowka, David, 214
Golembiewski, Robert, 32–33, 88,
    259, 260, 267–272
"Good Neighbor" policy, 53, 121
Gorsuch, Ann (Burford), 59
Governance model of public
    organizations, 249–250
Governance structures/networks, 250,
    251, 252, 255
Grazing fees, 108, 110
Grazing Service, 7, 22
Great Depression, 282
Great Lakes, 166, 178
Great Plains groundwater situation,
    172
Greater Las Cruces Industrial
    Development Authority, 155,
    157, 158
Greece, 282
Green Revolution, 284
Gregg, Frank, 85
Grossman, Joel, 293

Groundwater supplies
in New Mexico, 166–167
in Texas, 166
in the West, 166
Gutierrez, Rudy, 118

Halperin, Morton, 34–35
Hamiltonian assumptions related to
presidential power, 10
Hanke, Steve, 54
Hanks, Herrick (Rick), 114, 115, 116
Hannigan, Pete, 83
"Hard-look" doctrine, 48
Hargrove, Erwin, 231
Harjo, Susan, 219
Harlowe, Bryce, 48
Harmer, Sherman, 104
Harris, Dick, 149, 151
Harvey, Phil, 110
Hassell, Jean, 143, 144, 145, 150,
154, 242, 289
Hatch, Orin, 106
Healing v. Jones, 210 F. Supp. 125
(1963), 245
Health Maintenance Organizations
(HMOs), 287
Heclo, Hugh, 25, 35, 304, 308, 309,
312, 313, 315, 317, 318, 321
Heritage Foundation, 57
Hersey, Paul, 304, 309–313, 315,
316, 317
Hickel, Walter, 35
Hjern, Benny, 46, 231, 250
Hobbes, Thomas, 194
Hodel, Donald, 51, 58, 118, 139,
140, 188, 204, 210, 213
Hogan, William, 82
Hood, Christopher, 279
Hoover, Herbert, 47
Horner, Constance, 261
House Committee on Appropriations,
124
House Insular and Interior Affairs
Committee, 56, 142

Housely, Raymond, 159
Hudson, Ron, 150
Hueco Bolson, 167, 173, 182
Hult, Karen, 249, 252
Hummel, Ralph, 45
Hyperpluralism, 307

Idaho, 116
Ikle, Fred, 37
Imperial Presidency, 234
Implementation
as "assembly-line" process, 243
as "trading among objectives,"
254
"fixers," 242
"missing link" in study of, 231
"monsters," 318
"odd-man-out" game, 243
patterns of structural
interdependence, 243
strategies
backward-mapping, 254–256
bottom-up approaches, 232
forward-mapping, 253
reversible logic approaches, 232,
253, 256–258, 272, 320
tools, 279
top-down approaches, 58, 232,
249, 251, 272, 303, 313
Implementation structures, 250
Impoundment strategy, 42
"In-and-Outers," 306
Incremental policy change, 276,
287–288
Indian Claims Commission, 220
Ingraham, Patricia, 35, 39, 40, 303,
318, 319
Ingram, Helen, 265
Institutional presidency, 6
Intensive land management era, 22
Interior Department
Heritage Conservation and
Recreation Service, 57
Office of Water Policy, 57

Interior Department (*continued*)
Office of Water Resources and
Technology, 57
Planning and Environmental
Division, 56
reorganization, 7, 20, 38
research and development (R & D),
57
Resource Division, 57
Solicitor's Office, 57
Iran-Contra, 286
Issue networks, 9, 258, 281, 284,
285, 306

Jigsaw puzzle management, 36, 307,
308, 314
Johanson, Eric, 152–154, 159
Johnson, Lyndon B., 9, 30, 47, 234
Joint Chiefs of Staff, 32
Jones, Bob, 104, 110
Judicial review of agency decision
making, 23–24
Juvenile justice, 301–302

Kaufman, Herbert, 266
Kennedy, John F., 9, 30, 41, 47, 234
King, Bruce, 143, 211
King, Laura, 210
Kingdon, John, 221, 239, 276, 287
Kinney, Mayor, 158
Kissinger, Henry, 32
Knott, Jack, 36, 259
Kurlitz opinion, 178

Land acquisition
backlog, 133
critique of, 133–134
"deep pockets" phenomenon, 133
Land and Water Conservation Fund
(L&WCF), 16, 133, 135, 141,
161, 244
Land Classification and Multiple-Use
Act, 15, 22, 136

Land exchanges
difficulties with Elena Gallegos
exchange, 152–155
pace of (Carter years), 132
problems with large-scale
exchanges, 136–137, 147,
161
process, 132
staffing problems, 136
Land sales, 132
Land use plans (state or local), 131
Landau, Martin, 251
Landlocked urban areas, 129, 130
Las Cruces
Chamber of Commerce, 156
city commission, 144, 150, 155
Crawford Municipal Airport, 138,
139
demographics, 138
fiscal stress, 138
legal staff, 151
Las Cruces Industrial Park, 138, 286,
289, 297
"Lawless presidency," 305
Lea, George, 132
Legal Services Corporation, 301
Lehman, John, 37
Leshy, John, 25, 76, 193
Lindblom, Charles, 277
Lindholm, Vernon, 134
Linowes Commission, 91, 94, 96, 98,
99, 204, 247
Lonely organization syndrome, 250
Lopez, John, 97
Love Canal, 286
Lovell, Catherine, 163
Lowi, Theodore, 3, 10, 320
Lowry, Glenn, 302
Lujan, Manuel, Jr., 56, 140, 141,
142, 147, 148, 153–154, 162,
183, 222–225, 242, 244, 248,
289, 292
Luscher, Charles W., 116, 117, 122,
123, 154, 242, 289
Lynn, Laurence, 296, 307

MacDonald, Peter, 218–221
Management-by-Objectives (MBO),
    47, 57
March, James, 33, 276, 279
Mark Twain National Forest, 270
"Marrying the natives," 44, 46
Martin, Guy, 105, 124
Mature matrix, 268
"Maximum feasible participation," 47
Maynard-Moody, Steven, 94
McArthur, Johnny W., 135
McClure Amendment, 106, 246, 292
McCool, Daniel, 7, 20
McCubbins, Matthew, 91, 235
McLaughlin, Ann, 187–188, 190
McNamara, Robert, 41
Mechanistic model of public
    organizations, 249, 257
Medicaid funding, 49
Mesilla Bolson, 167, 171, 173, 182,
    183
Metzenbaum, Howard, 301–302
Micromanagement (congressional),
    76, 236, 261
Middaugh, Geoff, 90, 262, 271
Miller, Gary, 36, 259
Mine Health and Safety
    Administration (MHSA), 34,
    37, 297
Mineral appraisal difficulties, 137
Mineral Leasing Act of 1920, 14, 194
Minerals Management Service
    (MMS), 65, 93, 95, 96, 101
Minimalist state, 30, 76
Missouri River Basin, 178
Moe, Terry, 36, 260
Montana, 166, 189
Morton, Rogers, 194–196
Mountain States Legal Foundation,
    24, 52, 106
Multiple-use advisory boards, 110,
    124
Mulitiple-use and sustained-yield
    policy/management, 18, 87,
    88, 89, 193

Muris, Timothy, 37
"Mushroom" style of management,
    308

Narco-terrorism, 282
Nathan, Richard, 3, 4, 36, 234, 237
National Academy of Public
    Administration, 261
National Aeronautics and Space
    Administration (NASA), 31
National Association of Realtors, 135
National Center for Neighborhood
    Enterprise, 302
National District Attorney
    Association, 302
National Environmental Policy Act
    (NEPA), 16, 23–24, 136, 212
National Highway Transportation
    Safety Administration
    (NHTSA), 35
National Historic Preservation Act,
    16
National Juvenile Law Center, 301
National Park Service, 57, 58, 133
National Security Council, 30
National Wilderness Preservation
    System (NWPS), 193, 222
Native American Rights Fund, 219
Native Americans, 197, 204, 219,
    265
    Hopi, 215–222
    Navajo, 117, 193, 205, 206,
        215–223, 225, 227, 247, 251
    Pueblo, 117, 216
    Ute, 215
    Wasco, 218
Natural Resources Defense Council,
    210
*Natural Resources Defense Council v.
    Bergland*, 215
*Natural Resources Defense Council v.
    Hughes*, 196
*Natural Resources Defense Council v.
    Morton*, 23, 112, 215

Navajo-Hopi Joint Use Area (JUA), 27
Navajo-Hopi Relocation Act, 205, 216–217, 220, 227, 254
Navajo-Hopi Relocation Commission, 217, 223
Navajo Nation Justice Department, 220
Nelson, Robert, 203
Neo-Marxists, 260
Neutral competence, 4, 35, 306, 308
Nevada, 106
New Mexico
  as research focus, 7, 8
  economic boycott of El Paso, 167
  innovative groundwater policy, 168–169
  link between groundwater and surface water, 168–169
  natural resource endowment, 65, 82
  oil and gas production, 83
  revised water embargo statute, 181
  statute banning water exports (1953), 167
  water embargo statute, 175, 179
New Mexico-BLM Rangeland Consultation Memorandum of Understanding, 118
New Mexico Cattle Growers Association, 104, 105, 110, 118
New Mexico congressional delegation, 119, 120, 142, 143, 147, 183, 227, 233, 236
New Mexico Conservation Coordinating Council, 118
New Mexico Cultural Properties Review Committee, 214
New Mexico Department of Agriculture, 108, 118
New Mexico Department of Corrections, 144, 146
New Mexico Department of Game and Fish, 118, 120

New Mexico Generating Station, 211, 212
New Mexico Oil and Gas Association, 83
New Mexico State Land Office, 118
New Mexico State University Range Improvement Task Force, 114, 118, 121
New Mexico Water Law Study Committee, 181, 184
New Resource Economics (NRE), 7, 54, 56, 190, 191, 232, 263–265
Ninth Circuit Court of Appeals (U.S.), 217
Nixon, Richard, 30, 32, 35, 47, 195, 234, 235, 282, 300–301
Noncompetitive leasing (land), 132
Noncompliance delay effect (NDE), 294, 298, 299, 300, 303, 304, 309, 312
Nonmajoritarian interests, 127
Nonmarket failures, 259
Noonan, Peggy, 248
Noonen, Patrick, 133, 136
Nuclear power, 286, 299–300, 315
Nuclear weapons, 41, 47
Nunn, Sam, 262

Occupational Health and Safety Administration (OSHA), 31
Ochoco National Forest, 270
Office of Economic Opportunity (OEO), 30, 41
Office of Federal Contract Compliance, 45
Office of Juvenile Justice and Delinquency Prevention (OJJDP), 301–302
Office of Management and Budget (OMB), 31, 40, 41, 42, 45, 47, 60, 153, 181, 189, 307
Office of Personnel Management (OPM), 38, 39, 40, 57, 261

Office of Policy Development, 49
Office of Surface Mining, 53, 93, 95
Office of Technology Assessment
    (OTA), 247
Office of Trade Representative, 46
Office of Water Policy, 57, 171
Office of Water Research and
    Technology (OWRT), 171
Ogallala Aquifer, 178
Ogul, Morris, 234
Oil and gas royalties, royalty
    management, 91, 92
Oklahoma, 166
"Old style" reorganization, 31–33
Olsen, Johan, 33, 276, 279
Omnibus Budget and Reconciliation
    Act of 1981, 44
Onshore energy leasing, 95
OPEC states, 61
Oregon, 116
Organization of Petroleum Exporting
    Countries (OPEC), 203
Organized anarchy, 276
Ouchi, William, 265–266
Outer Continental Shelf (OCS), 236

Pacific Northwest, 166
Pacific Northwest Station (California),
    270
Packard Commission, 261
Packard, David, 261
Palumbo, Dennis, 269
Paragon Ranch, 218, 220–221
Parallel structures, 268
Parklands acquisition, 56
Parochial interests (versus
    majoritarian interests), 262
Pattison, Hoyt, 104
Perle, Richard, 37
Peters, Tom, 267, 270
Pfiffner, James, 35
Phillips, Howard, 41
Pinchot, Gifford, 18, 51
Pious, Richard, 31

"Police patrol" oversight, 91, 226,
    234, 288, 305
Policy
    as "bisociated recombination,"
        279, 282, 284
    as "consociated recombination,"
        279, 286, 287, 288
    as "gradualist transformation," 277
    as "hypothesis," 238
    as "idea set," 238, 248, 275, 277,
        284
    as "mutation," 277
    polycentric nature of, 249, 254
Policy entrepreneurs, 284
Policy mode, 277, 283, 284, 286, 287
Policy "softening," 238–239, 241,
    242, 244–248, 275, 281, 282,
    283, 286–289, 292, 297
Policy streams, 276
Policy tempo, 277, 283, 284, 286,
    287
Policy validity, 238, 239, 241–242,
    244, 245, 246, 248, 275, 284,
    286–289, 292, 297
Political model of public
    organizations, 249
"Politicizing" the bureaucracy, 35,
    306
Politicos, 55
Politics-administration dichotomy,
    307
Porter, David, 46, 250
Position reclassification, 38
Powder River Basin, 98, 202, 204,
    206, 209–210, 226, 246, 247,
    251
Preference lease sales, 146
Preference Right Lease Applications
    (PRLAs), 197, 205, 206, 208,
    209, 211–215
Presidential leadership (typology of),
    9
Presidentialists, 10, 41–42
Prior appropriation and beneficial use
    doctrines, 21, 122, 123

Privatization, 19, 54, 56, 113, 127, 252, 264
Professional-bureaucratic complex, 259
Program Associate Directors, 32
Program-Planning-Budgeting System (PPBS), 47
Progressive Conservationists, 18, 20, 51, 293
Progressive Reform Era, 23, 36, 272
Project management, 268
Public Choice, 54
Public land stewardship, 8
Public law litigation model, 23
Public participation, 23
Public Rangelands Improvement Act (PRIA), 17, 53, 84, 109, 110, 115, 118, 126
Public sector deregulation, 261–262, 269–273
Public Service Company of New Mexico (PNM), 205, 218, 220, 221
Public service model of appointee-careerist relations, 303–305, 309, 313–320

Rachal, Patricia, 296
Rainey, Glenn W., Jr., 269
Ranching industry
  control of rangeland policy, 21–22
  financial distress of, 12, 13
Rangeland Betterment Funds (8100 funds), 107–110, 113, 115, 123, 124, 127
Rangeland Improvement Policy (RIP), 107, 109, 110, 114, 115, 120, 122, 240, 287, 289
Rare and Endangered Species Act, 16
Rathbun, Dan, 123, 143, 145, 154
Rational choice theory, 87, 235
Rational ignorance, 259
Ravaging of the West, 25
Reagan Administration
  approach to administratively reorienting natural resource policy, 6, 250
  budget cuts affecting land exchanges, 144, 147
  budget cuts for water research and development, 173, 185, 190
  budget cuts to U.S. Geological Survey, 171
  federal water project assistance, 163, 165
  general approach to administrative presidency, 4, 257–258, 306
  general funding priorities, 44–45
  natural resource retrenchment initiatives, 6, 7
  position on El Paso-New Mexico water suit, 167
  position on Elena Gallegos exchange, 159–160
  position on federal nonreserved water rights, 178–179
  position on Sporhase case, 176–181
  prodevelopment energy agenda, 98, 246
  "Reaganizing" the federal bureaucracy, 34, 37–41
  reorganizations, 31, 34
  support for Native American issues, 218–219
  water project funding, 171
Reagan Doctrine, 282
Real Estate Appraisal Institute, 137
Realpolitik perspective on appointee-careerist relations, 308–309
Realpolitik school of organizational reform, 32
Recreation and Public Purposes Act, 14, 130, 131, 135, 157
Recreation grants, 56
Redhouse, John, 218
Reductions-in-force (RIFs), 5, 37, 38, 57
Reed, Bob, 115, 116
Regan, Donald, 51
Regional Coal Teams (RCTs), 197, 202, 204, 209, 211, 226, 246, 251

Regnery, Alfred, 301–302
Regulatory unreasonableness, 56, 100
Reilly, William, 133, 136
Reorganization "style," 94
Repoliticizing the bureaucracy, 36
Reservation era of land management, 21
Resource Management Plans (RMPs), 88
Revolt against bureaucracy, 23
Reynolds, Steve, 121, 168, 170, 182
Reynolds, Temple, 137
Richardson, Elliot, 35, 141
Richardson, William, 118, 222–225, 248
Rio Grande Commission, 172
Rio Grande Compact, 172–173, 179
Rio Grande River, 166, 167, 244–245, 252, 265, 292
Rio Puerco Grazing Association, 118
Rio Puerco Livestock Association, 118, 119
Rio Puerco pipeline system, 111, 112, 113, 121, 240, 287, 288, 294
Rio Puerco Resource Area (RPRA) characteristics, 105, 106, 111, 112, 284
Roberts, Paul Craig, 37
Robertson, F. Dale, 270–271
Rockman, Bert, 3
Role Clarification Study, 89, 97, 99
Roosevelt, Franklin D., 9, 37, 234, 283
Rosenbloom, David, 11, 260
Rural-urban water war, 166, 186, 284
Rusk, David, 141–142, 148, 244, 289

Sabatier, Paul, 123, 281
Sagebrush Rebellion
  defusion of, 108
  in Colorado, 59
  in Nevada, 106
  in New Mexico, 84, 104–106
  in the West, 103, 104
  in Washington, 52
  logic of, 8, 52, 107
San Juan Basin (SJB), 67, 160, 193, 205, 206, 246–247, 251, 252, 283, 292, 300
San Juan Wilderness Bill, 224, 225, 248
Sandia Wilderness Area, 141
Sandoval, Rusty, 119
Sanera, Michael, 36, 308
Sarat, Austin, 293
Schaafsma, Curtis, 215
Schattschneider, E. E., 231
Schedule C positions, 38, 40
Scher, Seymour, 234
Schickedanz, Jerry, 114, 116
Schlesinger, James, 30
Schmitt, Harrison "Jack", 83, 84, 105, 114, 139–144, 151, 153, 156, 162, 183, 242, 244, 246
School desegregation, 300–301
Schulman, Paul, 277
Schwartz, Thomas, 91, 235
Second American Republic, 3
Security and Exchange Commission (SEC), 156–157
Seidman, Harold, 32, 47
Senate Budget Committee, 56
Senior Executive Service (SES), 39, 40
Sierra Club, 214
Simplistic sovereignty, 259, 320
Skeen, Joe, 144
Smith, Bruce L.R., 29
Smith, Kenneth, 58, 218–219
Social services funding, 49
Society for Range Management (SRM), 124–125
Soil Conservation Service, 111
South Dakota, 189
Specter, Arlen, 301–302
Split estates, 207, 222–223, 226
Sporhase v. Nebraska, ex. rel. Douglas, 175, 176, 179–181, 183, 185, 186, 189, 244
Stahmann, William, 187

Steinberg, David, 151
Stephens, William, 121–123
Stockman, David, 44
Stout, Russell, 251
Strategic Defense Initiative (SDI), 279
Strategic deficit, 137, 213
Superfund scandal, 286
Supply-side economics, 29, 53
Supply-side management
   definition, 4
   elements of, 29–30, 50, 53, 67, 73,
      81, 90, 96, 113
   impact, 100, 101, 124, 127, 129,
      137, 151–153, 155, 158, 161,
      169–170, 189, 204, 209, 213,
      215, 226, 236, 249, 251,
      253–254, 257, 308
Surface Mining Control and
   Reclamation Act (SMCRA) of
   1977, 17, 197, 202, 204, 223,
   225
Surface transportation industry, 287
Surplus Airport Equipment Act, 138,
   139
SVIM, 105, 106, 191, 233, 244–246,
   284, 285, 292, 299

Taos, New Mexico, 220
Task Force on Regulatory Relief, 298
Taylor Grazing Act, 15, 21–22
Teague, Jonathan, 214
Tennessee Valley Authority (TVA),
   299–300, 315
Texas
   groundwater regulatory framework,
      169
   role in Rio Grande Commission,
      172
   water supplies, 8, 172
Theory X, 307, 309, 319
Theory Y, 306, 309
Thermal pollution, 299
Three Mile Island, 286
Tidwell, Moody, 218

Tienanmen Square, 287
Timber industry, 20
Times Beach, 286
Top-down budgeting, 42
Traditions in Public Administration
   legal, 11, 12
   managerial, 11, 18
   political, 11
Trail of Tears, 215
Truman Doctrine, 282
Truman, Harry, 30
Ture, Norman, 37
Type II errors, 251

Udall, Stewart, 104
Unreserved waters rights, 67
U.S. Geological Survey (USGS), 81,
   91, 92, 93, 96, 171, 182, 185,
   188
U.S. Public Health Service, 265
U.S. Supreme Court, 172, 216
U.S. v. New Mexico, 178–179
U.S. Veterans Administration, 39
Utah, 61, 106
Utah Cattleman's Association, 104
Utah Department of Natural
   Resources, 137

Valdez v. Applegate, 106, 113, 121
Validity of causal theory, 238, 241,
   288
Value/cultural overlays, 267
Vinson & Elkins (law firm), 177–
   178
von Weber, Carl Maria, 321

Walcott, Charles, 249, 252
Wallop, Malcolm, 134
War on Poverty, 30
Warwick, Donald, 260
Water market participation by state
   governments, 184–186, 245

Water rights (state), 121
Waterman, Richard, 305
Watt, James, 25, 51, 52, 53, 57, 59,
    93, 94, 95, 100, 106, 113,
    115, 117, 118, 134–135, 137,
    140, 159, 168, 173, 188, 204,
    207, 209, 210, 211, 219, 220,
    226–227, 233, 240, 246,
    248
Weber, Max, 259
Weinberger, Casper, 49, 294, 318
Western Governors Association, 187
Western States Water Council, 187
Wharton, Don, 221
White House Office (WHO), 6, 46
Wildavsky, Aaron, 302
Wilderness Act of 1964, 16, 195,
    203, 246

Wilderness exclusion issue in San
    Juan Basin, 206–208
Wildlife
    habitat protection, 56
    management in Rio Puerco, 117,
    120
Williams, Stephen, 184
Wilson, James Q., 296, 351
Wilson, Woodrow, 18, 305
Wittern, Klaus, 155, 156, 158, 244
Workshop on Public Land Exchanges,
    241
Wyoming, 61, 82, 93, 98, 189

Zah, Peterson, 221
Zero-based budgeting (ZBB), 47
Zone of indifference, 315

ABOUT THE AUTHOR

Robert Francis Durant was born in Northampton, Massachusetts, in 1949. He was graduated from Northampton High School in 1966 and received his B.A. in Political Science from Maryville College, Maryville, Tennessee, in 1970. He holds an MPA degree (1979) and a Ph.D. in Political Science (1981) from the University of Tennessee, Knoxville. From 1977 to 1981 he served as a research associate at the Bureau of Public Administration, University of Tennessee. He then joined the faculties at New Mexico State University (1981–1984) and the University of Georgia (1984–1991), where he was Director of the Masters of Public Administration Program and the Doctor of Public Administration Program, respectively. He is presently Professor and William Donald Schaefer Research Chair in Public Policy at the University of Baltimore. Professor Durant's research has been published in such scholarly journals as the *Public Administration Review, Administration & Society, Journal of Public Policy, International Journal of Public Administration, Social Science Quarterly, Legislative Studies Quarterly, Journal of Public Administration Research and Theory*, and the *Journal of Marketing*. He is also the author of *When Government Regulates Itself: EPA, TVA, and Pollution Control in the 1970s* (Knoxville: University of Tennessee Press, 1985).